BYNG OF VIMY
General and Governor General

JEFFERY WILLIAMS

A Leo Cooper book
published in association with
Secker & Warburg

First published in 1983
by Leo Cooper in association with
Martin Secker & Warburg Limited
54 Poland Street, London W1V 3DS

ISBN 436 57110 2

Photoset by Wilmaset, Birkenhead, Merseyside
Printed and bound in Great Britain by
The Camelot Press Limited, Southampton

Contents

List of Illustrations

List of Maps

To Irina
with Love

Foreword

LLOYD GEORGE WROTE in his war memoirs that there was no British general who could have replaced Haig in command of the B.E.F. His opinion of officers, from the Commander-in-Chief down, was based more on the frustration of a politician looking for easy options than on knowledge, but it had an undue influence on the popular view of where the responsibility lay for the enormous casualties of the First World War. He claimed later that, if it had been politically possible to do so, he would have made Sir John Monash of Australia Chief of the Imperial General Staff and Sir Arthur Currie of Canada commander-in-chief in the field. The reputations of the two Dominion generals are secure, but those of their British contemporaries have been viewed so often through veils of prejudice that none is untarnished in the eyes of the public.

As a Canadian who has known the British Army well for forty years, I find it difficult to believe that all its senior officers could have been so incompetent, unfeeling and unimaginative as they have been por-trayed. Hundreds of thousands of Canadian veterans would attest that one at least could not be cramped into that dismal mould. Inspiring, tough, competent and sympathetic, he made them into a superb fighting force and set them on the road to victory. In doing so, he won not just their trust and admiration, but their devotion.

While best remembered during his lifetime for his achievements with the Canadian Corps, Field-Marshal the Viscount Byng of Vimy was at the centre of several notable controversies, among them those of Gallipoli, Cambrai, the German offensive of March, 1918, and the 1926 constitutional crisis in Canada. His actions were opposed or criticized by ministers of the Crown and politicians as various as Sam Hughes and MacKenzie King, Kitchener, Lloyd George, Ramsay MacDonald, Philip Snowden and Winston Churchill. Many historians and generals have been critical of him. More often than not he was in the right, yet never a word did he utter in public to justify his actions nor to criticize others. Once he had retired from the Army, even his closest friends could not draw him into a discussion of the War. He wrote no memoirs, would permit no private history to be written of his Third Army and, on his death, had all his personal papers destroyed.

His reticence has made it difficult to ascertain details of his life and it is necessary sometimes to let the actions of his armies speak for his quality as a commander.

His old friend, John Buchan, had wanted to write his biography, but was prevented from doing so, first by becoming Governor-General of Canada himself and then by death. Years later Lt-Colonel Herbert Fairlie Wood, the Canadian military historian, having written his authoritative *Vimy*, began to research Byng's life, but again death intervened.

In 1971 Juliet Wood, his widow, herself a writer, invited me to take up his work. It was a gesture of true friendship to entrust the project to such untried hands and my gratitude to her is great.

Because no personal family papers exist (Lady Byng's were also burned) my need for help has been great. The openhandedness with which it has been given reflected in many cases a sincere belief that the life of this most widely loved and brilliant of soldiers should be recorded. It has made the research a pleasure.

Little progress would have been made without the assistance of the Canada Council who made a generous contribution to the cost of the project.

The Byngs were childless and their heiress was the late Miss Eva Sandford. For the final two years of her life, she offered her support and encouragement and, in the course of several conversations, told us of her life with the Byngs.

Mr Julian Byng of Wrotham Park, both namesake and godson of Lord Byng, opened his family records to us, has generously provided extracts from them and has gone to considerable trouble to ensure the accuracy of the material on Lord Byng's antecedents. His mother, Lady Elizabeth Byng, has helped with recollections of her uncle and her family history.

Simon and Bettine Birch, of Brantham, Essex, made possible our research at Thorpe-le-Soken. Through them we met Albert Orchin, Lord Byng's valet, whose remarkable memory and written recollections, and the tour he arranged of Thorpe Hall were invaluable sources.

Mme Georges Vanier's contribution was of a special kind. Now helping her son with L'Arche, his worldwide project for the disabled, she lives among them north of Paris. There she gave us a privileged view of the constitutional crisis of 1926 and of the devotion which Byng inspired in his friends. She has allowed us full access to the Vanier

Papers in the Public Archives of Canada–a particularly valuable source.

Lady Bigham, the former Miss Edith Drysdale, Byng's secretary at Scotland Yard, gave us much help with the period of his service as Commissioner of the Metropolitan Police.

An early and valuable contribution was made by W. N. Willis, who told of his service as a warrant officer of the 10th Hussars and, later, as a superintendent of a Rowton House, and loaned us his unpublished memoirs.

I am especially grateful for the gracious permission of Her Majesty the Queen, to make use of material from the Royal Archives at Windsor Castle, and for the help of Sir Robin Mackworth-Young and Miss Langton; to the Earl Haig for access to his father's papers in the National Library of Scotland and to its Keeper of Manuscripts, Dr Thomas Rae and his colleague, Mr Russell; to the Viscount Brookeborough for his recollections of his father's friendship with Lord Byng and for access to his family's papers in the Public Archives, Belfast.

Without the skill and sympathetic help of libraries and archivists, the task of research would have been impossible. They include, in addition to those mentioned above, at the Public Archives of Canada in Ottawa, Dr W. I. Smith, the Dominion Archivist and Dr Ian McClymont; at the Canadian War Museum, Mr L. F. Murray; at the National Defence College, Kingston, Mary Ann Higgs; at the Massey Library of the Royal Military College, Kingston, Mr Keith Crouch, Mr C. Watt and Major A. Bake; and at Queen's University, Kingston, Mrs Anne MacDermaid, the supervisor of archives; at the Royal Military Academy, Sandhurst, Mr J. W. Hunt and Mr M. G. H. Wright; at the Staff College, Camberley, Mr K. M. White and Miss Hills; at the Imperial War Museum, Mr Roderick Suddaby, Mr Willis and Miss Rose Coombs; at Eton College, Mr Patrick Strong; at the National Portrait Gallery, Mr Terence Popper and Mr Tim Moreton; at the Commissioner's Reference Library, Metropolitan Police, Miss Plank; at the Johnson National Scouting Museum, Irving, Texas, Mr Ilmar Pleer; and the Librarian and Staff of the Ministry of Defence Library, London.

Advice, help and encouragement have been supplied by many, including Major-General C. B. Ware, former commandant of the National Defence College, Kingston; Brig-General J. A. de La Lanne, Grand President of the Royal Canadian Legion; Dr R. H. Hubbard, Government House, Ottawa; Mrs Polly Labarge, the late Major John Swettenham and Lieut-Colonel Charles Askwith of Ottawa; Professor Roger Graham of Queen's University and Mrs D. C. Cameron of

Kingston; Mr and Mrs J. B. Williams of Calgary; Lieut-Colonel and Mrs E. H. Shuter of Toronto; Major-General E. K. G. Sixsmith; Lord Enfield; Lieut-Colonel Peter Upton, Royal Hussars; Lieut-Colonel R. G. Woodhouse, Somerset Light Infantry; Major John Sunderland, Royal Scots; Cdr and Mrs Barry Nation of Hatch Court, Somerset; Mme Irene Hagemann of Sarlat, France; Miss Ann Montgomery; Lieut-Colonel Howard N. Cole, Aldershot. I am especially grateful to my daughter and son-in-law, Stephanie and William Knight in London, not only for moral support but for much practical help.

To Captain R. C. Read, former Assistant Hydrographer of the Royal Navy I owe gratitude not only for the excellent maps which he has drawn but for his kindness and help during the production of the book.

To thank my wife for her help would, in a sense, diminish the credit she deserves for her part in the preparation of this book. Not only has she done all the secretarial work and typed every word more than once, she has been my full partner in research. It is her book as well as mine.

Chapter 1
The Early Years

CLOSE TO NOON Admiral John Byng, dressed carefully in civilian clothes, stepped from his cabin onto the quarterdeck of HMS *Monarque*, his bearing erect and confident. Saying 'Come along, my friend,' to the Marshal of the Fleet who seemed to hesitate by the door, he walked firmly to the cushion which lay on the deck. He bowed to the officers who stood nearby, then knelt to face the three ranks of scarlet-coated marines. Gently, he declined a friend's offer to tie the eye bandage, adding 'God bless you, don't stay any longer here, they may shoot you.'

For a few moments he prayed in silence, then, holding out his right arm, he deliberately dropped a handkerchief. Before it reached the deck six musket balls struck his chest.

In anger and grief, his family took him home and buried him by the Parish Church of Southill, in Bedfordshire. The inscription on his tomb reads

To the Perpetual Disgrace
of Public Justice
The Hon:^{ble} John Byng Esq:^r
Admiral of the Blue
Fell a MARTYR to
POLITICAL PERSECUTION
March 14th in the Year 1757 when
BRAVERY AND LOYALTY
were Insufficient Securities
For the
Life and Honour
of a
NAVAL OFFICER

When the Seven Years War approached in 1756, the British fleet had for years been starved of funds. Despite warnings, the Duke of Newcastle's government had ignored the imminent threat to the British base in Minorca. Too late, they despatched a scratch fleet of old, undermanned and leaky ships under John Byng on the impossible mission of relieving the island. Before they reached the Mediterranean, a powerful French fleet had landed fifteen thousand troops on Minorca and the island was over-run.

In a hard-fought action Byng succeeded in driving off the French fleet but suffered severe damage to his outgunned ships. So unseaworthy had they become that they were forced to return to Gibraltar for repairs and to land their wounded.

In the meantime the French admiral had claimed a victory. His reports were in London, were accepted as true by the King and Government and Byng's relief had been ordered – all before the British commander's account of the action was received.

Newcastle and his government realized that, if the truth were known, the public would hound them from office. To save themselves they shifted the blame on to the unfortunate admiral. He was tried by a naval court martial. under a charge which, if proved, would result in a mandatory death sentence. He was not found guilty of cowardice, disaffection, or negligence. At most he was thought guilty of an error in judgement. Clemency was refused and the Government was saved.[1]

Today the details of the case are forgotten but Admiral John Byng, while not the most distinguished member, is the best remembered of his family, for his name is coupled with Voltaire's sarcastic quip that in England they sometimes shoot an admiral *pour encourager les autres*.

At Wrotham Park, built, but never occupied, by the Admiral, are copies of anguished letters and appeals written in attempts to avert the tragedy. Eventually the bitterness and sense of loss died with those who had known John Byng. His story became for the family an especially personal cautionary tale.

Julian Hedworth George Byng was born at Wrotham on Tuesday, 11th September, 1862, the thirteenth child and seventh son of the Earl of Strafford, and a great-great-grandson of the unfortunate admiral's elder brother, Robert George. Their father, the first Viscount Torrington, had had a colourful early career in the course of which he held at one time a commission in the Army and in the Royal Navy simultaneously; he was, to quote Burke's Peerage, one of the most distinguished officers in the Naval annals of Great Britain, and rose to be First Lord of the Admiralty. Robert Byng had himself been Paymaster of the Navy and was appointed Governor of Barbados where he died in 1740 at the early age of thirty-seven, leaving three sons, the eldest of whom, George, was to inherit Wrotham Park on the execution of his uncle, while of the two younger sons, Robert was to die in the black hole of Calcutta in 1756 and the other, John, was to die at the age of fifteen at Bologna while on the Grand Tour; his portrait, painted in Italy by Angelica Kauffmann, hangs at Wrotham Park.

George Byng was Member of Parliament for the County of Middlesex, his co-Member being the celebrated John Wilkes. He married Anne Connolly, the daughter of William Connolly of Castletown in Ireland by his wife, Lady Anne Wentworth, co-heiress of her brother William Wentworth, Earl of Strafford, from whom, because of her sex, she could not inherit the title. They had four sons. The eldest, also called George, followed his father as member for Middlesex in the Commons, where he sat for fifty-six years and became Father of the House. The second son joined the Army but was killed in a duel in Guernsey at the age of twenty-five. Little is known of the third who died without marrying. The fourth, John, a great-grandson of the first Lord Torrington and the grandfather of Julian Byng, had a most distinguished military career. Entering the Army at the age of twenty-one, he served in the Walcheren Campaign where family tradition has it that he lost his toes through frostbite, thereby earning the nickname of 'Old Toes'.

In 1811, he became one of Wellington's generals in the Peninsula and won distinction for heroism in the assault on Bayonne. In the Army, he is best remembered for leading a Guards brigade in the stubborn defence of Hougoumont during the Battle of Waterloo. Later he entered Parliament as member for Poole and supported the Reform Bill.

He was unique in being the only one of Wellington's generals to be a Whig and not a Tory, and in order to increase the Whig representation in the House of Lords he was elevated to the peerage in 1835 under the title of Baron Strafford of Harmondsworth in the County of Middlesex. The revival of his maternal grandmother's family title provided a tenuous connection with his collateral ancestor, Thomas Wentworth, First Earl of Strafford, who was executed under the Long Parliament in 1641. Following the death of his elder brother George in 1847 he was immediately created Earl of Strafford and Viscount Enfield. Honours continued to come his way and in 1850 he was appointed Colonel of the Coldstream Guards and, in 1855, was promoted to the rank of Field-Marshal.

On his death in 1860 he was succeeded by his elder son, George Stevens Byng, who, like his father, had initially entered the Army, attaining the rank of Captain in the Rifle Brigade and becoming for some time honorary Colonel of the Royal Middlesex Militia. Entering Parliament in 1830 as Member for Milbourne Port, he was one of the junior Lords of the Treasury in Melbourne's first Administration and afterwards became Comptroller of Queen Victoria's Household and, for a short time, Treasurer of the Queen's Household. He lost his Parliamentary seat in 1852 but in the following year was summoned to sit in the House of Lords in his father's barony of Strafford.

Already the Byngs possessed wealth and property appropriate to their station. Wrotham had been enlarged and was now an even more imposing house than the 'stare about pile' described by one of the Admiral's brothers. Sitting on a rise where it overlooked the green acres of its landscaped park, and surrounded by broad lawns and gardens, it was lived in until her death in 1855 by the widow of George Byng. Above the Ionic columns of its Palladian front, a pediment sculpture of cannons, anchors and half-furled banners in bas relief spoke of the family's naval achievements.

In 1829 George Stevens Byng had married Lady Agnes Paget, daughter of the Marquess of Anglesey (another of Wellington's generals at Waterloo). They lived and entertained in considerable style both at the country house which they rented in Bedfordshire and at their house in Eaton Square. Captain Byng (as he then was) raced his horses and his yacht with considerable success and gambled, sometimes with less satisfactory results. Six children had been born before his wife died in 1845.

Three years later George, now known by the courtesy title of Viscount Enfield, married Harriet Elizabeth Cavendish, daughter of Lord Chesham.

Seven more children were added to the family in the next fourteen years, Julian being the youngest. This proliferation of Byngs placed a heavy burden on their father, now the second Earl of Strafford, for, as head of a noble house, he felt obliged to leave each of his children financially secure.[2]

So it was that, while Julian was born into a position of privilege, luxury and extravagance were unknown in his childhood. Most of his clothes were cast-offs and throughout his life his feet were to suffer from wearing the badly fitting boots which his brothers had outgrown.

The relative frugality of his early life and his place as the youngest of such a large family were to have lasting effects on Julian's character and on his attitude to the material things of life.

Agnes Paget's children, Julian's half-brothers and sisters, had taken up their careers or been married when he was born. The eldest, Agnes, had married Hedworth Hylton Jolliffe, MP for Wells. Her brother, Lord Enfield, was in Parliament. Henry was a lieutenant-colonel in the Coldstream Guards and Francis had just been appointed to a chaplaincy at Hampton Court. Julian's own brothers were packed off to school as soon as decently possible.

4

From the earliest Julian learned to be self-sufficient and yet to hold his own when the family was at home. His father's age – 56 when Julian was born – and stern and autocratic manner made him a remote figure of authority. His mother, by contrast, was warm, good-humoured and affectionate, and Julian was devoted to her, but he rarely saw her for more than an hour each day in the first few years of his life.

Perhaps because all members of the family were older and tended either to ignore him or give him orders, Julian's father did not appear to him to be much different in terms of age and authority than the others. He invariably treated 'Lord S' with respect but, unlike most of the family, never grew to fear him.

Julian's first introduction to schooling was in the classroom at home from which he took every opportunity to escape. He was taught to ride, to fish and, in due course, to shoot. Much else he learned unofficially – how to snare a rabbit and use a ferret.

In the summer of 1874, when he was barely twelve, Julian was sent to Eton. Here he spent the next four years in Coleridge House, a Georgian three-storied brick building on Keate's Lane. His tutor and housemaster was Henry William Mozley, a mathematics teacher.

Unlike most schools, where boys slept in dormitories, at Eton each had his own room. The authorities claimed that the practice was justified because it reduced the spread of infectious diseases. They did not see fit to say that it provided a refuge for the sensitive, the daydreamer, the scholar and the idler.

Latin and Greek were the staples of classroom work and took up two-thirds of the week's time. French, which had become compulsory two years before Julian arrived, mathematics and science made up the balance. Such fundamentals as English and religion were not taught in class but were the responsibility of the tutors. Nineteen of the thirty-one masters were clergymen, the ratio of teachers to boys was one to twenty-eight.

Julian was not a good scholar. Appalled by his poor reports, his father would fulminate in characteristic style, restrict his activities at home and cut his meagre allowance. But these measures had little effect on Julian's work. The priority of his interests were indicated one day when he traded his Latin grammar and his brother Lionel's best trousers to an itinerant hawker for a pair of ferrets and a pineapple.

When Julian left Eton in 1878, he had not progressed beyond the lower division of the fifth form. He was not distinguished in games, did not belong to the Cadet Corps and certainly never won a prize. He had acquired the nickname of 'Bungo' to distinguish him from his older brothers, 'Byngo' and 'Bango'.

5

At Eton today there is little to recall Julian's presence. Coleridge House has disappeared and, uniquely, so have Mr H. W. Mozley's records. 'Mr Byng minor' is shown in the school lists of the time and there is a short biographical note written about him in 1907 when he was a brigadier-general. He is to be seen in a photograph of Etonian generals of the First World War who visited the College after the Armistice.

In later years, Julian was to claim that he had been Eton's worst 'Scug' (freely translated, the term means 'undistinguished boy') a view which the College appears to share.

Lord Strafford's six older sons had known what their careers would be almost from birth but when Julian left Eton no decision had been made about his. By now his oldest brother, Enfield, was Under-Secretary of State for Foreign Affairs, Henry and Francis were in the Army and the Church, Charles was in the First Life Guards, Lionel in the Blues and Alfred was down for the 7th Hussars. With all his economies, Strafford did not think that he could support another son in the Army. The alternative seemed to be that Julian would have to go into 'business' but Strafford could not yet bring himself to face this humiliation, so no specific plans were made. The prospect had little appeal to Julian either. He desperately wanted to be a soldier. If he could not enter the Army as his brothers had done, he could at least get some military experience through the Militia. On 27th August, 1879, two weeks before his seventeenth birthday, he was commissioned as a second lieutenant in the 2nd Middlesex Militia (The Edmonton Royal Rifle Regiment).

Julian took his duties seriously, attended annual camps and was particularly well-regarded by his men. He enjoyed his first taste of the Army and longed for more. In June, 1881, he was promoted to lieutenant.

Apart from the Militia, he devoted considerable time to sports. He was an excellent horseman and both hunted and rode in point-to-points. He was a better than average shot, fished whenever he got the chance and played in the village cricket team.

In common with many of the noble families of Britain, Lord Strafford was keenly interested in amateur dramatics. A large number of the great houses contained their own private theatres in which the owners and their friends staged productions, often of quite a high standard. He had frequently taken part himself at Woburn Abbey, Nuneham and Panshanger. It was the age of the country house party. Guests who could sing or play an instrument were popular. Scratch entertainments of song and verse were composed and performed over a weekend. Everyone played charades.

Not surprisingly, Julian developed a liking for the theatre. When the family were staying in St James's Square, he often went to Drury Lane and soon developed a talent for writing sketches and the sort of doggerel popular in the music halls. He had a fair knowledge of music from the lessons he had taken at home. While he enjoyed the classics, in 1882, when he was twenty, his tastes leaned more to the banjo than to the violin.

That year his future was decided by chance at a Jockey Club dinner. The Prince of Wales, who knew Strafford well, asked what careers his younger sons had chosen. When he learned that nothing had yet been decided for Julian, he said that he would be glad to have him in his own regiment, the 10th Royal Hussars.

Strafford had serious misgivings about accepting the offer. The most he could possibly allow Julian was two hundred pounds a year and the Tenth was the most expensive regiment in the Army. Six hundred was considered the minimum allowance for the youngest officer – most had at least double that. Strafford's other sons had not shown the financial restraint which would encourage him to trust Julian to manage on so little. But it would have been impossible to refuse the Prince's offer without causing offence and that he was not prepared to risk.[3]

Julian was delighted when he learned the news. He had heard a good deal about the Regiment from both his uncle, Lord Chesham, and his cousin, Charles Cavendish, who had served in it. The Tenth had been commended for their service in the Afghan campaign four years earlier, and newspapers in England had been full of the story of the disaster when one of their squadrons had been swept away in attempting to ford the Kabul River. They had a reputation for efficiency which appealed to Julian's military interest, and for taking their polo and cricket seriously, both of which games he loved.

On 27 January, 1883, Julian was gazetted as a lieutenant and prepared to leave for India where the regiment had been stationed since 1873. Included in his uniform and kit were purchases which told something of what life there would be like – lance for pig-sticking 12/6, campaign knife 18/–, polo saddle 120/–, polo spurs 8/4, cholera belt (officers') 2/11.

The 10th (Prince of Wales' Own) Royal Hussars had been stationed in Lucknow for two years when Byng reported to them in March, 1883. The cantonment was located on the eastern outskirts of the city, its dusty roads shaded by flowering trees. There was about it an air of spaciousness – flower gardens surrounded most of the bungalows and the cavalry lines opened onto the beautiful grounds of the Bilkusha (or Heart's Delight) Palace. Beyond could be seen the domes and minarets of the many fine buildings of the old capital of the Kingdom of Oudh which lay along the banks of the River Gumti. In that direction too lay the Residency whose defence a quarter of a century earlier had inspired not only the British but Europeans and Americans as well as an example of Christian fortitude in the face of appalling conditions and overwhelming odds. The poems of Lord Tennyson and John Greenleaf Whittier were memorized in classrooms throughout the English-speaking world. It is not long since lines such as

> 'Dinna ye hear it? – dinna ye hear it?
> The pipes o' Havelock sound!'

and

> 'Ever upon the topmost roof,
> Our banner of England flew'

were learned by children in Auckland and Calgary, in Leeds and Boston. The flag still flew by day and night over the ruins of the shrine when Byng arrived.

J. W. D. Turner, an officer of the Regiment, later described him: 'He was a tall, slightly built boy of about 20 giving the impression, at least, of being dark because of an intent way of looking from under dark eyebrows with his head a little downward and having at that time the manner of one of retiring and thoughtful disposition'.[4]

He was greeted by Lt the Earl of Airlie, the adjutant, from whom he learned more about the regiment. Twenty of the thirty officers now serving with it had been in the Afghan Campaigns, as had W. W. Halls who would be his troop sergeant-major. It was Halls, then a signaller, who had received the message by heliograph telling of the disaster at the Kabul River, when nearly a squadron was drowned. Almost as many had died of cholera during the 'death march' returning from the Khyber in addition to the considerable casualties suffered in action. There had been no active service since that time. Only a few weeks before Byng arrived, the regiment had returned from camp where they had exercised in reconnaissance and outpost duties. The annual divisional commander's inspection was behind them and they were looking forward to the native cavalry polo tournament at the end of the month when they would play against the Bengal and Punjab Horse and the Central India Horse.

As a newly-joined subaltern Byng was soon at work learning his job. Riding school, foot drill on the square, fencing and single stick took up most of his time until the adjutant was satisfied that he could ride, drill and use a sword like an Hussar. He was as keen on polo as the other officers and now was able to put to use the knowledge he had acquired in the stables at Wrotham. Having grown up with horses, he had developed a discerning eye for horseflesh. Now he was able to buy two or three ponies cheaply and after training them for polo was able to sell them at a profit. He was popular with the other officers and, despite the frugality imposed by his small allowance, managed to do all that was expected of him.

As the hot season approached, routine in the regiment was modified to accommodate it. The first regimental parade of the day was at six a.m., followed by drill and manoeuvres for about an hour and a half. Officers then returned to their bungalows to bathe and change before having breakfast in the mess. From 9 until 10.30 the routine administrative tasks of orderly room and stables were carried out and by 11 o'clock all white men had taken shelter from the sun in their barrack rooms or bungalows. After lunch at 1.30 officers returned to their bungalows to sleep until 5 pm when polo and other sports were played. Dinner was at 8.30, usually with the band, and by 11 o'clock at the latest they were in bed.

The intense heat made life difficult in many ways. It was no longer possible to water horses in their lines but they had to be led to the River Gumti, a mile or more away, a trying and time-consuming process. Most Europeans suffered from the lassitude caused by the heat and from boredom with the monotony of their routine. Anything which could break it was welcome and there was general rejoicing when orders were received in June warning the regiment to prepare to return to England at the end of the year.

With the cooler weather of autumn, more active training was possible and Byng learned to appreciate the qualities of the Regiment's Walers, the wiry Australian horses on which the men were mounted. Social life in the garrison began once more, band concerts took place in the parks, and officers and men went out after black buck and shot quail in the neighbourhood. There was pig-sticking for the officers at Cawnpore.

Once a month, with the full moon for lighting, the Regimental Concert and Dramatic Club performed with the band. It was a kind of theatre which Byng enjoyed and for which he had a real talent. He organized a minstrel troupe as part of it, wrote humorous songs and sketches and performed himself, sometimes with his banjo. His 'The Stall Where the Old Mare Died' was a particular favourite with audiences.

On 4 December orders were received confirming that the Tenth would sail for England in two months time. Two weeks later, the officers gave a ball at the Chutter Munzil Palace to which people came from all over India. To greet the guests a picket, with its horses and men dressed as in the Afghan campaign, was posted by a campfire outside one of the verandahs. Indoors the oriental-style rooms were made even more glamourous with plants and shrubs from the horticultural gardens. Ice carvings lit by electric light were a feature of the decorations.

A farewell ball, given by the civilians of Lucknow, was followed by dinners with other regiments of the garrison. It was with some relief that the 10th Hussars left Lucknow at the end of January for Bombay where, on 6 February, they boarded the troop transport HMS *Jumna*. As they settled in, there was little regret at leaving the heat and dirt of India for the green fields of home. They could not know that they would fight a campaign in Africa before they would see the shores of England.[5]

Chapter 2
The Making of a Soldier

DURING THE PAST three years rebellions in southern Egypt and the Sudan had so grown in strength that the Khedive had only been able to contain them with British help. Early in 1884 a particularly dangerous threat to the ports of the Red Sea coast had prompted him to send an expedition of Egyptian soldiers and gendarmerie under Baker Pasha to the area. The hurriedly raised force met the rebels near the coast and suffered a bloody defeat. The soldiers, formed in square, had not had the stomach to meet the charges of the fanatical Sudanese tribesmen. The square broke and its survivors and most of the gendarmerie fled toward the base at Suakin which early in February was under siege. The War Office in London hurriedly directed the nearest available troops to reinforce the garrison of the port.

As HMS *Jumna*, carrying the 10th Hussars, the 2nd Battalion Royal Irish Fusiliers and an artillery battery, with their wives and children, approached Aden on St Valentine's Day, she was intercepted by the despatch vessel *Amberwitch* with instructions to call at that port for orders. There they learned that the troops on the *Jumna* were to proceed with all speed to Suakin to join the force assembling there under Major-General Sir Gerald Graham. Next day, having coaled ship and taken aboard camp equipment from the base, they sailed. By 19 February, the Tenth were ashore at the steaming East African port and taking over horses from the Egyptian gendarmerie.

With the help of the Navy, essential items of cavalry kit such as carbine buckets and nose bags were improvised. Two days later the Regiment re-embarked and sailed to the little port of Trinkitat, eighty miles to the south, where Graham had interposed his troops between the rebel force and Suakin. Within three weeks of Baker's defeat the British had assembled a force of one cavalry and two infantry brigades, artillery and stores ashore on the African coast, half way down the Red Sea.

11

It was dark when reveille sounded at 5 am on 29 February. During the night rains had drenched the soldiers sleeping in the open, and it was with difficulty that fires were relit to prepare breakfast. Wet and chilled, the men were quiet as they looked to their horses and packed their kits. Today they would march out to attack the Sudanese.

At 8 o'clock the order was given to advance. The infantry moved in a large square formation covered on their front and flanks by squadrons of cavalry. Julian Byng rode with the main body of his regiment to the rear. They were headed south towards the wells at El Teb where a large force of rebels were encamped. They had moved no more than a mile when the enemy opened fire with their Remington rifles from positions amid low sandhills thickly covered with scrub. They did no damage and retired slowly as Graham's force moved foward.

The axis of the infantry's advance avoided the scene of Baker's defeat but Julian and his men rode over the very spot. It was a horrible sight and the stench of decomposing corpses filled the air. For about three miles the route of the fugitives was marked by their scattered remains. Most had fallen on their faces as if cut down from behind.

Where Baker's square had been destroyed, the dead were heaped two or three feet deep. Scarcely a vestige of clothing remained on their contorted bodies. Of some only bare skeletons remained. All had been savagely mutilated. Nearby was a low mound bristling with sticks from which waved coloured strips of calico – the mass grave of the fallen rebels.

A heat haze was shimmering across the broken ground to the south as guns began to fire from the direction of El Teb. Shells burst near the advancing infantry and Julian could hear the staccato of a Gatling gun in the distance. With a crash, four guns of the Royal Artillery opened fire and, moments later, the machine-guns of the Naval landing brigade went into action. The infantry square halted and there was the sound of musketry in front. Through the dust and smoke Julian could see little from his position in rear, but after half an hour, during which the firing was intense, the infantry moved forward again on a new axis angled to the left. Later he learned that they had stormed the first position of the rebels. The squadrons which had been screening their movement returned to join the cavalry brigade.

At 12.20 pm, as the infantry moved across the ridge of the rebels' first position, a number of enemy were seen in the plain well to the right of the advancing square. Brigadier-General Stewart, commanding the cavalry, moved his brigade around the right of the infantry and gave the order to charge. The cavalry were in three lines. The 10th Hussars formed the first, the 19th Hussars the second and third.

Aligning himself on Major Slade, his squadron commander, Byng glanced back at his troop and then, in the words of Sgt. Major Halls, 'sat down in his saddle and rode like hell'.

After a gallop of three miles the 10th Hussars and the first line of the Nineteenth overtook the Sudanese and charged through them, cutting them down with their swords. When only a few of the enemy remained in front, the first two lines of sweating Hussars were brought to a halt. Only then did they learn that the third line was being cut up. As they advanced, the rear squadron had suddenly seen, away to their right, a body of enemy cavalry and spearmen approaching out of the bush. About a hundred horsemen carrying two-handed swords and riding bare-back were moving towards them, followed by twice their number on foot. The squadron of the Nineteenth swung to the right and met the enemy head on.

The remainder of the Nineteenth, followed by the Tenth, now wheeled about and found themselves faced by hundreds of Sudanese, mounted and on foot, charging toward them. As the Hussars advanced the rebel infantry disappeared, taking cover in the bush, and their horsemen rode straight through the British lines. Very little damage to either side resulted from this encounter and the cavalry galloped on to attack the rebel infantry who lay scattered among the scrub, hillocks and mounds of sand. The sharp thorns of the high mimosa bush made the cavalry horses swerve to avoid them and gaps appeared in the ranks. Choosing exactly the right moment to rise, the spearmen attempted to hamstring the cavalry horses or drive home their heavy spears. Like Zulu assegais in shape, these were given greater momentum by being weighted by a roll of iron at the end of the shaft. Other rebels threw boomerang-like clubs of mimosa wood at the horses' legs, bringing many animals to their knees, then attacked their riders with spears. More enemy appeared on the flank and the 10th Hussars wheeled to the left to attack them. On the flank of Julian's squadron, Lieut Probyn went down and Major Slade cut his way through to his side. At that moment Slade's horse was hamstrung and both he and Probyn were speared to death.

The two Hussar regiments charged again and again, doing little damage to the spearmen because of the unsteadiness of the gendarmerie horses which they rode. When finally they dismounted and opened fire with their carbines, the enemy scuttled off through the bush.

Rarely had irregular infantry resisted a cavalry charge as the Sudanese had done. Probably their courage and effectiveness were the result of experience in dealing with marauding bands of horsemen.

13

Whatever the reason, they provided a salutary lesson to those who believed that 'natives' always run away from cavalry.

For another month Byng and his troop were employed in reconnoitring and escort duties. On 13 March he was thrown when his horse was killed by a rifle bullet during the Battle of Tamai. Again he was under fire when the Tenth searched for and found another group of Osman Digma's rebels at Tamanieb, but his chief memory of that operation was of heat and thirst. The reconnaissance and subsequent attack had taken several days in arid country, under a blazing sun. Horses and men had been without water for forty hours when the rebel position was cleared and they won through to a stream which flowed beyond it.

With that action the last of the rebels had been dispersed and the campaign was over. The Tenth rejoined HMS *Jumna* and sailed for England on 29 March.[1]

Julian was now just over twenty-one. In later life he could seldom be persuaded to speak of his experiences in war and when he did he would usually divert his questioner with a joke. Once when asked about the Battle of Tamai he told of the Irish Fusiliers who formed one side of a square against which the Dervishes were mustering for one of their desperate assaults. 'In a brogue you could cut with a knife, a brawny sergeant shouted, "Now, boys, wait for my word to fire and when I give it, aim low and imagine every man jack of them is a landlord!".'

No record exists of Byng's reaction to the campaign. That he had done his duty and more is evidenced by his being mentioned in despatches in the London Gazette in July, 1884. He was fortunate that his first action came so early in his career, for it provided him both with the confidence of personal experience of battle and, if he needed it, a compelling incentive to study his profession.

The 10th Hussars arrived in Portsmouth on 22 April, 1884, and moved at once to their new station at Shorncliffe in Kent. Byng was soon involved in the training of young soldiers and new horses. As in India, sport was an important part of military life. Throughout the summer Julian played polo, and during the following winter followed the Regiment's drag hounds twice weekly over the Vale of Ashford.

In June, 1885, the Tenth moved into the South Cavalry Barracks at Aldershot. It was a modern structure when Byng first saw it, providing, for those days, excellent accommodation. (In 1940, known as Beaumont Barracks, it was occupied by Canadian troops, few of whom will shed a tear to learn that it was demolished in 1976.)

In 1885 the men and horses were as comfortably housed as any in the Army and the officers lived in considerable style.

14

The riding school, which still stands, was the scene that summer of the beginning of an interesting venture in royal education. At 6.30 am every morning H.R.H. Prince Albert Victor, Duke of Clarence, elder son of the Prince of Wales, was taught to ride like a cavalry officer by Captain Perry, the Riding Master.

Prince Eddie, as he was known, was Heir Presumptive to the throne after the Prince of Wales, and the 10th Hussars quite rightly regarded it as a unique distinction and indication of confidence that he should have been sent to join them as a subaltern. The Prince of Wales had always taken seriously his duties as Colonel-in-Chief and liked nothing better than occasionally to play at being commanding officer, even hearing disciplinary cases personally and drilling the regiment on parade. No officer had been appointed without his approval. By sending his son to the Regiment he was able to restrict the company which he kept to officers whom he had selected and over whose futures he could exercise a profound influence.

The Duke of Clarence served with the regiment for four years. During that time his father and his brother, Prince George of Wales, both later to be Kings, visited the regiment several times. Byng met them both on duty and in the easy atmosphere of the Officers' Mess and an enduring friendship with the future King George V developed from this period. Byng took no part in any of Prince Eddie's more informal social ventures outside the Regiment. Lack of money was one reason but he apparently lacked any real inclination to do so. He was not to attend a London ball until after his marriage.

Byng was fortunate in that two of his commanding officers, Lt-Cols A. E. Wood and R. S. Liddell were imaginative professionals. In 1886 the Tenth were given permission to carry out a 'cavalry raid' for three days in the area of Frensham and Haslemere to the south of Aldershot. In modern terms, it was a tactical exercise under active service conditions. It was a new departure in Army training and so successful that it became a pattern for all regiments of the cavalry.

During the same year Col Liddell bought a Nordenfelt machine-gun at his own expense and mounted it on a two-wheeled galloping carriage which had space for ammunition and a crew of two men. The Army liked it and six more were purchased and issued to other regiments. The Prince of Wales was so pleased with this development that he arranged for a Nordenfelt gun and carriage to be sent as a present from England to his nephew, Prince William of Prussia, later the Kaiser, who was then commanding the Hussars of the Guard at Potsdam.

Two events took place in October, 1886, which had an immediate effect on Julian's life. On the 20th he was appointed adjutant of the 10th Hussars. Nine days later his father died, leaving him a watch, one thousand five hundred pounds, since nothing had been paid for his commission in the Army, and two thousand more because, unlike his brothers and sisters, he had received no legacy from his grandfather, who had died before he was born.

The adjutant of a regiment is its commanding officer's staff officer – a term which implied that orders and instructions which he issued were backed by the authority of his C.O. In practice, the extent to which he exercised this prerogative depended on how much authority the commanding officer was prepared to delegate and how much he wished to retain to himself, and again on how much independence and authority he was prepared to give to his subordinate squadron commanders. Some of the hottest controversies within regiments centred around the role of the adjutant, but in the garrisons of Queen Victoria's Army in Britain, a fairly standard practice had evolved.

During most of the year a regiment was in barracks, usually in a garrison town such as Aldershot or Colchester. Its main preoccupation was in keeping the horses and men physically fit and drilled and disciplined to function in the field. The routines of stables, weapon training and the parade ground were conducted efficiently by the non-commissioned officers. Supplies and feeding were looked after by the quartermaster, routine reports and correspondence by the clerks, the whole under the general direction of the adjutant. Apart from the newly joined officers undergoing their initial regimental training, few, if any, others would be on duty in the barracks.

The remainder of the officers appeared with the regiment only when there was work for them to do – the occasional ceremonial parade, escort duties and so on. For about three months each year all were present for regimental training when the unit was exercised in barracks and in field manoeuvres at camp. Some officers studied for advancement. All were expected to spend several months of the year hunting, which developed their skill as horsemen and gave them an 'eye for country', and to be seen in the fashionable world during the London season. The quartermaster and the riding master were usually older men commissioned from the ranks and took little if any part in the officers' social activities.

In practice, the regiment was run by the adjutant and the N.C.Os. The post was not one which appealed to all young officers, for it meant giving up hunting, travel abroad on leave and much of the social life. By default it often went to an officer who could not afford these activities. But for the officer with ambitions in his profession, there could be no better training.

Byng was a superb adjutant. 'It was due largely to his efforts that, while posted close to the temptations of London, the defaulters' sheet was invariably clean. His efforts to provide sport and canteen facilities for the men, including his versifying efforts, were long remembered. To him was attributed the popular canteen chorus:

> "Ours is a happy, happy home,
> From the dear old 10th I never want to roam,
> What with drill and sports and cricket,
> For my '21' I'll stick it,
> Ours is a happy, happy home." '[2]

Another, 'His Busby Lines Were Hanging Down His Back' regularly brought down the house at Regimental Concerts.

Little was done for the off-duty soldier in the nineteenth century. He could not afford to go out in the evening yet in barracks there was nothing to do for amusement but go to the canteen and drink beer. The only other place he was allowed to be was his own sparsely furnished barrackroom. Inevitably drunkeness and fighting were common. Soldiers were often arrested by the military police on their way back from the canteen. Punishments were severe. Byng was sensitive to the unfairness and brutalizing effect of this neglect of the men's welfare and was prepared to use his new authority to alleviate the situation.

In each of the barrack blocks he cleared one room of its beds, arranged for some elementary furnishings in the way of chairs and tables and provided books. He explained to the men that they might use the room to read, relax and have a drink. Discipline and decorum would be their responsibility. Almost immediately the 'crime rate' in the Regiment plummeted. The men soon began to make the rooms more comfortable and as unlike their barrack rooms as possible. They became known as Blue Rooms and survive to this day as the squadron clubs of the Royal Hussars.[3]

Two other subjects which were a preoccupation of adjutants were drill and dress and Byng was punctilious in demanding the highest standards in both. Today this may seem anachronistic, but both subjects were regarded as having an importance far beyond that of mere display. The drill book was the cavalry tactical manual. Success on the battlefield often depended on the speed and precision of the movement of troops. The destructive force of a cavalry charge was far greater if delivered by disciplined troops riding knee to knee than by a mob of enthusiastic horsemen racing each other to be first to reach the enemy. Drill and discipline on the barrack square resulted in tactical efficiency and speedy reactions on the battlefield.

Dress was another matter. The time and attention paid to such minutiae as the length of a sword knot in Queen Victoria's Army should be considered in the light of the relationship between the Sovereign and her officers, for, from the time an officer received his commission from the Queen, he felt that he was directly in the Royal service. Even the style of the most routine letters which were addressed to the officer implied a Royal interest in his affairs:

'Captain A. B. Jones,
   Sir,
          I am commanded by His Royal Highness, the Commander-in-Chief, to inform you that your pay account is overdrawn to the extent of ten shillings and two pence and that an adjustment will accordingly be made in the amount deposited to your credit next month.
          I have the honour to be, Sir, your most obedient servant,
                                 H. H. Smith.'

The uniform was less the dress of the Army than the Queen's livery. Senior officers insisted that their juniors respect it as such. In the 10th Hussars no less an authority than their Colonel, the Prince of Wales, reinforced this attitude and records of the time show the many apparently trivial changes which were introduced to improve appearances.

Early in 1887 the regiment moved from Aldershot to barracks at Hounslow, on the western outskirts of London. Soon after they arrived, Byng became suspicious that contractors supplying meat to the 10th Hussars were cheating them on quality. During his next leave he attended Smithfield market in the early mornings and took a full course of instruction in meat inspection. He was able to prove his case and the contractors were changed. Later he attended a course at the Royal Military School of Music at Kneller Hall, partly because of his deep love of music and partly to enable him to improve the standard of the Regiment's band.[4]

While he was adjutant Byng became acquainted with Lord Rowton, a wealthy bachelor and sportsman. It was not long before they discovered that they had interests in common other than fishing and shooting. Rowton was helping Lord Iveagh, the founder of the Guinness Trust, in investigating the living conditions of the artisan classes in the working-class districts of London. Iveagh had established the Trust to provide better accommodation at lower rents for the skilled workers who had flooded into the city to work in its burgeoning industries, and who were now living in appalling conditions, the victims of unscrupulous landlords. It soon became evident to Rowton that, laudable though the aims of the Trust might be, it would only ameliorate the conditions of the families of working men. Yet below the poorest of these there were even more desperately unfortunate people, the down-and-outs who at best today would be called 'casual labourers'.

To measure the size of the problem, it was necessary for Rowton to visit the seamiest and most squalid districts of the East End, areas where policemen would not go alone, and where there was real danger to the visitor who did not belong there. The project appealed to Byng's instinct to help the underdog and he volunteered to help. For several weeks he accompanied Rowton on his investigations, learning far more in the process about how much of the population of Britain lived than most politicians, let alone officers of the Army.

Following their studies of the problem, Rowton embarked on his own project to build a gigantic model rooming house where respectable unmarried men could find cheap and comfortable lodgings. The first of the Rowton Houses was opened in Vauxhall in December, 1892, paid for by Rowton. The charge for a bed was sixpence per night, which included clean sheets, the privacy of a single room and central heating.

Unfortunately the company over the first weekend proved too rough for the supervisory staff. The superintendent gave a week's notice and the engineer departed with no notice at all. Anarchy reigned among the porters. Near to despair, Rowton appealed to Byng for help. Julian recommended that an ex-warrant officer or senior N.C.O. of the Army be put in charge and said that he had just such a man in mind – R.Q.M.S. Byatt of the 10th Hussars who was about to retire from the service. He proved to be ideal for the job and it became tradition that the staff of the Rowton Houses were retired soldiers.[5]

At Hounslow the Hussars were much involved with public duties in London and 1887 was particularly busy with the celebrations of the Queen's Jubilee. There were street linings, guards and escorts, inspections and visiting royalty. In June His Imperial Highness, Prince William of Prussia, in England for the Jubilee, visited the 10th Hussars at Hounslow. After a private session under Byng to learn the niceties of English drill, the Colonel of the Hussars of the Guard inspected the Regiment, rode with it through its manoeuvres and charged with it, riding beside the Commanding Officer. He afterwards watched the whole Regiment ride over jumps erected on the field. When the Regiment was reformed, the Prince made a 'most flattering and inspiriting address in English', then 'honoured the officers by taking luncheon with them'. A short time later he sent

19

them a portrait of himself in the uniform of the Hussars of the Guard with a suitable inscription.[6]

Portraits and others pictures donated by royalty to a regiment are frequently sources of embarrassment. They must be displayed in a prominent location or cause offence to the donor. The future Kaiser was particularly generous and few of the foreign regiments with which he had an honorary connection were spared. Sometimes high-spirited young officers volunteered to sacrifice their careers by assaulting a portrait with an axe and on such occasions adjutants had to place duty before inclination and restrain their enthusiasm. The Tenth were to wait until 1914 before a decent solution to the problem of the portrait was provided by the subject himself. Byng's own souvenir of the visit was much more desirable, for he could afterwards claim to be the only British officer to have put the Kaiser over the jumps.

Later that Jubilee year, when the Queen inspected a parade of forty-eight thousand troops at Aldershot, the 10th Hussars rode past under the command of the Prince of Wales, with Albert Victor, now a captain, commanding the right troop of the leading squadron.

As adjutant Byng was both the director and stage manager for the Regiment in these visits and ceremonials. He gained more experience of them in 1887 than most officers do in an entire career. It was not of much military value, but it did teach the virtue of taking pains. Mistakes or omissions in planning a ceremony result at worst in embarrassment, (as opposed to disaster in battle) but they can blight an officer's career just as effectively as ones which are made in action.

In 1888 the Hussars moved from Hounslow to York, the squadrons marching by different routes. When they camped at night, nearby landowners sometimes invited the officers for dinner and sent presents of food and beer to the troops. On 18 April, for example, the officers of Regimental Headquarters, including Byng, were entertained by the Duke of Portland at Welbeck Abbey. The weather was good and it proved to be a popular way of changing station.

The *Tenth Royal Hussars Gazette* later reported on the way in which Byng encouraged sport as a means of keeping the troops happy and occupied. 'In York, the adjutant particularly associated himself with all those who were keen on rowing, and the "White Rose Boating Club" was formed.' Unless duty intervened, the adjutant was always ready and willing to cox and coach.

'Under his supervision, the cricket of the Regiment attained a high standard. In one season, the regimental team lost only two matches out of twenty-one and these were to two very good Yorkshire teams. From cricket, Byng turned his attentions to football and very soon formed the first football team in the Regiment. The first game played behind the riding school in York Barracks proved such an attraction that very soon each squadron had its own team. Eventually a regimental side was chosen.'

At that time only officers might wear civilian clothes when off duty. Byng's hand could be seen in the extension of this privilege to N.C.Os of his Regiment.

In January Byng, at the age of 26, was promoted to captain. In March the Prince of Wales, now a Field-Marshal, arrived in York and took personal command of the 10th Hussars. Byng accompanied him as his adjutant as he inspected the barrackrooms and stables, attended mounted sports and rode at the head of his Regiment.

The Tenth had been pleased when they learned of the Prince's intention of visiting them, tempered by the news that he actually intended to live in York Barracks. The best rooms in the officers' quarters were cleared and freshly painted. Curtains and furniture were hired from Maples in London to produce what was probably the most comfortable suite of single officers' rooms in the British Army, all at the expense of the officers of the 10th Hussars. Julian was wryly amused when, during the visit, his Colonel-in-Chief said to him, 'You know, Bungo, I love coming here and roughing it with all you fellows'.

In December his father decided that Prince Eddie should take an extended tour abroad and spend the winter in India. Byng was invited to become one of his equerries, but declined on the grounds that he was studying for entrance to the Staff College and that he would not be able to do justice to both. Neither Prince Eddie nor the Prince of Wales resented Julian's decision. He resigned as adjutant in order to have more time for his studies.

In 1891 the Regiment moved to Ireland where the next two years were relatively uneventful. Much of Byng's time was now taken with studying for the Staff College entrance examination which he succeeded in passing. He spent some time away from the Regiment and was attached for experience to units of both the infantry and artillery.

In January, 1892, Major H.R.H. Prince Albert Victor died while at Sandringham on leave. The funeral in St George's Chapel, Windsor, was attended by much of the royalty of Europe and by all available officers of the 10th Hussars. The old Queen and the Prince and Princess of Wales were overwhelmed by grief which they sternly controlled during the service. It was significant of his opinion of Julian Byng that the Prince of Wales chose him to command the men of the 10th Hussars who carried Prince Eddie's body to its grave.[7]

In January, 1893, Byng reported to the Staff College at Camberley, Surrey, with the hope that in two years' time he would bear the

21

initials psc (for 'passed Staff College') after his name. They were the key to many of the Army's most interesting jobs, and the sign of a major step on the road to advancement in the profession.

Entrance to the College was normally by competitive examination, but a small number of candidates were 'specially selected'. Commanding officers could recommend officers for attendance whose experience, character and general competence made them particularly suitable for advancement and whose attendance at the College would be in the Army's interests. They nonetheless had to pass the entrance exams. Byng was one of those specially selected and his examination marks were about average.

The roll of students at Camberley with Byng included many names which became well known in the First World War – Rawlinson, Henry Wilson, Kiggell, Snow and Haldane.

The two years of Byng's course were a period of transition for the College. When he arrived the method of instruction was to expose the students to knowledge by means of lectures which they must supplement by individual study of campaigns and text books. Their qualifications depended on their passing examinations at the end of the final term.

In August, 1893, a new commandant, Col H. J. T. Hildyard, arrived and by the second year of Byng's course, a revolutionary system of instruction had been adopted. Many of the students had had experience in active operations and Hildyard appreciated that they could learn a good deal from each other. Henceforth much of their study was devoted to discussions chaired by an instructor. Final examinations were abolished and students were judged on their performance throughout the course. It was the basis of the technique used in the staff colleges of the Commonwealth today.

One can imagine the effect of such radical changes being introduced in the middle of a course. Many students and teachers viewed the changes with misgivings, but the more imaginative were enthusiastic about a development which would enable military study to keep abreast of the times and the progress of technology in the late Victorian period. Certainly it affected Byng in this way as later his admonishments to George Vanier in 1922 were to attest.

Another brilliant teacher at the College was Col G. F. R. Henderson. Since its formation, tactical studies had concentrated on the lessons of European wars, implying that there was little of value to be learned from conflicts which took place elsewhere. During Byng's course one of the main subjects was the German campaign of 1870–71 and the students visited Alsace and Lorraine to view the battlefields. But now Henderson also included for the first time a serious study of the American Civil War which ended in 1866 – one of the largest and most innovative conflicts of modern times.

During the summer of 1893 Henderson visited the United States to study the war on the ground. He took Byng with him and subsequently Julian helped him with the compilation of his classic work *Stonewall Jackson and the American Civil War*.

Byng took a full part in sports at the College. Every officer had a horse, both for use during tactical studies in the field and for exercise. All were expected to hunt with the 'Drag' of which Byng was secretary. A hunt is not always viewed kindly by those whose land it crosses but Byng, with his tact and personality, was successful in keeping the goodwill of the Berkshire farmers.[8]

Toward the end of April, 1894, Byng had arranged to spend a weekend with his old friend, Col J. P. Brabazon, commanding the 4th Hussars at Aldershot. On the Friday he was visited by a young cadet from the Royal Military College at Sandhurst who suggested that, since he had been invited as well, they might travel over together. His name was Winston Churchill.

Brabazon was an old friend of the Churchill family. Before going to Sandhurst, Winston had been offered a commission in the 60th Rifles, but had unfortunately not done well enough in the entrance examinations to qualify for an infantry cadetship and would thus only be acceptable to the cavalry. Evidently his father felt that his influence would enable Winston to obtain an infantry commission, but the young cadet made no secret of the fact that he would prefer to join Brabazon's 4th Hussars.

Byng was a superb horseman and Churchill gave every indication of becoming one too. He was a leader among the cadets in organizing point-to-point races and even a steeplechase and this love of mounted sports brought him into contact with Byng in his capacity as secretary of the Staff College 'Drag'. Winston dined with him on several occasions at the College. In December of that year Byng was one of the three judges of the riding competition for the R.M.C. cadets when Churchill came second with a score of 199 out of 200 marks – a good performance in a place where everyone rode.

It was evident that Byng was as popular at the College as he was with his Regiment. One of the other students later recalled that on the day of the 'break-up' inspection by the Duke of Cambridge, 'the students had assembled beforehand in the hall – artillery, sappers, cavalry, guards, Scotties, Marines, East Indians, West Indians – a variety of full dress kits seldom seen except at a Levee or a Durbar. We were getting rather bored when somebody called out "Bungo, where's your whistle?". Byng produced a tin whistle and, marching

23

around like a piper, soon started our feet tapping. Some followed him around the hall – a pied piper in cherry overalls – until presently he led forty or fifty earnest and studious British officers romping to his merry whistle out into the corridors.'[9]

Byng did well at the Staff College. Later he was to look back upon his two years there as the time when he began to focus his mind on the problems which the army would face in the future and was grateful to it for giving him a base of knowledge on which to build his further professional studies.

On graduating from the College in December, 1894, Byng returned to the 10th Hussars in Ireland to command A Squadron. There he remained for two years until June, 1897, when the Regiment moved back again to Aldershot where Julian left them for his first staff position – adjutant of the 1st Cavalry Brigade. Shortly afterwards he was appointed Deputy Assistant Adjutant-General of Aldershot Command, a move which foreshadowed his promotion from captain to major.

That year a new commander had arrived, Gen Sir Redvers Buller V.C. During the next two years, his staff, Byng included, were involved in the administration and training of the command which traditionally formed the basis of any expeditionary force sent from Britain.

In 1899 the possibility of war in South Africa became more apparent and preparations for it were a major preoccupation. Early in June Buller was informed that if it became necessary to send an army corps to South Africa he would be in command. Byng's days were filled with the work of preparing the force, but he did find time for a new interest.

Shortly after he left the cavalry brigade in 1897, its commander, Sir Reginald Talbot, invited Byng to dinner at Anglesey House. Anticipating a rather dull and formal evening, he found himself intrigued by another guest, Evelyn Moreton, who lived in nearby Church Crookham. She had heard of 'old Bungo' from officers of the 10th Hussars who told her he was a freak because he was bored with society and worked hard at his profession. She also knew that he was immensely popular, witty and had unusual charm. She obviously was prepared to be intrigued by him.

He was now in his late thirties and it seems unlikely that he had had any more than the most casual contacts with women. Perhaps it was that he found the conventional well-bred young ladies of the day shallow and uninteresting. He was certainly not practised in the arts of dalliance or courtship. Evelyn was puzzled:

'When we met of a morning out riding, if he was free, the fun began – though it wasn't always fun for me because I was bewildered, as he was never the same two days running. Talk of women being mutable – he could have given points and a beating to any one of them! On Monday he would be in his most enchanting mood; Tuesday he would treat me as a pal and a man; Wednesday he would hardly remember that I existed; Thursday he would be icily polite; Friday he would thaw a little and by Saturday be back in Monday's delightful mood! What could anybody make of such vagaries?'

For his part, Byng found Evelyn neither conventional nor uninteresting. She was twenty-seven when they met, the daughter of the Hon Sir Richard Moreton, Assistant Marshal of Ceremonies to Queen Victoria, and his Greek-born wife. Her grandfather, Thomas Ralli, was one of the heads of Ralli Brothers, the great Indian merchant house.

As a child she had lived in Ottawa where her father had been Comptroller to the Governor-General, the Marquess of Lorne, and her mother Lady-in-Waiting to Princess Louise. In 1881, her mother became Lady-in-Waiting to the Duchess of Albany and Evelyn began a lifelong friendship with her daughter, Princess Alice, and her constant companions, the children of the Duchess of Teck (the future Queen Mary and the Earl of Athlone).

This part of her background would not have seemed out of the ordinary to Byng. But the striking and statuesque Evelyn had a sense of adventure and a flair for the unusual. In 1887 she and her aunt, Lady Evelyn Moreton, had set off to travel around the world by ship, years before the first pleasure cruise. The route was much the same as the modern round-the-world yacht races – Cape Town – Hobart, New Zealand – Cape Horn – Rio. She had become drunk on rum punch when rounding the Horn, had delighted in the frontier atmosphere of Australia and been enchanted by the beauty of unspoiled Rio de Janeiro. When she arrived home to prim South Audley Street, just eighteen, with a swearing parrot and an assortment of Solomon Island weapons, her mother was scandalized.

Shortly thereafter she was ushered into society and her wealthy bachelor uncle, Pandeli Ralli, entertained lavishly for her. In 1885 Ralli had begun corresponding with an engineer major named Kitchener in Egypt about the murder of a mutual friend, Col J. D. H. Stewart, by adherents of the Mahdi. On his return to England, the two met and became close friends. Evelyn and her parents did not at first like this cold-eyed, hard-faced man with uncouth manners, who seemed to have so little in common with her very civilized uncle. But Ralli and Kitchener shared one passion – an implacable hatred for the Mahdi. It was not long before the rough edges disappeared from Kitchener's manners.

25

Ralli's liking for Kitchener became almost hero worship. He commissioned a portrait of him from Hubert Herkomer which he hung with one of Evelyn by the same artist in his home in Belgrave Square. When 'K' again returned from Egypt in 1898, a general and victor over the Mahdi at Khartoum, it was reported in the Press that he and Evelyn were engaged.

'As I was already head over ears in love with Julian Byng my wrath knew no bounds, and though my uncle also was furious at the episode, and considerably embarrassed, he had asked for trouble by the indiscreet placing of those two portraits. If we had married, what an awful misfit it would have been!'

Evelyn broke and trained young horses at her father's country house at Crookham and rode through the sandy, pine-covered hills west of Aldershot. Once an officer of the First Life Guards asked her to ride his second charger to see if it would carry a lady. It was a seventeen hand beauty and her father commented that she looked like a fly on a haystack. All went well until the Life Guards, on training, galloped over Long Hill. Seeing his stable companions, her horse joined in and Evelyn found herself caught in the ranks of a cavalry charge.

The inner circles of society in Britain in the Victorian period were largely the preserve of those English whose birth entitled them to the key. Foreigners were not easily accepted as fully-fledged members. Evelyn's grandparents were an exception, however, and her mother was allegedly 'the first Greek to marry an Englishman'. Until she was seventeen Evelyn normally conversed with her mother in French. Her enthusiasms and prejudices were more highly coloured than those of the average young woman and there was something of the Eastern Mediterranean in the vehemence with which she expressed them.

Through the summer of 1899 the situation in South Africa worsened. The British were reluctant to take any overt action which would precipitate an outbreak of war. Yet the garrisons in South Africa were outnumbered by the Boers and there was a fear that they might be overwhelmed before help could arrive.

Almost too late, on 7 October, Buller received orders from the Commander-in-Chief to mobilize. On the 11th forces of the Transvaal invaded the British colony of Natal.

Byng was appointed Deputy Assistant Provost-Marshal of Buller's corps and was immediately involved with the embarkation of the force. Headquarters left on 14 October but Byng remained behind to sail with its rear elements. In the intervening week his thoughts were often with Evelyn Moreton. Twice he started to ride over to Crookham to say he loved her and to ask her to wait for him, but turned back, afraid that if anything should happen to him, she would feel bound by the engagement.

When at last he came to say goodbye, Evelyn realized with rising dismay that he intended to say nothing of the future.[10]

Chapter 3
South Africa

WHEN BYNG LANDED at Cape Town on 9 November, 1899, he discovered a situation greatly different from that envisaged in England. British forces were surrounded in Ladysmith, Kimberley and Mafeking. The Boers had the upper hand and Buller was dividing his expeditionary force into what were relief expeditions rather than an army with the mission of winning a war by striking for the enemy capital of Bloemfontein.

Of more immediate interest to Byng were orders for him to take command, in the rank of lieutenant-colonel, of a new regiment of colonial irregulars whose formation had been announced the day before. It was to be called the South African Light Horse. Already more than two hundred men had assembled at Rosebank, outside the city where the new unit was to train.

The recruits were mainly South African but there were other colonials and a group of Texans who had brought shipments of mules to South Africa and now wanted to stay for the war. Many had had some military experience.[1]

Borrowing two horses, Byng and his new adjutant, Capt Villiers of the Blues, rode out to Rosebank. Word that two dandified Englishmen were coming to take charge of them had reached the men of the Light Horse and their arrival was watched with considerable interest. Walking through the camp, the tall slim lieutenant-colonel, in immaculate starched khaki drill, approached a group of some twenty men who were seated playing dice. They looked up but did nothing to acknowledge his presence.

Byng grabbed the nearest man by his collar, dragged him upright, kicked over the dice board and ordered the rest to get to their feet. Having tested his temper, his men were content to follow his orders.[2]

The ranks of the Regiment were soon filled. Most of the officers and N.C.Os were from South African militia units such as the Duke of Edinburgh's Own Volunteers and the Cape Town Highlanders.

There were also a number of loyal Afrikanders. The Stellenbosch Mounted Infantry joined to a man. In all eight squadrons, about six hundred men, were raised.[3]

The Light Horse were organized as cavalry but their main arm was the rifle. While they might carry out traditional cavalry roles such as reconnaissance, they were not designed for mounted combat. They would fight on foot.

Byng's new Regiment was recruited from tough, irreverent colonials, natural horsemen and, for the most part, good shots. They were used to thinking for themselves. There was no time to convert them into traditional Hussars or Lancers, even if he had been inclined to do so.

Byng recognized what a valuable military asset he had in his men. He set about channelling their natural skills into a force which could deal effectively with an enemy whom they so much resembled.

While his new Regiment cared little for military trivia, soldiers do value things which set them apart from other units. The Light Horse adopted the slouch hat, turned up on the left side with a plume of the long, black tail feathers of the Sakabula (*Diatropna Procue*). On it was their badge, a Maltese Cross, and below, the Zulu motto, USIBA NJALO NGA PAMBILI, or 'Feathers at the Front', with the letters SALH on the arms. At first they were known as 'the Sakabulas', but it was not long before the army dubbed them the 'Cocky-ollie Birds'. Byng was delighted.

Like most irregular soldiers, they had a light-hearted attitude to the rules of ownership of military property, including horses. Inevitably they were soon also known as 'Byng's Burglars'.

A committee of Johannesburg millionaires had offered to finance the new Regiment. In the course of his first meeting with them, Byng was asked by Sir Lionel Phillips how much money he would require for horses.

'I don't know,' said Byng, hoping for £20,000 as a beginning.

'Well, I think you'd better start off with enough to last for a week or so. Will £70,000 be enough?' Upon this, Phillips made out a cheque for that amount and handed it to the new C.O.

Clothing, saddlery, harness and wagons were made locally. Light ambulances were built, one even including a 'Roentgen' or X-Ray apparatus, whose owner arrived from England and was promptly taken on strength as medical officer. Byng's request to Ordnance for machine-guns was refused but he was told that he could accept a present for the Regiment. He cabled Vickers in England and two days later two Maxims on galloping carriages complete with harness and equipment left Southampton addressed to the Light Horse. Almost simultaneously Vickers sent a cable, 'From whom are we to receive payment?'

Byng replied, 'That is the very question I am asking myself.' The difficulty was overcome by Phillips and his friends.[4]

Mounted men were badly needed at the front and Buller decided to despatch the SALH to Natal. Four squadrons were hurriedly organized, equipped and mounted. Under Byng they embarked at Cape Town for Durban on 22 November, two weeks from the day the recruiting posters first appeared.

From Durban, a railway runs north-west through Pietermaritzburg, Colenso and Ladysmith to Johannesburg. Beyond Colenso the line crosses the Tugela River into territory where Boer forces were present in large numbers.

Late in November Clery's Second Division was camped at Frere, about 10 miles south of the river. With it was a mounted brigade which had been formed locally under the Earl of Dundonald, a colonel of the Second Life Guards. By 28 November it consisted of Bethune's and Thorneycroft's regiments of mounted infantry, and a composite regiment of Imperial Light Horse, Natal Carbiniers and regular mounted infantry. Later it was enlarged with the arrival of two cavalry regiments, the Royal Dragoons and the 13th Hussars.

> About this time [Dundonald wrote] Lieut-Col the Hon. J. Byng with 300 of the South African Light Horse joined my Brigade and formed part of it during nearly all the hard fighting in Natal. Col Byng was not only a good soldier but was possessed of that inestimable quality, clear common sense; he and his fine regiment, I soon found, could always be absolutely depended upon.

Be that as it may, the SALH were far from being trained and ready for the fighting which shortly must begin. While all could ride, several of the officers and most of the men had no knowledge of cavalry tasks. For the next two weeks Byng taught them how to form advanced and flank guards, pickets and patrols and the simple drills which all must know to avoid chaos. Particular attention was paid to dismounted action and to speed in deployment.[5]

General Buller arrived at Frere on 6 December and reconnoitred possible routes of advance across the Tugela River towards Ladysmith, which was besieged by the Boers. In general, the ground on the British side was open and sloped gently down to the river, but, opposite, steep hills dominated much of its length. About a mile east of Colenso the Tugela turns to the north and here the hill range extends across the river to a high rocky feature, Hlangwhane Hill.

On 14 December Buller decided to advance across the Tugela on

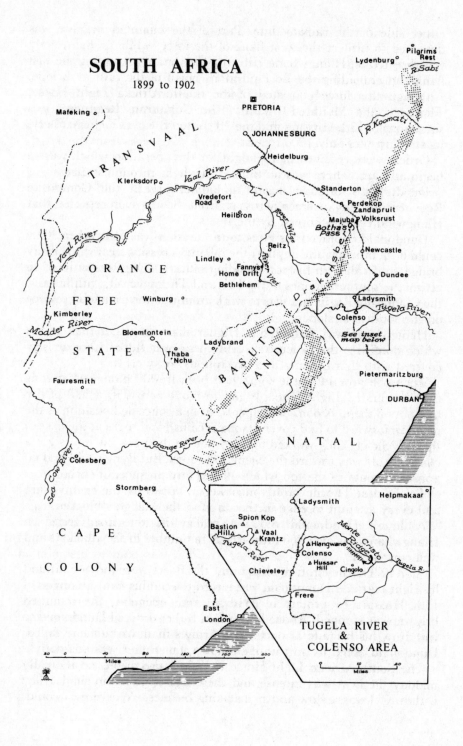

SOUTH AFRICA
1899 to 1902

Pilgrim's Rest

Lydenburg

R. Sabi

Mafeking

PRETORIA

JOHANNESBURG

R. Koomati

Heidelburg

T R A N S V A A L

Klerksdorp

Vaal River

Standerton

Vredefort Road

Perdekop

Zandspruit

Heilbron

Majuba

Volksrust

River Wilge

Bothas Pass

Vaal River

Reitz

Newcastle

Lindley

Fannys Home Drift

Bethlehem

Dundee

Ladysmith

Tugela River

O R A N G E

Colenso

See inset map below

Kimberley

Modder River

Winburg

F R E E

Bloemfontein

Ladybrand

B A S U T O

S T A T E

Thaba 'Nchu

L A N D

Pietermaritzburg

Fauresmith

DURBAN

Orange River

N A T A L

Sea Cow River

Colesberg

Stormberg

Ladysmith

Helpmakaar

C A P E

Spion Kop

Bastion Hill

Vaal Krantz

Monte Cristo Ridge

Hlangwane

Colenso

Tugela River

Hussar Hill

Tugela R.

C O L O N Y

Chieveley

Cingolo

Frere

East London

TUGELA RIVER & COLENSO AREA

Miles

either side of the railway line. Part of the mounted brigade was detached to protect the west flank of the force, while its main body was directed on Hlangwhane Hill with the aim of protecting the east flank and enfilading the Boer positions north of the railway bridge. Although this force consisted of the South African Light Horse, Thorneycroft's Mounted Infantry, the Composite Regiment, two squadrons of 13th Hussars and the 7th Battery, Royal Field Artillery, its strength was only 1000 men.

Orders were received at midnight for the operation which was to begin at 4 am. There was no time for daylight reconnaissance.

Dundonald's brigade began its advance with the Composite Regiment forming a screen across its front. Scouts soon reported that Hlangwhane was occupied by the Boers.

Dundonald deployed his guns to the south of the Hill, where they could both fire on it and support the infantry crossing near the railway bridge, and called in his commanding officers. Byng was ordered to attack the southern slopes of the Hill and Thorneycroft, with his and the Composite Regiment, was to work around to the east and advance on the south east slopes.

Hlangwhane was formidable. Higher than the other four kopjes which dominate the Colenso crossing, its lower slopes were densely covered with thorn, rising to a precipitous rocky crest.

The open ground to the south had been freshly ploughed and, as the dismounted Light Horse began to move across it, a hail of fire burst upon them. A pom-pom opened from a concealed position as the men ran forward to find cover among the bush and rocks at the base of the hill. Slowly they worked upward and in the next few hours got a considerable way toward the enemy positions. But Byng could find no approach route to the top which offered any prospect of success.

To the east Thorneycroft's men were stopped by the enemy's fire and every attempt to edge further around the Hill was blocked.

Although Dundonald did not realize it, the Boer force on Hlangwhane was over 800 men – equal in number to the attackers and well concealed.

At 7.40 Thorneycroft reported that the Boers were moving around his right rear and Dundonald was forced to send his two squadrons of 13th Hussars to protect it. Without reinforcement, the mounted brigade was stopped. About 11 am Gen Buller ordered Dundonald to withdraw his brigade at once. The Army's main assault had failed. Dundonald asked to wait until sundown, but Buller was adamant.[6]

The South African Light Horse were in a precarious position. By midday the heat was intense and there was little or no shade. The withdrawal was a slow and painstaking business. Where they could, men crawled to the rear. Elsewhere there were sudden rushes for cover. Byng managed to get most of his men away. But part of one squadron did not receive their orders because their squadron leader had collapsed with sunstroke. By the time they began to move, the enemy had cut them off by a rapid advance on their flank. Two officers and sixteen men were taken prisoner by the Boers.

The withdrawal had taken more than three hours and had cost more casualties than the attack. With such new troops, the wonder is that so many got safely away. Byng's cool leadership and the presence of a leavening of experienced men of all ranks brought them out.

The Light Horse were hot, tired and thirsty as they rode back to camp. Taking heavily defended positions was not their job and they had no reason to reproach themselves for not driving the Boers from Hlangwhane. In their first action, they had carried out one of the most hazardous of operations – withdrawal under fire. They had done it successfully and under control. Byng had reason to be pleased with his men.

He had spent the day trying to improve their positions and find ways of getting ahead. A bullet had clipped the heel from one of his boots and another had gone through his hat. It was not his fault that they were stopped.

Until after Christmas Buller's force did little but reorganize, regroup and train. The Cavalry were kept busy patrolling along the Tugela, but there was time for officers like Byng to reflect on the lessons of the battle and to train their men for the realities of the war in South Africa.

Within a few days the British Army had suffered three defeats at the hands of the Boers – Colenso, the Modder River and Stormberg. This 'Black Week' marked its first major reverses after a long series of little wars and it brought to light serious deficiencies in generalship, training and equipment.

There was nothing regimental officers could do about the inadequacy of maps, the shortage of artillery or poor generalship. But in the training of their troops there was much to be done. Byng was fortunate that his was an irregular force in which departures from army doctrine might be overlooked. Such was unlikely to be the case in the rest of Buller's army.

A joke current among the Boers was that it was an offence punishable by death to shoot a British general.

In Christmas week Sir Charles Warren, with his 5th Division, arrived to reinforce Buller. Stores and equipment poured into the railhead. Wagon trains pulled by huge steam traction engines moved ammunition and rations to forward dumps and the army's vast tented

33

camps. An observation balloon soon became a familiar sight overhead.

Another arrival was Winston Churchill, who had just escaped from a Boer prison camp and immediately presented Gen Buller with a problem. He wished to serve in the army, yet he was under contract as a correspondent to the *Morning Post*. After the Nile Expedition, the War Office had ruled that no soldier could be a correspondent and no correspondent could be a soldier.

The new regulation had been written because of Churchill's activities and now he was asking the former Adjutant-General to make an exception in his case. Evidently Buller felt justified in letting Churchill serve in an irregular force without pay. His words were, 'Alright, you can have a commission in Bungo's regiment. You will have to do as much as you can for both jobs, but you will get no pay for ours.'

Byng made him his assistant adjutant and allowed him to go where he liked when the Regiment was not actually fighting. Nothing could have suited Churchill better.[7]

Byng worked his men hard. When the Light Horse were not carrying out operational patrols and routine duties, they were training. The benefits were soon seen in action.

On New Year's Day a picket of the SALH on the extreme right of the army was attacked by 200 Boers. They fell back and the enemy followed. They did not observe that eight troopers had dropped behind the main body of the picket, concealing themselves behind rocks and ledges of a donga or gully. Twelve Boers attempting to move up this approach were met by a burst of rifle fire and made off with five riderless horses, two men on one horse and three lying still on the ground. There was no further interference with the picket.[8]

Buller now moved up the Tugela River to the west of Colenso and began an attempt to break through the Boer positions north of the river with a view to advancing on Ladysmith from the west. Dundonald's cavalry brigade on the extreme left was to secure that flank. Concealed by the foothills, they arrived nearly opposite a great bastion-shaped hill held by the enemy and separated from the cavalry by low ground. The hill dominated the attack now being made by the infantry and the enemy on it presented a serious danger. Dundonald ordered Byng to deal with them.

Sending two squadrons under Major Childe to advance dismounted on the hill, he led the other two with three machine guns toward the flank. Under accurate enemy shellfire, they crossed a mile of open ground to the shelter of a wood at the base of the hill. There Byng dismounted and worked his way forward. When he found a position

34

from which he could see the Boers on the summit, he deployed his men and sent Churchill back for the machine-guns. The hail of fire which he then opened on the enemy was so effective that Childe and his men were able to reach the top unharmed.

Byng's capture of Bastion Hill contrasted sharply with the operations of the rest of the army which culminated four days later in the bloody defeat of Spion Kop. From there, Buller moved four miles to the east and attempted again to cross the Tugela at Vaal Krantz. In anticipation of a break-through the cavalry were brought forward, but there were delays. About 4 o'clock on the afternoon of 3 February the SALH were told to bivouac as they would not be needed until next day.

The Regiment was travelling light and Byng and Churchill shared a blanket. When one turned over, the other was in the cold. Neither liked the arrangement. Byng was the colonel. Churchill was glad when morning came.[9]

The cavalry were not required, for this attempt also failed.

On 7 February Sir Redvers Buller heliographed to Sir George White, commanding in Ladysmith, his new plan for breaking through to relieve him.

First he would take Hlangwhane, the massive hill which was the scene of Byng's first action east of Colenso, then attack Bulwana from the south.

As a preliminary to the army's attack, Hussar Hill, a large wooded feature, would be seized to position the artillery. On 14 February the army moved east to occupy it. The SALH, thrown out far in advance, raced a considerable force of Boers to the hill. Byng quickly seized a commanding ridge where he positioned four Colt machine-guns, then drove an enemy picket from the hill. Half an hour later the leading infantry arrived and secured the position.

To reach the Tugela the army would now advance due north, the left or western division taking Hlangwhane, the right a ridge line which angled across their front from the extreme right to a point on the Tugela opposite their centre. The south-eastern end of this ridge rose to a hill, Cingolo, which was joined by a neck to the larger Monte Cristo ridge, which extended to the river.

The task of taking the two features was assigned to Gen Lyttelton's 2nd Division. The cavalry brigade was to remain in the right rear of the infantry and see that their flank was not rushed.

In the event Dundonald, urged on by Byng, Hubert Gough and Birdwood, his brigade major, departed from these orders and took two regiments, the SALH and Gough's Composite Regiment, by a circuitous route to the southern end of Cingolo. There they climbed

35

the extreme south-eastern point. It was hard going, the hill being covered with dense undergrowth and huge masses of rock over which the horses, led by their riders, scrambled as best they could. In places the path was so narrow that loads were dragged off the pack animals by the trees on either side.

Near the top of the hill was an open shelf which could not be seen from the heights above. Gough's men dismounted, scrambled to the summit and attacked the positions there. Meanwhile Byng took the SALH along the east slope of the hill, outflanking the Boer positions and firing into them from the rear. Assailed from two sides, the enemy wasted no time in withdrawing along the ridge in the direction of Monte Cristo. When Lyttelton's leading battalion panted to the top of the precipitous western slope, they found the hill occupied by the cavalry, who were now engaging the Boers on Monte Cristo with rifle fire.

It took the next two days for an infantry brigade to clear Monte Cristo, Byng's and Gough's regiments assisting on their right. Finally they worked right around the northern extremity to the Tugela.

The success was achieved at the cost of very few British casualties. On the face of it, it appeared to be a well coordinated attack, making the best use of cavalry in support of infantry. In fact, there had been no coordination. In the attack on Cingolo, Dundonald neglected to tell Lyttelton what he was doing and it was not until late in the afternoon, when the latter saw his infantry moving on top, that the situation became clear to him. By the time he was able to move forces into position for the attack on Monte Cristo, it was too late to continue that day.

It is of some historic interest that in 1900 three future army commanders, Byng, Gough and Birdwood, were working closely together and winning their first battles.

A week later the SALH were sent at top speed to drive off a force of four hundred Boers threatening the lines of communication near Frere, some 20 miles to the southwest. They rejoined the brigade on 26 February, their mission accomplished, and Dundonald walked over to their bivouac to see Byng. During their conversation Byng laughed and said, 'I must tell you what Winston said this evening. He wants to get the D.S.O. as it would look so nice on the robes of the Chancellor of the Exchequer. I told him he must first get into Parliament – if he could get any constituency to have him!'[10]

At last Buller's army of Natal had achieved a success. The hills across the Tugela were cleared by the infantry and on the 28th Dundonald's brigade crossed the river. By that evening two squadrons of Gough's Regiment rode into Ladysmith.

The SALH did not take part in Buller's triumphal entry on 3 March. They were patrolling well beyond toward the Drakensberg—the line of mountains to the west which marked the border of the Orange Free State.

During the two months which followed, the army rested, protected by the distant outposts of the cavalry. The blistering heat, poor food and isolation began to be felt by even the most robust of men and nerves became strained.

Early in May, Gough wrote in his diary:

(My) Regiment still remains on outpost duty, which I shrewdly suspect is on account of that extraordinary intriguer Byng having persuaded Dundonald to leave us here, because there being a big gymkhana on next Monday (7 May) the SALH wished to remain in the camp at Buy's Farm [sic] to practice for it and to all be there. I hate that way of Byng's of always trying to get the better of others while pretending the most friendly feelings. I have known several instances of this and would not trust him one yard as a friend . . .[11]

Poor Gough's prickly and suspicious nature made it difficult for him to form friendships with his equals and he never overcame his jealousy of Byng who was so easily able to do so. The entry in his diary was obviously written by a man under stress and could probably be disregarded as such, but for the importance of the relationship of the two men in later life. Even Gough must have known that, despite his opinion of Dundonald, neither he nor Birdwood, in charge of operational duties, would have connived at such shirking.

At the time of the entry Byng too was suffering from the effects of the campaign. At Byes Farm he was ill but refused to go to hospital. Toward the end of the war Dundonald, who had returned to England, wrote to him:

You have had your share and more than your share, and I who know what you have done as few others do, to the same extent, wish to see your life preserved for future use to the country—the hot weather has tried you—I saw it, but you would not give in, you remember Byes Farm.[12]

After two months of relative inactivity, Buller's army began to move from the Ladysmith area to clear the rest of Natal. Dundonald's force, now called the 3rd Mounted Brigade, consisted of the South African Light Horse, Thorneycroft's Mounted Infantry, the Composite Regiment and A Battery, Royal Horse Artillery.

On 11 May Buller set out with an infantry division and the Mounted Brigade to turn the left of an important position occupied by the enemy on the Biggarsberg range, which commanded the railway to north Natal and the Transvaal.

Forty miles east of Ladysmith, at Helpmakaar, two roads lead to the top of the hills. Buller's movements deceived the enemy into believing that he would use the more direct of these approaches, but instead he sent Dundonald along a much longer route, which wound its way south-easterly to the long sloping Uithoek valley, the SALH and Thorneycroft's Mounted Infantry moving along its eastern side.

The Boers referred to the Helpmakaar position as the Gibraltar of Natal. So confident were they of its strength that they did little to prepare it. When he learned of the British approach, the enemy commander, Commandant Ben Viljoen, badly out of position covering the wrong road, gathered his force of 500 men and raced to block the movement up the valley. The British cavalry and the Boers were in full view of each other as they raced for the neck which led to the Helpmakaar. The 3rd Mounted Brigade, advancing in a long line, enveloped the only trenches which the Boers had made and drove the few occupants away. Byng reached the summit of the Biggarsberg a few minutes before Viljoen occupied a few small kopjes across the path of the SALH. A sharp artillery duel took place, but the Boer guns were silenced by nightfall and during the dark the enemy slipped away.

At dawn the cavalry moved on northward along the Biggarsberg toward Dundee, 30 miles away, the SALH leading on the left front. The withdrawing Boers set fire to the veldt behind them, and soon sheets of flame and billowing masses of smoke obscured them from the cavalry and slowed the advance. At one point Thorneycroft's regiment emerged from the smoke to find themselves under heavy fire from an Irish unit of the Boer army. The SALH worked around the flanks, but the enemy abandoned his position before he could be cut off. Two miles further on he again attempted to stand, but was driven out by the same tactics.

25 miles beyond Helpmakaar the cavalry came under fire from enemy guns on a ridge across their front. The cavalry brigade's horse artillery was brought into action while the SALH extended and reached for the enemy flank. Night was falling as the Boers again withdrew and Buller ordered the cavalry to halt. Parched and blackened by burnt grass, they had covered nearly 40 miles during the day in waterless country, most of the time riding through smoke.

Dundonald's brigade entered Dundee on the 15th and on 17 May advanced to Newcastle, 37 miles distant. Two days later they crossed another 25 miles to the foot of Majuba Hill on the Transvaal border, scene of the British disaster of 1881.

The Boer position was strongly held and Buller decided to advance no further in that direction. He ordered the cavalry to withdraw. While the Royal Horse Artillery's guns were still in action, Byng concealed the SALH along the flank of the withdrawal route. When the guns retired, a large number of the enemy galloped forward to cut off the artillery, but rode into Byng's ambush. They suffered several casualties and soon broke off the action.

Buller now decided to outflank the enemy positions near Majuba by moving west into the Orange Free State via Botha's Pass through the Drakensberg Mountains, some 10 miles to the southwest. The approaches to the Pass on the Natal side were dominated on the east by the massive Van Wyck Hill and by a smaller conical feature called Spitzkop to the north.

For the operation the Light Horse were placed under command of Gen Hildyard of the 5th Division. On 6 June Byng reconnoitred Van Wyck as a position for heavy guns. Having driven enemy pickets from the hill with little trouble, he deployed his men along the north-western crest line, a front of about three miles, to cover the artillery reconnaissance.

The Boer commander, realizing the significance of the British moves, now made a determined attempt to retake the hill. Supported by a cleverly masked high velocity gun, the counter-attacking force climbed the south-western side, set fire to the grass and attacked the colonial cavalry. It was obvious to Hildyard that if he withdrew the reconnaissance force, it would not be so easy to occupy the hill a second time. He instructed Byng to hold it. In four hours of fighting, the SALH clung to their precarious positions until infantry arrived to relieve them. As night fell the Boers, who had been beaten back by Byng's men, retired and the SALH withdrew to bivouac at a nearby farm.

Next day, from its positions on Van Wyck, the heavy artillery of the Naval Brigade would be able to sweep the ridge of the Drakensberg and prepare the way for an infantry assault. One squadron of the South African Light Horse was ordered to seize Spitzkop, while the other two were to cover the left flank of the advance which would take them directly toward Botha's Pass itself.

Covered by the artillery bombardment, which began at 10 am on the 8th, the infantry attack was successful and the SALH occupied Spitzkop without opposition. Hurried along by Byng's rapid advance up Botha's Pass, the Boers were soon in full retreat.

On the 10th Buller's force, with Byng's regiment as vanguard, marched northward through the Orange Free State and entered the Transvaal at Gansvlei. Shortly afterwards the SALH were engaged by

Boers in position on a prominent hill astride their route. Byng immediately mounted an attack, supported by artillery, and drove them off. Pushing on into hillier country, he encountered a larger force in a stronger position. This time they were not so easily shifted and both sides came to close quarters. The SALH had six killed and ten wounded in the engagement, the Boers losing ten men killed before they withdrew.

Since before the assault on Botha's Pass the SALH had had more casualties than the entire remainder of the British force.

The country was now so easily defensible that infantry took the lead with cavalry brigades moving on either flank and the SALH protecting the rear – at that time by no means the least vulnerable portion of the force. After a sharp engagement at Alleman's Neck, Buller arrived at Volksrust on the railway, thus opening the way into the Transvaal. His next objective was Standerton, with its railway workshops, 50 miles to the northwest, on the line to Johannesburg.

On the 19th the advance began and on the 20th Lord Strathcona's Horse, commanded by Col Sam Steele of the Northwest Mounted Police, arrived from Canada to join Dundonald's brigade at Zandspruit.

On 23 June 3rd Mounted Brigade occupied Standerton where they remained until the 30th when they advanced to Heidelberg, leaving the SALH behind to protect the railway. In the next few weeks Byng picketed the line and made several reconnaissances against parties of Botha's forces which were reported in the area.

Lt-Col Norman Thwaites, who joined the SALH as a trooper, said that Byng loved danger for danger's sake.

'I remember a little affair near Standerton, when the SALH surprised a commando of Boers in the early morning. We rushed their lager and enjoyed the breakfast they were in the act of preparing for themselves. Before we got there, the firing had been fairly heavy and, having finished my two bandoliers, I sat up and began to take photographs of the scene. Suddenly a tall figure came into my line of snapshotting fire. "Why are you not firing?" asked Byng. "I am out of ammunition Sir," said I.

"Well there's a jolly over there with a boxful; go and help yourself," and Byng passed along the line, recommending the men to take good cover, the while he directed operations, hands in pockets.'[13]

By this time Byng's coolness under fire had become a legend in the Light Horse and his concern for his men had won their devotion.

On 27 July he accompanied G Squadron of his Regiment on a reconnaissance some four miles from Standerton. He was with one of the troops out of sight of the remainder when firing was heard ahead.

When he judged that they would soon be in view, Byng ordered his men to dismount and occupy a low ridge to their front. They had not been in position long when several Boers concealed in nearby kopjes opened fire on their horseholders. No enemy could be seen by the men on the ridge and Byng ordered the troop to mount.

As he climbed into his saddle Trooper R. W. Browne dropped his rifle and immediately got down to retrieve it. His horse, particularly excitable at best, now became frantic. Browne was unable to remount and his troop officer, Lt Wickham, told him to run alongside, which he did until the animal suddenly bolted, jerking him off his feet.

In spite of heavy fire which had now been opened on them, Cpl Dudgeon rode up and tried unsuccessfully to help Browne to mount behind him. The trooper, who had been ill, was by now exhausted. He told Dudgeon to save himself, saying that he would lie down as if shot.

'A moment or two afterward, the Colonel rode up to me, the only sign of any other of our men I could see was a grey horse clearing across the veldt with two men on his back. Before the Colonel could reach me, I shouted to him "For God's sake go, Colonel, save yourself." But he rode up to me and in a very quiet voice said, "Now try and run alongside me, take hold of my stirrup leather." I ran some little distance and, completely exhausted, I prayed the Colonel to leave me and save himself but he would not. After a slight pause he said, "Now have another try, I won't go too fast," and he put his horse into a gentle canter encouraging me all the time to keep on. I could not run when an officer rode up and called to the Colonel. I then begged him again to go which he did, seeing that I could advance no further, giving me a parting injunction to lie quite still. When the Colonel left, I am sure the Boers were not more than 300 or 400 yards away. . . . Few men have risked more during the war than did our worthy Colonel and Corporal Dudgeon.'[14]

Browne was captured by the Boers and within a few weeks was freed by British troops. On 20 September, 1900, he wrote to Byng, ending his letter

Words are too feeble to express to you my gratitude, but as long as my life lasts, I will feel grateful that you escaped in safety after risking your life to save your ever obedient servant, R. W. Browne.[15]

The Boer field army, with their government, was being gradually forced into the north-east of their territories where their only contact with the outside world was through Lourenço Marques, the Portuguese East African port. Lord Roberts was advancing on them from Pretoria tc the west while Buller, at Perdekop, was preparing to move northwards to join him. Byng received orders at the end of July to return to his brigade.

There were frequent brushes with Boer rearguards as the cavalry covered the advance. On 22 August, Major-Gen F. W. Kitchener, brother of Lord Kitchener, was sent with two battalions of his brigade, Byng's Light Horse and eight guns to clear the kopjes in the Komati valley. The country was extremely broken and the enemy were well emplaced, but Kitchener and Byng succeeded in dividing them and manoeuvring each band of Boers in succession from its position.

These operations took their toll of casualties. The SALH working through rough ground came upon a group of Boers who opened fire with rifles and three guns, killing one officer and wounding another officer and two men. Two guns of the 21st Battery came forward to assist and after a fifteen-minute duel with the Boer artillery, Byng's men drove them from the field.

The British Commander-in-Chief, Lord Roberts, now had three large forces near the railway line, half way between Pretoria, the Transvaal capital, and its eastern border. In this near mountainous country were remnants of the Boer forces. The area must be cleared and Buller was directed to advance with his column on Lydenburg, some forty miles to the north of Machadodorp.

For the next two weeks, the column, with Byng's Light Horse frequently in the lead, swept the area. By 11 September, when the 3rd Mounted Brigade descended into the Sabi valley, capturing large quantities of supplies and ammunition, they had blocked the Boer transport and guns into north-east Transvaal.

Buller was now directed to return to Lydenburg through the northern hills of the Mauchberg. The first part of the route led through the village of Pilgrim's Rest, past a rock-covered mountain which commanded the road for some miles. It was known to be occupied by the Boers. At 3 am on 28 September Byng led the SALH along a track which ascended the mountain some miles to the left of the road. After a four hour scramble in the dark, just before daylight, they came to the summit and surprised the Boer picket, which was just moving into position. In a short fire fight several Boers were wounded and the remainder withdrew.

The force arrived in Lydenburg on 2 October without further incident. It marked the end of the war for the Army of Natal. Buller returned to England and his force was absorbed into the main army in South Africa. The regiments of the 3rd Mounted Brigade were given other tasks and their commander, Lord Dundonald, went home.

Julian Byng had been at war for nearly a year. Of his performance Buller wrote:

Major (local Lt-Col) the Honourable J. H. G. Byng has commanded the South African Light Horse from its formation in November last. A cavalry officer of the highest qualifications, he has shown a singular ability in the command of irregulars. His regiment has done splendid service and I attribute this in great measure to Colonel Byng's personal influence. I strongly recommend him for award and advancement.

On 29 November, 1900, Byng was given the brevet rank of lieutenant-colonel as a reward for his service in the field.

The term of enlistment in the SALH had been for one year and in October and November the original members of the SALH were allowed to return to civilian life or to go home on leave. On 1 December, when Byng received orders to proceed into the Orange Free State to join in operations against the Boer leader, Christiaan de Wet, only 300 men of the SALH remained to take the field.

The character of the war now changed completely. With their field army destroyed, the Boers continued to fight, using the tactics of the guerrilla. Living off the country, bands of horsemen carried out raids deep into territory which the British thought was secure. Under skilled and resourceful leaders such as Christiaan de Wet and Jan Smuts, their elusive commandos struck where they were least expected, then vanished. The remainder of the war was devoted by the British to hunting them down and separating them from their sources of food, horses and manpower.

A new commander-in-chief, Lord Kitchener, had taken control of operations on 29 November and immediately began to organize his forces into columns as mobile as the forces of the enemy. Their size varied but usually consisted of a regiment or two of cavalry or mounted infantry with one or two guns or machine-guns.

Byng's first operation in the new campaign was to strengthen the force holding the Thaba 'Nchu – Ladybrand line east of Bloemfontein against a threatened attack by de Wet. The Boer leader passed northwards to the east of the line, and when Byng attempted to move against him, found his way blocked by a flank guard under Prinsloo, equal in strength to the SALH. He was recalled from attempting a pursuit and ordered to move south by rail into Cape Colony where another threat had developed. Two Boer forces under Herzog and Kritzinger had moved into British territory with the aim of stirring up disaffection among the Cape Dutch.

With three other columns under Col Douglas Haig, Byng took up the pursuit of Kritzinger. There were frequent skirmishes but the casualties of the campaign resulted more from heat, thirst and strenuous efforts of hunter and hunted. Dead and dying horses and abandoned waggons marked the trail which was followed by Byng's gaunt troopers. Then on 17 February word came that de Wet had crossed the Orange River into the Colony. Byng and his men were sent first via Murraysburg to Victoria Road to the west and then, towards the end of the month, by rail to Colesberg. He arrived with only 200 men, the remainder being held up when severe storms blocked the railway.

Further frustrations followed. With his handful of men Byng had to cover a frontage of 25 miles in trying to block de Wet's advance down the Orange. Units on his flanks were not in position. At 7 am on 27 February de Wet stumbled on a picket of fifteen of Byng's men at the junction of the Orange and Sea Cow Rivers. He captured seven and put the remainder to flight.

Byng's first news of the encounter came two hours later. Immediately he set off and rode for 45 miles that day in pursuit. But again de Wet had escaped and dispersed his band.

In April Byng was given command of a column of 503 men of his Light Horse, 450 Imperial Yeomanry and 17th Battery, Royal Field Artillery, with two guns and a pom-pom. The British had begun to quarter the country with lines of defended blockhouses, where possible connected by barbed wire fences, against which the mobile columns attempted to herd the agile Boers. Byng and his men were soon involved in sweeping the countryside to round up the commandos, and a small but steady toll of casualties and prisoners was taken. As a measure of the scale, when in May three burghers were killed and fourteen captured by two squadrons of the SALH at Metz Farm near Fauresmith, it was considered to be a remarkably successful coup.

In November Byng, with his column increased by Australian and Yeomanry units, moved through Heilbron and Vredefort Road to raid the basin of the Vaal River. One day, while accompanying twelve scouts of the SALH far in advance of the column, he surprised about twenty Boers watering their horses. Immediately he ordered the scouts to extend, then led them at top-speed down a slope towards the enemy, who, after firing a few shots, mounted and galloped away.

Within minutes the pace over rough country began to tell on the horses and both pursued and pursuers were soon strung out in single file with long distances between the riders. Byng, who was leading, overtook the hindmost Boer who threw down his rifle and surrendered, as did the others as they were overtaken.

Finally only four were left and they decided to make a stand in a farmhouse. Before they could take cover, Byng, armed only with his cherry-wood walking stick, was upon them demanding their surrender. They threw down their arms; then, seeing that he was alone and unarmed, they attempted to seize their rifles. At that moment, Byng's servant arrived, covered them with his carbine and completed the capture.[16]

It was about this time that a chance meeting rewarded Byng with a friendship he was to value for the rest of his life. Riding up to a railway station one evening, he found it abandoned except for a young Scots civilian sitting on his haversack who introduced himself as John Buchan. He wondered where he might find a meal and a place to sleep. Byng invited him to spend the night with his headquarters, which was markedly different in its comforts to Rideau Hall in Ottawa which each would one day occupy as Governor-General of Canada.[17]

In the first three weeks of January reports of de Wet being sighted drew the British columns off on pointless chases across the country until several were so exhausted they were obliged to refit. On the 20th Byng took the field, trying to pick up the slender threads of information which would lead him to de Wet. For ten days he swept back and forth between the Vlei and Wilge Rivers. Though he captured twenty-three prisoners he did not find the trail of the Boer leader.

Kitchener now massed all his columns in the area for a drive against de Wet, leaving Byng alone at Reitz, between the rivers, with orders to prevent de Wet and Mears joining forces, and above all to watch out for the latter and his guns. When they learned of the British concentration for another drive, Kitchener suspected that the Boers might think they could safely meet, in which case Byng would trap them.

Mears, with his men east of the Wilge, was almost encircled by British columns. He escaped to the west and received orders from de Wet to bring the guns through the line of blockhouses between Lindley and Bethlehem and push on southwest toward Winburg.

Mears moved at once and crossed the Wilge. As he approached the Fanny's Home Drift before first light on 2 February he walked into Byng's trap. When he tried to retire, he found his way blocked. The Boer force scattered, leaving two captured British guns and a Boer piece with their ammunition and crews in Byng's hands.[18]

Byng's column now consisted of 1284 mounted troops, 171 infantry, five guns and a machine-gun. For almost a year he had been commanding a force larger than his own regiment and his

45

success in doing so was marked by his promotion to the brevet rank of colonel.

For two weeks from 14 February three groups of columns under Byng, Rawlinson and Rimington swept east astride the Vaal River, then wheeled to the right to move down the west of the Drakensberg. On 23 February de Wet's men attempted to break through at Langverwacht, near Bothasberg. Their attack on Byng's line was repulsed and though de Wet himself escaped, the Boers lost 819 men.

It was Byng's last action in the Boer War.

Chapter 4
1902–1914

AFTER THE FIRST weeks of activity, following his arrival in South Africa, Byng had begun to write to Evelyn Moreton, little realizing that she had, in her words, been eating her heart out until she heard from him. Gradually over the months his letters grew in warmth until in January, 1902, he asked her to marry him, adding, 'Would she mind cabling the reply'. He received her answer in record time. The wording was peremptory: 'Yes please return immediately – Evelyn'. Possibly because it was despatched from Aldershot and its signature could have been that of Gen Sir Evelyn Wood, it was given priority and reached his column far out on the veldt within eighteen hours. Byng had it framed and kept it on his desk for the rest of his life.

After more than two years at war, his entitlement to leave was beyond doubt and Kitchener gave him three months in which to get married. On 12 March he sailed for England.

Evelyn found that constant campaigning with the unconventional South African Light Horse had wrought some changes.

'My prospective husband returned with some odd habits and a strong American accent – for there were many of that nationality among his men – and I remember the first day when we sat in the Crookham drawing-room he casually flung the dregs of his teacup in the fire – to my mother's speechless horror. She stared at him in a stricken silence of which he was blissfully unconscious and later said to me in a scandalized voice, "My dear child, he's a perfect savage! Will you ever be able to break him of such habits?" He didn't need much breaking once he found himself back in his customary environment, though I did discover that his ideas of things needed in a house were a trifle sketchy – for instance, it was quite a matter of debate as to whether or not curtains were needed in a drawing-room. He said no – I said yes. As a matter of fact throughout his soldiering life he had lived so long in barracks or mean lodgings that he had forgotten comfort.'[1]

The date of their wedding was set for 30 April. Following a honeymoon in France they would sail for South Africa where Evelyn would stay in Cape Town and Julian return to the war. A few days before the wedding Evelyn was unusually fortunate, for a prospective 'Army wife', to discover how Byng was regarded by the Secretary of State for War:

Dear Miss Moreton,

I want to write and tell you how lucky I think Colonel Byng is – and what a joy it must be to you how splendidly he has done in South Africa.

The C in C said to me just the other day 'Oh he's first rate'. I have before me a critique of him by another officer of standing and reliability 'He is one of the very best CO's out here. He has the gift of attracting the affection of his men and he is a conspicuously straight and reliable character.'

Don't let this get out in South Africa or the author will think I am giving away less favourable comments but I thought you would like to see it.

Indeed I wish you every happiness and a short trip if you have to go. . . .

Yours ever

St John Brodrick[2]

The Press was enthusiastic about the engagement which would 'ally two noble houses which bask in the sunshine of royalty'. The *Sketch* said that 'Miss Moreton is very good looking in rather more the Italian type than English – brilliant colouring, fine black eyes. She is an accomplished actress and has made her mark in some well known theatricals.' Another noted that 'Colonel Byng is an accomplished master of the graceful art of small sword exercise.'

No military band had been allowed in St Paul's Church, Knightsbridge, before that of the 10th Hussars played for Julian and Evelyn Byng's wedding. NCOs of the Regiment stood by each pew and formed an arch with their swords as the bride and groom came down the aisle at the end of the ceremony. Capt the Hon John Dawnay, a brother officer, was Julian's best man. The *Daily Express* commented that there were practically no decorations in the church – the colourful Hussars brightened it enough.

Other papers noted that much of London Society was there and called it a glittering occasion. Certainly there was sparkle in Evelyn's dress of white satin embroidered with diamonds and irridescent sequins, and in the brooches of the 10th Hussars badge in enamel and diamonds which Julian had given to each of the five bridesmaids.

The Church had done its best too, for the service was conducted by Bishop Randall Davidson, then of Winchester, but soon to become Archbishop of Canterbury.[3]

From the reception held in Evelyn's grandfather's house in Portman Square she and Julian left during the afternoon for their honeymoon abroad.

Byng had chosen Paris for the first stop of a few days, principally, so Evelyn claimed, because it led to the field of Waterloo where his grandfather had held the Farm of Hougoumont and where she could be educated in some of the family lore. Evelyn loved Paris and knew it well but it held little attraction for Julian. He was not interested in sight-seeing and while his French was serviceable, he could not keep pace with that spoken on the stage, so theatres did not attract him. 'He hated shops, and he wasn't the type to sit patiently in dressmakers' establishments during his wife's prolonged fittings.' One day, after being led around the Madeleine, boredom became too much for him. He asked in an all too audible voice, 'How do we get to the Morgue from here?'

Evelyn took him seriously. Soon they were walking along the Seine towards the Ile de la Cité where the small, one-storied Doric building stood on the tip of the island behind the Cathedral of Notre Dame.

Earlier in the nineteenth century it had been considered fashionable and a bit daring for foreign travellers in Paris to visit the Morgue and even in 1902 a constant stream of visitors poured in and out of its doors.

When they arrived in front of it, Julian obviously felt that the joke had gone far enough and said hesitatingly, 'Are you coming in?'

'Well you don't think I'm going to wait outside, do you?' Evelyn retorted.

He tried to dissuade her but now she insisted on entering.

Inside they found themselves in a viewing gallery separated by a glazed partition from a hall where the bodies of three unfortunates taken from the river were lying on black marble slabs. Naked except for pieces of leather across their loins, they were kept wet by a fine spray of water. Above them on pegs hung the clothes in which they were found.[4]

It was the first time Evelyn had seen a corpse and, while she did not find it as horrible as she had imagined it would be, she did not enjoy the experience. Like other English visitors, she and Julian found the most macabre aspect of the exhibition to be the complete indifference with which most men, women and particularly children viewed it.

The War in South Africa was coming to an end and for a time Byng considered applying for an extension to his leave. But in Paris Evelyn received a letter of good wishes from Kitchener which said that she must look on the short leave as a compliment because he could not spare 'Bungo' any longer.[5]

The honeymoon was over all too soon and they sailed for South Africa. Two days before reaching Cape Town a homeward bound ship signalled that peace had been signed. When they arrived, a message was awaiting Byng telling him to remain there until Kitchener came 'down country'.

For three weeks they stayed in the Lord Nelson Hotel where demobilized members of the Light Horse came in droves to see their old commander. Frequently he was intercepted in the corridor between his room and the bath and held a kind of levée in his dressing gown.

With him Kitchener brought orders for Byng to return to England and then to proceed to India to command the 10th Hussars who would be arriving there from South Africa in October.

The first ship available was the *City of Vienna*, a Ralli Brothers cargo vessel converted into a transport. With no freight aboard, she rolled through almost continuous rough weather and the Byngs and the eleven hundred guardsmen who were her passengers did not enjoy their passage to Southampton Water.[5]

Evelyn and Julian were in England for almost three months, buying tropical kit and making other preparations for the years which they expected to spend in India. Shortly before they left, Byng was invited by Edward VII, the enthusiastic Colonel-in-Chief of the Tenth, to spend two nights at Balmoral.[6] This was not necessarily an unusual honour for it is customary for the sovereign to receive the new commanding officer of one of his own regiments. However, the King would have been less than human if he were not especially pleased with the success of an officer whom he had personally chosen for a commission. For Byng, as for most soldiers, the command of his Regiment was his most cherished ambition. He had never been happier than when he set off with his new wife to join the Tenth at Mhow in the heart of the Central Provinces of India.

The routine of garrison life had changed but little since Byng had first joined twenty years before at Lucknow. After an early ride with Evelyn, his mornings were devoted to soldiering, afternoons to polo or cricket. Social life was limited since the other married officers of the Regiment had left their wives in England until they had seen for themselves what conditions were like in one of the country's least promising stations.

There was little of the glamorous East about Mhow. Set in what is now the province of Madhya Pradesh, all was sand-coloured and drab under a blinding sun. On the southern horizon a hint of blue hills marked the Vindhya Range but elsewhere nothing relieved the monotony of the scene but the heat haze which shimmered and distorted the unvaried flatness of the plain.

With the end of the South African war, many regular soldiers were due for discharge and the Regiment was well under strength when it arrived in Mhow. The next few weeks were devoted to absorbing drafts of men from England, getting to know its new horses, and to the innumerable administrative tasks associated with taking over equipment and quarters in a new country. With his usual energy, Byng hurried the process, prompted by the knowledge that the Regiment might soon have to take the field.

To the north lay the princely state of Indore ruled over by a particularly sadistic Maharajah, Shivaji Rao Holkar. His oppressive measures against his subjects included punishments such as imprisoning victims in cells alongside hungry tigers, separated from them only by rickety partitions which sometimes collapsed. So appalling was his misrule that it could not be allowed to continue and in January, 1903, the Mhow garrison – infantry, cavalry, artillery – marched out to persuade him to abdicate in favour of his 12-year-old son Tukoju Rao. The argument was compelling and, using ill health as an excuse for abdication, he invited his son to take the throne.

The experience had been useful for the Tenth as training, even though they had not been called upon to fight. It also contributed to a misunderstanding on the part of Evelyn which she retained for the rest of her life.

Lord Kitchener had arrived in India as Commander-in-Chief on 28 November, and shortly thereafter invited the Byngs to stay with him for the great Delhi Durbar, when King Edward VII would be proclaimed Emperor. It would involve an absence of at least two weeks from Mhow at a time when Byng, knowing that trouble was brewing in Indore, was working hard to prepare his newly arrived Regiment for operations. He refused to go and asked Evelyn not to attend either. He seems not have explained the real reason to her, perhaps because of security, but she believed it was because he hated pageantry of any kind and was content with his work. Doubtless she would have been more upset had she gone to the Durbar alone and her husband had marched out to war while she was away. Nonetheless, she missed a remarkable pageant which she would have attended in great style and in the utmost comfort. Though she felt that Julian had been unreasonable in refusing her permission to attend, it was a trivial matter which did not affect their relationship. Years later however, it was to have some serious consequences.[7]

At almost the same time, on 26 December, 1902, another great British soldier, Field-Marshal Lord Roberts, the Commander-in-Chief of the Army, was taking a hand in Byng's future. He wrote to Lord Knollys, the King's private secretary, recommending him for command of the cavalry brigade at Salisbury in one or two years' time when the barracks would be ready and its units had returned from South Africa. He said that he realized that the King would not want him to be removed from the 10th Hussars at present but 'perhaps His Majesty would not object to his being given a brigade command a year or two hence, and superseding some 31 cavalry officers senior to him.'[8]

In normal circumstances a commanding officer could expect to spend three or four years with his regiment during which he could implant his own stamp on its style of life and its methods of operation. Whatever goals Byng may have set himself with the Tenth, it now seemed likely that, unknown to him, he would not be given as much time to achieve them as he expected.

Characteristically, one of the first changes he introduced affected the comfort of his men. The high collars of their khaki drill jackets were hot and uncomfortable in the blistering heat. He had them altered so that they could be worn open and issued the men with collars and ties similar to those worn by officers. It was a revolutionary innovation for the times and, while very popular with the troops, it caused some wagging of heads at army headquarters. Kitchener came to see the change for himself, liked it and approved it for the rest of the army.[9]

Later in the year came a further indication that Byng was destined for advancement when he was given command of a cavalry division temporarily formed for the manoeuvres of the Punjab Command in December.[10]

While the Regiment was happy and efficient and Byng's star was clearly rising, India brought bitter disappointments to him and his wife. Both wanted children but though Evelyn conceived more than once, her pregnancies ended in miscarriages. So badly were these mishandled by the doctors in Mhow that her future hopes for children were forever frustrated.[11]

Another blow to them both was the disastrous ending of Byng's service with his beloved Hussars. On 13 January, 1904, in a polo match, he and his horse crashed to the ground and he was carried from the field in agony, both bones of his right forearm dislocated backwards. An operation which involved cutting down on the joint, sawing through the olecranon process, replacing bones in situ and wiring the separated fragments together appeared to be satisfactory but in the view of his doctors long and careful massage and passive movement treatment would be necessary to alleviate the stiffness of the joint. Byng would have to go to England, without delay. In the meantime he was unfit for service with troops.[12]

On 5 March the Byngs sailed from Bombay in the S.S. *Persia*. The most significant occurrence on the voyage was Byng's meeting with Edgar Horne, the President of the Prudential Assurance Company, with whom he formed an enduring friendship. Every autumn thereafter until 1913, he and Evelyn were to go to Horne's estate at Stiffkey on the Norfolk coast for partridge shooting. There they developed a love for the coast, its flat fields and its marshes which eventually drew them to finding a home in East Anglia.

Byng's return coincided with a decision by the War Office to form an army school for cavalry to be located initially in a tented camp at Netheravon on Salisbury Plain. Three weeks after he arrived in England, Byng was appointed its first commandant and arrangements were made for him to receive treatment on his arm at a nearby military hospital.

For five months Byng suffered torments as he struggled to make his arm useful again. Gradually some movement returned to the elbow but no amount of will power and determination could make it whole. When he next appeared before a medical board on 1 September, they found that his right arm was shortened and was somewhat atrophied, but the limitation in the movement of his elbow joint was expected to improve. To Byng's immense relief, they found him fit for general service.[13] In a cupboard he was afterwards to keep a bottle labelled 'The olecranon of a male adult of forty' (which he called 'Byng's Bottled Bones').[14] Why he kept it, it is not possible to say, but it may have been as a reminder of a victory of will power over body, where defeat would have spelled the end of his military career.

The function of the Cavalry School was to improve the standard of training of squadron officers and to bring into balance the experience of South Africa with the accepted tactical teachings for a European war. Writing about it in the October, 1907, issue of *White Lancer*, Col John Vaughan said of Byng that he 'had the task of trying to make bricks without straw, an operation at which, however, he was strangely successful'.

The School could not long remain under canvas and in October it was moved into barracks in Borden Camp in Hampshire which was then under construction. From their comfortable house beside the sparkling Avon in the Wiltshire Downs the Byngs moved into damp and dreary quarters, surrounded by a sea of mud and rejoicing in the graceless name of 'Hogmere Lodge'.

In the spring of 1905 Byng was promoted to brigadier-general and given command of the 2nd Cavalry Brigade with Headquarters at Canterbury. The Byngs moved into an attractive eighteenth century house set in a small old-fashioned garden at Bridge, a quiet village south-east of the city on the road to Folkestone and Dover.

Early in his period of command, Byng presided over an interesting departure from the normal routine of training. In August, 1905, he brought two of his regiments to Dover to train for amphibious operations. The disembarkation of cavalry over beaches was notoriously difficult, yet it was a task which might be required in a raid on an enemy coast.

There was a holiday atmosphere about the training which hundreds of spectators turned out to watch. For several days Byng practiced his troops in slinging horses and in the use of boats, rafts, pontoons and piers. All horses were swum in the sea, an exercise which the people of Dover found particularly fascinating.

On 26 August, watched by Lord Methuen and Sir Robert Baden-Powell, the Inspector of Cavalry, the training was concluded with a brigade landing exercise.[15]

Byng's period of command was adjudged a success by the Army. In June, 1906, he was made a Companion of the Order of the Bath, and a year later he was transferred to the 1st Cavalry Brigade in the Aldershot Command. There he and Evelyn moved into Anglesey House where they had first met in 1897.

For an officer as imaginative as Byng serving under Sir John French, who then commanded at Aldershot, was a galling experience. Despite his successes as a cavalry leader in South Africa, where he exploited both their mobility and dismounted fire power, French insisted that in Europe cavalry would fight mounted. To him their arms were the sword and the lance, the steel weapons, the arme blanche. This latter term gave its name to a controversy which divided the army on the subject of the employment of cavalry in war and on how it should be trained in peace.

Proponents of the arme blanche believed that cavalry should be trained for its traditional roles of screening and reconnaissance. In these, its most likely opponents would be enemy cavalry and these it must attack swiftly, boldly and with the confidence of superior training in its weapons of steel. To agree that a principal role was dismounted action would be to forfeit cavalry's ability to exploit the unexpected and would result in a diminution of the cavalry spirit of boldness, of independence and the capacity for rapid decision.

It was a point of view which was widely held in Britain and was the accepted doctrine of the German and French armies.

Others held that, while there would still be a need for cavalry to perform its traditional tasks, it must also be able to fight dismounted as infantry, using its rifles and machine-guns. It could act as a mobile reserve which could move its firepower rapidly to threatened sectors of the field, or it could defend (as opposed to observe) a flank or could seize and hold a distant objective until infantry could arrive. And, heresy of heresies, it could destroy enemy cavalry with bullets.

Byng was of the latter school. Sir John French was his commander. The result was frustration. Not until French departed was enough ammunition allotted to train cavalry troopers to shoot as well as the infantry. By that time, the summer of 1909, Byng had moved again.

In the South Cavalry Barracks during this time were stationed the 16th Lancers, commanded by Hubert Gough, who had led the Composite Regiment in South Africa. He showed that he was as competent in peacetime as he had been in war and Byng recommended him for promotion and the command of a cavalry brigade.[16]

On 1 April, 1909, Byng was promoted to the rank of major-general, having this time been brought up twenty-four places on the seniority list. He was to take command of the East Anglian Territorial Division in August, 1910, and in the meantime would be on half-pay. Having no other home, he decided to move to the vicinity of his new headquarters at Warley. A few weeks later he and Evelyn leased Newtown Hall, a pleasant house on the outskirts of the sleepy old town of Dunmow in Essex. Their landlady was the famous and beautiful Countess of Warwick, whose brother-in-law, Alwyne Greville, Byng had known in the 10th Hussars as equerry to the Duke of Clarence.

At Dunmow, for the first time since he joined the Army, Byng enjoyed the pleasures of a comfortable home and the freedom to do as he liked. His only military duty was that of the part-time editor of the *Cavalry Journal*. Both he and Evelyn were pleased to find that they had happened upon a literary and artistic circle who had gathered at this secluded spot. Among the friends they made were the editors of two national newspapers, H. A. Gwynne, of the *Morning Post*, and R. D. Blumenfeld, of the *Express*, and writers such as H. G. Wells, Samuel Bensusan and Henry de Vere Stacpoole.

There was hunting in the area with the Essex Hounds and London and the theatre were easily accessible. Byng read extensively and welcomed the opportunity of broadening his already wide range of interests.

The Boy Scout movement, formed by Sir Robert Baden-Powell, was beginning to gain momentum when Byng moved to Dunmow. He was deeply, if quietly, religious and he found that the ideals of the movement were ones to which he had subscribed all his life. He accepted the appointment of District Commissioner for North Essex and began to organize it with characteristic thoroughness. The object was to form troops in every community in the county so that as many boys as possible could join. To give the project the prestige which would encourage local support, he persuaded a galaxy of prominent people to help. Princess Alice became the President of his North Essex Boy Scouts Association and its vice-presidents were her husband, then known as Prince Alexander of Teck, the Earl of Warwick and Field-Marshal Lord Kitchener of Khartoum.[17]

Sir George Arthur in his *Life of Kitchener* (Macmillan 1920) credits Byng with interesting the Field-Marshal in the Scout Movement after his return from East Africa in April, 1911. While staying with the Byngs at Newtown Hall that spring, he went with them to morning service. On coming out from the church he said, 'You know, Bungo, when I hear that response "Because there is none other that fighteth for us, but only Thou, O God," I rather wonder where we generals come in, don't you?' That the aloof and flinty old warrior might become concerned with the welfare of boys was inconceivable to most of the Army. Yet that summer he became president of the 1st North London Boy Scouts and had them to camp at his estate, Broome Park.

In 1910 some 400 Scouts camped at Hatfield Park, Lord Salisbury's estate. The *Evening Standard* of 4 August reported an incident which showed Byng in characteristic form:

> Camping with the Scouts of the district over which he is Commissioner is Major-General the Hon Julian Byng. On Monday morning he arrived in camp with sixty of his Scouts and at once volunteered to take charge of all fatigue work for the day so that the other Scouts might be free to take part in the rally. In the afternoon a messenger was despatched to ask if General Byng would honour the rally with his presence. Word came back that the General had been discovered working in his shirt sleeves in a rubbish pit and that he sent a message saying he was afraid he could not manage to get there because he was one of the fatigue party.

In October, 1910, Byng officially took command of the East Anglian Division but was able to continue his voluntary work with the Scouts since by that time the most demanding tasks of organization had been completed. In the following July he made one of his last appearances with them when he took 240 of his boys to the great rally of 30,000 Scouts at Windsor held in honour of the coronation of King George V.

As part of the Territorial Force, the East Anglian Division's wartime role would be the defence of the British Isles. Its home was that part of eastern England which would be the obvious target of an invasion or raid by the Germans, who were seen to be the most likely enemy.

The Division's authorized establishment was 534 officers and 17,217 men, all part-time volunteer soldiers, with a sprinkling of Regular Army staff officers and instructors. Byng worked hard to popularize the Territorials and to train its officers by lectures, courses and tactical studies. At the end of July, 1911, when the Division assembled for its annual training at Thetford, its enrolled strength was 473 officers and 14,804 men, of whom 10,000 came to camp. More would have been there but for an early harvest.[18] A Press report commented that Byng 'is an indefatigable worker and during this year's camp has been with the troops all day and well into the night. Gen Byng has an unusual facility for public speaking and few soldiers can talk to other soldiers in a manner so lucid, enlightening and concise.'[19]

Before another annual camp took place, Byng received an interesting if puzzling telegram at Dunmow.

Cairo, 4 July, 1912
'Congratulations very glad to think you will be with me in Cairo.
Kitchener'

Ten days later came a letter dated 13 July from the War Office.

'Dear Byng,
    Will you inform me confidentially whether it would be agreeable to you to be considered for appointment to command the force in Egypt. The vacancy is due on the 8 November next. Pay £3 daily with allowances.
                              Yours sincerely,
                              Military Secretary.'[20]

On 27 July the *Essex Chronicle* announced the appointment, observing that Byng was the youngest general on the staff of His Majesty's Regular Force.

Simultaneously with the telegram from Kitchener, Byng was made Colonel of the 3rd Hussars, an appointment which caused considerable comment in the Army and the Press. The colonel of a regiment does not command it in an operational sense but is a senior officer who can represent it when necessary in the higher echelons of the Army and in public, and supervises such important matters as the selection of officers. He is a trustee of its traditions and long-term interests. For an officer from another regiment to be appointed to the post can only have been regarded at first as an affront by the officers of the Third. Evidently their dissatisfaction, if any, was short-lived for Byng was to hold the position for more than ten years.

Late in October, 1912, the Byngs left Victoria Station for Cairo, where they expected to spend the next four years.

Egypt's strategic position astride the trade and invasion routes between Europe, Asia and Africa had for centuries rendered it the object of dominance by foreign powers. With the creation of Britain's empire in the East, so grew the importance to her of the overland route from the Mediterranean across the isthmus of Suez to the Red Sea. The Germans did not exaggerate when they referred to the Canal as the jugular vein of the British Empire. Through it flowed the bulk of the trade between Europe, Asia, Australia and New Zealand. In war it would be the route taken by troops from India and the Pacific Dominions to the main theatre of conflict in the west.

Successive British Governments had recognized that security was not simply a military matter. They believed that an Egypt which was prosperous and peaceful would be more secure than one where discontent and political turmoil might undermine Britain's strategic interests.

While Egypt was in theory still a province of the Turkish Empire, Britain had become her 'protector'. No written convention spelled out the terms of the British occupation and Kitchener, her chief representative, bore only the title of Consul General, as did the agents of other European powers. Theory had it that his authority was no larger than that of his colleagues which was entirely diplomatic. In practice, however, he represented 'the ultimate authority in the country in all those matters . . . which the protecting power chose for the moment to regard as calling for the exercise of its control.'[21]

In the fifty years of its occupation, Egypt had become vastly better off, but both the now impotent ruling class and the small part of the general population who thought about the subject, gave the British no credit for their well-being. They saw only that their country was occupied by a nation alien in race and religion.

The Egyptian army was British-trained and was firmly under the control of its Sirdar, Gen Sir Reginald Wingate. With the Police, it was able to deal with internal security matters both in Egypt and the Sudan.

As an ultimate deterrent to disaffection, and to protect the Canal, there was a British garrison of 5,000 men. Known as the 'Force in Egypt', it consisted of four infantry battalions, a cavalry regiment, two batteries of artillery and administrative units.

These and other British troops in the Eastern Mediterranean, such as the garrison of Cyprus, were Byng's command.

The mere existence of the force was enough to prevent overt interference by foreign powers in Egypt, but to deter the organization of insurrection within the country it was useful to remind the population of its presence. 'Showing the Flag' through military displays was one method and Byng himself was obliged to take an active part, as the force commander, in the social and diplomatic life of the capital.

Kitchener's predecessor, Sir Eldon Gorst, had tried to show his regard for the feelings of the Egyptians by adopting an exaggerated simplicity in the style of life of the British Agency. In doing so he showed little appreciation of the character of the people to whom the change spelled not sympathy but weakness. Kitchener's experience in

Africa and Asia had taught him that a measure of pomp was necessary for prestige and was even conducive to popularity. The change from Gorst's drabness was sudden and startling. Kitchener and his staff were always impressively turned out and mounted. The plain semi-European dress of his servants was replaced with scarlet and gold Turkish costumes and once more the carriage of the British Consul General was preceded by running syces in Oriental livery.

In nothing was the contrast between his austere nature and his policy more apparent than in his official entertaining. By any standards, it was lavish and promised to be more so when the new ballroom which he had ordered as an addition to his residence was complete.[22]

By an act of singular ineptitude, the Office of Works had allowed the force commander's house to pass into the hands of the Suez Canal Company and when the Byngs arrived in Cairo nothing had been found to replace it. Kitchener insisted that they stay with him at the British Agency until a suitable place became available. From that time and even after they had moved into their own home Evelyn acted as Kitchener's hostess whenever one was required.[23] In effect, she was the senior British wife in Cairo and became the leader of its society.

While his duties as force commander were of far more interest and concern to Byng than the social tasks which were imposed upon him, it is worth noting the experience which both he and Evelyn gained in the cosmopolitan diplomatic and political life of Cairo. Years later, in Canada, it was to prove invaluable.

Some twenty years earlier Evelyn and her parents had spent a winter in Cairo with her uncle, Pendeli Ralli, who had entertained extensively. The city was little changed and, being fluent in French, the principal foreign language of Egypt, she fitted easily into the social scene.

She entertained distinguished visitors as various as J. Pierpont Morgan and Midshipman Prince Albert, the future King George VI, who, as the society press had it, attended a magnificent ball, which Kitchener gave, 'under the shelter of her wing'.

Soon she was the driving force in the Soldiers' and Sailors' Families Association and the Cairo Branch of the Society for the Prevention of Cruelty to Animals. In 1913 she acted as delegate from Egypt at the International Congress on the White Slave Traffic held in London. She was no mere figurehead but raised money for her charities and personally lobbied legislators to support her causes, particularly against cruelty to animals, with such success that Julian predicted that she would end with a knife in the back from an angry donkey-boy.

When a small force, such as the British maintained in Egypt, is faced with the likelihood of being outnumbered on the outbreak of war, it has a compelling incentive for efficiency. The rigorous exercises which Byng set it and his insistence on the highest standards in its training and administration were soon apparent. In January, 1914, Gen Sir Ian Hamilton spent a few days in Egypt and wrote the following to the King's private secretary:

> I must again break my custom of not troubling you with familiar Mediterranean topics, just to send you a line containing news which I think the King will appreciate, viz., that Julian Byng has more than fulfilled the promise of last year and is, in every respect, the most successful commander we have had in Cairo for many years.
>
> I cannot too highly praise his military work. I do not say he is a great administrator, or a constructive, original thinker. But short of that he has all the qualities:– intense keenness, exceptional ability, great commonsense, unfailing physical energy.
>
> On the social side he and his wife (although unfortunately the War Office has let the beautiful General's house slip through their fingers, so that they have an inferior base of operations to their predecessors) fill their position in just the way I am sure the King would wish it to be filled. Amidst all these wealthy, cosmopolitan visitors, as well as amongst all the diplomatists, Suez Canal magnates, Levantines etc. etc., they stand out as very important people and they do this in virtue not so much of their social position or official rank, as simply because they are both high class, charming people.[24]

In the spring of 1913 Byng gave serious thought to retirement from the Army. When the four years of his posting to Egypt were complete he would be 54 years of age, and there seemed to him little chance of his gaining further advancement, or even of obtaining another interesting job. When Evelyn left Cairo in May to spend the summer in England, he asked her to look for a possible permanent home. Both had learnt to love East Anglia through their shooting holidays at Stiffkey with the Edgar Hornes and it was on its coast that she focused her search.

Based at Newtown Hall, which they still had on lease, she spent some weeks ranging the countryside and eventually found a near derelict Georgian manor house at Thorpe-le-Soken near Frinton on the Essex coast. The garden was overgrown, its 2½-acre lake covered with slime, but it filled Julian's requirements in that there was shooting nearby, it was close to the sea, there were two good golf courses within three miles and, though London was seventy miles away, he could reach it in an hour and ten minutes by train.

The property, plus a big farm, was up for auction within a week. Evelyn made an absurdly small bid for the house, two hundred acres of land and three tumble-down cottages and was somewhat dismayed to find herself their owner. Early in September Julian arrived for a month's leave and Evelyn was relieved when he unreservedly gave his approval to the house.

So they came to possess Thorpe Hall whose history could be traced back to Saxon times. It would never be an ostentatious 'great house' but, chiefly by Evelyn's efforts, it would become a haven of peace and comfort surrounded by one of the most beautiful gardens in England.

In October, having seen the King, Byng returned to the hothouse atmosphere of Cairo. Behind the outward friendliness of diplomatic custom, several powers were attempting to undermine the British position in Egypt. Their agents sought to encourage rebellious elements in the country and to make deals with the Khedive and the host of political opportunists who surrounded the Court. In this sort of activity the Germans were more energetic than most.

Relations between the British and German Agencies, if rather formal, were not outwardly unfriendly. The Byngs had a week at Luxor in December, 1913, and included at their table for Christmas dinner Baron and Baronin von Falkenhausen.[25]

The side entrance of the German Agency abutted the Byngs' house in Kasr-el-Doubara and the Cairo police spent some time in their drawing room recording the visitors who called next door.[26]

In April, 1914, Evelyn was preparing to return to England in a month's time to spend the summer when she became convinced that she would never return to Egypt. So strong was the feeling that she arranged to sell everything which she would not need in England. 'Kitchener was rather puzzled by this conviction and tried to chaff me out of it, saying – which was quite true – that we had close on three more years of the appointment to run; but nothing could shake that queer intuition, and at last he asked me whether he too would not come back and, though I was less certain about him, I doubted if he would. Nor did he, as it turned out.'[27]

In early June Kitchener returned to England where, as the international situation worsened, he was retained by the Government. When Britain declared war on Germany and the Austro-Hungarian Empire on 4 August, the responsibility for protecting British strategic interests in Egypt lay entirely in Byng's hands. His first action was to put into effect plans to protect the Canal and the state railways from sabotage and to order the internment of enemy aliens, many of whom had been under surveillance for months.

With these precautions taken and the garrison at their war stations, Byng awaited developments. The first came in the form of a warning order from the War Office that the Force in Egypt would be relieved by troops from India. Then on 12 August a telegram from Kitchener who had become Secretary of State for War ordered Byng to return to England to command a cavalry division as soon as he had been relieved in Egypt. Lt-Gen Sir John Maxwell, his replacement, arrived on 8 September, and Byng sailed on the first available ship.[28]

Chapter 5
Cavalry Leader 1914

BY THE END of September, 1914, the bulk of the British Regular Army had joined the Expeditionary Force in France. Overseas garrisons were being drawn home, their places being taken by units of the Dominions, the Indian Army and the Territorials.

All reserves had been mobilized. The Territorial Force was as yet unready to take the field and, despite the strength of the Fleet, a German invasion was thought to be possible. The War Office planned that the Regular units returning to Britain be formed into new divisions, at first for home defence, later to be deployed against the enemy, not necessarily in France.

The first two of these formations were the 7th Infantry and 3rd Cavalry Divisions. Into them were absorbed the last Regular units based in Britain. The War Office envisaged that they would not be sent abroad for at least two months.

When Byng arrived in England he was told that the 3rd Cavalry Division, now forming at Ludgershall, north of Salisbury, was to be his new command. Its 7th Cavalry Brigade, consisting of the 1st and 2nd Life Guards and the Royal Horse Guards (The Blues), was up to war strength and had been in camp since the beginning of September. Their commander, Brig-Gen C. T. M. Kavanagh, was an old friend of Julian's. They had been subalterns together in the 10th Hussars and he had succeeded to the command of the Regiment after Julian's polo accident in India.

The 6th Cavalry Brigade had just begun to form. So far only two of its regiments had arrived in the country, the Royal Dragoons and the 10th Royal Hussars, who had been together for two years in South Africa. Its third unit, the 3rd Dragoon Guards, had been delayed in sailing from Alexandria and was not expected to arrive for another month. Brig-Gen Ernest Makins arrived to take command of the Brigade on 21 September.

Of the two horse artillery batteries, one had been disbanded a few months earlier and was hurriedly being reconstituted, but was far from ready for war. The other supporting units of the Division, engineers, signal, medical, transport and veterinary, were being improvised. No sooner had the Engineer field squadron been formed than it was taken away for another division already in France. All units were deficient in stores and transport.

Even more serious, the 8th Brigade, his third formation, was not due to be formed until November and its Yeomanry regiments were as yet untrained.

When Byng arrived at the County Hotel in Salisbury, where the officers of his headquarters were billeted, it was late afternoon on Tuesday, 29 September. About 8 pm Lt-Col H. S. Davey, his senior administrative officer, arrived from Ludgershall where he had been working for the past four days at forming the headquarters and trying to get a grip on the problems of the Division. That evening and the next day Byng spent in discussions and in visiting the two brigades. The headquarters became more mobile with the arrival of its complement of riding horses.

Evelyn had arrived with Julian, hoping that they would have some weeks together before the Division was sent abroad, but events were moving faster than either of them could know. On Thursday, 1 October, a wire came from the War Office asking if the 3rd Cavalry Division would be ready to move in 48 hours. Byng replied that they would not and sent them a list of the appalling shortages of men and equipment which would be essential for operations.

At three o'clock next afternoon he received a warning order to be ready to move at very short notice to an unknown destination.[1]

On the Continent the focus of the opposing armies which had been concentrated on the approaches to Paris began to shift toward Belgium.

Following the retreat from Mons in August, the French and British regrouped and turned to the attack. Into a gap between two of the German Armies, the BEF drove forward and recrossed the Marne.

Everywhere the Germans began to fall back. The pursuing Allies gained bridgeheads north of the Aisne on September 13 but within two days were halted by the entrenched, if exhausted, enemy along a line which ran from Soissons through Rheims to Verdun.

Throughout these battles, Gen Joffre, the French commander, had sought to find and envelop the western flank of the Germans. With stalemate on the Aisne, he continued his probes while the enemy resumed their attempts to sweep round the ever-extending seaward wing of the Allies. By the end of September the opposing armies had reached Lens.

The French and British commanders now decided on a bolder manoeuvre – to disengage the BEF and move it north into Belgium, well beyond the flank of the battlefront. There it could begin to drive behind the German right wing, or be in position to go to the aid of the Belgians defending Antwerp, should that prove necessary. The move would shorten its lines of communication to Britain and make it easier to reinforce.

The Germans, invading in August, had driven the Belgian Army into the western part of the country. The bulk of it held the great port and fortress of Antwerp, which was masked by a German force which seemed content to do no more than tie the garrison to its positions.

On 28 September the situation changed dramatically. The Germans brought up siege artillery and began a systematic destruction of the Antwerp defences. The guns of the fortress could not reach the enemy batteries and it was evident that, unless the siege could be raised, Antwerp must fall. The Belgian Government, the Court and the field army were in danger of being trapped. They began to plan a withdrawal to Ostend, leaving the fortress troops, some 80,000 men, to carry on the defence as best they might. On the 30th the Belgian Prime Minister asked the British and the French for help.

The loss of Antwerp would be disastrous to the Allies. The force attacking it was little more than four divisions in strength, scarcely more than would be needed to mop up after the heavy artillery had done its work. It might be possible to relieve the fortress by a relatively small force, attacking from the direction of Ghent against the German left rear where lay the enemy's heavy guns.

On September 30, the British Government offered to send the 7th and 3rd Cavalry Divisions if the French would also help. Two days later, it was decided to send a force of Royal Marines and heavy artillery to reinforce the defence of the port. On 4 October, the Government decided to follow them with the balance of the newly formed Royal Naval Division and to despatch the two divisions offered on the 30th to raise the seige. They would be commanded by Lieutenant-General Sir Henry Rawlinson and were to cooperate with a French force of one division and a brigade of Fusiliers Marins.

The warning order which Byng received on Friday, 2 October, was followed by near frantic activity in his Division. Suddenly the miserly trickle of equipment and other resources burst into a flood.

By the afternoon of the 5th, when the Division began to entrain for Southampton, its Field Ambulance (the medical unit) could not move because it had no harness. The Engineer Field Squadron was not yet formed, but most other essentials had been received. Embarkation began at 10 am on the 7th, Byng's headquarters being on S.S. *Honorious*, 'a small dirty boat'.

Byng and his staff could do nothing to influence the embarkation authorities, whose only concern was to load the Division as quickly as possible in the few available ships. Troops and equipment of different units were thoroughly mixed up in the process. Eventually, after a five- hour wait for darkness at Dover, the fourteen ships of the convoy were escorted by twelve destroyers to Ostend and Zeebrugge where they arrived at 4 am on 8 October. The four transports which were unloaded at the latter port had been picked at random and contained parts of several different units. New horses and saddlery for the Royal Dragoons and 10th Hussars were shipped direct to Belgium to meet the units on arrival. The landing of the cavalry was protected by the 7th Division which had landed the day before.

By the previous evening it had become obvious that the relief of Antwerp was impossible, so Rawlinson was ordered to cover the withdrawal of the Belgian and British troops from the city, then to join Sir John French's force and form its left column in an advance to the east. At 11.25 pm on the 8th, he arrived at Byng's headquarters, the Terminus Hotel in Ostend, and briefed him on the situation.

Next morning, the 3rd Cavalry Division moved to Bruges where they billeted on the outskirts of the town.

On the 10th, when Rawlinson's force (now designated 4th Corps) began its move southward, the armies of four nations were converging on the same small area of the Flanders plain. Determined to retain at least one corner of their country, the Belgian field army was withdrawing to hold a line from the coast at Nieuport along the River Yser and its canal almost to Ypres. The French division, originally destined for the relief of Antwerp, was in Ypres itself. On the left of the main French forces, their Tenth Army was extending their line to the north. They had reached the La Bassée canal and their cavalry was covering the detrainment of the BEF at St Omer. The Germans were keeping pace with the French and the cavalry of both armies were probing to the north.

Following the surrender of Antwerp, the German 3rd Reserve Corps was about to move south and west after the Belgians. Behind them, and unknown to the Allies, was to follow a new Fourth Army composed of four newly raised Corps. The orders of its commander, Duke Albrecht of Württemberg, were to break through the Allied left flank between Menin and the sea and capture Calais.

Byng's task was to protect the 7th Division as it moved to the south. Enemy cavalry had been reported in Hazebrouck and Bailleul but little else was known about their movements. Obviously they could be encountered at any time. To find them, Byng sent patrols far in advance and to the flanks of the marching troops. His regiments were now performing a classic task of cavalry for which they were superbly trained. That they were bold and skilful was soon to be proved.

But a division is much more than a collection of regiments. If its skills and fighting power are to be used effectively, staffs, communications, supporting arms and services, and the brigade and divisional commanders need to be practiced in working together.

The first time the 3rd Cavalry Division was exercised in its operational role, the part of the enemy was played by the German Army. Fortunately the Division was to have a few days to shake down before it met them in strength.

The green and fertile Flanders plain into which the cavalry advanced was sprinkled with tiny hamlets, isolated houses and woods. Hedgerows, frequently with trees in them, separated the small fields. Only a few low hills and ridges rose from the plain and even from these the view was often obscured by trees. For the most part the main roads outside the towns were straight and flat, the stone pavé of the surface being only wide enough for a single vehicle.

An army could lie hidden in this close country and horsemen sent to find them would only discover their presence by stumbling on them or by coming under fire.

Byng's two brigades worked down the roads between Bruges, Thourout and Roulers, then to Menin and Ypres, ensuring that the country was clear of enemy. To protect the marching infantry, Byng could not move his main strength too far in advance, but small patrols were sent well ahead. On 10 October six armoured cars, armed with machine-guns and manned by Royal Marines joined the Division. Next day two of these surprised a German cavalry patrol south of Ypres, capturing two officers and three men of the 7th Jaeger Regiment, the Division's first sight of the enemy. Two days later, as the 6th Brigade was marching from Roulers to Ypres, an officer's patrol of the 10th Hussars stumbled upon German cavalry on the outskirts of Comines and lost one man captured.[2]

When the Division marched into Ypres they learned that the country to the west was clear. On the morning of the 14th Byng's cavalry moved through heavy mist and rain to meet Allenby's Cavalry Corps moving up from the south.

'So far the War has not presented itself in all its grim reality. We have only heard the rumbling of the guns smashing Antwerp or smacking the Boche on the Aisne. The first Uhlan captured and the first scouting cyclist

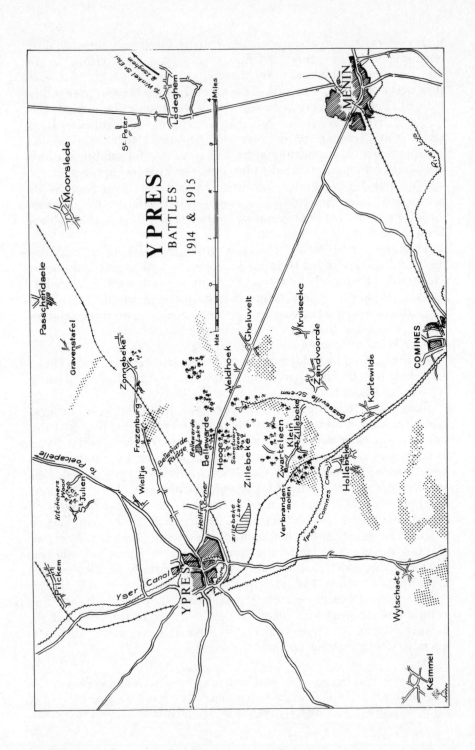

YPRES

BATTLES

1914 & 1915

scotched have been objects of curiosity and perhaps the only thing realized is the importance of the map-reading, which in barracks seemed so boresome,' commented an officer of the 7th Cavalry Brigade.[3]

By that night the 7th Division was covering Ypres. A French Division on their left connected them with the Belgian Army along the Yser Canal. On the right Byng lay between Kemmel and Wytschaete, in touch with the Cavalry Corps. A continuous line of allied troops now extended from Switzerland to the sea. Opposite them the Germans were known to be moving rapidly to cover the new line in the north, but were falling back in front of the 3rd Corps of the BEF, as it advanced to the River Lys, just south of the Franco-Belgian border. As the only enemy troops known to be advancing on Ypres were the three divisions of the Antwerp siege corps, there seemed a good chance of separating them from the main German Army.

On the afternoon of 15 October Sir John French ordered his force to advance to the east. The French and Belgians agreed to join in on the left. The 7th Division was to move eastward between Courtrai and Roulers, with the 3rd Cavalry Division on its left, north of that town.

Early next morning, through a cold, dense fog, Byng's cavalry rode north through Ypres to the area of St Julien. From there patrols of the Household Cavalry probed toward the north-east and established that the enemy were in Staden and Oostnieuwkerke. That night as they billeted in Passchendaele, some German Hussars arrived looking for lodgings. A picket of the Blues emptied a few of their saddles as they wheeled about and departed to the east.[4]

In England it was public knowledge that Byng was commanding a cavalry division on the Continent. On 17 October, in an article in *Town and Country*, H. G. Wells gave his opinion of him.

Here is a man who is nothing if not a soldier. My idea of him, knowing him intimately, has always been that he goes to bed at night and dreams of long vistas of soldiers, and he gets up in the morning and still thinks of soldiers. He knows Clausewitz by heart, he is a master of tactics, he has studied every battlefield in the world, he assisted Col Henderson in writing *The Life of Stonewall Jackson*, he has the physique of a machine and the brains of twenty men, which fits him eminently to be a cavalry leader.

Byng's opinion of Wells, expressed some years before, was that he 'talked through his hat'. Fortunately, with his first battle of the war looming so close, he did not see the article immediately or his comments would have been even more pungent.

Skirmishing with German cavalry continued while Byng and the

7th Division waited for the 3rd Corps to move into position on their right. On the 18th Byng moved to the western outskirts of Roulers which was now occupied by the French. It was almost midnight when a motor cycle despatch rider carrying Rawlinson's orders for the next day arrived at Byng's headquarters. He was to advance to the Roulers-Menin road at 6.30 am and then push forward strong reconnaissances to Ledeghem, Winkel St Eloi and Iseghem, protect the left flank of the 7th Division as it advanced to Menin, occupy Roulers and maintain touch with the French to the north.

C Battery, Royal Horse Artillery, joined the division early on the morning of 19 October and now both brigades had their own artillery support.

As they advanced, the cavalry were soon in action. On the right the 10th Hussars, advancing from St Peter, made contact with a German cyclist battalion as it emerged on the west side of Ledeghem. The Germans quickly deployed into the turnip fields surrounding the village and began firing on the leading troop of B Squadron, which was near an estaminet outside the village. Lt-Col Barnes sent his machine-gun troop to help B Squadron pin down the Germans while Major C. B. O. Mitford's squadron galloped around the village to seal off their line of retreat.

The 300 yards between the machine-gun troop and B Squadron's position was devoid of cover and their commander gave the order to gallop.

On reaching the estaminet, several of the troop horses failed to respond to the aids to halt. Their riders were faced with the choice of being carried into the German lines or throwing themselves off, which they did, and the horses galloped riderless into the German lines, one old grey horse trotting about amongst the turnips and Germans snorting defiance. In the end, they all returned unharmed.

Meanwhile the excitement of going into action for the first time had caused even the seasoned soldiers of 12 years service and upward to omit quite a number of the details of elementary training. However, both guns were mounted at last. During all this, the senior sergeant had nearly burst himself with expletives and excitement. At last with a hoarse cry of 'Here, give it to me,' he hurled Nos. 1 and 2 from the nearest gun, seized the traversing handle with his left hand and pulled the crank handle smartly over with his right. The failure of the gun to respond to the pressure of the firing button, caused another and more terrible explosion of language. No. 1 politely referred his commander's left hand to the belt and suggested a repetition of the movements with his right. All was well. For the first time we were sending real bullets at a real enemy. The cyclist battalion was completely stopped.

Ledeghem was soon cleared of the enemy; three men had been wounded and two Germans with a number of bicycles were captured.[6]

On the left the 7th Cavalry Brigade encountered the head of the German 53rd Reserve Division advancing from Iseghem (five miles south-east of Roulers and 7 miles north-east of Ledeghem). By 10 am they had been forced to retire about three-quarters of a mile to a better position and Byng learned that the French on his left were being heavily attacked. Three hours later news came from 4th Corps that a strong enemy force had been spotted from the air, advancing toward him.

By then the French on the left had withdrawn, leaving the 7th Cavalry Brigade's flank uncovered. Kavanagh was obliged to retire to the high ground east of Moorslede, leaving the 6th Brigade isolated to the east and Byng ordered Makins to pull back gradually to join them.

Byng's lightly armed cavalry were now being attacked by infantry brigades supported by artillery. Keeping just out of their reach, he withdrew the division slowly to Poelcapelle and Zonnebeke.

Major-Gen Capper's 7th Division on Byng's right fared no better and the night found them three and a half miles to the rear of their start line of the morning. Only by superhuman efforts had they been able to drag back their howitzer batteries through the mud which began to be in evidence. The attempt at an offensive in the face of superior numbers had not gone well.

Prisoners revealed that Byng's division had met the 46th Reserve Division of the 23rd Reserve Corps and the 52nd Reserve Division of the 26th Corps and that each was followed closely by another division. They also revealed that, instead of only the one corps from Antwerp, the Allies in the north were faced by five and a half army corps.

The 3rd Cavalry Division was fortunate to have had only eighty-three casualties in imposing at least a seven-hour delay on the advance of two German corps.

Sir John French distrusted the new intelligence and ordered his Army to resume the attack on 21 October. The 1st Corps, under Sir Douglas Haig, having arrived in the Ypres area, was now to come into action on the left of the 7th Division. Byng was to cover its advance and to capture Menin if possible. In the meantime he was to hold his positions, while awaiting the arrival of 1st Corps.

At 4.30 am his men began digging trenches along the west of the road north of Passchendaele in order to support the French. It was their first such experience and they were poorly equipped for it, having only bayonets and a few requisitioned tools. There was no barbed wire. Their horses were hidden half a mile to the rear.[7]

At 8 am enemy artillery began firing upon the cavalry line and continued until about noon. Suddenly, without warning, the French on the right and left of 6th Cavalry Brigade retired, leaving it and the left of the 7th exposed. Byng had no option but to pull back to the line Zonnebeke – St Julien – Poelcapelle.

For a time the fighting appeared to die away, but suddenly it broke out again with great violence on both flanks of the division. Again without notice, the French retreated, this time from Poelcapelle, exposing the 6th Brigade. Heavy shell fire obliged Byng to move his left back close to Langemark, while on the right a determined attack developed against Zonnebeke.

During the afternoon Haig rode out to meet Byng and agreed to reinforce his right flank. By 7 pm divisional HQ was established at St Julien and the arrival of two battalions of the Coldstream Guards enabled Byng to secure his position.[8]

The Germans made a night attack on Langemark, which was repulsed, though some adjustment had to be made to the division's line.

Early in the morning of the 21st the Division was relieved in the line and moved back to Ypres where it would be ready to support the right flank of Haig's Corps, which was beginning its advance in the direction of Thourout. French still believed that the Germans would retreat in the face of this attack and that there would be little more than rearguard fighting.

By 5 am Byng was at Hooge, about 3 miles in the rear of the centre of the 7th Division's line. Three hours later the infantry came under heavy attack by the enemy who were massively supported by artillery. About noon Brig-Gen Lawford, commanding 22nd Infantry Brigade near Zonnebeke, asked for assistance. His trenches had been badly enfiladed all morning by artillery and machine-gun fire from Passchendaele on the left. Byng sent the 1st Lifeguards forward immediately and, having been forward to see the situation himself, moved the remainder of Kavanagh's Brigade to support Lawford.

About 1.30 pm, as he was returning to Hooge, he learned that Gough's 2nd Cavalry Division on the right was being furiously attacked by two German cavalry divisions. Due to a misunderstanding of orders, one brigade had withdrawn from the key position of Hollebeke Château and the village of that name on the Ypres-Comines Canal, exposing the flank of the 7th Division. Byng immediately sent the 6th Cavalry Brigade at the gallop to the threatened area where they helped to recapture the village and the canal crossings, but Gough's attempts to retake the Château failed.

By nightfall the 6th Brigade was holding the line from the Château to Zandvoorde. The trenches of the exhausted Scots Guardsmen whom they had relieved had been well dug for those days and were deep and narrow. It was the first occasion in the war when the men of the Brigade were separated from their horses.

On the left of the BEF five German divisions, at great cost to themselves, had been able to halt the advance of Haig's two divisions. Taken with the evidence of the strength of the German attacks against the rest of his line, it was enough to convince the Commander-in-Chief that he was outnumbered. At 8.30 pm Sir John French placed the BEF on the defensive.

The 3rd Cavalry Division was now responsible for the 3,000 yards of front between Zandvoorde and Hollebeke. One brigade was in the front line, the second being in reserve at Klein Zillebeke. Divisional headquarters was in Zillebeke which, the War Diary notes, was a filthy village.

When a cavalry regiment of 540 men is dismounted to fight on foot, its horses must still be looked after, so that it can at best deploy about one third the strength of an infantry battalion, and its supporting artillery is much lighter than that of the infantry. The frontages which battalions and regiments might be expected to defend were prescribed in training manuals, but around Ypres these became meaningless. Units were so reduced by casualties that often their positions were barely as strong as an outpost line. At best their defences were short disconnected lengths of trench, three feet deep and hastily constructed. There were no dugouts, no communication trenches, nor any prepared second line. In a few places there was a single strand of barbed wire in front, elsewhere there was none. Troops fought in small groups, scattered along the front, the gaps between them often amounting to several hundred yards. By day these were covered by artillery and the crossfire of rifles and machine guns, but at night the few patrols which could be spared were unable to prevent penetration by the enemy.

Fighting was almost continuous, hardly interrupted at night, and there was no rest for the troops. Only after dark was it possible to bring forward food and ammunition and to remove the wounded. From now until 21 November, when the first battle of Ypres officially ended, the intensity of the battle scarcely waned. Every day, in every position along the front, there were bursting shells, blown-in trenches, fatigue, hunger, wounds and death. The beating-off of German attacks by fire were such regular occurrences that often they were not recorded in unit war diaries.

For ten days Byng and his five regiments, their strength diminishing with casualties, held the same sector of the front. Senior officers were not immune from enemy fire. On the morning of the 23rd

Kavanagh, his two staff officers and Lt-Col Brassey, commanding the 1st Life Guards, were slightly wounded by shellfire, while having their positions pointed out to them.

Outwardly Byng appeared totally unconcerned by the danger of the situation. One evening he took John Bigge, his ADC, with him for a stroll near Klein Zillebeke while shells fell unpleasantly close. The young officer grew increasingly nervous for his own and his general's safety, but Byng seemed deep in thought and he did not like to intrude. Eventually they came to a sunken road and Byng turned and said, 'What do you think? Wouldn't partridges come over here nicely?'[9]

The presence of the Germans in Hollebeke Château was a serious threat to the right of the position. During the morning of 22 October Byng arranged for the guns of a Naval armoured train to supplement the fire of C Battery, RHA, in supporting an attack by C Squadron of the Royals to drive them out. It succeeded with little opposition.

Three days later, in a reorganization of the front, Byng came under the orders of Lt-Gen Allenby, the commander of the Cavalry Corps, whose other two divisions held the line to the right. He also learned that the shortage of artillery ammunition had become so serious that expenditure was to be restricted to 30 rounds per gun per day and that only bodies of troops attacking in close formation or enemy guns limbered or visible in action might be engaged.[10] The enemy suffered no such disadvantage.

Believing that the enemy had shot his bolt, General Foch (commanding the French army in the area) and Field-Marshal French had ordered their troops to resume the offensive. At 12.30 pm on the 26th Allenby issued orders for a general advance to conform with that of the 7th Division on the left. Less than half an hour later, before the attack had begun, Byng received a message from Capper of the 7th Division to say that the front of his 20th Brigade at Kruiseeke had been broken in three or four places. While he was endeavouring to seal off the penetration it might be necessary to fall back after dark. He added, 'I will endeavour to keep you informed. Can we arrange a rapid method of communication? Have only cyclists.'

Byng rode to the headquarters of the 7th Cavalry Brigade and instructed Kavanagh not to attack, but instead to assemble his brigade at the crossroads at Klein Zillebeke.

Two hours later Capper asked Byng to cover the flank of the retirement of 20th Brigade. Because of his wide front and small numbers, Byng could spare only one regiment, the Blues, who he sent mounted behind the lines eastward towards Zandvoorde. Crossing the north-west shoulder of the Zandvoorde Ridge, the leading squadron opened out and in the fading light cantered toward the enemy trenches, being met by heavy rifle and shellfire. They turned and rode at a gallop for a quarter mile, parallel to and 200 yards from the Germans. Then, swinging toward the trenches occupied by the 6th Cavalry Brigade, they dismounted, left their horses under the cover of a hedge and farm, and opened fire with their rifles. The other two squadrons galloped further east, extending the front to the right and flanking the German advance. The enemy turned to engage them, but light was already beginning to fail and no attack followed. After dark, the regiment was withdrawn to Klein Zillebeke, having drawn the enemy away from the 20th Brigade with the loss of 8 men and 25 horses. Byng was well pleased with their performance.

The withdrawal of the 20th Brigade created a gap on Byng's left which extended almost to the Menin road. His troops in Zandvoorde were now terribly exposed. Either their left must be covered or they would have to be withdrawn. While the demonstration by the Blues was taking place, Byng drove to Ypres to see the 7th Division to agree on a plan for repairing the situation. Capper assured Byng that the gap would be filled, but, because of the shortage of troops, the link-up did not take place until next morning.

The trenches which the cavalry took over at Zandvoorde had been dug on the forward face of the ridge, where they were exposed to direct observation and fire by the enemy. Byng wanted to move them to the reverse slope but this was not practicable immediately because it would endanger the 7th Division's newly restored position on the left. Little could be done except deepen the trenches and begin construction of second and third lines in their rear.[11]

At 7 am on 29 October Byng took the commander of the 1st Corps engineers into the village of Zandvoorde to discuss again the possibility of moving his positions to the reverse slopes and to suggest alterations in the 7th Division's line. But any possibility of doing this vanished when it was learned that heavy firing, which had been heard from early that morning, marked the beginning of a major German attempt to break through south-east of Ypres, later to be known as the Battle of Gheluvelt.

During the morning reports came in of heavy fighting near the Ypres-Menin road and of the 7th Division being driven back from the high ground near Kruiseeke. Two counterattacks were to be launched against this, one by the 1st Division from near Gheluvelt, and the other by the 7th Division. Haig asked Byng to cover the right of the latter and he detailed the 6th Cavalry Brigade for the task, the 7th supporting them by fire from the Zandvoorde position.

With the 10th Hussars leading and the Royals in support, the Brigade advanced dismounted through the woods in touch with Lawford's 22nd Brigade. The opposition was not heavy and the line was re-established. At Byng's request, Allenby moved the Cavalry Corps reserves of five squadrons, some guns and half a battalion of infantry to Klein Zillebeke, in order to be closer to the threatened point.

Both French and Foch were unaware of the strength of the enemy force which had begun to attack. Indeed, some allied advances had taken place that day and British counterattacks had all been successful. Owing to fog and later to clouds, little information came from air reconnaissance and that which was received indicated no important movements of German troops.

The right of Byng's position east of the Ypres-Comines Canal was held by a squadron of the Royals in Hollebeke Château. Next were the Blues, then, with the ground rising to the village of Zandvoorde on its well-marked ridge, came the 2nd and 1st Life Guards. Behind them, across the meadowland through which flowed the Basseville stream, the remaining five squadrons of the 6th Cavalry Brigade were at Klein Zillebeke on the ridge to the rear. On Byng's immediate flanks were the 2nd Cavalry Brigade and 1st Royal Welch Fusiliers of 22nd Brigade.

By moving at night and hiding in towns and villages during the day, an entire army group under Gen von Fabeck had succeeded in concentrating undetected. Their first objectives were to be Zandvoorde and the Messines ridge to the south, followed by a thrust through to the Kemmel heights. Having thus cut off the Allied troops in and north of Ypres, they would turn and drive them either against the coast or into Holland.

Facing them were the 7th Division, already weakened to less than half strength, and the three cavalry divisions which in all had fewer rifles than a German infantry brigade. With two under-strength Indian battalions in support, the odds were approximately six to one in rifles and field and horse artillery in favour of the enemy. Fortunately for the British their weakness and almost entire lack of reserves was concealed by the close nature of the country which also favoured the better trained troops.

During the night of 29 October Byng received several reports of movements of the enemy towards the Zandvoorde position. Shortly before 6 am he rode forward to carry out his customary visit to the outposts. He was within three-quarters of a mile of Zandvoorde, when the ridge and the ground immediately in its rear erupted under the fire of 260 heavy guns. So violent was the concentration that Byng

76

could not get to the HQ of the 7th Brigade and returned to his own at Klein Zillebeke.[12]

The intense bombardment continued for over an hour. Casualties mounted alarmingly as the Life Guards' trenches were blown in, just as Byng feared they would be.

It was obvious that under such fire the only alternatives were annihilation or withdrawal. The second line was being manned when, at 8 o'clock, the bombardment ceased and the German infantry advanced. Against the remnants of the Household Cavalry came the entire 39th Division, plus three Jaeger battalions. Retirement was imperative. The two squadrons on the right managed to extricate themselves, but the remainder, a squadron each of the 1st and 2nd Life Guards, and the machine-gunners of the Blues, were cut off and annihilated. Not a man escaped and not one of the few prisoners taken by the enemy was unwounded.

As the 7th came back to their support lines in the valley of the Basseville stream, Byng moved his reserve forward to cover their withdrawal and prepared to hold the position on the Klein Zillebeke ridge. Sheltered by trees and on flat ground, its fields of fire had been sacrificed in favour of concealment and protection from artillery.

The first moves to stop further German penetration having been taken, every effort was now turned to recapturing the Zandvoorde ridge. Before 9 am Lawford of the 22nd Brigade moved three battalions to support Byng's cavalry and to attempt to regain Zandvoorde village. Allenby placed his reserve of three regiments under Byng to join in the counterattack on the right of the 6th Cavalry Brigade. At 9.15 Haig ordered the 1st Corps reserve of two battalions and a field company of engineers under Major-Gen Bulfin to support the operation.

In the meantime the Welch Fusiliers, holding the line north of Zandvoorde, had been exposed by its capture. With their trenches blown in, the enemy raking their position from the flank and rear, and a battery firing on them from higher ground, the battalion was overwhelmed. Fifty-four were taken prisoner and but eighty-six answered roll call in the evening.

While some advances were made in the counterattack, every attempt to recover Zandvoorde proved impossible. Then, at about 10.30, the enemy launched the 2nd Bavarian Corps up the axis of the Ypres-Comines Canal. Following an intense bombardment, its 4th Division advanced against what remained of the 3rd Cavalry Division. The German infantry strove hard to capture Hollebeke Château but elsewhere the attacking troops noticeably lacked enthusiasm. The squadron of the Royals beat off the attack and C Battery, RHA, did much execution, catching the enemy in the open as they crossed the

Zandvoorde ridge. Nonetheless, the position of the 7th Brigade forward of the Basseville stream became precarious and Byng withdrew them through the 6th into the Klein Zillebeke line to refit, refill with ammunition and become the division's reserve.

On the right the 2nd Cavalry Division were forced to give up the high ground around Hollebeke village, causing the squadron of the Royals to evacuate the Château. To relieve the pressure, Byng sent two squadrons of the Life Guards who had so recently retired from the bloody Zandvoorde ridge down both sides of the Ypres-Comines railway. At 7 pm the two tired regiments of the 6th Brigade were relieved by battalions of the Grenadier and Irish Guards and the division moved back into reserve near Klein Zillebeke.

The morning sun burned away the early mist of 31 October to produce a fine, warm day, which, for the British, would see the most desperate of the hard-fought battles of 1914. Before it began, not only had casualties reached frightening proportions, but complete tactical units had disappeared. Four of Haig's thirty-six infantry battalions had been practically annihilated, as had two of Byng's fifteen cavalry squadrons, yet the German attacks had achieved little at terrible cost. At Gheluvelt and Messines they failed, and even their limited success at Zandvoorde and Hollebeke had been stopped dead by Bulfin's and Lawford's brigades. But, despite protests by commanders, the German High Command was determined to renew the attack and it was announced that, to encourage his troops, the Kaiser himself would be present, as indeed he was – at Crown Prince Ruprecht's battle headquarters 120 miles away.

Two major thrusts were made by Fabeck's Army Group. The first, between Messines and the Comines Canal, aimed at seizing the Messines – Wytschaete ridge. It succeeded only in taking part of Messines.

The second was directed at Gheluvelt which had become vulnerable from the south-east after the capture of Zandvoorde.

The 3rd Cavalry Division, which had been warned to take part in an advance that morning, soon had its orders changed. At 8 am Byng was instructed by Allenby to move closer to the Menin road where he would be able to support 1st Corps. He moved to Hooge with his 6th Brigade and concentrated the 7th east of Zillebeke.

At about 9.30 Allenby reported a heavy attack against Wytschaete where the situation was becoming critical. He ordered as much of the division as possible to return to his assistance. Byng, however, had come under the orders of Haig who ordered him to remain. Kavanagh, who had seen Allenby's message en route, marched at once and was allowed to proceed.[13]

A desperate battle now developed at Gheluvelt. With an average strength of only 200 men, the five British battalions defending the village were overwhelmed by the massive German assault and wiped out. For a time the enemy penetrated beyond the village and occupied its Château, but a counterattack drove them back. With his last reserves gone, Brig-Gen Fitz Clarence, commanding the 1st Guards Brigade, galloped back to his headquarters and informed Gen Lomax of the 1st Division that the village was lost. Lomax told Fitz Clarence to call on the reserve of the 2nd Division, then rode back with his staff to that division's headquarters to consult with its commander, Gen Munro. Fifteen minutes later, as they were conferring, the headquarters at Hooge Château was struck by heavy shells. Lomax was mortally wounded, Munro badly stunned and, of the operations staff officers of the two divisions, only one was not killed or wounded.

At about the same time Fitz Clarence ordered the 2nd Battalion Worcestershire Regiment 'to advance without delay and deliver a counterattack with the utmost vigour against the enemy who was in possession of Gheluvelt and re-establish our line there'. It seemed a forlorn hope.

At Haig's HQ reports spoke of a mounting disaster. Following the news that Gheluvelt was lost came a report that the line there was broken and counterattacks had failed. Haig's only reserve was the much tried 3rd Cavalry Division, of which the 7th Brigade had gone to Allenby's assistance. He instructed Byng to place the two regiments of the 6th Brigade in a position along the road running south from Veldhoek to support the 1st Division.

As Byng moved off, further reports arrived saying that the gap near Gheluvelt had been widened by the annihilation of the units covering the village and that 7th Division, which so far had only been shelled, was now under infantry attack on its right flank.

There was now little to stop the Germans. The 1st Division's last reserve of fighting men, two field companies of the Royal Engineers, had been sent to Gheluvelt. Orders were prepared for a last-ditch stand to be taken up less than 2,000 yards from the walls of Ypres.

About 2 pm French arrived on foot at Haig's headquarters, the White Château near Hellfire Corner. Haig and Gough, his chief staff officer, were seated at a table littered with the remains of a glass chandelier brought down by a shell. Having no reserves himself, the Commander-in-Chief could do nothing but turn to the French for help. He hurried back to his car.

Haig was waiting for his horse, to ride forward and take personal command of the 1st Division, when Gen Rice, his chief engineer, galloped up and reported that the counterattack of the Worcestershire

Regiment had been successful – the enemy were running away from the village and help was needed to consolidate the success. Haig's ADC ran after the Commander-in-Chief and overtook him with the news just as he reached his car.

But the day had not ended. All morning a heavy bombardment had fallen on the British lines between Gheluvelt and the Comines Canal. Six battalions under Bulfin now occupied the front which Byng had held the day before. On their left lay what remained of Capper's Division. Shortly after noon, waves of German infantry began to advance against them and, to the north, masses of field-grey figures could be seen streaming toward Hooge, south of the Ypres-Gheluvelt road. As the German attack developed, the front line of the 7th Division was exposed to enfilade fire and began to give ground.

As the 22nd Brigade fell back Bulfin withdrew his left flank to avoid it being turned. In places, guns of the Royal Artillery were in the front line firing over open sights and still the enemy came on. But their determination seemed to be wavering. Col Jeudwyne of Haig's staff had come to see the situation and Bulfin asked him to send forward the 2nd Gordon Highlanders who were three-quarters of a mile to the rear. Bulfin then told his two left flank battalions, the Sussex and Northamptonshire, that the Gordons were coming, and ordered them, when they heard cheering behind, to give the enemy the 'mad minute', 15 rounds rapid fire, and when the Gordons reached them, to drive the enemy from his position with the bayonet.

Having given Bulfin's instructions to the Gordons, Jeudwyne rode back until he met Haig and his staff on the Menin road close to what was afterwards known as Sanctuary Wood. Later he was to write:

> I made my report to Sir Douglas and he asked me whether I could lead the cavalry to where Bulfin was counterattacking. I said I could. He called up Gen Byng and gave him orders to join in Bulfin's counterattack with his cavalry. I went with Byng, his staff and the leading squadron along the eastern edge of Sanctuary Wood until we were in rear of Bulfin's front and indicated the direction in which his counterattack was taking place and then went on to inform Bulfin that the cavalry were coming.[14]

Fortunately the woods concealed the fact that the Gordons, yelling as they moved to the attack, numbered only eighty men. A roar and crackle of rifle fire exploded from the line of the Sussex and Northamptons. The Germans, their ranks swept as from the fire of dozens of machine-guns, began to waver. Then the two battalions with the Highlanders went into them with the bayonet, just as Byng arrived to join in the charge on the left. Most squadrons leapt from their horses to attack with the infantry, but two, with swords drawn,

1. Julian's grandfather, known in the family as 'Toes' – Field-Marshal Sir John Byng, Earl of Strafford. *(Paul Mellon Centre for Studies in British Art Limited)*

2. George Stevens Byng, 2nd Earl of Strafford – Julian's father. *(Paul Mellon Centre for Studies in British Art Limited)*

3. Harriet Cavendish, daughter of Lord Chesham, Countess of Strafford –
Julian's mother. *(Paul Mellon Centre for Studies in British Art Limited)*

4. Julian and his elder brother Lionel.

5. Wrotham Park, seat of the Straffords, Byng's birthplace.

6. 'The Joint Stock Company'—Elizabeth, Margaret, Susan, Julian and Lionel, the family drama company at Sherborne about 1890.

7. Julian as adjutant of the
Tenth Royal Hussars.

8. Charge of the Tenth Hussars at El Teb, Byng's first action, in which the
two other officers in his squadron were killed.

9 & 10. The Herkomer portraits of Kitchener and Evelyn Moreton commissioned by her uncle, Pendeli Ralli in 1890 which led to the rumour in the press that they were engaged.

11. Julian, the Earl of Airlie, Colonel Gough, Lieutenant Prince Albert Victor.

12. Commanding Officer of the South African Light Horse and his Assistant Adjutant at Spion Kop. 'No one ever cursed me as heartily as Bungo did in the Light Horse days' – Churchill.

charged through an open part of the wood. At one point two machine-guns brought the advance of the Royal Dragoons to a halt. C Battery, RHA, assisted by some of the Royals, dragged one of their guns to within a hundred yards of the firing line and blew the Germans from a shooting lodge where the machine-guns had been pinpointed.

Success was beyond belief. Bulfin's and Byng's men advanced nearly half a mile and the 7th Division were able to reoccupy most of the ground lost that day.[15]

By evening the line was once more secure and Byng brought back his weary regiments to Hooge to become once more the mobile reserve of 1st Corps.

The day of crisis was over, but with their fighting strength still further reduced, and their supply of artillery ammunition fast running out, the outlook for the British was bleak.

The 1st day of November brought no reprieve. As the morning mist cleared the German bombardment was renewed and by 11 am the junction of Bulfin's force and the 7th Division was under attack by at least a division. Byng sent Makins with his brigade to reinforce Bulfin.

His force, the entire reserve of the 1st Corps, was now reduced to the seven squadrons of the 7th Brigade.

With a renewal and extension of the German attack at 2 pm, this last reserve was sent to help the 7th Division. Though few in numbers, the cavalry brought just the amount of reinforcement needed to stop the enemy. Gradually the fighting died down and the division was withdrawn to the neighbourhood of Hooge for the night.

Again next day the Germans attacked and at 1.30 pm the line about Veldhoek was reported to be giving way. The need for reinforcements was urgent and critical. The route to the threatened area – straight up the Menin road – was under heavy shellfire. Byng despatched Kavanagh with the suggestion that the less time he spent en route the better for all concerned. The enemy attack was halted and again the division concentrated near Hooge in reserve.

Byng's men were not to be in action again for nearly three days, although detachments moved temporarily to support the forward divisions. The condition of the infantry was now so serious that commanders felt that they could not plan on them holding out in the face of further attacks. In addition, gun ammunition was in such short supply that Haig sent back one-third of the field artillery of his divisions to an area south-west of Ypres where they would be out of range of the enemy guns to which they were unable to reply.

In these circumstances, the arrival of the 3rd Dragoon Guards under Lt-Col O. D. B. Smith-Bingham to join the other two regiments of the 6th Cavalry Brigade was warmly welcomed by Byng. By 9.30 pm next evening they were in the line, the 10th Hussars on their right, having relieved the 3rd Infantry Brigade.

Byng had only the 7th Brigade in hand as yet another critical day of battle developed. A new German attack was directed up the Comines Canal. From Messines to the Canal the line was held by five French battalions under Gen Moussy, connecting with a force of five British battalions to the north of it, under Lord Cavan.

A thick fog screened the German attack which by afternoon had driven the French back to Zwarteleen and almost to Verbranden-molen, only 3,000 yards from Ypres and nearer to it than Hooge Château. The Irish Guards on Lord Cavan's right had been forced back beyond their support trenches.

About 4 pm Byng received word that the French were falling back rapidly on Cavan's right and he at once sent the 7th Cavalry Brigade to his support. By now their numbers were so depleted that they could only muster 600 rifles. Ten hours later, having stopped the enemy in a desperate battle, they had lost a further seventeen officers and seventy-eight men. Their three commanding officers had been killed or wounded and in the 2nd Life Guards, of the four officers remaining, only one was a regular.

In the meantime, the 6th Brigade had been holding their trenches at Veldhoek in the face of considerable hostile shelling, but no direct attack developed. They were relieved about 11 pm by infantry and returned to their horses. Their casualties had been four officers and sixty-five other ranks.

The next four days saw brigades and regiments moving to support threatened sectors of the line, or relieving infantry battalions desperately in need of rest. On 11 November the Germans attacked once more in strength. Cavan's force, of which the Royals and 10th Hussars formed part, had a rough time. Like the rest of the line, they had been heavily shelled from 6.30 am onwards and were under a constant rain of rifle bullets, the fire interfering with the bringing up of ammunition and rations and with rest and feeding.

During the morning, from the woods behind the German trenches which were only 100 yards from those of the Royals and 10th Hussars, troops of the German 39th Division advanced in mass, to be mown down before they reached the British line. Again and again they came forward but made no progress. By the end of the day the German attacks had completely collapsed, spelling the end of any real likelihood of success for them in the First Battle of Ypres.

As if to mark the change in the situation on the Ypres front, the weather broke. On the 12th cold, driving rain added to the misery of the troops, trenches filled with water and the countryside became a sea of mud. Every morning for the next few days the enemy reopened his general bombardment, but no attacks developed. Two more regiments arrived to join Byng, the North Somerset Yeomanry for the 6th Brigade and the Leicestershire Yeomanry for the 7th, and were soon employed in the trenches. Then came some news few by now had expected to hear: Foch had agreed to relieve the British cavalry who were to go back into billets in the Hazebrouck area. There might also be some leave.

But the battle had not yet ended. On the 17th, a violent attack by Pomeranians burst upon the 6th Brigade. The enemy pressed forward so close to the trenches, in front of which there was no wire, that the field police could be seen threatening the men and urging them to advance before they broke in the face of the cavalry's rifle and machine-gun fire. During the day the brigade lost a further ten officers and 129 men.

At last on the 21st the Division began to move back from the front to rest, refit and organize the new 8th Cavalry Brigade.

It was a long, cold ride from Ypres to Hazebrouck. There had been a hard frost on the 18th, followed next day by a heavy snowstorm, leaving the ground covered and the roads glazed with ice. There was little to hint that the worn, mud-caked men in ragged khaki riding a little heavily on their thin, bedraggled mounts were the cream of the British cavalry.

To the east the tattered columns of men in field grey moving away from the front were as worn, filthy and haggard as the British, but to the shock of their losses was added the dispiriting knowledge that they had failed.

For both sides, the First Battle of Ypres had set a terrible pattern for war. Despite all that training can do to prepare men for the conditions of battle, all armies in peacetime wonder what the next war will be like. The question is seldom answered correctly. As the BEF sailed for France in August, 1914, it would have stretched imaginations too far to foresee that within four months they would have fought a month-long battle of unremitting violence, at the end of which, on average, only one officer and thirty men who landed with each battalion would remain, that they would be the victors, yet the enemy would not have sued for peace.

It would have been thought impossible for the Army to survive as a fighting force or for the war to continue. Yet Ypres showed that it could. Further, given the threat, the price in blood was accepted. Soon replacements for the casualties began to flow from Britain and new divisions from there and the Empire expanded the Army's strength, all determined to do their best to fight as well as the Regulars had at Ypres. That resolve produced victory and the death of a generation.

Those who survived the battle bore its mark. The old Regular Army had been a close community of which the wives and children of the officers and men were part. Friendship, marriage and common interests bound the Army and their families together. The human suffering caused by the destruction of the Regulars at Ypres was perhaps not apparent to all the public. But the survivors knew, and it bred in them an implacable resolve to win the war. Any compromise would be unthinkable after the losses of Ypres.

In command of a division Byng had proved to be as cool and resourceful in battle as he had in the South African War. Haig obviously thought that he was a good man to have at his side in a tight corner, for on 30 November he wrote to French recommending that he be decorated:

> Throughout the operations east of Ypres, he has commanded his division with skill and gallantry and has at all times moved to the support of the other arms with great promptitude and often without waiting for orders to do so when the situation was urgent. General Byng was always well forward where he could best command his brigades and for the last two weeks or more lived in a dugout as his post of command was under the enemy's shellfire. By his merry wit and cheerful bearing, he not only encouraged those under his orders, but also all with whom he came in contact, an asset of much value in the circumstances in which we were placed during the fighting around Ypres.[16]

There was little to laugh at in the news in 1914 but an item in the *Morning Post* of 3 November caused Byng a chuckle of satisfaction. It reported indignant complaints in the German press of his 'illegal' action in expelling the diplomatic and consular representatives of Germany and Austria from Egypt.

Byng's inner thoughts and feelings were not exposed for all to see, but he was greatly troubled by the price in lives paid by his soldiers and by the death of so many of his friends. John Buchan later wrote, 'I have seldom read anything more moving than his letters from the Front in which he spoke of the terrible losses in the battles of Ypres.'[17]

Casualty figures give some measure of the ordeal through which his division had passed. Between 14 October and 30 November, for most of the time only five regiments strong, it lost 2005 officers and men killed, wounded or missing. During the same period, the eighteen regiments of the 1st and 2nd Cavalry Divisions along the River Lys lost 1612.[18]

At the end of November, rather than take leave in England, Byng arranged to meet his wife in Boulogne. She sailed on the Leave Boat in a howling gale and arrived on the quay in 'pitch darkness and pouring rain, stumbled over railway lines to the grubby blacked-out hotel where Julian had engaged rooms to find no sign of, or from, him. The four hours I spent waiting were grim before he came at last, and we snatched a few hours' happiness, though they were shadowed by all he told me as to the seriousness of conditions at the Front.'[19]

After publication of the Commander-in-Chief's despatches, Byng was congratulated by his old friend R. D. Blumenfeld of the *Daily Express*. On 6 December he replied, discounting his part in the battles:

Dear Oom,
       Sir John was very kind to me in despatches . . . personally I don't see that I have done anything except to keep my blokes' spirits up. They have fought perfectly splendidly and I don't think any troops except them and the 1st Army Corps could have stuck the 31st October – we hadn't a soul in support and the line broken in 3 places – but the Germans had lost their leaders and were meandering about in any direction and when I took my 6th Bde in at 4 pm we came on a heap of them in a wood doing nothing and beat to the world. . . . The attack of the Bavarians on the 6th, the Guard on the 11th and the Pomeranians on the 17th were all critical for a short time but they got hell from the trenches and lost direction and cohesion and were shot down in lumps. Of course they inflicted a heavy loss on us – but it was nothing to what we gave them.
    Evelyn was at Boulogne for 24 hours which was splendid.
    Love to Daisy and lots to yourself
                        Yrs ever
                        Bungo.

For the next three months the 3rd Cavalry Division was not engaged with the enemy. Replacements came to fill the ranks, losses of equipment were made good and the days were spent in training and sports. It was soccer weather and in two matches between the headquarters of the 2nd and 3rd Cavalry Divisions Byng and Gough played in their respective teams. So unusual was it for generals to play 'footer' that *The Times* reported it and commented on the remarkable physical fitness of the two cavalry generals.[20]

On 19 April, 1915, Allenby was taken ill and Byng was given the temporary command of the Cavalry Corps.[21] It was now part of the general reserve of the BEF and there was no plan to employ it in action for the next few weeks. Spring was in the air and the warmth and sunshine lifted the spirits of the troops as they made ready for the fighting which was bound to come.

North-east of their billeting area, around Hazebrouck, the British Second Army and the French held much the same line covering Ypres as when the fighting ended on 11 November, 1914. On the left of Plumer's 5th Corps which held the southern two-thirds of the salient was the 1st Canadian Division. From their flank on the Ypres-Poelcapelle road, two French divisions facing generally north continued in the line until it met that of the Belgians at Steenstraat on the Ypres-Yser Canal.

Enemy activity on Thursday, 22 April at first seemed little different from that of the preceeding few days. Ypres itself was shelled by heavy guns in the morning and the roads and bridges north and east of the town were treated by the enemy's light artillery. The Canadians working in their shirt sleeves in the warm sunshine had little reason to suspect that an enemy attack was coming until about 4 pm when heavy shell fire began to fall on their positions and those of the French. Then at 5 pm the Germans for the first time in war released more than 160 tons of chlorine gas into the light breeze which carried it toward the two divisions on their left. Completely unready to cope with this new weapon, the French troops fled and within a few hours it was apparent that the Germans had penetrated to within four miles of the backs of the British holding the southern flank of the salient. A gap of 8,000 yards had opened between the left of the Canadians and the Yser Canal.

Equally unprepared to face poison gas and despite very heavy casualties, the Canadians managed to stem the German advance and hold the St Julien – Ypres road until British reinforcements arrived.

At about midnight on the 22nd Byng was ordered to concentrate the Cavalry Corps west of Yser Canal where, for the next few days, he remained ready to block any penetration of the Germans in that direction. The cavalry presence there reflected the British anxiety for the left flank which the performance of the French had done little to allay.

On the 4th Allenby returned from hospital but two days later was moved to 5th Corps and Byng's position as commander of the Cavalry Corps was confirmed.

The Second Battle of Ypres, 1915, was in reality a series of battles, those of Gravenstafel Ridge and St Julien extending from the first gas attack of 22 April until the 30th. With the failure of the French counterattacks, the British line became untenable and was withdrawn to the Frezenberg Ridge. The battles from 8 to 13 May were named after that Ridge and were followed on 24 and 25 May by the Battle of Bellewaarde Ridge. Troops of Byng's Cavalry Corps were involved in them all, but, with the exception of the last, he was not in direct command of troops engaged with the enemy.

From 4 May the new Frezenberg line was heavily shelled by the enemy, whose main attack began on the 8th. In the next few days entire brigades were annihilated, almost all reserves of artillery ammunition were used and the Germans came close to a breakthrough. On the 12th a dismounted force of the 1st and 3rd Cavalry Divisions under Major-General de Lisle relieved the exhausted infantry of the 28th Division, between Bellewaarde Lake and the Ypres–St Julien road near Wieltje. Next morning they and the 80th Brigade on their right were attacked by three German divisions. In the desperate fighting which followed, the losses in Byng's old division were severe and included one brigadier and seven of its commanding officers. But, apart from a few minor withdrawals, the line held.

The Cavalry Force, as Gen de Lisle's command had been called, was now dissolved and the Cavalry Corps itself became responsible for the centre of the 5th Corps front. Byng relieved his 1st and 3rd Divisions with the 2nd and began to take back the ground which had been lost to the Germans on the 13th. By the morning of the 24th the 2nd Cavalry Division had been relieved by the 1st astride the Menin road just east of Hooge. At 2.45 am an explosion of fire by guns and small arms burst from the enemy front as they released the heaviest concentration of cloud gas yet seen. Almost immediately their infantry assaulted.

Again the cavalry casualties were heavy and the 2nd Brigade in particular was badly punished by gas. Shortly after 10 am the German 39th Division broke through between Hooge and Bellewaarde. The gap was covered by the 4th Dragoon Guards and the penetration was contained. Just after dark a counterattack by the 9th Cavalry Brigade drove back the enemy from the Menin road, who, fleeing to the rear, were shot down by their own side. Byng then relieved the 1st Cavalry Division by the 2nd.

That night, the German Fourth Army issued orders that offensive operations at Ypres would cease.

On 27 May Byng's men reoccupied the village of Hooge and pushed forward north of the Menin road. For the next two years, the lines drawn by the opposing armies around the Ypres Salient were to remain virtually unchanged.

On 22 May Byng had written again to R. D. Blumenfeld with news of their mutual friends in the Tenth Hussars and some comments on the war:

22 May, 1915

They have made me temporary Lieutenant Gen: – very kind of them but I was quite happy where I was.

I have had absolutely no time to write anything in the shape of a letter as

87

they gave me command of nearly all the line east of Ypres on the 15th so as to relieve Snow and Bulfin who needed a rest badly. I held the line with the Cavalry Corps, two Brigades of the 28th division, two Brigades of Territorials. So far it has gone all right, and I was relieved of half my line last night, but take it up again tomorrow (23rd) till the 28th when I hope they will bring the cavalry back to their horses. . . .

It has been very hard work up here and a great deal of responsibility. One doesn't get to bed till late as there is always a good deal of shooting of an evening and the Boches never stop bombarding Ypres and its roads. But as we only use them for ambulances and rations of an evening it has next to no effect.

I suppose the Ice-Cream men are coming in, but the French say they don't care whether they do or not as they will only fight Austrians. If they would send some Army Corps to the Vosges and Alsace they could release French troops for the Arras push, but they don't think they will do that.

Evidently the only way to end this war is to kill Boches, consequently every Boche-killer sent to the Dardanelles is a man wasted. Hence the Bumstunt of the politicians. . . .

Perceval Landon and John Buchan appeared yesterday disguised in uniform and posing as correspondents. They now allow a gang of melancholy looking penmen to joy-ride about the lines, but they seem harmless and have not got the blatant bounderishness of Bennett Burleigh and others of his kidney. The destruction of Ypres seemed to have impressed them, but when one sees it every day and smells it every night it loses any impression of interest. Still its an awful picture of wanton destruction and at night between the shells it is curious as there isn't a soul about. A few cats live in the ruins and you hear the nightingales or some other birds all night long. Heaps of rats come up after the dead bodies and the stink is like nothing on earth.

His caustic comment about the Dardanelles strategy and his misgivings about the Italians were strangely prescient for both were to have unfortunate influences on his future.

As in 1914, credit for the successful defence belonged to the fighting soldier and his regimental and brigade commanders. Above that level, generals could do little to influence the battle other than by moving what reinforcements there were to the battle area, and ensuring that food and ammunition got forward to the troops. Without adequate aerial observation and photography, it was impossible to determine the enemy's dispositions and movements. For the same reasons, coupled with inadequate communications, they rarely knew the exact location of their own troops. The employment of reserves and the organization of counterattacks had to be left to commanders on the spot. It was not until later in the war that corps and army commanders could influence the day-to-day fighting of a defensive battle.

While in these actions there had been little opportunity for Byng to demonstrate his skill as a tactical commander, there was little doubt in the minds of his superiors as to his ability. On 8 June, 1915, Gen Lambton, the Commander-in-Chief's Military Secretary, wrote to the King that he and French considered Byng, Snow (28th Division) and Alderson (Canadian Division) to be the most suitable of all to command the new Corps which were now being formed.[22]

In April Lt John Bigge, Byng's ADC, asked to be allowed to return to his regiment, the King's Royal Rifle Corps. Within a month he was killed at Festubert. Capt Sir Basil Brooke, 10th Hussars, who had fought with his regiment in the desperate battles around Ypres, replaced him and was to remain with Byng for the remainder of the War. In May the Marquess of Titchfield, Royal Horse Guards, who had come to France with the Composite Regiment of Household Cavalry in August, 1914, joined Byng's personal staff as his second ADC. He was soon nicknamed 'Chopper'.

Brooke and his sister Sylvia kept up a lively correspondence during the War. When he learned of his appointment on 21 April, he wrote to her

> I am going to General Bungo as ADC. . . . He is one of the nicest men I have ever met and I don't think I would have cared to go to anybody but him. It seems rather velvet but it will be most interesting and I think I shall like it.

It was not long before he realized that the job was no sinecure. 'The General moves right up during the day'. Two weeks later, when the Cavalry Corps were improving forward defences, 'Oh darn, must stop. Just off with the General to see digging – hope they don't shell us.'[23]

In the second week of July Byng returned to London to receive the KCMG from the King. Alighting from a taxi outside Oddenino's Restaurant, he was knocked down by a motor van and stunned. A waiter rushed forward with some brandy as Byng climbed to his feet, remarking, 'I really wish I was back in France. It's much safer there.'[24]

Basil Brooke would not have agreed. On 27 July he told his sister, 'I have been up trenching a good deal lately with the General which is sometimes pleasant and sometimes quite the reverse.' Chopper Titchfield agreed with him; they took turns in escorting Byng on his tours of the trenches. He later told his father that Byng made a habit of visiting the forward trenches every day, often at night. Especially after dark this was particularly dangerous and the General proceeded at the slowest possible walk. Titchfield found it nerve-shattering work and was always glad when it was over and they were safely back in their headquarters, even though it too was frequently heavily shelled.[25]

But a change to an even less pleasant scene was soon to come. Four lines scrawled by Brooke on 15 August told of the speed of their departure: 'I am just off to the Dardanelles in two hours, only four hours notice, with the General.'[26]

Chapter 6
Gallipoli

ON SUNDAY, 25 APRIL, 1915, three days after the first gas attack at Ypres, a British, Australian, New Zealand and French expedition landed on the Gallipoli Peninsula, its aim to capture Constantinople, open a passage to the Black Sea and forge a link with their Russian allies.

The operation followed an unsuccessful attempt by the Navy to force a passage through the straits of the Dardanelles by ships alone. The Turkish defences would have to be overpowered by the Army before the Allies could enter the Sea of Marmara and open the Bosphorus.

From the conception of the original strategic plan, the First Lord of the Admiralty, Winston Churchill, had used all his formidable powers of argument and persuasion to win approval for it from the Cabinet. Lord Kitchener, the Secretary of State for War, had agreed, as eventually had the others. But the Cabinet were not unanimously enthusiastic for a diversion of effort from the crucial theatre of war in France. The plan did not have the whole-hearted support of the Naval staff and Kitchener committed the Army without consulting his professional advisers at the War Office.

The controversial nature of the strategy bore in itself the seeds of its failure. As operations in the Eastern Mediterranean developed they were plagued by inadequate resources, changes in plan and delayed decisions.

Its two chiefs proponents, Kitchener and Churchill, were the political heads of the Army and Navy. Through their persuasion, the Cabinet had taken the decision to pursue the Mediterranean strategy, without an adequate appreciation of the resources it would require. When what they supposed was needed proved insufficient, they could only draw on what might better have been used in France and then, tragically, they despatched it too late.

In taking the decision to mount the Gallipoli operation, Kitchener had no intention of diverting significant forces from the Western theatre. Dictatorial though he may have been, he would probably have listened to the advice of the General Staff had he trusted them. But the best brains in the Army had been taken from Whitehall to command and staff the BEF and he regarded their replacements at best as inexperienced and more commonly as second rate.

Once committed to the operation, which so often seemed within sight of success, it was difficult for him to draw back. Having launched it without advice, Kitchener knew that the responsibility for it was entirely his own. Success in the venture became essential, not only for the strategic rewards it would bring but for his own self image of professional infallibility. In the past he had usually been prepared to listen dispassionately to officers who opposed his opinions. As Byng was to discover, his commitment to Gallipoli now resulted in near animosity to anyone who took a contrary view.

The first landings took place at what became known as Anzac Cove, on the Western side of the Gallipoli Peninsula and at its southern tip, Cape Helles. Opposite the latter, on the Asiatic mainland, the French went ashore at Kum Kale. Far less than expected was achieved. The best chance of success seemed to lie in exploiting the landings at Anzac, but there was insufficient room in the beachhead to hold the number of troops and guns needed to develop an offensive.

Early in May Sir Ian Hamilton, in command of the operations, informed Kitchener that he would need more troops. The future of the whole enterprise was questioned by the Government and not until 7 June was it decided to send two more divisions to Gallipoli. Later, on the urging of Churchill, the number was increased to five, three of them forming the 9th Army Corps. But they could not arrive until the end of July and in the meantime the Turks continued to build up their forces and defences.

The task of the new corps would be to seize a beachhead at Suvla and support the Anzacs in a drive to take the hills which dominated the peninsula and the Dardanelles.

Hamilton was delighted with the reinforcements, even though their arrival would be dangerously late. He was much less pleased with the choice of their commanders and cabled Kitchener that the corps commanders should have 'a good stiff constitution and nerve. Everything is at such close quarters that many men would be useless in the somewhat exposed headquarters they would have to occupy on this limited terrain – I can think of two men, Byng and Rawlinson. Both possess the requisite qualities and seniority.'[1]

Kitchener refused to ask French to spare either and insisted that the command of the corps should go to an officer senior to Lt-Gen Sir B. T. Mahon, the commander of the 10th Division of 9th Corps. Only two lieutenant-generals in the Army List filled the requirement. One was unfit for the climate of Gallipoli. The other was Sir Frederick Stopford, a successful and dedicated staff officer who had retired in 1909. Recalled to the service in 1914, he was now 61 years old and in indifferent health. He had never commanded troops in war.[2]

The commanders and senior staff officers of the new divisions were, in the main, elderly Regulars, neither eager nor young enough for hazardous enterprises. Their troops were the young volunteers of the New Army who had flocked to the colours in 1914. Their courage was unfortunately wasted by the lack of drive of their commanders and by their own inexperience. Though they got ashore at Suvla almost unopposed, they barely secured the first rim of hills overlooking it. Within hours the possibility of success had disappeared.

Kitchener agreed that Hamilton should remove Stopford and at last sent out commanders who had proved that they could win battles. Byng would replace Stopford and he would bring with him Major-Gens F. S. Maude and E. A. Fanshawe, both of whom had commanded divisions in France.

Hamilton noted in his diary that day: 'Cables to and from K. about our new generals. Byng, Maude and Fanshawe are coming. A brilliant trio. Byng will make everyone happy; he never spares himself.'[3]

Evelyn was horrified. She wrote in 1945:

Then Julian was suddenly ordered to go to the Dardanelles, and when I received his telegram giving me the bitter news I felt as if his death warrant had been signed, for at that time no place was more hopeless strategically and from the point of view of health, for the men were dying like flies on those hideous beaches, in the water-logged trenches; and every horror was rampant.[4]

When Byng arrived at Suvla Cove on 24 August he was met by Major-Gen de Lisle who had been commanding the 9th Corps since Stopford left on the 16th. The scene which greeted him was far different from anything he had seen in France. There the army's stores were moved through ports to depots which were run like well-ordered warehouses, safe from interference by the enemy, from whence the requirements of the fighting formations were delivered by rail and road. But here at Suvla stores were being unloaded from lighters by hand onto a rickety pier at West Beach. Gangs of listless, half-clad men lounged about, sweaty and begrimed by the heat and all-pervading dust. Mules and carts milled about ramshackle shelters clustered on the hillsides. It was more typical of a middle eastern bazaar than an army base.

93

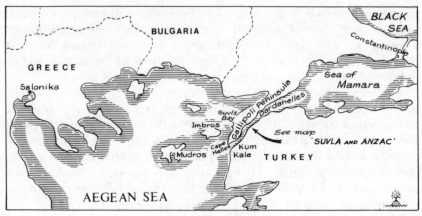

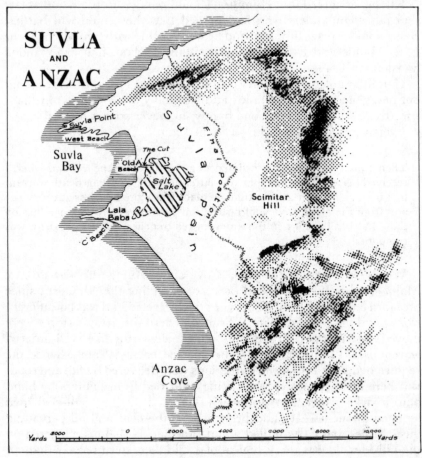

Crowded into a total area of little more than a square mile were the stores, reserves, medical installations and headquarters of more than six divisions. To the south, across Suvla Bay, Byng could see the low conical shape of Lala Baba. On its western slopes were the headquarters of three divisions, three artillery brigades and several reserve battalions of infantry. Near the base of the hill, not far from the men's bivouacs, were the horse lines, where they and the wretched mules suffered the torments of flies and insufficient water. There was almost no cover from shellfire and most of the beach area could be observed by the enemy. Fortunately the Turks were running short of artillery ammunition.

From the commander-in-chief downwards, practically everyone in the expeditionary force was suffering from dysentry – 'the Gallipoli Gallop'. With its debilitating effect combined with the strain of fighting, the heat, dust and flies, the army was worn out, their normal vitality gone. Few men could walk more quickly than a crawl.

Byng scarcely needed to hear the opinions of the divisional commanders to realize that his force was incapable of offensive action.

> General Byng, it will be remembered, had been specially asked for at the middle of June when the August operations were first projected, but the request was then refused. Now, ten weeks later, it had been granted. The experienced pilot had arrived. But the ship to be steered into port was already hard on the rocks.
>
> (Official History)[5]

The front line had been advanced but little from that established in the landings of early August, when the 9th Corps had occupied the western promontory of the Gallipoli Peninsula. Were it not for Suvla Bay at the apex, the ground occupied would have been an equilateral triangle, the front line forming the base and the coast its equal sides. From the 11th Division's position anchored on the cliffs of the northern coast, the line crossed the broken ground of the Suvla Plain and rose again to some lower hills where the 2nd Mounted Division joined flanks with the troops of the Australian and New Zealand Army Corps – the Anzacs. The tip of Suvla Point was less than $3\frac{1}{2}$ miles from the front line. Inland from Suvla Bay was Salt Lake which was dry in summer. Beyond it, to the north and east, was the low-lying Suvla Plain, the largest part of the Corps area, dominated from the east by the enemy-occupied hills. In few places had proper trenches been dug and in many battalion areas the ground was so rocky that the only protection was formed by breastworks. The artillery was scarcely better off, it being practically impossible to find gun positions which were not open to enfilade fire.

95

Three days before Byng's arrival at Suvla the 9th Corps had suffered a bloody reverse in attempting to take Scimitar Hill which dominates the Suvla plain. Of the 14,300 men who took part in the attack, no less than 5,300 were killed, wounded or missing. In proportion to its size, it was the most costly and least successful of all the Gallipoli battles. The casualty rate related to the force involved exceeded that of the worst day of the First or Second Battles of Ypres.

There were other similarities between the Ypres Salient and Suvla. In terms of infantry, the British force was roughly the same size, the front line of comparable length, situated at roughly the same distance from the key communications point – in one case, the town of Ypres, here the beaches and installations of Suvla Bay. At Ypres, a line of ridges provided observation over all the low ground to the north and east of the town, as the hills overlooked the Suvla plain. At Ypres, the vital ridges were held by the British but here, from their positions on the heights, the Turks looked down as in an amphitheatre at the British below.

Commanders in France believed that if the Ypres ridges were lost, the Salient would be untenable.

The comparison cannot be taken much further. The Turks, brave as they were, did not have the resources of the German Army, but their strength was increasing and there were ominous signs of improvement in their artillery. Yet Byng's Corps was incapable, without rest, reinforcement and far more artillery support, of even capturing the dominating hills.

On 31 August Basil Brooke gave his impressions of Suvla in a letter to his sister –

I have at last arrived in this God-forsaken place . . . We are shelled all day as there is no room back which is rather upsetting to one's nerves. Thank goodness they have not got as much as the Bosch, or as big, but quite enough to be unpleasant. One landed just outside our Mess while we (were) having tea and perforated my washing. Here we wash in salt water and collect fresh water for a weekly bath when the clothes are washed as well. We are absolutely cut off and live in caves. . . . It is very hilly and one can see practically the whole line.

It is rather amusing trying to spot where the Turks' guns are firing from . . . and then wire down to the ships who proceed to lambaste it lifting great chunks off the sides of the hill. It is very pleasant being able to see the effect.

The old Turk is a great gentleman. He never shoots at the hospital ships in the bay, or at the hospitals, very different from our friend the Bosch.

I saw an attack by the Australians the other evening. It was a very fine sight. Our ships shot beautifully and made their trenches appear a sheet of flame. The attack was a complete success.

It is very pretty looking down on the bay in the dark with a glorious sunset and the warships shooting. Later on, the hospital ships all light up with green lights and a large red cross on their sides.

When I wrote to you last, I had no idea that we were going off and suddenly we got the wire, motored to Paris and trained to Rome where we stopped the day and looked round and then on to Taranto where we stopped for a day and a night on the Flagship. We then went on in a patrol boat to Mudros where we transferred to a destroyer, then to GHQ on an island [Imbros] and finally on here.

We go and do reconnaissances in a destroyer which is great fun. I saw the monitors fire the other day. They shoot bang across the Peninsula and yesterday sank 3 ships. . . .

I must quit as I am a bit drowsy having walked most of the day in the sun – This goes by King's Messenger. When you write put the envelope inside another addressed to Lt Gen The Hon Sir Julian Byng, IX Corps, Dardanelles, c/o The Secretary, War Office, Whitehall. It will then get out in a week instead of a month.

Earlier, within a week of arrival, Byng had instructed his staff to prepare a secret contingency plan for evacuating Suvla.[6]

His line of reasoning was simple. The operations in Gallipoli were yielding few strategic benefits to the Allied cause and were a running sore in terms of casualties. The Army must either drive on and seize its final objectives (and there seemed little likelihood of being given the resources to do this) or the troops should be withdrawn and used elsewhere. What a difference even one of the Gallipoli divisions would have made at Ypres!

It was soon apparent that a firm hand was on the wheel at Suvla as measures were taken to make the 9th Corps' position tenable. Gradually a coordinated defensive system was developed from the hasty positions which had served so far and a start was made at improving the protection of the force from shelling. Not only the men needed shelter. On 29 August one Turkish shell killed 113 mules.

In some places local advances were required to make the line more defensible. These attacks were well planned and carried out with little loss, but Byng refused to countenance any larger operations until he had sufficient artillery ammunition to ensure success. This was slow in coming and he was soon under pressure to undertake a large-scale offensive.

While Sir Ian Hamilton forebore from ordering Byng to attack, he did make his desires known, and a general does not lightly ignore the wishes of his commander-in-chief. Later Byng was obliged to restrain his more aggressive divisional commanders. The mounting pressure can be inferred for Hamilton's diaries:

'26 August, 1915. Sailed for Suvla and went straight to see Byng. During the two days he has been here, he has been working very hard. Our old A beach was being briskly shelled as we walked down to our boats. Between Hill 10 and the sea there were salvoes of shrapnel falling and about every 30 seconds a big fellow, probably a six incher, made a terrible hullabaloo. The men working at piling up stores carried on.'

Next day he signalled to Kitchener:

'Byng is getting everything in order and has infected all around him with his own energy and cheeriness and has quickly grasped the whole situation.'
'31 August, 1915. I am very anxious indeed he should work his men up into the mood for making a push. He charms everyone and he is fast pulling his force together. Maude, Fanshawe and de Lisle seem to be keen to do something but Byng, though he is also keen, has the French standards for ammunition in his head. He does not think we have enough to warrant us in making an attack. Also he does not realize yet that if he is going to wait until we are fitted out on that scale, he will have to wait till doomsday.
'5 September, 1915 . . . Byng has a keen sense of humour; he is energetic and by his looks and manner attracts all ranks. No one could wish a better corps commander. . . . But his sojourn on the Western Front has given him inflated standards as to the number of guns and stocks of HE shell which are essential to success; especially with troops who have suffered heavy losses. Perhaps he is right.
'This para from a letter written to the great man (Kitchener) tonight explains more generally what I feel: – Maude is burning to get on and do something and I heard him myself ask Byng when he was going to let him have a dash. As to Byng, I think myself he is not quite sure yet about the spirit of his men. I have been trying to spur him on for the last day or so although only by very gentle hints as I think, with a man of Byng's great reputation, one must leave him to himself as long as possible. I daresay he may be quite right and very wise. Still these reinforcements have brought the Suvla Bay troops up to no less than 37,000 men and I am most anxious that they should do something soon, a little more rapid than sapping out slowly toward the enemy's lines – which they are doing.
'After my talk with Byng, we went on to meet Fanshawe and de Lisle. Maude came along with me as far as the crest line. I asked him about his division. He replied, "If you give the order now, and will arrange for a little artillery support, my division will storm and hold onto any thousand yards of Turkish trench you like to point out – tomorrow." I could have embraced him, but I had to go steady and explain to him that a corps commander must judge all his divisions and that taking the situation as whole, Byng did not think it fair on the men to let them have a dart yet – not, at least, til they had more munitions at their back. Byng has had wide experiences in the West and he looks on it as trying the men unfairly to ask them to attack without preliminary bombardment on a scale which we cannot at present afford. "Yes," said Maude, "that is all very well, but after all you must

remember the Turks have neither the artillery nor the munitions the Germans have at their command on the Western Front."

' "Well," I replied, "you put your points to Byng and you know I am a man who never yet in my life refused a good brave offer like yours." He has a great admiration for Byng and so, though sadly, he went away.'

A week later, Hamilton's sense of frustration was becoming more apparent. '23 September, 1915. Have written K to tell him how day succeeds day, never without incident, but never with achievement; how we are burnt up with longing to get on and how we know that he is as anxious, yet, as I tell him, we can't force the pace. How can we? We have not the wherewithal – the stuff. Byng would like to have four days successive bombardment for an hour and then attack, and speaks of one HE shell per yard as pat as if they were shells we could pick up on the sea shore. I have assured him it is no earthly use; that he shall have his share of what I have got, but that stuff for bombardment is simply not in existence – not here, at least.'

But much as commander-in-chief and divisional general might give vent to their frustrated ardour, there are hints in what Hamilton wrote that he knew that Byng was right. The cemeteries at Gallipoli already showed the cost of attempting to take Turkish positions with bayonets alone. There might indeed have been enough ammunition to permit Maude to take his one thousand yards of Turkish trench, or any particular hill position, but beyond there would be more positions to be taken before the Corps could shake free of the enemy defences. What was needed was sufficient ammunition to sustain an offensive which would bring victory. Without it the issue would be in doubt and Byng was not prepared to accept the casualties of such a dubious enterprise.

In the meantime there was much to be done to prepare for a winter campaign. Timber for huts, corrugated iron, road building material, rails for a tramway and rolling stock, pumps to drain trenches and thousands of stoves, winter clothing, tents, horse blankets and additional engineers – all were requisitioned. Every day Byng visited the trenches with Brooke who wrote, 'Sometimes we get straffed, sometimes we don't. I am getting pretty used to it again but it always frightens me. I always either feel it is going to burst in the pit of my stomach or else in my ear hole!'[7]

As Byng worked tirelessly to improve conditions for his troops, Brooke and Titchfield attempted to make conditions a little more pleasant for their commander. With the help of friends on a naval ship anchored in the bay, they had glass windows made for the general's dug-out which were installed while he was away. Feeling pleased with themselves, they expected to be praised. Unfortunately they missed seeing him come back and the first intimation they had of his return was the sound of crashing glass and swearing, as Byng smashed the windows with his swagger stick. With a furious face, he demanded to know who had done this, and, when they confessed, he told them that when he wanted to live in more comfort than his men he'd let them know.[8]

During September and early October new units arrived to replace some of those decimated in the fighting in August, principally yeomanry regiments for the 2nd Mounted Division and the Newfoundland Battalion for the 29th Division, but, far from building up the forces in Gallipoli, troops were taken away for a new expedition to Salonika.

Both the German naval and general staffs viewed with increasing alarm the possibility of an Allied victory at the Dardanelles. Now, confident that they could defeat any attack which might be brought against them in the West, they turned their attention to opening a land route to Constantinople. On 6 September the Bulgarians agreed to join with the Germans and Austrians in attacking Serbia. In the last week of September they mobilized and Greece and Serbia called on Britain and France for help. They agreed and each removed a division from Gallipoli. It marked the beginning of the end of the Dardanelles campaign.

The 10th Division, from Byng's 9th Corps, was selected for the new venture and by the end of September had left Suvla.

Byng commented to Blumenfeld:

> This expedition was sent to enable us to sing 'We're here, because we're here' which I believe is a famous Music Hall ditty. There is no other possible reason for this Brobdignagian Bumstunt – oh, the pity of it –
>
> We were taught at the Staff College the famous maxim that campaigns were won by 'Superior numbers at the decisive point'. Here we have inferior numbers at four decisive points.
>
> Verily, we are the sport and plaything of irresponsible politicians and agitated Diplomats.[9]

By 7 October it was apparent in London that if Hamilton were to have any chance of opening the Dardanelles before German help reached the Turkish Army, he must be heavily reinforced. There was, however, another option to be considered. The War Office asked for his opinion as to the number of casualties which would be suffered in an evacuation of Gallipoli. He replied that he estimated these would amount to about one half of his force. With luck he would do better, but on the other hand, with inexperienced troops at Suvla and Helles, there might be a catastrophe.[10] The Government now decided that an unbiased view must be taken of the situation. They recalled Hamilton and ordered Gen Sir Charles Munro, commander of the Third Army in France, to replace him. Before leaving, he spent several days in London finding out all he could about the situation in the Eastern Mediterranean. He found nothing to change his firmly held opinion that the war could only be won in the West and that, if practicable, the Gallipoli venture should be abandoned. Until Munro arrived at Gallipoli, Kitchener directed that Lt-Gen Birdwood, commanding the Anzac Corps, should act as Army commander.

For some days there had been ominous signs that the weather might break. On 8 October gales washed away ninety feet of the West Beach pier at Suvla, damaged the tramway and drove three motor-lighters ashore. The situation of the 9th Corps had improved, but it was still far from ready for a major operation. If all its units had been at full strength, they would have numbered 74,448, yet on 10 October, their strength was 41,622. 300 men per day were being evacuated sick and artillery ammunition expenditure was limited to two rounds per gun per day. This situation was little better when Sir Charles Munro arrived at his new headquarters at Imbros on the 28th. He had been there less than twenty-four hours when he received a telegram from Lord Kitchener –

Please send me as soon as possible your report on the main issue at the Dardanelles, namely, leaving or staying.

Next day Munro visited Helles, Anzac and Suvla, staying long enough to visit the headquarters and take a quick glance at the immediate neighbourhood. At each location he interviewed the divisional commanders privately in the corps commander's dugout and asked two questions – were their troops physically and morally fit for a sustained effort to capture the enemy's positions? Alternatively, presupposing that no drafts could be sent to them and the Turks received strong reinforcements, with German heavy guns and ammunition, could they maintain their positions throughout the winter?

Each divisional commander gave the same answers. In their present state of health, the troops could not be depended upon for more than twenty-four hours sustained offensive effort. They could promise to hold their positions in existing circumstances, but if the Turks received unlimited ammunition, while they themselves received little, invariably they then paused and shrugged their shoulders and added that they could only say they would do their best.

On 31 October Munro cabled that he recommended evacuation of the Gallipoli Peninsula. Kitchener was appalled and replied asking if Munro's corps commanders were also in favour of withdrawing. The message arrived on the evening of 1 November and Byng and Birdwood were ordered to come to GHQ while a staff officer was sent to see Gen Davies, commanding at Helles. A near gale was blowing which the previous night had wrecked a destroyer on the shore at Suvla Bay and done serious damage to the piers.

Byng took Brooke with him.

(We) couldn't get a destroyer 'til 10 pm as she was shooting on our flank. It was damnable rough and getting out of a picket boat into a destroyer in a rough sea is no joke. However, I am getting pretty nautical. After a very rough passage we got there about midnight.[11]

Munro showed Byng and Birdwood the recommendation he had sent to Kitchener and told them to state in writing if they agreed, or disagreed. He said that they should give their personal opinions without in any way deferring to his. Byng began to write

I have had the question of evacuation in my mind since arrival two and half months ago.

He paused and ran his pencil through the words, then went on, without hesitation

I consider evacuation advisable. As regards Suvla, a voluntary and *not* costly retirement is feasible at the present time. But it seems possible that with German help to the enemy, a compulsory and therefore costly retirement may be necessitated.

Birdwood was fearful of the effect that the evacuation (which the Turks would claim as a complete victory) would have on Moslem feeling elsewhere. He opposed it, adding that a withdrawal would be fraught with difficulty and danger and that, with the season of bad weather approaching, a withdrawal might be interrupted with heavy losses.

Davies' views were soon received – he was in favour of evacuation.

Munro reported his corps commanders' opinions to Kitchener and added that he estimated that the casualties resulting from an evacuation might amount to 30 or 40% of the force. Then, handing over temporary command of the Expeditionary Force to Birdwood, he sailed for Egypt to consult the commander there on the possible effects in Egypt and the Arab world of an evacuation of Gallipoli.

Early next morning an urgent ciphered telegram from Kitchener arrived for Birdwood. It began:

Most Secret. Decipher yourself. Tell no one. You know Munro's report. I leave here tomorrow night to come out to you – Admiralty will I believe agree naval attempt to force Straits.

He went on to outline a new plan for an army attack to assist the Navy, adding that he refused to sign an order for evacuation. Munro would be appointed to command the Salonika force.

On 9 November Kitchener arrived at Mudros from Marseilles and embarked on a series of conferences on the subject of evacuation. Plans for attacking the Turks and for defending Egypt were discussed. Between the 11th and 13th he visited the three corps and came to the conclusion than an evacuation might be less costly than had at first been feared.

At Suvla conditions were becoming more uncomfortable. On 15 November Byng reported 'unusually heavy and accurate shellfire on the supply depot near C Beach, South pier badly damaged by storm, work on A Beach stopped by heavy sea, no landing possible at present.'

On the 22nd Kitchener cabled to the Government recommending that Suvla and Anzac should be evacuated. He was now of the opinion that the chance of success in the Peninsula had been jeopardized by refusing Hamilton the reinforcements he requested in August. It was now too late to try again.

Next day he appointed Munro to command all forces in the Mediterranean outside of Egypt and Birdwood to command at Gallipoli. On the same day a cable arrived from the Prime Minister saying that the War Committee were in favour of evacuating Gallipoli but that the matter had to be referred to the full Cabinet for confirmation. He expected the final decision would be telegraphed after their meeting next day.

Already, on Kitchener's instructions, progress had been made in withdrawing surplus stores and ammunition from the Peninsula. Orders were now issued to press on with this preliminary work with all speed. Arrangements were made for reception of the troops on the nearby islands and in Egypt. Fifty-six hospital ships were summoned to the area and a deception plan was put into operation. Then came frustration. Despite the unanimous recommendation of the War Committee, the British Cabinet could not make up their minds. The whole policy for the Mediterranean theatre was back in the melting pot.

At Suvla the arrival of cool weather and the disappearance of flies in the first weeks of November had brought an improvement to the health of the troops. There was little infantry fighting and it seemed to some that weather was becoming the real enemy. Almost weekly the piers at the landing beaches were washed away. A violent storm broke out on the 27th and for three days it was impossible for a boat to approach the

Gallipoli beaches. At Suvla the position became alarming as the cold north wind drove torrential rain before it. On the northern coastal ridge, there was no shelter for the troops exposed to the fury of the storm, while below them on the plain, trenches were soon flooded and the dry water courses became raging torrents. At one place a wall of mud and water several feet high rushed down a nullah carrying drowned Turks and pack ponies with it into the British lines. Positions became untenable and the centre of the front could only be held by snipers. The Turks, too, had been flooded out and in places, the dazed and near frozen garrisons stood about in the open, observing an unofficial truce.

Many men had been drowned in the trenches and the severe cold and driving snow which followed the floods proved too much for men whose health had been undermined in the summer campaign. Whole units were out of action and streams of utterly exhausted men struggled back across the plains toward the beach. Many collapsed on the roadside and froze to death. Casualties soon filled the hospitals and overflowed into any place where there was shelter. Store tents and supply depots were filled, yet more and more sick poured into the beach area for whom no shelter could be found. The suddenness of the emergency overwhelmed the means of dealing with it. It became impossible even to supply men with warm food and drink. Help could not reach Suvla from outside, nor, while the storm lasted, could the sick be moved away.

Just before the storm began, orders had been received for all surplus stores to be sent back to Mudros. The first items to be cleared from the beach were the latest arrived consignments – the winter clothing for the force. In the course of the storm there were more than 5,000 cases of frostbite and over 200 men drowned or were frozen to death.

On 30 November the wind dropped. For the next three weeks the sea sparkled by day in warm autumn sunshine.

Days went by without a decision from the Cabinet. On 2 December Kitchener cabled Munro to say that the Government now wanted to know whether, if four divisions from Salonika were sent to Gallipoli, could he attack again at Suvla and increase the depth of his position. At once Munro replied that he was against any renewal of the attack at Suvla and marshalled convincing arguments to support his case. But again Kitchener would not rely on Munro's opinion and asked for those of Birdwood and Byng.

Birdwood's view was that it would be a 'complete gamble' but, given fresh troops and plenty of howitzer ammunition, they could advance. Landing the troops would be as easy or difficult as evacuating them.

Byng maintained, as he had always done, that, with more men and ammunition, he could gain ground on his left, but he considered that the landing of the four divisions would be difficult. Almost weekly piers at

Suvla had been washed away, roads were nearly impassable and there was not enough shelter from weather for the troops already there.

With the season so far advanced, neither general was prepared to recommend the operation.

At last the Cabinet reached a decision. Suvla and Anzac should be evacuated but, partly for naval reasons and partly to avoid admission of complete failure, Helles was to be held for the present.

On 8 December Birdwood ordered the withdrawal to begin.

Before Kitchener left the Mediterranean, he had ordered that a preliminary evacuation of surplus stores should commence. This by now should have been well advanced but on 1 December, with the Cabinet far from convinced that the Gallipoli operations should be ended, he cabled that his previous orders were to be held in abeyance. There was no alternative but to return to the Peninsula the stores and equipment which had been removed and to begin once more landing the large quantities of material which would be needed in the winter. Now these operations were again to be put into reverse.

The scheme of withdrawal which Byng had devised at the end of August was fairly conventional. It involved withdrawing from the front line to two successive defensive lines, the final position being close to the embarkation beaches. When Munro indicated that evacuation was being considered, Byng began the construction of these rearward defences. By this time the Salt Lake at Suvla had flooded, dividing the 9th Corps area into two almost equal halves. The only means of communication between them was via a bridge across the Cut. All troops to the north of the Salt Lake would withdraw toward the northern arm of Suvla Bay, called Reserve Area A and the troops to the south or east of the Lake to the southern arm, Reserve Area B.

While the stage was thus being set for a fighting withdrawal, Byng appreciated that, with care, it would be possible to progress the evacuation well towards completion before the Turks became suspicious. To this end the enemy could not be allowed to observe any change in the routine activities of the Corps. The amount of rifle and artillery fire to which the Turks had become accustomed would have to be maintained. The number of ships lying off the beaches and the activity of the back areas in daylight must not vary from the normal. Carried to its logical conclusion, the aim should be to get the last man off the beach before the enemy realized that the evacuation had begun.

Given the distance of the front line from the beaches in the Suvla area, the possibility of achieving this seemed remote, for it implied holding the front line until late on the last night of the evacuation. At

Anzac, immediately to the south, Lt-Gen Godley, now commanding the Anzac Corps, concluded that no other course was practicable. There was no room between the front line and the beach for reserve lines of defence. Here deception became imperative if those remaining on the last night of the evacuation were not to be overwhelmed by a Turkish attack. If the enemy detected that Byng's front line had been abandoned, they would inevitably probe the Anzac position which, by that time, would be too lightly held to be defended. Thus the plan evolved of holding the front line at Suvla until the final hours of the evacuation.

Once started, the final stage would have to be completed with all possible speed to reduce the likelihood of detection by the Turks. Because of the uncertainty of weather, it could take no more than 48 hours. The maximum number of men which the Navy could remove from Suvla was 10,000 per night, thus the final garrison was fixed at 20,000.

The preliminary stage, which had been interrupted, involved taking off all troops, animals and material not needed for a defensive winter campaign. With the Government's decision to withdraw, the removal could now begin of everything not needed for the defence of the beachheads during the final stage. On 9 December there were 41,000 men and 91 guns in the Suvla beachhead, half of which were to be embarked in the ten days which would ensue before the commencement of the final stage.

The weather was ideal and embarkation proceeded like clockwork. By day the Turks could see, as usual, two or three storeships anchored in Suvla Bay and the normal amount of movement and fires in the rear area. At night the beaches were alive with activity as men and animals, guns and vast quantities of stores were loaded into lighters to be carried to the transports waiting offshore.

By the morning of 18 December all was ready for the final stage which would begin that night. Enough troops remained at Suvla to resist a serious attack, but any engagement would delay the withdrawal. The chances of discovery by the enemy were increasing with every hour and the Force meteorologist predicted that the good weather would soon come to an end. There was now little more that Byng could do. Arrangements were complete for the embarkation of his men. There were fortified areas near each beach, stocked with rations where any troops left behind might maintain themselves until they could be embarked later. A hospital for 2,000 patients with sufficient personnel to look after them was there to take care of casualties who could not be embarked on the second night. Everything which could not be taken away was prepared for destruction.

Byng had moved his headquarters to a sloop offshore but each night was on the beaches until 3.30 am. On the 18th he and Commodore Roger Keyes spent some hours walking around the Corps area and the sailor congratulated him on the imaginative and meticulous arrangements for the evacuation. 'There seemed nothing for his Corps to do but march down to the boats and set light to the bonfires.' Byng told him that he intended to spend the last night on shore and would be the last to embark. Keyes observed that he would have trouble with Capt Unwin, the naval transport officer, who would claim the beach party's prerogative of being the last to leave. Byng said he would gladly defer to Unwin whom he greatly admired.[12]

As dusk fell the first troops to be embarked started to move. In silence they came back in close formation to assembly areas from whence they were directed in groups of 400, the capacity of a motor-lighter, to the beach. All night the embarkation went on without interruption by the enemy, exactly as planned. There was not a casualty and the only contact with the enemy was the arrival of two Turkish deserters.

As the morning of the 19th dawned, no longer could it be said that the 9th Corps was capable of defending itself. If its soldiers reflected upon it, they must have been grateful that, in terms of daylight, this was one of the shortest days of the year. A low-hanging mist partially obscured the Turkish view of the beaches and the Suvla plain. Every effort was made to simulate normal activity. Mules and carts were driven back and forth and groups of men were detailed to show themselves at conspicuous points in the base area.

In the morning a newly arrived battery of Austrian six-inch howitzers shelled Lala Baba and a nearby pier. Every round exploded, an unpleasant change from the unreliable ammunition used by the Turks, but so few men were left in the area that only one was wounded. 9th Corps' guns replied to such effect that the Turks did not suspect that so few remained.

As night fell embarkation resumed. With the first troops went the remaining heavier guns, but a few light field guns stayed in action until nearly midnight when they too were sent away.

On the rocky hillsides where trenches were close to the enemy, troops muffled their boots with sandbags and lay sacking on the trench floor to deaden the sounds of movement. As the infantry in the front line withdrew, a scanty rearguard spread out to wide intervals and kept up the usual rate of sniping. At 1.30 am the front line was abandoned but sporadic firing continued from rifles equipped with improvised timing devices to pull the trigger.

The troops from the front moved back through small garrisons which remained in the trenches, protecting the beach area. There officers who knew the numbers of each withdrawing group checked them off and, when the last man had passed, the gaps in the wire were closed. Their task completed, these garrisons then withdrew.

Byng had been ashore with Brooke since dusk, using an old Ford car to get about the area. Having visited the forward checkpoints, they returned to the beach, the car loaded with some rifles and wheels which they had found dumped beside a track. When, all the men having reported in, Byng and his ADC walked up to the supply dump to see if everything was ready for burning, there was no one between them and the Turks.

Shortly afterwards the dump was fired and the rearguard, with details of the Royal Army Medical Corps, who now would not have to remain, climbed into their lighter. Byng and Brooke boarded a picket boat and watched, by the light of the burning supply dump, as Unwin and the beach party prepared to leave in another. As it was about to pull away from the pier, a soldier fell overboard and Unwin dived in and hauled him to safety.

The evacuation was completed without the loss of a man or an animal or a gun.

On boarding HMS *Collingwood*, Byng told Roger Keyes about Unwin's rescue (he had won a VC in the landings at Helles) and added, 'You should send him home; we want several little Unwins'.[13]

A withdrawal in the face of the enemy is one of the most difficult and dangerous operations of war. That from Gallipoli roused the admiration of professional soldiers everywhere, even in Germany:

> The English had therefore in all probability realized the hopelessness of the struggle before the last weeks of November and about the middle of December, they had prepared their retreat in an absolutely admirable manner. For this, praise must be accorded to them. As long as wars exist, their evacuation of the Ari Burnu (Anzac) and Anafarta (Suvla) fronts will stand before the eyes of all strategists of retreat as a hitherto unattained masterpiece.[14]

Everyone who took part in the evacuation deserved a measure of credit for its success. Birdwood, and Godley who succeeded him in command at Anzac, were two of its principal architects. But, though not the force commander, the chief of these was Byng. He had begun to study the problem shortly after his arrival in August. Alone of the senior commanders, he believed the operation could be carried out without great loss and devised a plan to achieve the result. His optimism and enthusiasm were infectious and turned the outlook of other commanders from an acceptance of the inevitability of disaster to a belief in the possibility of success.

There was now a clear indication that Byng was a commander of outstanding quality. Gallipoli provided the first evidence of the imaginative and meticulous planning and preparation for battle which were to mark his later career. In addition to technical skills, his qualities of intellect and character had now become apparent. Sent by Kitchener to revive a failing enterprise, he showed remarkable objectivity in concluding almost at once that its abandonment was more likely than its success. Then in the face of mounting pressure from both his commander-in-chief and his subordinates, he refused to allow men and ammunition to be wasted in attacks which could not achieve the ultimate objectives of the operation.

From Egypt where Byng's 9th Corps was reforming along the Suez Canal, Basil Brooke wrote:

> The General is in great form and jolly glad to get out of that b——y Suvla. There has not been much mention of his name as he does not advertise. . . . I hope he gets all the credit he deserves for it.[15]

From one source Byng expected no gratitude. When Kitchener visited him in November, Byng had told him that evacuation was essential, but the Field-Marshal had disagreed, claiming that the results would be calamitous. Byng answered that if he were allowed to conduct it according to his own plan, he believed it could be managed with a minimum of casualties. Had the operation failed, Byng knew his career would be over. Now that it had succeeded, he knew he would never be forgiven.[16]

In the meantime the war was entering a new phase in France. The BEF was expanding and officers junior to him already had been given command of armies. Byng was well aware that, successful as the withdrawal had been, evacuations do not win wars and military reputations are not built by association with failed enterprises.

Mercifully he had not long to wait. Orders arrived for him to return to France to take command of the new 17th Corps.

On the way he had a few days in England. On the morning of 25 February he spent some time with the King, who was keenly interested in his experiences, but neither then nor in March, when he returned to receive the KCB for his services at Gallipoli, did Kitchener send for him. Julian and Evelyn, who had known him so well for years and had been part of his household in Egypt, were never to see him again.

On 6 June, 1916, Evelyn received a telegram from her brother-in-law, Charles Byng: 'Admiralty report Kitchener and staff drowned in Cruiser *Hampshire* sunk off Orkney Islands.'[17]

Characteristically Byng never spoke of the horrors and frustrations of Gallipoli, or of its effect on his career. His only recorded comment was: 'My great uncle was shot for running away from Minorca. I was given a decoration for running away from Gallipoli. Now which is right, because surely they cannot both be?'[18]

Chapter 7
The Western Front

THE FIRST FEW months of 1916 saw the BEF, now commanded by Sir Douglas Haig, reinforced by seventeen divisions of the New Army and the Territorial Force. As they arrived in France, these were grouped into corps of three or four, one of which, the 17th, concentrated around Doullens where Sir Julian Byng, their new commander, joined them on 25 February. A week later they moved north of Arras as part of Allenby's Third Army to relieve the French 12th Corps between Roclincourt and Cabaret Rouge.

The men of Byng's divisions, the 25th, 46th (North Midland) and 51st (Highland), found that the trench line which they took over from the French on the slopes of Vimy Ridge was little more than a series of shell holes connected by inadequate ditches, knee-deep in sloppy mud. The protective fences of barbed wire were thin and inadequate. Over all hung an appalling stench from dead bodies which had lain unburied for months and from the absence of even rudimentary sanitary arrangements.

The British soldiers' first impressions were more of discomfort than danger. Bloody fighting had taken place here earlier in the war but the French now knew it as a quiet sector. There was little firing and the Germans walked about freely in the open, well protected by wire. For the French, the memory of the tens of thousands of casualties they had suffered in coming this far up the slope of the ridge cooled any thoughts of reaching the top where they might see the village after which it was named.

The infantry of the 17th Corps began immediately to improve their defences and make them habitable: and they opened fire at the first sight of an enemy. It was not long before the Germans began to call the Vimy sector 'a windy corner of the Western Front'.

'Live and let live' as a policy had no appeal for Byng or for the untried and ardent young soldiers of his divisions. Neither, as it transpired, did the Germans favour it, but had been using it to mask

111

their preparation of a hideous fate for the infantry who faced them below.

In the past the French and Germans had driven saps under each other's positions, then exploded huge mines, the craters of which formed part of the front line. Recently French activity had diminished but, while the Germans had smiled down at them from above, they were pushing on below. Their works were much deeper and much further advanced than the mining system which the British now acquired.

Fascinated by Vimy Ridge and the problems it presented, Byng spent hours reconnoitring it until he knew every contour.[1] With a major offensive planned to begin on the Somme, he would not have the resources to capture it. Yet if the British were to remain on the Ridge, they would have to win the underground war. Withdrawal was not a practical option, for Haig wished to deceive the enemy that it was here that he intended to attack.

The necessarily slow and deliberate progress of the British tunnellers in attempting to overtake the German head start – to blow their mine before the enemy blew his – lent a kind of desperation to the struggle below ground. Above, the infantry of both sides knew what was being prepared for them. Often they could hear the sound of pick and shovel below the surface. When it stopped they would suffer an agony of anticipation until it resumed or the world erupted under them. When a mine was fired, infantry would rush to consolidate near the lip of the crater, often to find that only its enormous hollow of pulverized earth separated them from a shaken but dangerous enemy.

In the two months which followed his arrival on the slopes of Vimy Ridge, Byng persuaded, begged and cajoled Headquarters Third Army and GHQ to provide him with more resources to counter the German saps and push forward his own. Eventually no less than ten tunnelling companies, British, Canadian and Australian, were engaged. Gradually the British miners gained supremacy but the strain on the infantry in the front line was almost beyond bearing.

Daily Byng visited a section of his front. It was strenuous and dangerous work. Basil Brooke and Chopper Titchfield, who took turns to accompany him, began to be affected. Those who have spent some time in a front-line position, facing the enemy, know that the anticipation of 'going up the line' and the hazards of the route forward are often more disturbing than the daily routine of the forward trenches. Nor do men look forward with any pleasure to the return journey. Frequent ventures from safety into unknown danger and back again, strangely enough, are harder on the nerves than living with known hazards. The number of cases of battle exhaustion among

112

infantry company quartermaster sergeants, who take forward rations and supplies each night, can in part be attributed to this.

Brooke's sister, Sylvia, had written to him, as he had told her to do, enclosing the envelopes in ones addressed to Byng. On 25 March, 1916, little more than three weeks after the move to Vimy, Byng wrote to Sylvia –

My dear *Miss Sylvia Brooke* –
You see that having begun by giving you all your titles, names etc. I can now easily drop the 'Miss' and the 'Brooke' and get down to calling you Sylvia which I shall probably do in the near future.

First – Let me thank you a thousand times for all the envelopes you sent me to Suvla. I read and re-read your carefully worded address – that the contents should have to be passed on to Basil seemed as nothing when I was allowed to keep the envelope. Even the stamp and the postmark were not without an influence of warm cordiality.

You are wrong. I have never asked for cheerful correspondence. It is only subalterns who are allowed to be 'lonely'. Nobody ever heard of a lonely Major, and a lonely General is unthinkable. I would like to be a lonely General, but they won't let me – Straaf them. . . .

Now I want to tell you about Basil. I had to pack him off a week ago as he was getting a nasty irritating inflammation behind his eye. I don't think it is serious if it is seen to at once and if he gives them time to make a good job of it, but it is no use his bustling out here before he is right. Since he left he seems to have mislaid his 'Stylo' as he hasn't given us any indication of his whereabouts. I have written to my better $\frac{1}{2}$ (a nice woman who shares my home and banking account) telling her to try to find him as soon as he writes and not to let him be foolish in trying to get back, but a word from you would probably be beneficial. The weather here is foul and the trenches fouler, so he probably would only get bad again if he was to return – besides I have Chopper (Do you know Chopper? – he is married so you can't be a Duchess there). He (Chopper) has developed a snuffle, a cold, damp unlovely snuffle, only Duke's eldest sons could carry it off with eclat. That snuffle is always about this house, you come upon it everywhere.

You will get this letter about the 28th perhaps. Yours of the 29th is expected with eagerness. Let me know about Basil.

Bless you

Yrs. Ever
J. Byng.

On 8 April he wrote again:

You are quite wrong, My dear Sylvia. I am not in the least like a butler (other Generals may be, but I doubt it) you ask Basil. If you want to know what I am like, look at Bairnsfather's pictures in 'the Bystander'. He draws me every week.

113

Now Sylvia, listen to me. Basil is fussing about his being away for a considerable time and thinks I will get someone else in his place, which I certainly shall *not* do as I am far too fond of him. Don't show him this but keep him at home till he is really well. He has not recovered Suvla properly, and wants an absolutely easy time, watching a blackbird's nest or potting the bulbs (do you pot bulbs?) or something restful and peaceful. He also wants to be with you as much as possible so as to be taken care of. I think his nerves got a bit of a shake at Gallipoli which was quite possible & it was too quick to get him out here again. Keep all this to yourself, Sylvia, and don't let him worry. The snuffle is getting drier and more snort like but is still unlovely.

12.IV

I started this letter, My dear Sylvia, some days ago and meant to finish it, but there is a beastly war on here and I had to bolt off to watch people trying to kill each other, and now I have nothing to say.

Lots of love to you and Basil

Yrs Ever

JB

If you go on calling me 'General Byng' I shall become inflated with choleric wrath.

Good luck Sylvia.

Later that month, he sent the following to Basil Brooke:

The only news we have to talk about are the Boche mines. The total sprung on my front is now 21. So far, our casualties have been wonderfully small. About 700 in the 46th Division, 500 in the 51st and 120 in the 25th. Of these many are at duty and the total deaths is under 100. We had a bad night on Wednesday in the N area opposite the ridge – about 100 casualties. Two Boche mines and an attack – as an attack it was a failure as they never got over the lip of the crater. A good Lewis gun on the flank got them as they came along and forty-five Boches were killed there (the men claim a hundred). But we suffered a lot from the minnenwerfer and men buried.

There is no doubt that all this mining tells on the men's nerves as they don't know what is going to happen next and the fright of being buried alive is to them unnerving. Still up to now they have been splendid but are looking a bit 'googley' about the eyeball.[2]

It is a pity for us that the French left us a legacy of a honeycomb of mines with no effort to countermine. 'Their ways are not our ways' and the capture of a bit of ground is nothing to them, whereas we always fight for it.

A few days later near the abbey at Mont St Eloi a sudden squall of enemy artillery fire caught Byng and Titchfield in the open. For several minutes the shelling went on and, when it ended, the ADC lay unconscious among the rubble. Gradually he came around and Byng helped him back to their car. Though dazed and shaken, he asked not to be evacuated. In the hope that he would not be badly affected, Byng kept him at his headquarters for a few weeks. Eventually it became plain that he would not soon recover from his shellshock and the medical authorities recommended he return to England for treatment. It was the end of his service at the Front.[3]

Late in May, 1916, Byng received orders to report to HQ Canadian Corps at Ypres and take command. In his three months with the 17th at Vimy he had secured their position in the chalk heart of the Ridge and on its western slopes. He could not know that before the year was out he would return.

His instructions were followed by a message from GHQ:

Heartiest congratulations on your promotion to be Lieut-General for distinguished services in the field and good luck – D. Haig[4]

As a Regular soldier it signified his permanent promotion.

The move to the Canadian Corps was one he had not sought. On 26 May he answered Blumenfeld's congratulations:

Why am I sent to the Canadians? I don't know a Canadian. Why this stunt?

Am rather sorry to leave the old corps as we were fighting like hell and killing Boches. However, there it is. I am ordered to these people and will do my best but I don't know that there is any congratulations about it. For God's sake keep the advertisement out of it – it makes it much harder.[5]

In the spring of 1916 the Canadian Corps consisted of three divisions, to which a fourth was soon to be added. While it had some unusual units such as its motorized machine-gun brigade, its size and organization were almost identical to a British formation. But there were important differences.

In the BEF most Corps were little more than a headquarters to which three or four divisions were assigned for specific operations. There were frequent changes and the officers and men who fought under their control seldom knew or saw their corps commander of the moment, or his staff.

The divisions of the Canadian Corps belonged to it permanently, giving it a potential for cohesion quite apart from its separate national identity. Its commander could control the training and administration of his officers and men, their welfare and their preparation for battle in a way which was not possible for his counterparts in the British Army.

But the Corps suffered from divisive influences which plagued each of its commanders. Some were political, others were rooted in the military organization in Canada and in the improvizations of mobilization.

Before the War the small Canadian regular army existed only to train the part-time soldiers of the Militia, units of which existed in almost every town of any size in the country. Training usually took place entirely within local districts. Only rarely did officers from different parts of the country meet, let alone have an opportunity to see other units. Soldiers in the West suspected that regiments in the East were better equipped, probably because of political influence. The latter thought that western units were not as well trained as they themselves were. Such misconceptions could have been erased by good leadership and a well-ordered mobilization.

In August, 1914, the Canadian Government, and most of the people, were seized with the need for speed in sending a force to fight in Europe. None was more affected than the energetic and self-confident Minister of Militia and Defence, Sam Hughes.

His military experience was that of a colonel in the Militia. Yet in politics and war he believed himself to be infallible and the Defence Staff in Ottawa to be incompetent. To him the long-standing plan to mobilize the units of the Militia was too deliberate and pedestrian to meet the urgency of the time. He scrapped it. The Adjutant General, the key figure in mobilization, was sent away, to Valcartier, Quebec, to organize a huge camp for the expeditionary force. Hughes set about organizing completely new units outside the Militia organization but using its men. Normal channels of communication were ignored as he sent torrents of telegrams direct to individual officers and officials. Not being regular soldiers, militia officers had taken part in politics and Hughes did not hesitate to show preferment to Conservatives over Liberals, if they were approximately as competent.

Hughes got results. The 1st Canadian Division was in France by 16 February, 1915, in advance of the first of the British Territorial divisions. But it was to be some time before the jealousies arising from Hughes' partisanship disappeared from the Canadian Expeditionary Force.

At Ypres in April, 1915, the Canadians showed the world that, despite their inexperience, they were indeed soldiers of quality. When the 2nd Division joined the 1st in France they were formed into an Army Corps with their own supporting troops. On the recommendation of Sir John French, Lieut-Gen Alderson of the 1st Division was given the new command and two of its brigadiers, Arthur Currie and Richard Turner, VC, were promoted to command the divisions. A third was formed in France in the following winter.

In April, 1916, the 2nd Canadian Division fought its first major battle. Attacking near St Eloi, where, incredibly, Second Army had blown a series of mines in marshy ground with little thought of the quagmire which would result, they were embroiled in a dispiriting series of bloody engagements in water-filled shell holes and mine craters. They were not successful. Alderson (who, it will be remembered, was a British officer) asked Turner to write an adverse report on one of the brigadiers, but he refused. The Corps Commander then asked for Turner to be dismissed, but the Commander-in-Chief, aware that among the Canadians there was some resentment against the British over the battle, decided that it was better to retain 'a couple of incompetent commanders' than risk a feud.

Haig recognized that it was impossible to keep both Alderson and Turner. On 9 May he told the King in a hand-written letter what he proposed.

> Another day I visited the Canadians. Their 2nd Div^n (Gen Turner) have had a hard time at St Eloi. But all were in the best of spirits and determined to give the enemy more than they had received in hard knocks from him. Although Turner is not the best possible Com^d of a Division, I think it would be an error to change him at this moment.
>
> On the other hand General Alderson, Com^d the Canadian Corps, which is soon to be increased to *four* Divisions, has so much political work and administration arrangements to discuss with the Canadian Govt. that it will be well nigh impossible for him to carry it out, and also command the Corps in the Field. I therefore think the suggestion to appoint him Inspector Genl of all Canadian troops in England and France a very good one. The Canadian Govt. has given me a free hand in the choice of his successor. I propose to recommend Genl Byng for the appointment. I think he will do it well and is sure to be most popular.[6]

Since 4 April the Canadians had been holding a 5½-mile sector of the Ypres Salient from half a mile south-west of St Eloi, through the Bluff and Hill 60 (which was in German hands) to 500 yards north-west of Hooge on the Menin road. The 2nd Canadian Division's battle in the St Eloi craters had been followed later in the month by German attacks on the 1st and 2nd Divisions which were beaten off. As an indication of the intensity of the day-to-day operations in the Salient, May was described as quiet, yet, during it, the Canadians suffered nearly two thousand casualties.

When Byng arrived at his new headquarters on 28 May he was greeted by Brig-Gen Charles Harington, the Brigadier-General, General Staff, whom he had known for many years. But apart from him he had met few officers of the Corps. Even Currie, Turner and Mercer, the divisional commanders, were strangers to him.

Immediately he was involved in a controversy which had developed between the Corps and the Militia Department in Ottawa, who persisted in naming inexperienced or incompetent officers to the command of units in the field.

A letter to Blumenfeld written five days after he arrived told how seriously he viewed the situation:

PRIVATE   Cdn AC 1 June 1916

Dear Oom,

Thanks for yours.

I presented a sort of ultimatum the other day saying I did not think I could carry on unless promotions and appointments were in my hands.

The men are too good to be led by politicians and dollar magnates, and if the credit of the Corps is to be augmented, the men must be led by leaders.

I don't want Imperial officers but I want to shove on the Canadians who have proved their worth and get rid of the Bumstunts. There it is. GHQ may not support me and I am probably up against the Canadian Govt. If they refuse, I shall offer my resignation as I feel strongly about it.

The GOC Anzac has an 'Order in Council' authorizing him to promote and appoint – without something of that sort I cannot help these people – they are (I think) all with me but powerless to do anything.

Having no axe to grind of my own, I can face it with equanimity and am only trying to do my best for these men who have fought for 18 months.

Keep this to yourself and write again.[7]

Blumenfeld asked Byng to take Max Aitken, who would be visiting the Corps, into his confidence, suggesting that he should be able to help. Byng gladly agreed to do so.

On 18 June, Byng wrote of their interview:

He seemed to realize that the state of affairs was impossible, and I hope he also realized that I would resign if the present state of affairs continued. There is nothing else for it – to officer these splendid men with political protegés is to my mind little short of criminal. . . .[8]

From the first day it was apparent to the Canadians that their new commander was uncommonly thorough. The comprehensive briefings which Harington provided were followed by shrewd and penetrating questions and comments by Byng, which left his headquarters in no doubt as to what he expected of them. Then, having learned as much as he could, he set out to see the Corps for himself. Because of the problems of the 2nd Division at St Eloi, he began by

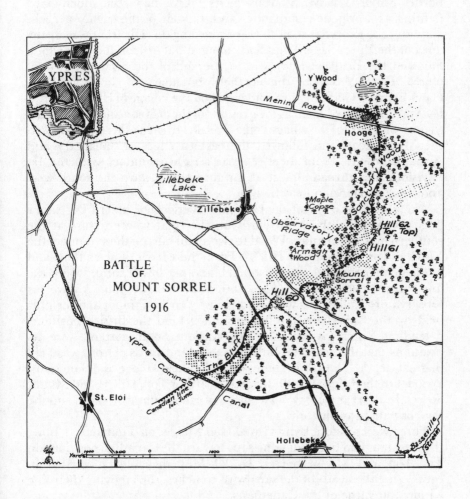

YPRES

Y Wood

Menin Road

Hooge

Zillebeke
Lake

Zillebeke

Maple
Copse

Sanctuary Wood

Observatory
Ridge

Hill 62
(or Top)

Hill 61

BATTLE
OF
MOUNT SORREL

1916

Armagh
Wood

Mount
Sorrel

Hill 60

Ypres - Comines

The Bluff

Canadian line 1st June

Canal

St. Eloi

Hollebeke

Bassevilte
Stream

Yards 1000   500   0   1000   2000   Yards spending the last two days of May with it. During his visit he saw every battalion. When he left, his uniform dirty with the mud of the front line, the word spread that, if nothing else, the new Corps Commander had himself seen the quagmire of the St Eloi craters.

Next morning he visited the 3rd, which had yet to fight a divisional battle. Major-Gen M. S. Mercer, its GOC, had seen much hard fighting as a brigade commander and, in view of the enemy's recent activities, he expected soon to be engaged again. His front was at the apex of the Ypres Salient and had changed but little in the year which followed the British withdrawal at the end of the Second Battle of Ypres. From Y Wood, the northern boundary of the Corps, the Canadian and German lines converged on the village of Hooge. Only a few yards separated them in the grounds of the château and through the eastern outskirts of the village ruins. Parallel to each other, they crossed the Menin road and followed the eastern edges of Sanctuary and Armagh Woods. From there, Mercer's right boundary with the 1st Division, they turned almost at a right-angle toward the south-west and the 2nd Division near St Eloi.

Along most of its front the Germans overlooked the 3rd Division's line, except for a thousand yards on the right where it rose at the southern end of Sanctuary Wood to two small hills on the summit of the Ypres Ridge, Tor Top and Hill 61. From there it continued a thousand yards further south to Mount Sorrel, another low feature, where the line turned west. From Tor Top a prominent spur known as Observatory Ridge runs westward toward Ypres. From it and the hills held by the Canadians the flat ground behind the British positions defending Ypres lay open to observation. So important were its positions that the 3rd Division's four thousand yards of front was held in great depth. The 7th Brigade on the left held Hooge and Sanctuary Wood. On their right the 8th Brigade held Tor Top, Hill 61 and Mount Sorrel. In the rear were two battalions of each of these brigades and the four battalions of the 9th.

Three weeks before Byng visited Gen Mercer on Thursday, 1 June, the Germans had begun digging saps toward the Canadian positions on Tor Top and Mount Sorrel. By 29 May they had succeeded in connecting the heads of the saps with trenches, thus moving their line within 150 yards of the Canadians.

When Mercer explained the situation, Byng asked him to carry out a reconnaissance with a view to a local attack. He then left to visit the headquarters of the brigades in front of Ypres. He was at 8th Brigade when Mercer arrived to arrange for the reconnaissance with its commander, Brig-Gen Williams. He asked Byng if he would join them. After giving it some thought, Byng replied, 'No, you had better go yourselves tomorrow and make your own proposals. I will come round and see them on Saturday.'

In effect he was giving the two untried commanders the opportunity to make their own plan, uninfluenced by his presence or his comments. They would learn much in the process and gain greatly in confidence if it proved to be successful. He could make changes later if it had serious flaws.

There were many indications that the enemy was planning an attack on the Canadian front. Far to their rear two lines of trenches resembling the positions near Tor Top had been photographed from the air but a close watch revealed no special troop movements. On 31 May the enemy brought large-calibre trench mortars into action, and on 1 June eight observation balloons could be seen and German batteries were registering on points in the Canadian line and behind. But there was no indication that an attack would come as soon as it did, or in the middle of the day.

Opposite the Canadians was the German 13th Corps under Gen Freiher von Watter. His troops, all from Württemberg, were well trained and took special pride in their separate national identity. By capturing Tor Top and pushing along Observatory Ridge they would secure observation behind the British line and could reasonably expect that a general withdrawal in the salient would result. They hoped 'to fetter as strong a force as possible in the Ypres Salient and thus reduce the numbers available for a British offensive', an obvious reference to the preparations which were now well advanced for the offensive on the Somme.

At 8 pm on 1 June the German guns fell silent, arousing the suspicions of the troops in the Canadian front line. With each hour of silence tension increased until, at 3 am, the enemy guns resumed their usual activity. So normal did the situation appear that at 6 am Generals Mercer and Williams set out for the 4th Canadian Mounted Rifles on Mount Sorrel. They had just reached the front-line trenches when the storm burst. The trenches of the CMR vanished and their garrisons were annihilated. A German eye witness wrote, 'The whole enemy position was a cloud of dust and dirt into which timber, tree trunks, weapons and equipment were continuously hurled up, and occasionally human bodies.'[9] Only seventy-six of the 702 officers and men in the battalion came through unscathed. Williams, wounded in the head, was taken prisoner. Mercer had been stunned, his ear drum shattered by a shell-burst, and taken to an aid post. He insisted on leaving to return to his headquarters, but soon had his leg broken by a bullet. A little later, as he lay on the ground, he was killed by shrapnel.

During the morning the enemy's devastating artillery fire obliterated the defences of the two mounted rifle battalions of the 8th Brigade and the right forward company of Princess Patricia's. All forward observation officers of the artillery were killed or wounded and their telephone lines destroyed. Shortly after 1 pm the Germans exploded four mines close to the trenches on Mount Sorrel and the Württemburgers attacked. Six battalions advanced against Mount Sorrel and Tor Top, five more were in close support with a further six in reserve. Confident that their artillery had obliterated all resistance, the enemy infantry came forward in four waves, about seventy-five yards apart, the first carrying hand grenades, wire cutters and flame throwers. Their pace was almost leisurely.

There was time for only a few rounds of rapid fire from the survivors in the front line before the assault was upon them. Men of the CMR, their rifles damaged, used them as clubs, but they were soon overwhelmed. Only on the left was the attack halted by the stubborn resistance of the Patricias. The machine-guns with their left company, outside the zone of assault, broke up the advance of the German right flank. On the right they stubbornly contested every foot of the communication trenches which ran back from their obliterated front line until they brought the German advance to a halt.

On the left No 2 Company, now commanded by a sergeant, poured a heavy fire into the flank of the Württemburgers.

To the south the enemy had overcome all resistance. Tor Top and Mount Sorrel were in their hands. Moving down the western slopes of the ridge, they began to move into open ground west of Armagh and Sanctuary Woods and threatened to take the Patricias from the rear. Pressing forward on Observatory Ridge, they captured a section of 18-pounders of the 5th Battery, Canadian Field Artillery, (this was the only time in the First World War that guns of the Canadian Corps fell into enemy hands. They were subsequently recaptured. A German regimental historian later wrote, 'Here too the Canadians did not surrender, but at their guns defended themselves with revolvers to the last man.'). As they moved into the open the Germans came under fire from the 5th CMR near Maple Copse and from two platoons of the Patricias, deployed to protect their battalion's right rear. The enemy halted and hastened to dig trenches to defend the newly won ground.

North of the initial attack a German attempt to break through the left company of the Patricias was beaten off by rifle and machine-gun fire. During the night the enemy laid a curtain of fire behind the company and attacked it three times. In spite of flame throwers and close-range machine-gun fire from three sides, the Patricias held out. But, with ammunition almost gone, and no hope of reinforcement, their position was hopeless. Just before daybreak and under the threat of a fresh attack, they withdrew over the shell-torn fields to their rear, taking their wounded, their weapons, stores and equipment with them. Passing through the enemy barrage, they tumbled into the reserve trenches, 500 yards to the rear, without the loss of a further man.[10]

At Corps, Division and Brigade headquarters, behind the fighting zone, little was known of the situation at the front. All telephone lines had been destroyed and the curtain of artillery fire laid down by the Germans effectively isolated the battlefield from contact by men on foot. It was mid-afternoon before it became certain that Generals Mercer and Williams were missing. Byng ordered Brig-Gen Hoare-Nairne, the divisional artillery commander, to take command of the 3rd Division, but not until about 6 pm was Lt-Col J. C. L. Bott of the 2nd CMR able to get forward to take over the 8th Brigade. For several critical hours both Division and Brigade were without their commanders, seriously hampering the conduct of the defence.

From the start it was plain that the situation was serious and within an hour of the German assault, the reserve battalions of the 7th and 8th Brigades began to arrive in previously arranged blocking positions, while two batteries of the Motor Machine-Gun Brigade moved to cover a 600-yard gap in the defences centred on Observatory Ridge.

By late afternoon the extent of the enemy's success was known and Byng ordered the 3rd Division to prepare to counterattack that night or early the following morning. After visiting the HQ of the 3rd and 1st Divisions, and consulting some of the brigadiers by telephone, he told Hoare-Nairne to plan on using a brigade of the 1st Division against Mount Sorrel and one of the 3rd against Tor Top and Sanctuary Wood, but deferred issuing orders until the new divisional commander had determined the condition of his units and consulted with Currie of the 1st Division.

At 6.30 pm Hoare-Nairne reported that, with Currie's agreement, he proposed to attack Mount Sorrel and Tor Top at 2 am with the 2nd and 3rd Brigades of the 1st Division while three of his battalions restored the front in Sanctuary Wood.

Moving forward from behind Ypres, over difficult routes in the dark, the progress of the infantry was slow. Two battalions were caught in artillery barrages which the Germans laid behind the Canadian front and suffered heavily, particularly in officers. When it became obvious that zero hour would have to be postponed, there were further delays in communicating the changes in time. Finally it was decided by HQ 3rd Division to launch the assault by signal, when all attacking troops were ready. Not until after 6 am was this condition met. Immediately the artillery began a final half-hour of intense fire on the enemy positions and at 7.10 am the firing of the signal, six green rockets, was ordered. By now it was broad daylight and the troops would be advancing over open ground.

Many of the rockets proved defective, and fourteen were launched before six ignited. Instead of bursting simultaneously, they appeared intermittently and battalions were not sure that they were intended as the signal. As a result, the attacks of the four assaulting battalions were launched at different times allowing the enemy to concentrate machine-gun and rifle fire on them separately. All the attacks reached the German positions and in places penetrated it, but, in the hand-to-hand and grenade battles which followed, the Canadians were too weak in numbers to maintain a foothold and most were killed or made prisoner. By 1 pm the survivors had fallen back to their start line, except on the left of the Patricias' sector, where the Edmonton Regiment clung to the trenches leading to the old front line.

While the attack failed to drive out the Germans, it did secure a firm line almost a mile forward of the temporary positions which had been occupied after the German attack.

The bright sunshine of 2 June had given way to rain on the 3rd. The ground in which the troops toiled to improve their trenches was clay which soon turned to the consistency of cream cheese. Setting themselves to defend their gains, the Württemburgers fortified their positions with barbed wire and machine-gun posts and dug eight communication trenches forward from their former front line.

The German success had given them a dangerous advantage in observation and had brought them almost to within two miles of the gates of Ypres. Not only Byng, but Haig and Plumer, commanding Second Army, were seriously concerned. They allotted additional artillery to support the Corps plus a British infantry brigade in reserve.

Byng at first planned to attack on 6 June, but the bad weather continued, grounding the Royal Flying Corps. Without observation from the air, the heavy artillery could not register their targets and the attack was postponed until the 7th.

In the meantime the Germans struck again. At 3.05 pm on 6 June two companies of the 28th Battalion in the eastern outskirts of Hooge were practically wiped out by the explosion of four large mines. The remainder of the battalion with the 31st on its right defeated German attempts to reach the support line, but Hooge had fallen to the enemy, who had taken one more step toward domination of the Ypres Salient. It was not the first time that the Germans had occupied the rubble of the village. Byng decided to leave its trenches in their hands for the present while he concentrated on regaining Mount Sorrel and Tor

124

Top. Haig agreed and loaned him the 2nd Dismounted Cavalry Brigade to act as a counterattack force in that area in case of further trouble.

Major-Gen Currie of the 1st Division was given the responsibility for recapturing the Canadians' lost positions. Because of the depleted strength of some of his units after the unsuccessful counterattack on 3 June, Currie formed two composite brigades from his stronger battalions. On the right Brig-Gen L. J. Lipsett would take back Mount Sorrel while Brig-Gen G. S. Tuxford attacked Tor Top. The 58th Battalion of 9th Brigade was to complete the recapture of the trenches in Sanctuary Wood. The whole would be supported by 218 guns, probably the greatest number yet employed on such a narrow front.

Currie's plan provided for the two attacking brigades to start at different times and join up at the point of the assault. Brig-Gen H. E. Burstall, the Corps artillery commander, later told what transpired at the coordinating conference where it was discussed:

> Addressing the assembled orders group, Byng said 'It has been found that when an attack does not start together, generally it will not assault together and so fail. I would prefer to see the two brigades start together, but I realize you have made the reconnaissance and if you still think your plan the better, then it becomes my plan and I authorize and approve it. Think it over and let me know the result of your decision later.'
>
> That evening an amended plan arrived at Corps headquarters on the lines Gen Byng had advised and the attack was a complete success.
>
> I have always thought his action on this occasion showed most marvellous strength of character as well as military knowledge. He hardly knew us and yet he was willing to stake his professional career on a plan he believed to be faulty, rather than force a better one on troops who did not believe in it, and to whom he was a stranger.[11]

Burstall did not mention that, though Byng had been at war since October, 1914, the attack was the first which he had conducted. The temptation for him to intervene directly in the planning of Currie's counterattack must have been great.

During this time a letter arrived from Sylvia Brooke which told of Basil's eagerness to return but aroused Byng's suspicions about his ADC's health. He replied:

> . . . Now look here – don't let Basil come back before he is really well. It is rather strenuous here and things buzz, not much sleep & rather beastly.
>
> However we are killing a lot of them. You will see what to do. I can get on quite well with my Canuck A.D.C. Chopper has gone home rather washed out in everything but his nose. Be a good girl and write as often as you can. I want 'cheerful correspondence.'

The attack on Mount Sorrel again had to be postponed because of the weather. On the 7th and 8th it improved enough for No. 6 Squadron Royal Flying Corps to observe for the registration of artillery targets. During the next few days, though there was almost continuous rain, the guns could fire and, between the 9th and 12th, bombardments of the enemy positions were carried out to deceive him as to the hour of attack.

Byng decided that, despite the foul weather, action could be delayed no longer. On the 11th, he set zero hour for 1.30 am on the 13th.

For ten hours of the preceding day the German positions were bombarded. At 8.30 pm the attacking battalions moved into their forming-up places to wait in pitch darkness, soaked by driving rain, for their zero hour, 5 hours later. At 12.45 am a final intense bombardment began. So accurate was it that the two leading waves of the 16th Battalion were able to move forward and lie down close to the German positions inside the enemy defensive barrage. At 1.30 am the Canadian infantry began to plough forward through the mud and rain into the German positions. There was little resistance. Nearly 200 prisoners were taken and the survivors struggled back to the old German line. It was the first attack in real strength which the Canadians had made in the War and it was a complete success.

In accounting for their failure to hold their gains, the Germans referred to Allied superiority in artillery, aircraft and ammunition supply, adding 'Even the weather favoured the enemy. Continuous rain assisted to wear down the troops exposed to heavy hostile fire night and day.' It is doubtful that the Canadian infantryman, soaked by driving rain as he lay in the mud of no man's land, would have been very sympathetic.

As soon as the Germans realized that the Canadians were back in their old positions, they opened fire with the full weight of their artillery and continued the bombardment for almost twenty-four hours. Early on the morning of the 14th they launched a counterattack on Mount Sorrel. Sadly for them, Byng anticipated it and had arranged a concentrated bombardment of the enemy positions opposite, to begin at 6.45 am, the precise time chosen by the Germans for their zero hour. They remained quiet until 9 o'clock when a second attempt was defeated by artillery fire. The Battle of Mount Sorrel was over.

Earlier, on 4 June, Byng had received a message that Charles Harington, his BGGS, was to be promoted to serve Gen Plumer of Second Army in a similar capacity. When Harington heard the news from him, knowing his sense of humour, he did not take it seriously and was surprised when his replacement, Brig-Gen P. P. de B. Radcliffe arrived.[12] Plumer realized that it was not a good time for the new Corps Commander to lose his experienced chief of staff. He telephoned Harington and told him that he might stay on for a few days with Byng, saying, 'You had better look sharp and get Mount Sorrel back or I shan't have you at all' – the sort of senior officer's remark which makes a recipient wonder if it was intended to be taken seriously or not.[13]

In the short time that he had been with the Corps, Byng had come to admire the Canadians for their fighting qualities and their high morale.

But there were deficiencies. Their competitiveness and unreasonable pride in their units often resulted in grudging cooperation between them. Their effectiveness was hampered by the inadequate professional training of their officers, while their enthusiasm and initiative, unfettered by discipline, resulted too often in unnecessary casualties. All of these could be remedied. Byng appreciated that, when they were, he would have under his command the most effective force of its size on the Western Front.

More difficult to cope with would be the political interference of which another sign was a message Byng received shortly after Gen Mercer's death: 'Give Garnet 3rd Division – Sam'. Sam was the Minister of Militia and Defence, Garnet was his son, a brigade commander in the 1st Division. Byng ignored it and appointed Brig-Gen L. J. Lipsett whom he considered to be better qualified.

As their commander formed an instant liking for the Canadians, so they also immediately took to him. Blumenfeld told Evelyn that he had received the following letter, dated 16 June:

A man came back from Ypres this morning and he tells me that 'the Byng Boy is here' is now the watchword of the Canadian Corps and that Bungo Byng himself says it will take months to live it down.[14]

Soon the Canadians took the name to themselves and to the end of the War, more than a year after their commanders had again changed, they referred to themselves at the Byng Boys (the name came first from the title of a popular show in London).

For three months more, the Canadians remained in the Ypres Salient. Holding their positions as thinly as possible, they harried the enemy by raids, bombardment and mining. On 12 August the enemy attacked Hill 60 and were repulsed by the 60th Battalion, well supported by artillery. That afternoon Byng, with Basil Brooke, who had returned earlier in the month, went forward to see the situation for himself.[15] A reporter from the *Toronto Telegram* found him, brushing the dust off his uniform and readjusting his helmet and gas mask, having just crawled back past dead men and over shattered heaps of sandbags

127

and wire from the advance post which the Canadians were holding within fifteen yards of the Germans.[16]

For the most part, though, the Ypres Salient remained relatively quiet. In February the Germans had launched their costly offensive at Verdun which continued until after the beginning of the British and French attack on the Somme on 1 July. The resulting commitment of the major resources of both the Allies and Germans left little to spare for operations elsewhere.

For the Canadians it was a period of intense activity of another kind. Byng set about improving the training and discipline of his Corps with a ruthlessness and energy which astonished those who had been deceived by his casual manner and appearance. As one veteran put it, Byng brought the gospel of smartness to the Canadian Corps. He maintained that clean uniforms, burnished weapons and saluting made for efficiency in fighting. He formed a Corps school to provide units with instructors in weapons, physical training and trench warfare. Its second purpose was to help bind together the divisions and battalions of the Corps by enabling their members to live and train together and develop common approaches to problems. He paid particular attention to the training of junior officers and, in the infantry, reorganized the basic unit, the platoon, to give it more independence. In doing so, he began a trend toward the more flexible tactics which proved so successful later in the war.[17]

Few Canadians had been trained as staff officers and most of the key appointments in the Corps were held by officers of the British Army, many of exceptional ability. Three, Edmund Ironside, John Dill and Alan Brooke, were to become field-marshals in the Second World War. On the whole Canadians were well served by their headquarters staffs, but even in the best of circumstances, fighting men tend to harbour a suspicion that those who work behind the lines in comparative safety and comfort do not understand their problems. If the staff officers come originally from the units which they serve, they are much less likely to be regarded as a race apart. Byng decided to replace the British officers with Canadians as quickly as possible and increased greatly the number of them on staff courses.[18]

Byng's method of inspecting his units was a curious mixture of outward casualness and skilful probing at detail. A senior medical officer, Andrew Macphail, described in his diary his first sight of the new Corps Commander in July, 1916. His unit was formed up on parade, expecting to watch him arrive escorted by his staff, trotting down the road on sleek chargers. Two troopers might be riding some yards in advance of the General to clear the way while following him, a mounted orderly would carry the commander's pennant on a lance. It was a sight which they had often seen before. But not this time:

> He came into the horselines through a hedge, jumping the ditch as unaffectedly as a farmer would come on a neighbour's place to look at his crops . . . this is a soldier – large, strong, lithe, with worn boots and frayed putties.

> Not only did he look at the men and their weapons, he wanted to see their mess tins, to make sure that every man had one and that it was clean.

Inspections and visits to units were not always formal occasions.

> I remember him best as I saw him one beautiful day in July, 1916. The corps had been withdrawn from the Ypres Salient and was behind the line, training in several new styles of attack which we were to make use of on the Somme front. Companies, battalions, brigades and divisions were training intensively from morning 'til night and Byng was every place at once. His very presence inspired enthusiasm and confidence. My battalion had fallen out for a short rest and haversack ration and as I was at some distance when the bugle sounded, I was the last man to finish. Byng sat by himself, lost in thought, throwing an occasional glance at me. He wished to have a short conference with the officers, but was too much of a gentleman to proceed until the last one had finished his meal.

> Finally, however, his energetic impulsive nature won out and he walked over to me and addressed me by name: 'For God's sake man, bolt it. This war can't wait.'

> Needless to say, I bolted it.[19]

The Corps Commander's lack of interest in food was the despair of ADCs who accompanied him on his travels. If some soldiers happened to come by on foot as they were eating their sandwiches by the roadside he was apt to say, 'Well, let's get going – give the rest of this to those men,' and the hungry young officer, smiling wanly, would hand over their lunch to the troops.[20]

In one sense Byng was less fortunate than other corps commanders in that he had to concern himself with administrative problems peculiar to an independent national force. The most irritating of these concerned the supply of reinforcements from the Canadian base at Shorncliffe in England. Its improvised and unnecessarily complex organization, suffering from lack of experience and a multiplicity of authorities exercising control over it, seemed incapable of producing sufficient trained replacements for the Corps in France. Yet there were more Canadian troops in England than there were on the Continent.

Harried by superior headquarters and the criticism of the divisions in the field, the overtaxed staff of the Depot drew in on itself, defensive and jealous. They spent more effort on justifying the standard of training of their product than on improving it.

Out of the 20,000 men at Shorncliffe, a quarter were permanently employed on odd jobs about the camps, their training neglected. Six hundred more were kept as bandsmen.[21]

Four separate Canadian authorities in Britain corresponded with Byng's headquarters, often at cross-purposes, on the same subject. He made an appeal for help at an unusually high level.

On 28 July, 1916, Haig wrote to the King in his own hand:

> From the XIV Corps H.Q., I went to Gen[l] Byng's H.Q. with the Canadian Corps. I found a greatly improved atmosphere there since he assumed command. Before, there was always a certain amount of jealousy and friction between the several Canadian Divisions. I am glad to see that one result of the recent hardships suffered by that corps has been to weld the units more together, and to bring out the necessity for trained officers, instead of those agreeable to the Politicians of Ottawa! . . . Byng mentioned the unsatisfactory matter to me and that is the condition of the Canadian Depot at Shorncliffe, and the state of feeling which exists between the units training there and the Canadian Divisions in France. Perhaps Your Majesty might be able to say a timely word which would ensure the Depot at home regarding its own interests and those of the Canadians in France as one and the same.[22]

The Canadian Government was also aware that all was not well with their organization in Britain and had already sent Sam Hughes to England to remedy the situation. Eventually it improved, but not until after Hughes had been forced from office in November, 1916.

In the middle of August the new 4th Canadian Division joined the Corps. Four days later the Minister of Militia and Defence came to give Byng the benefit of his experience and prejudices. In the course of a long dissertation on how Canadians should be handled, Hughes asserted, 'I am never wrong,' at which Byng commented, 'What a damn dull life you must have had, Minister!' Hughes lay back in his chair, roaring with laughter.[23]

It was only coincidence that by the end of that month the detested Ross rifles with which the Canadians had been equipped were replaced by Lee Enfields and their ageing Colt machine-guns by the latest Vickers. Improved trench mortars were issued to all battalions. While these improvements had been put in train before Byng came to the Corps and while he sought no credit for them, they were ones which the troops could appreciate. By now, few of his men had not seen him and heard him speak. The stories they began to tell about him were to become legends.

130

One favourite concerned his inspection of a unit's transport, whose harness was not in good condition. He looked it over thoroughly, fingering a buckle here and turning up a strap there, indicating that things should be better kept. An NCO said, 'Sir, the leather is so old that it won't take a shine.' Byng looked at him thoughtfully, 'Well, I'm old, but I'm not dirty.' It was enough. In short order the straps and leather gleamed and worked easily and the story ended, 'You could shave yourself in our brass.'

Another concerned saluting. Soldiers who failed to salute Byng were likely to be surprised by being saluted themselves and would sheepishly respond. But sometimes Byng's temper showed through. More than once he was heard to reprimand a soldier sharply, saying, 'I have saluted the Canadians so often myself, I would now greatly appreciate one in return.'

The training, discipline and morale of the Corps were soon to be tested. At the end of August they left the Ypres Salient and marched south to the Somme where, on 30 August, they began to relieve the 1st Anzac Corps under the command of Gen Sir Hubert Gough's Reserve Army.

Chapter 8
The Somme

OF ALL THE battles of the First World War, those fought in 1916 near the River Somme have become fixed in the minds of the British peoples as the most tragic and wasteful – the epitome of horror and military ineptitude. That the casualties and, often, the conditions in which the battles were fought were appalling cannot be disputed, but the Somme earned its special reputation on its first day when the British losses numbered 57,470. The New Armies of Britain, raised in 1914 from its untrained and ardent youth, suffered a bloody reverse. The shock left an indelible mark on the minds of the articulate and questioning volunteers, but in the main their patriotism and their courage remained intact. Later, in poems, books and plays, they wrote resentfully of their loss of innocence when the reality of war shattered their heroic ideals.

The horrors of a battle are not equally perceived by all its participants. It is possible to find old soldiers who will say, 'The Somme? That wasn't so bad,' adding, 'You should have been at so-and-so'. It then transpires that there his company was destroyed and for twenty-four hours he was left wounded in no-man's-land. Yet he and his friends had been lucky on the Somme and 'so-an-so' is not mentioned in the Official History.

Armouring themselves with their humour, the soldiers did not look about for tragedy outside their own platoons. Their jokes and their superstitions were macabre: 'It is considered bad luck to be killed on Friday.'

For the individual the Somme was no worse than Passchendaele, or Gallipoli, or the Menin Road in 1914. But its scale was terrible. For the first time British armies of the size of those of the French and Germans were thrown into a massive offensive. Their casualties were no higher than those which the continental armies suffered in similar battles – at Verdun for example. They were an inevitable result of battle on that scale in that period of military development, a concomitant of war. For the British they expunged the last vestige of the illusory existence of military glory.

All the Allied Powers agreed that early in 1916 they would launch major coordinated offensives against their enemies. In February Falkenhayn, the Chief of the German General Staff, attacked at Verdun with the avowed intention of killing so many Frenchmen that France would be forced out of the war. Soon Marshal Joffre called on Haig to advance the date of their joint offensive, but because of Verdun, instead of the French playing the larger part, their participation would be diminished to eight divisions compared to thirty of the British.

The area of the Somme held few strategic possibilities and the offensive had no major geographical objectives. Its aim was to inflict heavy losses on the Germans, to prevent their forces being transferred to other fronts and to relieve the pressure on the French at Verdun.

The front chosen for the attack extended from Gommecourt in the north, midway between Arras and the Somme, to a point some four miles south of that river. Protected by two great belts of barbed wire, each thirty yards wide, the German forward position consisted of three lines of trenches. A thousand yards to the rear was a line of strong points. About a mile behind these were yet more belts of wire protecting the strong Second Position in which there were dugouts twenty to thirty feet deep in the chalk soil. Each could protect twenty-five men from artillery fire.

Haig's two-to-one superiority in heavy artillery would be able to cause heavy casualties to the enemy but would be insufficient to smash his defences. Falkenhayn decreed that a line must be defended rigidly and, if breached, must be restored at all costs. The stage was set for a killing match.

By the end of August, despite some early successes on the right, there had been little forward progress and on the left the line stood much as it had on 1 July. At the deepest point of penetration there had been an advance of about four miles. The Germans had lost 200,000 casualties, the British nearly the same and the French more than 70,000.

Early in July the Germans abandoned their offensive against Verdun but had been unable to move significant forces from the west to meet the attacks of the Russians and Italians in the east and south. In August Falkenhayn was replaced as de facto supreme commander of the German forces by Field-Marshal Paul von Hindenburg. The cost to Germany of Verdun and the Somme was mounting catastrophically. On 21 August Falkenhayn wrote:

Beneath the enormous pressure which rests upon us, we have no superfluity of strength. Every removal in one direction leads eventually to dangerous weakness in another place which may lead to our destruction if even the slightest miscalculation is made in estimating the measures the enemy may be expected to take.

The avowed objectives of the Somme offensive were being achieved.[1]

Few Canadians felt any regret at leaving the stinking shell-torn military desert of the Ypres Salient. By rail, they moved south to detrain near Abbeville, their spirits lifting as they breathed in the scented air of the smiling cornlands of Picardy.

From there they marched almost due east, moving off early in the morning in order to make bivouac or billets before the heat of the day. The weather was excellent for route marching and the troops, hardened by training, enjoyed it. At villages such as Pernois on the River Nievre they swam or lazed on the banks, laughing at the horseplay in the water. Then on the fourth day they came to Albert.

The atmosphere was exhilarating – guns, transport and men filled the roads, all moving in one direction – towards the front. Bivouacs were crowded with infantry and there were even large numbers of cavalry, obviously there to exploit a breakthrough.

Few Canadians saw the River Somme itself. Flowing between Péronne and Amiens to the south, it was in the French sector of the battlefield. They were to be much more concerned with the road which runs straight north-east from Albert to Bapaume, between the villages of Pozières and Courcelette, and the ground north of it which rises gently to a crest, then falls away to the valley of the River Ancre.

More than sixty years after the War the road between Courcelette and the Ancre at Miraumont crosses a broad plateau, whose wide unfenced wheatfields could be mistaken for the Canadian prairie. No sign of the War can be seen until the gates of Adanac Military Cemetery. Its white headstones, bordered by flowers and set in green close-clipped lawns, mark the graves of 1071 Canadians, among them eighteen-year-old Piper James Richardson of the Canadian Scottish, who won his VC piping his comrades forward to capture Regina Trench.

To the Canadians who entered Albert after their pleasant march through Picardy, life seemed far better than it had ever been in Belgium. They were soon to be disenchanted. To the east, not a green thing remained. Churned by high explosives, the ground had become a greyish sea of shell holes – landmarks gone, villages rubble, few roads even passable and not a sign of the copses, farms and windmills which showed on their maps.

The Canadians had come to the Somme with further fresh British divisions to deliver a strong attack about the middle of September.

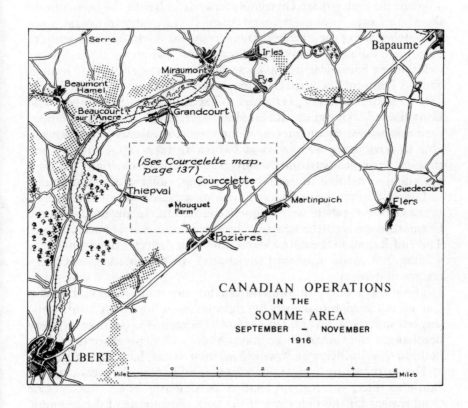

Serre

Irles

Bapaume

Miraumont

Pys

Beaumont
Hamel.

River Ancre

Beaucourt
sur l'Ancre

Grandcourt

*(See Courcelette map,
page 137)*

Ancre

Courcelette

Thiepval

Guedecourt

Mouquet
Farm

Martinpuich

Flers

Pozières

CANADIAN OPERATIONS
IN THE
SOMME AREA
SEPTEMBER — NOVEMBER
1916

River Ancre

ALBERT

Mile 0 1 2 3 4 5 Miles

They would form the right-hand corps of Gough's 'Reserve' Army, attacking in conjunction with Rawlinson's Fourth Army on their southern flank. Their task was to assist Rawlinson's main effort and secure, near Courcelette, ground which would give observation over the German Third Position, the main barrier which now confronted the Allies.

Haig suggested to Gough that the Canadians should be given a chance to settle in before undertaking any offensive operations. In the event, this did not mean that they were to have a quiet time.

While the 2nd and 3rd Divisions prepared for battle, the 1st took over the whole Corps front from the 1st Anzac Corps – three thousand yards of trenches along the Pozières Ridge from 700 yards west of Mouquet Farm to the Fourth Army boundary east of Pozières.

Mouquet Farm was a heavily fortified strongpoint in the German Second Position. Six Australian assaults had failed to take it and their 13th Brigade was trying yet again to capture it on 3 September. The Canadian 13th Battalion (Royal Highlanders) was temporarily under their command. Again success eluded the Australians but they were able to seize some 300 yards of Fabeck Graben, a German trench running north-eastwards in the direction of Courcelette. The Canadian battalion, in helping to extend this holding, suffered 322 casualties.

The relief of the Australians was completed under heavy shellfire. In the next few days there were frequent counterattacks and on the 8th the Germans recovered the nearly obliterated section of Fabeck Graben. The 2nd Battalion then attacked south of the Albert – Bapaume road, gaining 500 yards of enemy trench and the Commander-in-Chief's congratulations.

Three days later, in preparation for the main attack, the 2nd Canadian Division took over the right sector of the Corps front, while the 3rd moved in on the left. Almost unceasingly, German artillery bombarded the Canadian positions and by 13 September the Corps had lost 2,821 officers and men. And their attack had not yet begun.

The forthcoming operation, which would later be known as the Battle of Flers-Courcelette, had a particularly novel feature – the employment for the first time of the tank. Forty-nine of the ungainly monsters were available, of which seven were allocated to the Canadians. Weighing 28 tons, the Mark I Tank was 26½ feet long, 14 feet wide and 8 high. Its 105 horsepower Daimler engine gave it a speed of 3.7 miles per hour on roads, little more than normal infantry marching pace. On shell-torn ground it could barely achieve one half a mile per hour. There were two versions, the 'male' armed with two 6-pounder guns and four machine-guns, and the 'female' with six machine-guns only. Each was crewed by an officer and seven men of the

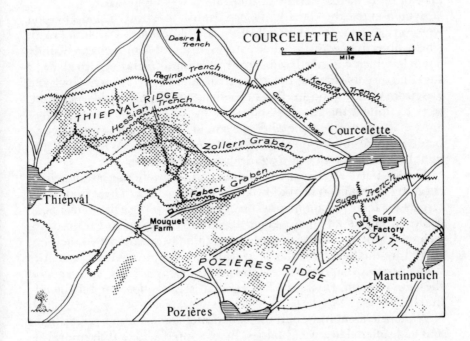

COURCELETTE AREA

Desire Trench

Regina Trench

Kenora Trench

THIEPVAL RIDGE

Hessian Trench

Grandcourt Road

Courcelette

Zollern Graben

Fabeck Graben

Sugar Trench

Thiepval

Candy Tr.

Sugar Factory

Mouquet Farm

POZIÈRES RIDGE

Martinpuich

Pozières

Heavy Branch, Machine-Gun Corps which later became the Tank Corps. Shipped to France in mid-August, there had been time only for the crews to learn to drive and acquire some skill in gunnery.

A creeping artillery barrage was to precede the infantry advance which would be in accordance with an instruction issued by General Headquarters in May: 'in many instances experience has shown that to capture a hostile trench a single line of men has usually failed, two lines have generally failed, but sometimes succeeded, three lines has generally succeeded but sometimes failed and four or more lines have usually succeeded.'[2] Not yet was the idea of advancing in small groups, instead of in waves, accepted; infiltration was unknown.

Byng allotted the Canadian Corps' tanks to Turner's 2nd Division who were to make the main effort astride the Albert–Bapaume road. Their objective was the defences in front of Courcelette–Candy Trench, which ran north-west from Martinpuich through the ruined sugar factory, beside the Bapaume road, and Sugar Trench which ran west from Candy. The 3rd Division, whose 8th Brigade held their front, were to protect the left flank of the 2nd.

At 6.20 am on 15 September, zero hour for the attack, a shattering bombardment burst upon the German positions. Within seventy minutes, the 4th and 6th Brigades reported success.

The six tanks attacking with the Canadians were put out of action, either by mechanical breakdown or becoming stuck. Three had found targets for their machine-guns, one also laying 400 yards of telephone cable during its advance. Their appearance had given the troops a feeling of superiority and security (according to one report), a view not shared by the five men who preceded each tank to remove casualties from its path. A captured German soldier was bitter at the unfairness of the new weapon, saying in English that it was 'not war but bloody butchery'.[3]

While the assaulting battalions had met some stubborn resistance and had suffered heavy casualties, Byng appreciated that the morale of the Germans must have suffered a severe blow. To maintain the momentum of success, at 11.10 am he ordered the attack to be resumed that evening, its objectives being Courcelette and Fabeck Graben, a fire trench which joined the western edge of the village to Mouquet Farm. The 5th Brigade (Brig-Gen A. H. Macdonell) of the 2nd Division would attack on the right, the 7th Brigade (Brig-Gen A. C. Macdonell) of the 3rd Division on the left.

The Canadian Official History records that the attack was launched in broad daylight without any jumping-off place, a feature described by the Army Commander as being without parallel in the present campaign. The 5th Brigade took Courcelette and the 7th all but 200 yards of Fabeck Graben. The speed with which the attack had been mounted – the troops had only just been able to reach their starting positions on time – had caught the Germans still shocked and disorganized after their earlier defeat. Yet soon they counterattacked and a bitter struggle went on for three days around Courcelette. The 22nd (Canadien Français) Battalion beat off fourteen counterattacks, seven in the first night. On the 16th the final 200 yards of Fabeck Graben were taken and the 2nd Canadian Mounted Rifles bombed their way into part of Mouquet Farm.

During the next few days the area was soaked by heavy rain. The 3rd Division attempted to capture the trench line beyond Fabeck Graben, Zollern Graben, gained a temporary footing, but were forced back from most of it. On the right the 1st Battalion captured the enemy front line trenches east of Courcelette.

The Canadian Corps had acquitted itself well in its first major action on the Somme. Haig wrote in his despatch that the fighting of the 15th September and the days immediately following had resulted in 'a gain more considerable than any which had attended our arms in the course of a single operation since the commencement of the offensive.' The week's fighting had cost the Corps 7230 casualties.

As a subordinate commander in a large army, Byng had little scope for his tactical skill, let alone strategic brilliance. Assigned a very narrow front, he had no choice but to assault directly the objectives he was given. Even the formation in which his infantry advanced was imposed, as was the pattern and scale of his artillery fire. He could but allot objectives to his divisional commanders, coordinate their plans and spur them on. Even in forcing the pace and seizing Courcelette on the 15th, he was conforming to the known wishes of both Gough and Haig.

Such success as had been achieved had been at heavy cost. Could they afford victory? Outwardly he remained the confident, cheerful, hard-driving commander. The only obvious sign of his disquiet was the amount of time he spent in reflection. During the Somme campaign Canadian Corps headquarters was at Contay, where, in the grounds of the old château, Byng might often be seen bare-headed, pacing back and forth, absorbed in thought, having previously issued instructions that he was not to be spoken to, not even saluted, unless the interruption was justified by urgent need.[4]

His concern for the welfare of his men, which he had shown from the beginning of his service, was not simply a professional requirement related to maintaining their fitness to fight. It was rooted deep and affected his conscience, his sympathy and his emotions.

139

During the relief of the 2nd Canadian Division after Courcelette he passed a company coming back from the trenches, several of whom were wounded. Byng half-turned, half-stopped, as he returned the men's salute, hesitated for a moment and then went on. Presently he turned to the officer he was with and said, 'I really ought to have said something to the boys, but I daren't. I believe I would have broken down if I had.'[5]

The German second main defensive position followed roughly the line of a ridge from the bend in the River Ancre north of Albert, south-eastward toward the Somme. The heavily fortified village of Thiepval at its northern end gave its name to the ridge and to the battle which was to begin on 26 September.

While the enemy second position had been breached, it was necessary to clear the Germans from the entire crest-line to hide the British rear areas from their view and to give observation over the valley of the River Ancre. The British 2nd Corps on the left had the unenviable task of taking Thiepval and other notorious strongpoints such as Mouquet Farm. The Canadians were to break the German defences which lay along a low spur projecting eastward from the main ridge. The three trench lines which comprised them, Zollern Graben, Hessian Trench and Regina Trench, with Kenora Trench which branched from it, became the successive objectives of the 1st Canadian Division. The 2nd's task was to take the trench system which joined them to the Bapaume road beyond Courcelette.

The attack of 26 September made good progress. Much of Zollern Graben and Hessian Trench were taken and by the evening of the 27th the Germans had withdrawn to Regina and Kenora Trenches. Attempts to drive them further were repulsed with heavy losses.

On 1 October and again on the 8th the Canadians attempted to take Regina Trench but were frustrated by fresh German troops in undamaged defences covered by uncut barbed wire. Their casualties were enormous.

On 10 October the 4th Division arrived and relieved the 1st and 3rd in the line. On the 17th the Corps moved away from the Somme to take over a sector of the First Army's front between Arras and Lens which included Vimy Ridge. Left behind were the 4th Division and the artillery of the other three. In the next six weeks the 4th systematically destroyed and captured Regina Trench. On 18 November, in blinding sleet, its infantry ploughed through the frozen mud beyond to capture Desire Trench, the next newly-dug German line.

The last day of the Battles of the Somme came on 19 November. Both sides were worn out but the 4th Division had shown such resilience that it was not relieved in the line until 28 November, when it began to move to the Arras front.

In all, the Canadians suffered 24,019 battle casualties on the Somme.

They had done what they had been asked to do, but from Corps Commander to private soldier they carried away a sense of frustration at the way in which they had been employed. Confined as between two rails by their narrow right and left boundaries and by the tactical strictures of Gough's headquarters, they advanced as an assault machine, the force of which was dependent on the number of lines of men who were fed into it. For Byng and his Canadians, it was the first experience of sustained offensive operations under the intimate control of a higher headquarters. Their first instinctive conclusion was that there must be a better way to win battles.

Before the Canadian Corps left the Somme Byng and his divisional commanders were looking for more effective methods of attack than those which they had been obliged to use. In its present stage of development and insignificant numbers, the tank provided no solution. They must look to improving the techniques of employing the resources which were available to them.

Byng ordered his staff and each division to make detailed studies of every aspect of the offensive battle and to analyze the recent actions fought by the Corps. The reasons for their lack of success were many. The artillery had failed to gap the German barbed wire or to destroy Regina Trench. German shelling had inflicted heavy casualties on units moving up from reserve. Objectives had been hard to identify. Reinforcements had been inadequately trained. Most important of all, the infantry formation for attack was suspect.

Chapter 9
Vimy Ridge

THE CANADIANS WERE soon settled in their new position, grateful for the relative quiet which gave them time to rest, re-equip and absorb reinforcements. On 30 October, Evelyn received a welcome telegram 'Arriving leave train afternoon 1st – Byng'.

Evelyn met him in London from where they went by train to Thorpe-le-Soken. Their car had been laid up for the duration of the War and they walked the half-mile home from the station. There had been many changes. The younger men and women of their staff had left for the Services or to work in factories. Much of the grounds, including even the rose garden, had been ploughed up for growing vegetables.

For most of his leave Julian was in old clothes, working in the garden and felling trees. On Sunday he and Evelyn rode over to Beaumont to attend church, where, as he did each week, the vicar read out the list of his parishioners who were serving in the Forces, one being simply 'Julian Byng'.[1]

On Friday, 10 November, they went to London for the baptism of Chopper Tichfield's daughter, Lady Alexandra Margaret Anne Cavendish-Bentinck. Earlier in the day Byng saw Lord Stamfordham, the King's private secretary, who sent the following to the Sovereign at Windsor:

Memorandum.
I saw Lieut-General Sir Julian Byng. Bearing in mind my conversation with the Prime Minister two hours previously, I asked for his views as to the best strategic means of bringing the War to an end. He gave as his unqualified opinion that this could only be done by maintaining the present plan of a vigorous offensive on the Western and Eastern fronts. He strongly deprecated any repetition of subsidiary campaigns, such as that of Gallipoli Peninsula, or any further developments of an offensive based upon Salonika. It was true that the advance on the Somme was slow, and only achieved at considerable cost, but the loss to the Germans was that of the flower of their Army, which is opposite to us. The Allies have lost men but

gained ground and gained prestige, whereas the Germans have lost men, lost ground, and lost prestige. We have a Commander-in-Chief in whom the Army has the greatest confidence. The spirit of the Army is excellent. Of his own command, the Canadian Corps, he spoke in the highest praise, and if the present (policy) of continued, persistent, determined wearing away of the German strength is persisted in, his opinion is that it is the surest quickest road to victory.[2]

His view was one which few soldiers would dispute. The War could only be won by defeating the main forces of the enemy. What he recognized but did not say was that less costly methods of doing so must be found.

Shortly after his return to France, Byng was summoned to a conference on future operations by Sir Henry Horne, commanding First Army. There he learned for the first time of the major offensive being planned for the spring of 1917. The main effort was to be made by the French armies under Gen Nivelle. Large British forces would take part. The Canadians on the left would form a strong defensive flank for the Third Army's effort by capturing the northern half of Vimy Ridge. A British Corps would take the remainder. On 19 January, 1917, First Army informed Byng that his objective had been extended to include the whole crest of the Ridge.

Byng's efforts to improve the battle effectiveness of the Canadian Corps now had the focus of a specific task – the capture of what could be argued was the most dominant and tactically important feature on the whole of the Western Front. Already he knew it well.

Between the River Scarpe and the smaller Souchez to the North a nine-mile barrier of higher ground bars the western edge of the Douai plain. Its northern half rises abruptly above the village of Vimy and dominates the lower slopes which point to Arras in the South. To the east it overlooks the industrial cities of Lens and Douai.

Allenby, of Third Army, was unwilling to advance east of Arras so long as Vimy Ridge remained in enemy hands. For the Germans it was the lynch pin joining their northern defensive line, which ran north through Belgium to the sea, to the new Hindenburg system in the south. To them it was not only of tactical importance. As long as they held it they could operate the Lens coalfields which were important to their war economy.

In October, 1914, Vimy Ridge and Notre Dame de Lorette, the feature which extends from it across the Souchez River, were seized by the Germans. During the spring and autumn of 1915 the French, at the cost of 150,000 casualties, recaptured most of the Lorette Ridge, but were halted on the western slopes of the Vimy feature.

The bravery of the French troops who tried three times to take the

143

Ridge in 1915 was not in doubt. Joffre and Foch attributed their failure to insufficiently accurate and inadequate artillery preparation. Yet the expenditure of ammunition had been enormous. For the assault on 25 September and its preliminary bombardment 147,500 rounds of heavy artillery ammunition had been used, in addition to 565,000 rounds fired by their field guns.

The similarity to the Canadian experience on the Somme was not lost on Byng. It was obvious that, before an attack on the Ridge could be planned, radical improvements in tactical methods were required. Their development had already begun.

Having determined the reasons for failure on the Somme, Byng began to seek solutions to the problems which they revealed. At first those of the artillery seemed to be the most intractable. The heavy guns had failed to destroy Regina Trench in the Somme battle because too few of the rounds which they had fired had fallen in it. Field guns firing shrapnel had not cut paths through the enemy's barbed wire. Heavy guns with shells designed to penetrate deep into the ground did somewhat better but slowed the infantry's advance with nearly impassable craters. They were the only weapons which could reach the enemy's guns, but they had done little to save the infantry from the heavy casualties which they suffered from shelling.

Yet the solutions to most of these problems were near to hand. Gen A. G. L. McNaughton, who later commanded the Corps Heavy Artillery, wrote:

General Byng was one of the first to grasp the significance of the lessons of the Somme and, with Major-General Edward Morrison, set about perfecting our artillery organization. As the number of guns available began to increase, the existing artillery units had to be expanded and new ones raised. Technical skill had to be developed and previous lessons and teachings modified to suit the changing conditions. The field and horse gunners, accustomed to fighting under circumstances which enabled them to observe every round, had to cease from scoffing at corrections for temperature, barometric pressure, velocity and direction of wind, wear of guns and type of shell and fuse. And the heavy artillery, used to the utmost deliberation, had to learn speed. Accuracy of fire on unseen targets, and the ability to shoot close over the heads of our own infantry, had to be acquired, and an organization built up which could effectively handle large masses of artillery.[3]

In the months before Vimy the artillery units alloted to the Canadian Corps were inspected, instructed and nagged by the Corps' own instructors of gunnery until their performance reached a standard acceptable to Byng.

Cutting wire was another problem. Shells which burst in the air or deep in the ground either failed to cut it or dug enormous craters. What was needed was a fuse which would explode a shell the instant it struck the earth, so that its blast and splinters would tear great holes in the wire entanglements. Byng's gunners knew of the existence of such a fuse which had just been developed, the No 106. It had been tried with success in later stages of the Somme, but was not yet in full production. The problem was to get enough of them for the attack on the Ridge. Through every channel available to them, Byng, Morrison and their staff officers pressed for the supply of the fuses. In January they began to arrive in quantity and with them a growing confidence that, on the day of assault, the infantry would not be stopped by the German wire.

The final artillery problem was that of the enemy guns. In attempting to neutralize them the artillery relied, in the main, on the Royal Flying Corps to find their targets and direct their fire. An organization had been developed to locate enemy batteries by taking bearings of the flash of their guns. Lt-Col A. G. Haig, Sir Douglas's cousin, had developed a counter-battery organization in 5th Corps with such success that the remainder of the BEF were authorized to do the same. McNaughton was chosen to form the organization in the Canadian Corps. It was a happy choice for not only was he a competent artillery officer, he also held a Master's degree in electrical engineering and was the pioneer in the use of the oscillograph in Canada.

When he visited Col Haig he learned that a new technique of finding enemy guns was being developed. Microphones at different locations recorded the sound of them firing and of the explosion of the shell. The heart of the system was the oscillograph.

McNaughton invited the three scientists who were working on the problem to come to the Canadian Corps to help him complete his counter-battery organization. Lawrence Bragg and Charles Darwin were distinguished physicists; Professor Lucien Bull had developed the oscillograph at the Sorbonne.[4] They had not been warmly received elsewhere. McNaughton commented that to many gunners of the old school, 'The idea of carrying an electrocardiograph into the line, setting it up and depending on a photograph of the vibrations of an oscillograph to tell you where the enemy guns were was treason, literally treason.' Sir Lawrence Bragg said, 'An almost impassable barrier had been encountered between the military and scientific minds. The military thought us scientists far too visionary and gadgety to be of any help in the field; the scientists could not understand why their brain waves, which seemed to them such war winners, made no impression on the military.'

The organization which McNaughton set up soon payed in results. It could not be matched elsewhere either by the Allies or the enemy and it was on its success that McNaughton's fame as a scientific gunner in the

First World War largely rests.[5] By watching the movements of enemy guns, the targets they chose and so on, McNaughton could predict with accuracy what the enemy was planning to do. One of the most frequent visitors to his office, listening and encouraging, was Byng.[6]

Byng's intelligence organization was unique in the British armies. Under the personal control of his own intelligence officer were air photo interpreters, interrogators, scouts, snipers, observers and collators. Working closely with the counter-battery organization, they assembled a detailed picture of the German defences on the Ridge and of the strength and habits of the garrisons who manned them.

The process continued to the day of the assault, the most valuable information coming from the infantry themselves. After an initially quiet period when they first moved into the Vimy sector, Byng's battalions began a succession of raids and reconnaissance patrols partly to gain information and partly to harry the enemy. His intelligence staff would meet them on their return and add their new-found knowledge to the developing picture of the enemy.[7]

No function which contributed to the Corps' effectiveness – engineers, signals, supplies, medical and transportation – escaped Byng's personal scrutiny. All services improved and in doing so developed confidence in themselves and pride in the Corps.

The foregoing developments were largely technical in nature. Problems had been defined and engineering or scientific answers had been found. Faith, confidence, imagination, and knowledge of human nature were required, in addition to scientific method, in the solution of a more fundamental problem – improving the tactics of the infantry.

More than any other branch of the army, the infantry of 1916 suffered from the losses of the first months of the War. The skills of mobile warfare – fire and movement, independent action by platoons, flexibility – died with the officers and NCOs of the British Regular Army. There had seemed little scope for such tactics in the positional warfare of the Western Front and there was no time for nonessentials in training the new mass armies of the Empire. For them the attack was an assault of a few hundred yards. The leading troops should arrive at the enemy position as soon as possible after their supporting artillery fire lifted. Since a barrage and a German trench were both lines, so should their formation be a line. Hence the tactics of the Somme – the assault in waves.

Advancing in the centre of his platoon line, perhaps a few paces in front, a lieutenant could do little but encourage his men by his example. At that he could usually be seen by only a few of them. There was no possibility of control or of manoeuvre.

If the enemy wire was cut and his trench destroyed, the tactic

146

worked. But something always went wrong. The wire was never entirely cut nor were all the defenders destroyed. If the platoon came under fire from a flank they could do little about it. Hence the need for succeeding waves.

Byng knew how pre-war infantry were trained and in 1914 had seen for himself the skill with which small units dealt with the Germans near Ypres. The problem was not so much in the training of the men as in that of their officers and NCOs. Already he had made a start in improving the training of platoon commanders at the Corps School. But did the minor tactics taught before 1914 apply to the deliberate attack in positional warfare?

He set each of his divisions to study the problem and all concluded that, with modifications, they did. Watched by Byng, their ideas were demonstrated at the Corps School. Then, in January, he sent Arthur Currie, the able commander of the 1st Division, to visit the French at Verdun to discover what they had learned. Their experience confirmed that infantry should advance in small groups, taking advantage of the lie of the ground, toward objectives which should be natural features, not trench lines which were often obliterated.[8]

The assault machine was scrapped. Henceforth platoon commanders and their NCOs would be given a chance to use their brains instead of only their courage. If time was needed for teaching, time would be found, as it would be for training company and battalion commanders.

As always, the latter would play a key role in the operations of the Corps, and Byng went to considerable pains to get to know them and brief them on his ideas. During the winter months he invited small groups of COs to stay for a week at his headquarters. Much of their time was spent with the Corps Staff on the study of tactical problems and methods of improving the administration of their units. Byng himself was often present and was able to talk informally with each in his mess. The surroundings were far from luxurious, but the atmosphere was cheerful and relaxed.

Concurrently with his measures to improve the Corps, Byng was making his plans to take the Ridge sometime after 15 March.

Horne's preliminary instructions provided for two separate operations against Vimy Ridge. In the first, known as the Southern Operation, the Canadian Corps would take all of the main crest with the exception of 'The Pimple', a 120-metre hill at its northern end. It, with the Bois-en-Hache across the Souchez, would be taken later in the Northern Operation by the British 1st Corps. Byng would need all his Canadian divisions in the initial assault, so Horne allotted him the 5th British Division as a reserve. Massive artillery support would be provided.

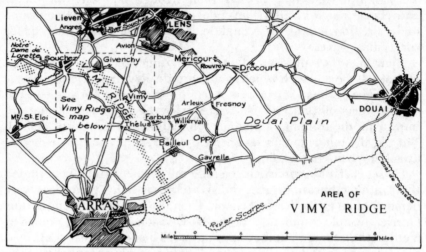

Lieven
Angres
Aix Noulette
LENS
Avion
Notre
Dame de
Lorette Souchez
Givenchy
Mericourt
Rouvroy
Drocourt
MY RIDGE
Vimy
See
Arleux
Fresnoy
Vimy Ridge
map
Farbus
Willerval
Douai Plain
DOUAI
Mt.St.Eloi
below
Thélus
Bailleul
Oppy
Canal de Sensée
Gavrelle
Miles 0   2   4   6   8 Miles
River Scarpe
ARRAS

AREA OF
VIMY RIDGE

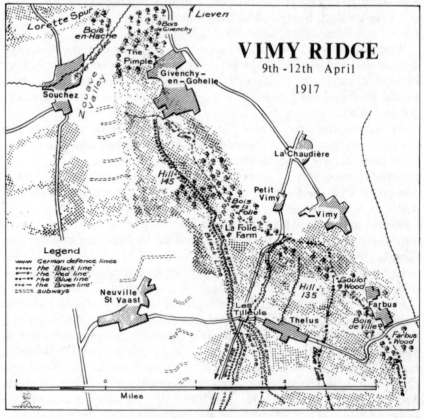

Lorette Spur
Lieven
Bois
en-Hache
Bois
de Givenchy

The
Pimple
Givenchy-
en-Gohelle

VIMY RIDGE
9th - 12th April
1917

Souchez

River Souchez

Zouave Valley

La Chaudière

Hill
145

Petit
Vimy

Bois de la
Folie

Vimy

La Folie
Farm

Legend
www German defence lines
o-o-o the 'Black line'
•-•-• the 'Red line'
•••• the 'Blue line'
oo-oo the 'Brown line'
----- subways

Neuville
St Vaast

Goulot
Wood

Hill
135

Farbus

Les
Tilleuls

Thelus

Bois
de Ville

Farbus
Wood

Miles

The 3rd and 4th Divisions already held the sector of the line from which they would attack. Early in March the 1st and 2nd Divisions moved from north of Givenchy-en-Gohelle to take up positions on the right.

Opposite were the three German divisions of Group Vimy commanded by General of Infantry Karl von Fasbender. He had been there since 1914, apart from a few bloody weeks on the Somme when he had won the '*Pour le Merite*', the highest German award for bravery. His 1st Bavarian Reserve Division, too, had been in the Arras area since the first months of the War. They now held Thélus, opposite the 1st Division, and Bailleul – facing the 51st Highland Division of Third Army. In the centre the 79th Reserve Division held the highest points of the Ridge, while on their right the 16th Bavarian Division held the remainder, including 'The Pimple'.

'Group Vimy' was under Gen von Falkenhausen's Sixth Army, part of Prince Rupprecht's Group of Armies responsible for the northern third of the German front.

The 79th Reserve Division, raised in Prussia, had served for two years on the Russian front before coming to Vimy in February, 1917. The 16th Bavarian had been organized in January from divisions shattered at the Somme and Verdun. So far, as a division, it had only met Canadians, whose raiding tactics and general aggressiveness its troops deplored. One night they left a large sign in no-man's-land, printed in English: 'Cut out your damned artillery – we, too, are from the Somme.'[9]

The defences of the Ridge had been designed for Falkenhayn's stone-wall tactics, which proved so disastrous on the Somme. A more elastic system was planned but work on it had not yet begun. In the face of the increasing destruction caused by the British and Canadian guns and frequent alarms caused by infantry raids, the garrison could do little more than maintain their existing defences.

Three main lines opposed the Canadian Corps. In the First, or Forward, Zone, seven hundred yards deep, were three rows of trenches, with machine-gun emplacements and wire. Tunnels and communication trenches joined them and deep dugouts protected the garrison.

Behind and parallel to the Ridge was the Second Line, its dugouts huge underground chambers, some large enough to shelter entire battalions. Again it was strongly protected by wire. To the rear, well out on the plain, was the Third Line, extending from Lens to Méricourt, Oppy and Gavrelle. At the widest, some five miles separated the Third Line from the First. Further east a fourth position was under construction – the Drocourt–Quéant Line which was to contain any success which the Allies might achieve in the Lens-Vimy area.

Of the nine infantry regiments forming the divisions of Group Vimy, only five were on the Ridge. Each held its First and Second Lines with one battalion, its Third Line with another. Its third battalion was billeted in villages two hours march to the rear. The five divisions of Sixth Army's counterattack force were ten to twenty-five miles behind the front. Falkenhausen believed that an Allied attack, which clearly was in the offing, would be contained for some days in the Forward Zone, hence there was no need to place his reserves closer to the front.

Byng's plan for taking the Ridge was sent to Horne for approval on 5 March. With some modifications to the artillery programme, this 'Scheme of Operations' became the basis of his orders for the attack.

He defined the principal objectives as the village of Thélus and Hill 135 north of it, which were vital to the advance of Third Army on the right. But the approaches to both of these were overlooked from Hill 145 and La Folie Farm, hence these must first be secured. The third objective was the German guns in the Farbus and Goulot Woods. To capture these the attack must be pushed through to the German Second Line by nightfall on the first day.

The four Canadian divisions, in numerical order from the right, would attack together. The 5th British Division in Corps reserve would allot its 13th Brigade to the 2nd Canadian Division to take part in the attack on the final objective. The operation would be carried out in four stages, each of which related to an element of the German defensive system. A report line for each was indicated by a coloured line on the map. Attainment of the first, the Black Line, some 750 yards from the Canadian front trenches, would mean that the German forward defensive zone had been captured. The next, the Red Line, ran to the north along a German trench called Zwischen-Stellung to the crest of the Ridge, including La Folie Farm and Hill 145. For the 3rd and 4th Divisions attacking on the Corps left, this would be the final objective. On the right, a third report line, Blue, included Thélus and Hill 135 and the woods above the village of Vimy. Finally, the Brown Line marked the final objective: the German Second Line and the guns in Farbus and Goulot Woods.

The four divisions would assault together at 5.30 am. In thirty-five minutes, they were to reach the Black Line where a pause of forty minutes was scheduled to ensure that both the infantry and the artillery barrage would resume the advance together. Twenty minutes later they were to be at the Red Line. This would bring the 3rd and 4th Divisions to the far side of the Ridge at 7.05 am. In the 1st and 2nd Divisions, after halting for two and a half hours, the reserve brigades, with 13th British Brigade on the left, would pass through to the Blue Line. Here they would pause again for 96 minutes before advancing beyond the Ridge to the Brown Line, the final objective, which they should reach by 1.18 pm. On the right the 17th Corps, whose report lines joined those of the Canadians, would be using similar timings.

Machine-guns would move forward to each objective with the infantry to ensure that no German counterattack would succeed. A final line of outposts would be established beyond the Ridge, supported by a defence line just east of the crest. A new main line of resistance would be located one hundred yards down the western slope. To help in their attack on Thélus, the 2nd Division would have eight tanks attached, but, because of the difficult conditions of the ground, no reliance was placed upon them.

For once Byng felt that he had sufficient artillery. The guns of seven divisions plus eight independent field artillery brigades gave him 480 eighteen-pounders and 138 4.5-inch howitzers for close support of the infantry. To this was added the immense fire power of eleven heavy artillery groups – 245 heavy guns and howitzers – and the artillery of the 1st British Corps, a further 132 heavy and 102 field guns. In comparison to the Somme, where there had been a heavy gun to each 57 yards of front and a field gun to 20 yards, at Vimy there was one heavy gun to 20 yards and a field gun for every 10 yards of front. 42,500 tons of ammunition was provided as a basic allotment for the operation, in addition to a daily quota of 2465 tons.

The concentration of such large quantities of stores and ammunition brought about a near crisis in the transportation system behind the Canadian front. Roads had to be built and maintained involving shipping in some eleven train-loads of gravel and engineer stores every day. It was not enough. Byng formed a temporary forestry unit from lumberjacks in the Corps to cut timber to build three miles of plank roads. Twenty miles of tramway were operated and forty-five miles of water pipelines. But the greatest engineering feat was the excavation and extension of protective tunnels under the Ridge.

Unlike the steep eastern slopes, those on the west rose gently toward the crest. From their positions above the Canadian lines, the Germans could see anything that moved on the surface of the ground. Communication trenches offered some protection but were often made unusable by observed artillery fire. In similar situations on the Somme infantry moving forward had suffered heavy casualties long before they reached the front line.

The British had dug a few tunnels as shelters in the chalk soil of the Ridge, but by far the greater number were low galleries driven under the enemy lines preparatory to exploding mines. Twelve of these were

151

now developed and extended to provide a covered route to the front line. Called subways, they were six feet six inches high and three feet or more in width. Adjoining chambers were dug for headquarters, signal exchanges, advanced dressing stations and ammunition storage. Some, such as Grange Tunnel, had more than one level with a tramline for moving stores and casualties. There were large chambers and connecting galleries where troops could wait in safety. Telephone lines and even water pipelines were bracketed to the walls. And they were all lit by electric light supplied by petrol-driven generators located in caves near the entrance.

Exits from the tunnels led to the front and support lines and to mortar and machine-gun posts.

Huge craters in or near the front lines were the result of two years of warfare. As the Brigade Major of 4th Canadian Infantry Brigade examined an air photograph of the German positions on his front, it occurred to him that the old mine galleries leading to it must still exist. By probing below the Canadian front line trench, a three-foot-square timbered shaft was discovered leading to a crater known as 'Phillips' in the German Line. The dangerous work of clearing the debris from the German end took several days of painstaking work which, as it neared completion, was done only at night. Finally a small hole was opened on the side of the crater. On the opposite side could be seen the silhouette of a German sentry. Not only could the assaulting troops of the 4th Brigade shelter in the tunnel leading to their front line, but now they could cross below no-man's-land unharmed by the enemy's defensive fire.[10]

Along the front similar galleries were opened to serve after the assault as communication trenches or for the protection of signal cable.

In his 'Scheme of Operations' Byng laid down measures to coordinate the advance of his divisions, ending with the paragraph which was revolutionary at that stage of the War:

> In the event of any Division or Brigade being held up, the units on the flanks will on no account check their advance, but will form defensive flanks in that direction and press forward themselves so as to envelop the strong point or centre of resistance which is preventing the advance. With this object in view reserves will be pushed in behind those portions of the line that are successful rather than those which are held up.[11]

Even in the Second World War there were commanders who had not learned to reinforce success.

Early in the development of the plan, subordinate commanders were fully briefed on its details and rehearsed their units in their roles. Byng had a full-scale replica of the battle area laid out in fields behind the lines and kept up to date by air photographs and patrol reports. Enemy positions were indicated by white tapes or flags. Whilst in reserve, units of every size, from platoon to division repeatedly rehearsed their tasks. Everything possible was done to promote realism. Mounted officers with flags moved forward at the pace of the rolling barrage. Everyone carried what they would need in battle, and every foreseeable stage of the advance was simulated, from climbing out of the jumping-off trench to crossing broken ground and dealing with enemy strong points. Almost daily the Corps Commander was there to watch.

At First Army headquarters a plasticine model of the Ridge was constructed, showing in minute detail every known enemy trench, dugout and strongpoint. All officers and NCOs taking part in the attack were given ample time to study it and work out plans to deal with the problems they would soon have to face. Often Byng himself took part in their discussions, not only to guide them but to discover any weakness which he could remedy.

Byng treated the Canadian soldier as an adult capable of thought. It was foreign to his nature to patronize anyone. For his part, the Canadian was sceptical of the concept that rank in itself gave any man the right to lead. He himself had volunteered for the war which he saw as a dirty business which must be finished as quickly as possible. He was willing to do his part in winning it and he resented any implication that anyone, officers included, had a greater interest in the outcome than he did. He had a proprietary right to share in the business. All he asked of his officers was that they know their jobs and do them. Byng impressed him as being a straightforward fellow who knew his work and had the interests of his troops at heart. By taking these men into his confidence Byng inspired them in a way which never could have been achieved by rhetoric or any other shallow device. A wide-scale issue of maps of the battlefield had a psychological impact on the soldiers quite separate from their satisfaction at receiving a useful tool. Formerly maps were for officers; marked maps were protected and rarely seen by the men. Now they were being given to corporals. It meant that they were trusted and had been given a share in the responsibility for the enterprise.

Only the date of the attack, now set for 9 April, was not revealed. As it approached everyone knew his role in the assault as well as those of his commander and his neighbours. The thoroughness of the training was unprecedented in the British armies.[12]

During the first three months of 1917 the fighting had not stopped whilst preparations for the attack were being made. Almost nightly, somewhere along the Canadian line, a raiding party would burst into a

German position, blow up a dugout and its occupants and hustle a bewildered prisoner back across no-man's-land. Armed with weapons of their own choice, clubs, grenades and explosives, but rarely rifles, and unimpeded by equipment, they relied on speed and the isolation of the German post by a curtain of artillery fire. Their success rate was high but there were disasters when an alert and determined enemy caught the raiders in the open. The enemy artillery invariably retaliated and, in the two weeks ending 5 April, the Canadians had 1653 casualties, mostly incurred during or as a result of raids.

Despite the development of the counter-battery organization, the artillery still relied on the Royal Flying Corps to find hostile batteries and direct the fire of their guns against hidden targets. No 16 Squadron, attached to the Canadian Corps, suffered heavy losses to German fighters, which, though outnumbered, were faster and more heavily armed than the protecting British machines. As April began, so did the intensity of fighting in the air. Concentrating their strength to support the battle and to prevent the German air force from interfering, the RFC brought over 700 machines into action, more than half of them fighters. So began what they later called 'Bloody April'. Somewhat more than 100 German fighters, well commanded and audaciously flown, wreaked a terrible execution. Flying a red Albatros, Baron Manfred von Richtofen claimed thirty kills that month.

On 20 March the artillery began the systematic destruction of the German defences. Until 2 April, to conceal their strength, half the supporting batteries remained silent. Then, a week before the attack, their full weight came down on the hapless garrison of the Vimy fortress. Trenches were pulverized and great gaps were torn in the protective wire. When the destruction of one area was complete and the guns switched to other targets, machine-guns laid down barrages of bullets to prevent the Germans from repairing the damage. Villages behind the Ridge were destroyed, roads and communication trenches obliterated. Ration parties carrying food to the front now took six hours to make what had been a fifteen-minute journey. Meals when they arrived were cold and often spoiled. Frequently for companies in the front line, hunger was added to the sleeplessness and strain of what the Germans later called the week of suffering.

In the comparative safety of their dugouts, the German infantry waited, listening for the beginning of the intense bombardment of their trenches which would precede an assault. Its ending would be the signal to rush to their trenches and pour a withering fire on the infantry approaching up the slope, just as they had on the French.

154

Byng and his staff knew what had happened in 1915 and that the German tunnel and dugout exits were all within the 750 yards of the forward defensive zone which was to be crossed in the first thirty-five minutes. Obviously there was no hope of the infantry reaching and blocking them unless tactical surprise was achieved. To deceive the enemy as to the time of the attack, they decided to dispense with the intense heavy artillery bombardment which customarily preceded the assault.

On 5 April Byng received orders from Henry Horne which affected the 4th Division. No longer would the attack on The Pimple be the responsibility of 1st British Corps. It was to be taken by the Canadians after Hill 145 had been captured. Byng warned Gen Watson of the 4th Division who assigned the task to his reserve brigade, the 10th.

Already Byng's efforts were being appreciated. On 2 April Haig's military secretary wrote a personal note to Stamfordham for the King's information:

Dear Lord Stamfordham,
     The French Government nominated Byng last week for Commander of the Legion of Honour. Sir Douglas concurred and his name should shortly be submitted for His Majesty's approval and permission to accept it. This is his third Foreign decoration in addition to a KCB, KCMG and promotion to Lieut-General, so he has not been done badly. He deserves it all, he has worked a miracle with the Canadians. Personally I have always thought he should be an Army Commander.
                              Yours sincerely,
                              W. E. Peyton[13]

As night fell on 8 April the assaulting battalions began to move to their forward assembly areas. Not all could use the protected subways and the usual German artillery and machine-gun harrassing fire caused casualties. In silence the leading companies filed through gaps in their wire and lay down in the shell holes of no-man's-land waiting for the signal to assault. A bitter north-west wind drove gusts of snow and sleet across the frozen mud of the battlefield. The men shivered somewhat less than they otherwise might; each had had a hot meal and a ration of rum.

By 4 am on the four-mile front of the Canadian Corps, 52 battalions, 30,000 men, had deployed in the dark, their leading companies within a hundred yards of the German outposts, without giving the alarm.

Byng liked to be near his troops. The advanced headquarters where he lived was at Berthenval Farm west of the Arras-Souchez road along which were the tactical headquarters of each of his divisions. The most distant was within three miles. During the night the bare wood floors of

155

the dairy farm echoed as reports arrived on the progress of the assembly for battle. As dawn approached on 9 April there was nothing for the Corps Commander to do but say a prayer, which he did, and wait.[14]

Despite the subways, the counter-battery fire and the torrents of shells which had bombarded the Ridge, no one, least of all Byng, expected anything other than a hard-fought battle in the morning.

At 5.30 am 983 guns and mortars opened fire in support of the infantry. The main field artillery barrage fell on the German's foremost trenches where it remained for three minutes, then lifting one hundred yards every three minutes, it rolled through the enemy forward zone. Before its first move the infantry were on their feet and advancing. Other guns and howitzers concentrated their fire on known strongpoints and defences, their fire lifting precisely as the barrage arrived so that the defenders were unaware of a change. Simultaneously, all known German batteries and ammunition dumps were bombarded by high explosive and gas shells. With their horses affected by gas, the enemy artillery could neither change position nor get up ammunition. With their observation posts destroyed and telephone cables cut, they knew little of the situation at the front. Most of the SOS rockets which rose above the lines of the desperate German infantry failed to call down the shells which might have helped to stem the Canadian attack.

There are different ways of describing the Battle of Vimy Ridge. The simplest is to say that the three Canadian divisions on the right took all their objectives on schedule – Thélus and Hill 135, La Folie Farm and the German guns in Farbus and Goulot Woods. But the 4th Division on the left, ran into difficulties and did not take Hill 145 until the afternoon of the 10th April. Then, on the 12th, they took The Pimple and the whole of Vimy Ridge was in Canadian hands.

For many of the twenty-one battalions which led the attack the assault was the easiest part of the battle, despite the condition of the ground. The continuous shelling had pulverized the badly drained earth into great puddles of clammy mud. Shell holes, shattered trenches, the tangled remnants of wire obstacles and vast mine craters had to be negotiated or by-passed in the dark. Byng had chosen a zero hour of 5.30 am to give the infantry enough light to see their way, but insufficient for the Germans to distinguish targets clearly. Now dense clouds and driving rain and sleet obscured the half-light which precedes the dawn. Yet so well rehearsed were the infantry that few became lost.

The assault on the German front line was so swift that, apart from sentries who were quickly over-powered, little resistance was offered. Leaving guards on tunnel and dugout exists, the leading companies pressed forward to the second line. Here some of the garrisons were still underground but, though opposition increased, it was overcome in hand-to-hand fighting. Snipers and strongly emplaced machine-guns now took an increasing toll of casualties, but the advance kept moving as small units and even individual soldiers silenced the opposition.

Along the front of the 1st, 2nd and 3rd Divisions the entire German forward defence zone, 750 yards deep, was taken by 6.25 am. Fresh units now took over the lead.

It was now light enough for the troops to see well ahead, but the Germans were less fortunate as the wind drove snow diagonally across the front and into their eyes. On the 1st Division's front the Bavarians did not see the attack coming until it was almost upon them. Most were either captured or fled – nearly a full battalion was seen moving back over the skyline toward Farbus Woods. The 2nd Division, fighting hard, cleared the hamlet of Les Tilleuls, captured two German battalion headquarters, two field guns and some 500 prisoners as they pressed forward to the Red Line.

The 3rd Division's advance had gone well and they had reached the Red Line, the crest of the Ridge, by 7.30 am, half an hour before the two divisions on their right. As planned, two Vickers machine-guns accompanied each battalion to be ready to repel counterattacks. The two with 1st CMR on the right of the division reached the Arras – Lens road ahead of the infantry and promptly engaged a large party of Germans assembling on the slope below. They claim to have inflicted a hundred casualties. The German account was more graphic. While 2nd CMR were capturing 150 prisoners at one of the exits of the Schwaben Tunnel, at another exit:

> No sooner had it been decided to abandon the battalion headquarters at the tunnel entrance than the first English appeared 200 yards away and brought a machine-gun into action at the Ruhleben House. Pursued by the fire of this troublesome gun, the battalion commander, his staff, and twenty men went back along the communication trench, knee deep in mud, toward the second line position; but most of the staff and all the men were killed or wounded before reaching it.[15]

La Folie Farm was taken by 2nd CMR.

The 7th Brigade suffered considerable loss as it entered the Bois de la Folie and the Germans counterattacked. One attempt was launched against the junction of 4th CMR and the Royal Canadian Regiment. Another was aimed at bombing the RCR from their trenches in the wood. Both were repulsed.

On the left of the RCR, Princess Patricia's Canadian Light Infantry made good use of Byng's new infantry tactics. Advancing by section rushes – one section of a platoon pinning the enemy down while the remainder dashed forward – the two leading companies closed on the enemy. As they entered the Bois de la Folie, they were met by heavy fire but reached their final objective with only fifty casualties, a high proportion being officers and NCOs.[16] Help was needed to consolidate the position. Pte F. W. Laycock who had 'jumped-off' with No 3 Company at Zero Hour described his part in it:

Our objective was Zwischen Stellung, a German trench half-way to La Folie Wood. We took it and I was with Macdonald who had joined the Pats with me from the 68th Battalion. We got dug in when an officer came and ordered us up to help take La Folie Wood. Macdonald and I went on up. We got a little too far over to the right and found an RCR machine gunner all by himself. So we said 'You're all alone; we'll stay and help.' He got mad and told us to get the hell out of his shell hole. He said 'The RCR don't need help from you damn Pats.' So we left him and went up and got off a few shots at German artillery horses. Then we raided a German post and took some prisoners. One of the bastards shot me. Macdonald finished him off.'[17]

As the 3rd Division dug in and sent forward patrols down the slopes toward Petit Vimy, the 1st and 2nd Divisions resumed their advance to the Blue Line which they secured shortly after 11 am. Just before they reached it, the sun broke through the storm clouds. As the troops topped the ridge, they could see below them red-roofed houses set in green fields, untouched by war. The only enemy were a few parties straggling away to the east. From the German side

The cessation of the snowstorm lifted the veil which had until now hidden the landscape, and we saw a remarkable sight. The air was suddenly clean and clear, filled with spring sunshine. The high ground about Thélus was covered with English stormtroops standing about in large groups. The officers could easily be distinguished waving their short sticks in the air and hurrying from group to group to give instructions. For a few moments, the artillery fire almost ceased on both sides and complete silence fell upon the battlefield, as if all were lost in wonder. The battle itself seemed to hold its breath.[18]

At Byng's headquarters reports of success were accompanied by pleas from senior officers to speed the attack by abandoning its rigid timetable. Leading troops reported that the Germans appeared to be on the run. They should not be given a chance to stop for breath or to turn and fight.

The orders which Byng had received were explicit. He was to capture Vimy Ridge and hold it as a bastion on the flank of the Arras offensive. The War had already seen too many initial successes ruined by

158

German counterattacks. His plan provided time for each objective to be made secure before the advance to the next began. To remove all restraints now would mean abandoning this precaution and scrapping the complex artillery fire plan which had ensured the infantry's success so far. Byng refused to do so.

Ninety minutes after the Blue Line had been taken the advance to the Brown Line began. On the right Griesbach's 1st Brigade advanced on Farbus Wood. The crews of the German guns concealed in it had been driven to cover by the barrage and the guns were captured without difficulty.

On their left, German artillery in the Bois de la Ville opened fire at point blank range on the 6th Brigade, whereupon the leading troops charged downhill and bayonetted or captured the gunners. Continuing through the wood, they captured 250 prisoners, including the commander and staff of the 3rd Bavarian Reserve Regiment.

Further north, the West Kents and Scottish Borderers of the British 13th Brigade rushed the guns in the Bois du Goulot, the crews surrendering or escaping hurriedly down the hill under heavy fire.

The 1st and 2nd Divisions had now captured the whole of their final objective. Patrols were pushed beyond the German Second Line to set up observation posts as the troops prepared their new positions for defence.

On the left of the Corps, the 4th Division's attack was not going well. The main objective was Hill 145, the highest point on the Ridge. From it the Germans could see everything that moved in the valley of the Souchez and in Zouave Valley, which ran behind the Division's front. Were they to lose it, the position would be dramatically reversed, for the Hill afforded a commanding view not only of the rest of Vimy Ridge, but of the German rearward defences on the Douai Plain.

As the most important feature of the Ridge, it was the most heavily defended. Running across its south-east slope were two trenches of the German First Line. Two more ringed its rounded top. Old mine workings provided almost complete immunity from shelling for their garrisons while on the reverse slope a system of deep dugouts (the Hangstellung) protected the reserve companies.

At the slightest provocation the German artillery would lay a barrage down Zouave Valley which could have disastrous consequences during the assembly for an attack. Subways and communication trenches ten feet deep now reduced this danger, but so closely did the Germans scrutinize the area that nowhere else on the Vimy front would surprise be more difficult to achieve. Because of the lie of the land no-man's-land was wider here, 750 yards across. With great difficulty the Canadians had succeeded in digging assembly trenches for the assault within 150 yards of the German line – a long distance given the state of the ground.

The Germans were aware of this work on the trenches, but made no attempt to interrupt it, even by artillery or machine-gun fire. Unknown to the Canadians, the 16th Bavarian Division was set to drive them from their positions above Zouave Valley. Their plan was based on the extensive use of gas, but the wind persisted in being unfavourable.

Major-Gen David Watson hoped to over-run the forward German positions by surprise and hold their reserves at bay with artillery and machine-gun barrages until consolidation was complete.

On the right, part of Brig-Gen Victor Odlum's 11th Brigade swept over the crest of Hill 145 and secured a foothold in the trenches beyond. But its left-hand battalion met disaster. Machine-guns in an undamaged enemy strong-point virtually wiped out its assaulting companies. Exposed to heavy fire from the uncaptured positions on the summit, the successful troops on the right were in danger of being cut off and had to be withdrawn from the far side of the hill.

All day the brigade fought to extend their hold on Hill 145 but by nightfall were stopped just short of the crest.

The 12th Brigade on the left of the division had been delayed by heavy fire from the Germans still on Hill 145 and from The Pimple but eventually reached most of their objectives. The Pimple was blocked off and contact established with 1st British Corps to the North.

During the day each of the leading brigades had been reinforced with a battalion from the 10th Brigade, but the 4th Division's main objectives had still to be taken.

It was obvious to Watson that Odlum's exhausted battalions could do no more. Yet the remainder of Hill 145 and La Folie Wood beyond must be cleared before he could take The Pimple. The only troops available were the two uncommitted battalions of the 10th Brigade, which he had been saving for that operation. At 6 pm on the 9th he ordered Brig-Gen E. Hilliam to take the 11th Brigade's final Red Line objective.

Victor Odlum, like David Watson, was a newspaper publisher in civilian life. He had been a company commander at Ypres in 1915, been wounded several times and was one of the prime architects of the trench raid as practised by the Canadians. More than once as a brigadier he had led small raids himself. Austere and a teetotaller, he was known as 'Old Lime Juice' by his troops because of the restrictions he placed on their rum ration. But he was no armchair soldier and he decided now that he would make sure that the 10th Brigade would at least have a secure start line.

'In the end, towards morning,' he recalled, 'I went forward to see

160

what the position was. I had two or three officers with me. As I got up on top of the hill, I could see that we had not got over; we were bent back on the top. The Germans were still up there. I went around and started on the left flank of my brigade, and, unit by unit, I took them forward and placed them in position one after the other. Then I went along and took the last one over the crest of the hill.' The disorganized Germans had evacuated the trench beyond the crest and Odlum's men were able to prepare it for defence in time to beat off a half-hearted counterattack.[19]

In the early afternoon Hilliam's two battalions crossed the Souchez Valley in artillery formation – that is, dispersed into groups of twelve men – and by about 2 pm had moved up the casualty-strewn slope to the road near the summit. At 3 o'clock the artillery opened fire on the Hangstellung beyond the crest and at 3.15 the 44th (Manitoba) and 50th (Calgary) Battalions charged down the slope. Within minutes the 50th on the left lost a third of its strength. In plain view from the flat ground below the Ridge, fire poured up at them. A German battery, like toy soldiers, could be seen firing at them from a barnyard.

Leaping into the enemy trenches, they cleared them with bayonet and bomb. Within 30 minutes the Hangstellung fortifications were captured and by late afternoon the 44th had cleared the remainder of La Folie Wood. The 12th Brigade was now able to move its right flank forward and at last the Red Line was secure.

As light was failing in the evening, the two battalions were relieved and began to move back behind Zouave Valley to reorganize and re-equip for the attack on The Pimple on 12 April.

The 'Southern Operation' was complete. The main part of the Ridge was in Canadian hands and on the right the 51st Division had also reached its objectives. To a remarkable extent the battle had progressed as planned and, except in the case of the 4th Division, there had been little need for intervention by Byng or his divisional commanders.

Later historians were critical of Byng's rigid adherence to the timetable which prescribed that his men should take six hours to secure their final objectives. Had Falkenhausen, the German army commander, not been too sanguine about the ability of his forward troops to hold the Ridge, two of his reserve divisions near Douai might have reached Vimy by rail within four hours.

Byng's insistence on ensuring the defence of successive objectives had just such an intervention in mind. To have planned on taking the Ridge within four hours would have seemed foolhardy before the battle. Perhaps Byng thought that his opponent's confidence in the strength of the Vimy defences might slow his reactions.

Unfortunately we do not know. Faced with the fact of this first major success in the War for British arms, such speculation seems trivial. But could Byng have done more?

The British Official Historian, Capt Cyril Falls, suggested that an opportunity for a cavalry breakthrough had been lost at 7.15 am. In fact there was, in practical terms, no possibility of a large force of cavalry passing quickly through the Canadian front and Byng, the most experienced of cavalry commanders, knew it. The ground which they would have to cross was about as passable as a marsh and would not permit guns and transport to accompany them for at least twenty-four hours.

But there was a possible use for a small force of cavalry, for which Horne had already issued instructions. If the enemy withdrew to the Oppy-Méricourt line, the Canadian Corps was to attack The Pimple, occupy Vimy and Willerval and send the Corps mounted troops to secure a flank position along the Vimy-Rouvroy road facing north.

Due to the appalling conditions of the ground, the only possible route they could follow would be along the now non-existent road from Neuville-St Vaast to Thélus and Farbus, thence to Willerval and the north. At 2 pm Byng ordered his only available cavalry, a squadron of the Canadian Light Horse, to send patrols as far as Willerval to see if this route was passable for horses. He telephoned First Army to say that he might be able to use a cavalry regiment and asked that one be made available. Horne in turn asked GHQ but the reply was slow in coming. In the late afternoon the 9th Cavalry Brigade was allotted to First Army.

In the meantime two troops of C Squadron of the Light Horse advanced to Thélus and at 4.20 sent patrols forward to Farbus Wood, from whence they advanced on Willerval, thirteen men to the north, seven to the south. The first group charged and captured ten Germans in the centre of the village but retired when a machine-gun came into action against them. The southern patrol met a line of German infantry. Only two of them returned to Farbus Wood, on foot. The northern patrol lost its officer, five men and several horses.

Sadly, by the time the cavalry had reached Thélus it was possible from elsewhere on the Ridge to see enemy in and about Willerval but the squadron was out of communication with Corps headquarters and no one stopped them.

Subsequently the German command structure was disturbed by a report which passed quickly through it: 'a strong force of English cavalry has broken through into Willerval'. Three battalions were ordered to counterattack to recapture the village. The advancing troops were seen from the Ridge. They did not reach the new Canadian line.

On 12 April the 44th and 50th Battalions and two companies of the 46th left their rest areas at 1.45 am, moved northwards to the village of Souchez, crossed Zouave Valley and climbed the slopes above to within two hundred yards of the crest. There they waited in assembly trenches for another zero hour. Their objective was to capture the northern end of Vimy Ridge – the Pimple and the spurs which splayed out from it overlooking the Souchez River and the village of Givenchy.

The 44th, on the right, was to make contact with the left of the 12th Brigade at Givenchy, the 50th, reinforced by the two companies of the 46th, would clear the northern spur and link with the 1st Corps in the Souchez Valley. Simultaneously the 73rd British Brigade would capture the Bois en Hache, the end of the Lorette feature opposite the Canadians.

A westerly gale was driving a blizzard of snow and sleet towards the German positions as the preliminary bombardment began and, if anything, it increased in force as the infantry began to advance at 5 am through the heavy clinging mud. So unexpected was a night attack in such appalling weather, that the garrison, a fresh battalion of the 5th Guard Grenadiers, were surprised. With their two forward trenches obliterated by the bombardment, their resistance was unorganized. Small groups emerged from shell holes and the few habitable dugouts, and there was vicious hand-to-hand fighting. On the left the two companies of the 46th (Saskatchewan) lost heavily in crossing no-man's-land but worked steadily forward and established their Lewis guns above the Souchez. The 50th (Calgary) squelched through the mud of the Bois de Givenchy and were on their final objective by 5.45. At 6 am the 44th (Manitoba) had secured the Pimple.

As day broke the storm lifted and, under a bright sun, the three Western battalions could see what they had achieved. To the south was the summit of Hill 145 which they had cleared thirty-six hours earlier. Ahead lay the Douai plain stretching to the eastern horizon. Below them from the left were Angres, Lievin and Avion, lying in front of Lens and its coal mines. German troops and transport were hurrying to the east.

To the north the British had cleared the Bois en Hache and the 2nd Battalion Prince of Wales' Leinster Regiment (Royal Canadians) joined the 46th on the Souchez.

Crown Prince Rupprecht wrote in his diary on 10 April, 'No one could have foreseen that the offensive would gain ground so quickly.' Early that day O.H.L. (German General Headquarters) had ordered withdrawal to the second line along the eastern slopes of the Vimy and Lorette Ridges. But already part of it had been evacuated. A counterattack to recapture it was considered but dismissed as impracticable. Next day Rupprecht ordered his forces to withdraw to the Oppy-Méricourt Line by the morning of 13 April. It would be far enough into the plain to prevent effective observation from the Ridge and would be strong enough to resist anything but a full-scale attack with intensive artillery preparation.

A quick advance in strength by the Canadians was not practicable. Even with 5,000 men working on them, the almost obliterated roads would not be passable to heavy guns and ammunition for several days.

The Corps moved forward as the Germans withdrew, capturing large quantities of weapons and stores. By the evening of the 14th the Canadian artillery had brought nine captured guns into action, ranging from 8-inch howitzers to 77-mm guns, bombarding enemy batteries and trenches and German billets with their own gas shells. It was no lighthearted affair – they had been well-trained during the winter for this eventuality.

That afternoon, when patrols had determined the location of the enemy's new line, Byng ordered the Canadian Corps to prepare a main defensive line running north through Willerval and the eastern edge of Vimy to the Bois de L'Hirondelle on the south bank of the Souchez. Apart from a temporary absence at Passchendaele, the Corps was to hold this line until the final advance of the War began in 1918. It marked the end of the Battle of Vimy Ridge.

Byng was elated at the result as this extract from a letter he wrote to Evelyn on 15 April shows:

I am sending you some specimens which you can tear up or put in the book. The unsolicited testimonial of the Boche General commanding one of the divisions opposite me is good – a thoughtful paper but not quite correct. A good lady has written asking me to contribute something written for her local newspaper and addresses the envelope to me 'on top of the Vimy Ridge.'

Well, Thursday night was the climax. I had just finished a scribble to you when I heard they were massing to counter-attack the Pimple. Everything was ready and everything went at them at 2 am Friday morning. They chucked it and took to their heels and raced for Lens leaving everything. By 9 am we were in Givenchy-en-Gohelle, Petit Vimy, Vimy and Willerval and the Canucks were moving up the Douai Valley. Thank God nobody lost his head and the good old Canucks behaved like real disciplined soldiers. I then pulled out the 4th Canadian Division, who were stone cold, and shoved in a British division and continued the pursuit in proper formation towards Lieven and Arleux. The gentle Boche has brought down a lot of fresh troops and holds the line in strength. . . . Horne has been more than helpful and backed me up in everything and now, having got old Squibs (Congreve) South of me, who sees eye to eye, I am quite happy again.

I went over the Pimple yesterday. It IS a sight: the dead are rather ghastly but a feat of arms that will stand for ever. Poor old Prussian Guard WHAT a mouthful to swallow being beaten to hell by what they called 'untrained Colonial levies'.

Yesterday was a great day. Seven captured Boche batteries in action firing Boche gas shells into Boche batteries!! We knocked one of them out entirely at 7 o'clock with their own gas and the Canuck gunner sent me in the comic report beginning – 'Our 5.9 and 4.2 batteries very effective on German guns.' I shall get their 'captured Boche' 8″ howitzers in action today against them. So much for the Boche report that all the captured guns were disabled. They have left me over a thousand rounds per gun and the number of guns now mounts up to fifty besides howitzers. The 'Booty' (as the Boche calls it) is enormous. Every sort of weapon – wireless, telephones of all descriptions, changes of linen for quite half our men, complete maps, electric light, trench tramways, dumps of every sort and a complete new issue of greatcoats.

Talking about dumps, our one and only Dump got shelled the day before yesterday and was very angry and excited. I told him that if he himself looked less like a Tank it wouldn't have happened. This has quietened him.

Later . . . I have been inundated with congratulatory letters and am sending you a few; you can tear them up. Tim Harington's are very nice. I was sorry to lose him and he loved this corps. Old Plum sent a nice message of course. . . . The Canucks are saying very nice things to me, and one informed me that they couldn't have done without the discipline and training which had been instilled into them for the last eight months. That is most satisfactory as it shews they are beginning to realize that bravery is not the only thing that is wanted and that without discipline it means loss of life without the compensating success. They are just bursting with bon-homie and grinning from ear to ear.

('The book' in the first sentence is Evelyn's scrap book; the reference to the 4th Canadian Division being 'stone cold' is army jargon, in this context meaning 'tired out'; 'our one and only Dump' is Walter Denison, his Canadian ADC. The letter is particularly interesting as the only one from Julian to his wife known to exist, even in the form of this extract which Evelyn gave to Lady Perley, wife of the Canadian Overseas Minister in London, who sent it to Sir Robert Borden.)[20]

Indisputably Vimy was a great and striking victory for Byng and his Canadians. On a four-mile frontage they had taken what the Germans

165

regarded as an impregnable position, over-running it from its front-line trenches to its supporting artillery positions in a single day. They had then gone on to advance for almost a further five miles. The Corps had inflicted heavy casualties on the Germans including the capture of more than 4,000 prisoners and had seized large quantities of stores and equipment, including 54 guns, 104 trench mortars and 124 machine-guns. The cost had been 10,602 casualties, of whom 3,598 had been killed.

To the south the Third Army had won a significant success on the 9th but then bogged down. Later in the month Nivelle's great offensive ended in a débâcle. In the circumstances the Canadian success at Vimy stood out brightly in a scene of unrelieved gloom.

Congratulations poured in to Byng's headquarters from the King, the Commander-in-Chief, the Governor-General, and from across Canada. The French Press was full of praise and gratitude for 'Canada's Easter Gift to France'. Significantly, members of the French General Staff returned to the Ridge which had cost them so many lives to discover how it had been won.

The battle was and remains a classic example of the deliberate attack against a heavily defended position. The earlier history of the War abounds in examples of objectives being taken at great cost, only to be lost through failure to prepare for an enemy counter-stroke. Now an Allied force had shown that it could move 'readily from swift and sustained assault to aggressive and concerted defence'.

For the future a standard had been set in meticulous preparation, training and staff work, receptiveness to new techniques and tactical innovations which would have important results.

'The Byng Boys', as the Canadians were to call themselves until the end of the War, were justly proud of their achievement. No longer was that maddening deprecatory attitude of Canadians to their own kind to obscure the fact that as soldiers they were unexcelled. Their newly-won self-confidence gave them the will to be a Canadian as opposed to a British force. In British eyes, they had won the right to be trusted with an independent role.

Independence is not just a political fact but a state of mind. Few nations are totally free in the sense that they can do what they like without regard to reactions beyond their borders. Even the greatest powers are aware that they live in a world community. For every act they commit in defiance of the wishes of others, there are hundreds of instances of them shaping their policies to avoid offence or to gain approval. The bounds of their independence are limited to the extent to which they believe these constraints are necessary.

166

Before the First World War Canada was as independent of Britain as her people chose to be. Only two powers could affect the welfare of Canadians in any measurable degree – Britain and the United States. Both guaranteed Canada's independence and Britain stood ready to resist any serious attack from the United States. There was no perceived need for Canadians to be concerned with countries other than these two and they were content to leave their other international affairs to the British.

The only military threat to Canada was from the United States. The history of the preceding century, in which British troops had stood with Canadian militia in defeating invasions and raids, had proved it to be real. In its face, Canada had become a willing, albeit junior partner in the defence organization of the British Empire. But Canadians were not willing to pay the price in peacetime of having regular forces of a size which could produce generals and trained staffs. Britain was prepared to provide them and Canada was content to accept.

Now no longer was this true. By April, 1917, Byng had replaced most of the seconded British officers in the Corps with Canadians and had shown them at Vimy Ridge that they were competent to manage their own military affairs. The British Government and the Commander-in-Chief were witnesses. Later, when a Canadian commander protested at the way the Corps was to be employed, Haig grudgingly gave way. To him the Canadians seemed to be conducting themselves more as 'Allies' than as fellow-citizens of the Empire.

But it was not only the Canadian army which had won independence at the Battle of Vimy Ridge. For the first time Canada had performed a significant act of her own on the international stage. The world recognized it and henceforth would identify Canadians as a separate people. The vast country which spreads so wide between the Atlantic and Pacific was drawn together by a new feeling of nationhood. Her people saw now that an independent road had been opened to them and that the time had come for them to follow it.

Haig resumed his offensive on 23 April with a main attack by the Third and First Armies astride the Scarpe with the object of driving the Germans back to the Drocourt-Quéant Line. After hard fighting, the First Army succeeded in capturing Gavrelle on the Arras–Douai road. Five days later the attack was resumed with the 13th Corps charged with taking Oppy and the Canadian Corps Arleux.

In what the British official historian described as 'the only tangible success of the whole operation' three battalions of the 1st and one of the 2nd Canadian Division took the heavily defended village.

Five days later fresh brigades of the two divisions attacked the Méricourt-Oppy line at Fresnoy. The operation was part of a further major continuation of the Arras offensive involving the Fifth, Third and First Armies. Everywhere, except at Fresnoy, the British met with disaster. At the insistence of Gen Gough of Fifth Army, Haig altered zero hour for the attack from dawn to one hour earlier, in effect making the operation a night attack. There was inadequate time to prepare for the change; the troops were inexperienced in night operations and, in the event, on large stretches of the front they were silhouetted against the setting full moon. In many areas artillery preparation was inadequate and vigorous German counterattacks eradicated most of the small gains which were made.

At Fresnoy the Canadians were able to turn the changed zero hour to advantage. While the Germans were expecting an attack, they did not believe it would come before daylight. So swiftly did the assault fall upon them that the artillery defensive barrage which they put down within a minute of zero caused casualties only to the supporting companies. The darkness made their musketry ineffective.

Again careful rehearsals and the superior training and briefing of the Canadian junior officers and NCOs had its effect. In the dark they found their way through the gaps which had been blown in the German wire. Enemy strongpoints were outflanked and captured. Fresnoy and the German trenches beyond were taken. Only on the left were the Canadians halted by new barbed wire and heavy enfilade fire.

Determined German counterattacks during the morning and afternoon were defeated by machine-gun and rifle fire, supported by accurate artillery barrages.

The British Official History commented:

> The capture of Fresnoy was the culminating point of the brilliant series of successes by the Canadian Corps during the Arras battles, and the relieving feature of a day which many who witnessed it consider the blackest of the War.[21]

These were the last significant operations conducted by the Canadian Corps under Byng's command. On 6 June he wrote to Evelyn: 'the dreaded blow has fallen'. Twice Douglas Haig tried to remove him to take command of an army but he had managed to evade the attempts. Now he received a peremptory order to hand over the Corps within three days and take command of the Third Army.

He was glad that there was so little time to visit his regiments to say farewell. He wished only to slip away as quietly as possible to avoid the emotional strain of saying goodbye, which he feared he could not hide. Major-Gen Sir Arthur Currie was to replace him and for this Byng was grateful. The burly commander of the 1st Canadian Division had already proved his quality as a soldier.

Gen A. G. L. McNaughton summed up the feelings of Canadian soldiers toward Byng when he spoke of him as the 'wonderful commander who did so much to establish our identity, our unity of purpose and our general attitude towards life and our mission in it. He was in fact literally adored by all the Canadians who were in France.'

On 9 June, 1917, Lt T. A. Rowatt of the 38th Battalion wrote to his parents:

Yesterday we went out to see Sir Julian Byng . . . and to hear him say goodbye to our Division. He has been promoted from a Corps to an Army Commander. He was greatly affected with emotion and only said a few words among which were that we had gained his promotion for him and that he would never forget it as long as he lived. He said the last year (during which he was Canadian Corps Commander) was the happiest of his life, if any year could be happy during the war; he wished us all goodbye; good luck; a speedy termination of the war and all success and happiness afterward. It was a dramatic sight to see the scene in front of an old château on the lawn completely surrounded by trees, the officers drawn up in two double lines on either side. He came in quietly, walked up between the two lines, turned about and faced the château and without looking at anyone started to speak. It appeared he was afraid to look at anyone lest he become overwhelmed with emotion. After he had spoken, he walked away alone, head down and everyone could only stand and stare until one of the other Generals walked off with him. Then we all ran around to a road leading from the château to cheer him as he passed. He is a wonderfully solid looking man, with, I should say, a rather large head, not tall, but rather stocky looking. Simple, unaffected and of course, sad looking and mannered as was natural. He said when he started to speak that he had come to honour the saddest and hardest thing he had ever done.

The scene at headquarters of the 1st Division was recalled by Canon Scott, its senior chaplain:

I shall never forget his farewell to the 1st Canadian Division at Château D'Acq, near Villers aux Bois. We were told one morning that General Byng was coming to say goodbye. With Gen Currie in the centre, we stood in a semi-circle in front of the door. General Byng drove up and, getting out of his car, he came forward with evident deep emotion and said, 'Gentlemen, I have just been offered the exalted position of Army Commander of the Third British Army in the field. It is an honour which I have never expected. I have not come to say goodbye. I do not want to do that for the honour has been won for me by you and I have come to say thank you.' He then shook hands with us all in silence, and we all felt so deeply the separation from our gallant Corps Commander that nobody could raise a cheer, and we watched him drive away in silence.[22]

Chapter 10
Cambrai

TOWARD THE END of June Evelyn Byng accompanied Princess Alice on a visit to the King and Queen of the Belgians at La Panne, in the small strip of their kingdom which still remained in their hands. The two ugly little villas which they occupied on the seashore were not far from the front line and an occasional shell burst on the beach or splashed into the sea nearby. The Earl of Athlone, husband of Princess Alice, had been there since 1914 as British Liaison Officer to the Belgian Army.[1]

On 5 July, 1917, a luncheon party was given by the King and Queen of the Belgians for King George V, which was attended by the Prince of Wales, the Athlones, Gen Sir Henry Rawlinson and Lady Byng.[2] Julian had been invited as well.

> 'I hadn't said a word to my lord and master that I was going to Belgium, because I guessed there would be a song and dance, as he might think it risky and when he heard, from the King's invitation and my covering letter, that I was there, I received a furious reply, saying nothing would induce him to come to La Panne. It was exasperating to know he was so near, in some ways, but sticking his toes in out of sheer cussedness! But it was very like him.'[3]

Byng that day had more serious matters in mind for on it his front was widened to include that covered previously by Rawlinson's Fourth Army. With five corps under command, he would now hold the right of the British line from its junction with the French near St Quentin to Arras forty miles to the north. On 7 July the ration strength of the enlarged Third Army was 629,408 men and 161,532 horses.

For twenty miles behind his position lay an area of complete devastation. In March, when, to shorten their front, the Germans withdrew to the Hindenburg Line, they laid waste the ground which

171

they abandoned. War material was removed, towns and villages were evacuated and razed, wells filled in or polluted, roads and bridges cratered and demolished. A tremendous amount of work would be needed to develop adequate communications and installations for the needs of the Army.

British operations in the summer and early autumn of 1917 were dominated by Haig's offensive in the Ypres area, remembered now as 'Passchendaele'. Its primary aim was to recover the Belgian channel ports, but of equal importance was its other purpose of taking the weight of the German Army from Britain's allies.

Byng's Third Army on the southern flank was not directly involved but of the sixty divisions in the BEF all but nine took their turn in the battle. When they were so exhausted and depleted that they could do no more, they were, if they were lucky, sent to a quieter sector to recover their strength. Most of Byng's divisions took their turn in Flanders, having previously been through the Arras battles.

Opposite them, manning the formidable defences of the Hindenburg Line, most of the German divisions had also suffered at Ypres and were recuperating in the 'Flanders sanatorium', as they called this part of the front.

There is a fine line between resting troops and letting them lapse into a live-and-let-live philosophy which saps their morale and renders them vulnerable to surprise. At a conference at 6th Division's HQ on 24 July at which Haig was present, Byng discussed the problem with his corps commanders. Haig noted in his diary

> Byng's policy is to encourage his men to make successful raids and so raise their morale and teach them how easy it is to enter the German trenches *if the operation is well thought out* and troops practised beforehand.

In effect he was introducing the Third Army to the practices which had proved so valuable in the Canadian Corps.

Within a few weeks the infantry's skill at raiding improved greatly and with it their confidence.[4] Visiting American generals were invited to watch an operation south-east of Monchy le Preux on 14 October. Safely positioned in a communication trench 700 yards to the flank, they saw three battalions – Norfolks, West Kents and East Surreys – block off sections of the German line with box barrages and seize sixty-four prisoners with little loss. They were much impressed.[5]

In taking over Rawlinson's line, Byng had inherited a proposal for an offensive near Cambrai. It's origin was an instruction issued by Haig on 25 April to the Fourth and Fifth Armies to devise a scheme for breaking the German defences south-west of that city. Subsequently

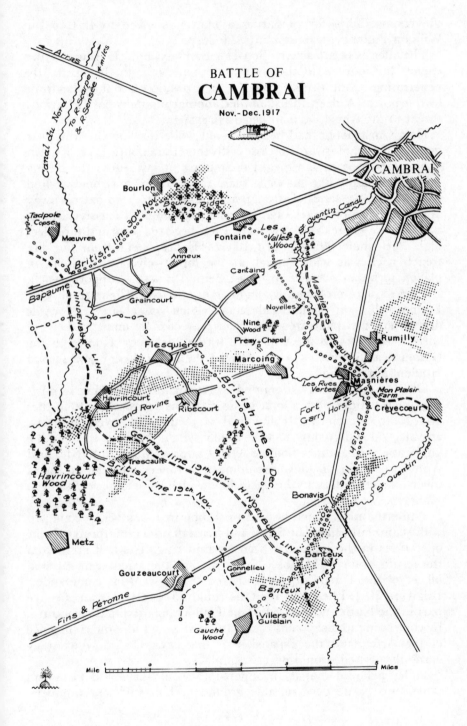

BATTLE OF
CAMBRAI
Nov.-Dec.1917

Arras

Canal du Nord

To R. Scarpe
& R. Sensée

4 miles

Tadpole Copse

Moeuvres

Bourlon

Bourlon Ridge

British line 30th Nov.

Anneux

Fontaine

Les Valles Wood

St Quentin Canal

CAMBRAI

Bapaume

HINDENBURG LINE

Graincourt

Cantaing

Noyelles

Nine Wood

Premy Chapel

Masnières – Beaurevoir

Rumilly

Flesquières

Marcoing

Les Rues Vertes

Masnières

Mon Plaisir Farm

Havrincourt

Grand Ravine

Ribecourt

German line 19th Nov.

British line 6th Dec.

Fort Garry Horse

Crèvecoeur

HINDENBURG LINE

Trescault

British line 19th Nov.

Bonavis

British line

St Quentin Canal

Havrincourt Wood

Metz

Gouzeaucourt

Gonnelieu

Banteux

Banteux Ravine

Fins & Péronne

Villers Guislain

Gauche Wood

Mile   1   0   1   2   3   4   5   Miles

the responsibility for preparing a plan was given to Lt-Gen Sir William Pulteney, commanding 3rd Corps.

The idea was attractive. Between Banteux and Havrincourt the enemy line curved to the west and then again to the north. By penetrating it, the British would be in a position to roll up his front to the north. A deep thrust beyond Cambrai would pose a serious threat to the whole German defensive system.

Haig's instruction had been received while the Fourth Army was fighting its way forward to close with the Hindenburg Line. Known to the Germans as the Siegfried Stellung, it lay across the rolling green downland like an ugly scar. Covered by a strongly wired outpost zone – a series of strongpoints designed to keep patrols away and slow a major attack – its front line lay behind a massive area of barbed wire – four to six rows of it, each 12 yards wide and three feet high, the whole filling a belt 100 yards deep. The front line fire trench itself was wide enough at the top, twelve feet or more in places, to be an obstacle to tanks. Behind it was a support trench, similar in size, protected by another hundred-yard barrier of wire. Forming the rear of the battle zone, which was about 2,500 yards deep, were two more trenches, each protected by immense belts of wire. Two miles to the rear were further defences. Known to the Germans as Siegfried II, they formed the forward edge of a second Hindenburg position.

On 19 June Pulteney submitted a plan for taking the Havrincourt-Flesquières Ridge with a force of six divisions as a prelude to further attacks to the north. It involved a methodical, even leisurely, advance – slow-but-sure tactics which would convert the smiling landscape into another Somme. GHQ approved and ordered Third Army to begin making preliminary arrangements for it as a diversion, subsidiary to the operations which were about to begin in Flanders.

While the plan which he had thus inherited was being examined with scant enthusiasm by Byng and his staff, two other proposals for operations in the same area were germinating. The first grew from the fertile brain of Lt-Col J. F. C. Fuller, the senior general staff officer of the Tank Corps. He shared the view of his commander, Brig-Gen H. J. Elles, that the tank could no longer play an effective part in the battles now mired in the Flanders plain. On the contrary, by continuing to disappoint the infantry, it would lose the confidence of the Army and the expansion of the Tank Corps, which they earnestly desired, would never take place.

Fuller believed that if an opportunity could be found to launch tanks into battle over suitable ground and in sufficient numbers, they would do so much damage to the enemy that their position as a fighting arm would be established beyond doubt.

On 4 August he drafted a proposal for an attack in the area south of Cambrai and Elles took it to GHQ. Major-Gen Davidson, the head of Haig's operations section, liked it but thought that Kiggell, the Chief of the General Staff, would not support it. Fearing that this would be the end of the matter, Fuller arranged for the scheme to be shown to Byng. It won his enthusiastic support.

Next day Byng went to GHQ to see the Commander-in-Chief to whom he suggested a tank attack south of Cambrai for 20 September. Later he recalled:

Sir Douglas Haig was much taken with the idea and was backed up by General Davidson. Then Kiggell came in and, when he heard of the project, he shook his head and said: 'The British Army cannot win a decisive battle by fighting in two places at once; we must concentrate every man in the Ypres area.'

The project was not approved.[6]

Closer to the eventual scene of the battle, Lt-Gen Sir Charles Woollcombe, commanding 4th Corps, was looking for ways to harry the enemy. A proposal for a major trench raid by the 9th (Scottish) Division had been discarded because of the difficulty of achieving surprise, but the project had prompted Brig-Gen H. H. Tudor, the commander of its divisional artillery, to study other possibilities.

In the past it had been virtually impossible to conceal from the enemy the concentration of artillery necessary for a major attack. Guns could only be certain of neutralizing a target if they had ranged on it beforehand. Inevitably this 'registration' warned the enemy that something was afoot. But by combining the skills of the surveyor with accurate maps and good gunnery it was possible to lay a gun on a distant unseen target with reasonable certainty of hitting it. The technique, though proven, had never been used on a large scale.

Tudor now suggested assaulting the Hindenburg defences in an entirely new way. Tanks, covered by smoke, would break a way through the wire for the infantry, who would be supported by artillery barrages. But because of 'silent registration' no gun would fire before zero hour. Surprise would be complete.

Tudor's plan was to seize the Flesquières Ridge first. Then the attacking force would swing to the left and roll up the German line to the Scarpe, between Arras and Douai to the north, while cavalry operated toward Cambrai. Woollcombe reduced its scope to little

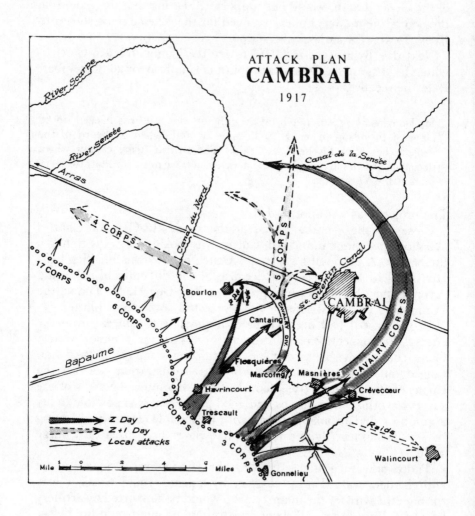

ATTACK PLAN
CAMBRAI
1917

River Scarpe

River Sensée

Canal de la Sensée

Arras

Canal du Nord

4 CORPS

17 CORPS

6 CORPS

5 CORPS

St. Quentin Canal

Bourlon

1st CAVALRY DIV.

CAMBRAI

Cantaing

CAVALRY CORPS

Bapaume

Flesquières

Marcoing

Masnières

Crèvecœur

Havrincourt

4 CORPS

Trescault

Z Day
Z+1 Day
Local attacks

3 CORPS

Raids

Walincourt

Mile 1 0   2   4   6 Miles

Gonnelieu

13. Brigadier-General commanding 1st Cavalry Brigade, Aldershot, 1907.
— P. A. de Laszlo.

14. Suvla Bay – Lala Baba, the hill which sheltered three divisional headquarters, three artillery brigades and several battalions of infantry. Troops on the beach are the Scottish Horse who have just landed, 3 September 1915. The beach was under shell fire and casualties soon occurred. *(Imperial War Museum)*

15. Drying blankets at Suvla after the storm at the end of November 1915. *(Imperial War Museum)*

16. Being welcomed aboard HMS *Cornwallis*, the last ship to leave Suvla Bay. Behind Byng is his ADC Basil Brooke. *(Imperial War Museum)*

17. The Somme—49th Battalion (Edmonton Regiment) going over the top near Courcelette, October 1916. *(Public Archives Canada)*

18. *(above)* Canadian infantry advancing during the Battle of Vimy Ridge –
9 April 1917. *(Public Archives Canada)*

19. *(below)* Battle of Vimy Ridge – Germans surrendering. *(Public Archives
Canada)*

20. Canadians on the Ridge looking east over the town of Vimy and the Douai plain. *(Imperial War Museum)*

21. Sir Arthur Currie who succeeded Byng in command of the Canadian Corps. *(Imperial War Museum)*

22. Belts of wire protecting the Hindenburg defences near Cambrai. *(Imperial War Museum)*

23. Rehearsal for Cambrai – a tank of F Battalion, Tank Corps at Wailly, 21 October 1917. *(Imperial War Museum)*

24. After Cambrai, B Squadron Fort Garry Horse led by Lieutenant Harcus Strachan who won the VC in the action. (*Public Archives Canada*)

25. The Prince of Wales, the Earl of Athlone, Byng and King George V with a German helmet on Thiepval Ridge, scene of some of the bloodiest fighting of the Somme battles. (*Imperial War Museum*)

26. The ramshackle train which served as Byng's advanced headquarters in the final months of the War. (*Imperial War Museum*)

27. General Sir Henry Rawlinson, Byng, Field-Marshal Sir Douglas Haig. General Sir Henry Horne, Lieut.-General Lawrence and General Sir William Birdwood—Cambrai, 31 October 1918. (*Imperial War Museum*)

more than the seizure of the Hindenburg system between the Canal du Nord and the St Quentin Canal. He forwarded it to Byng on 23 August.

The possibilities offered by the new tactical methods and the firm rolling downlands of the battle area caught Byng's imagination. The German garrison in the immediate area amounted to no more than two divisions which could not be significantly reinforced for forty-eight hours. If surprise were complete and the advance swift it might be possible at last to unleash a large force of cavalry into the enemy rear areas and gain a spectacular success.

After consultations on the ground with Elles of the Tank Corps, he put his ideas to Haig who was favourably impressed. 'But the fact remained that at this time it did not seem possible that our Army could undertake this; the difficulties of railway transport, and everything of that sort, seemed so great that it was almost decided not to attempt it. However, the Commander-in-Chief told us to think it out and carry on with what few preparations we could make. And we did so.'[7]

On 16 September Byng again saw Haig with his detailed plans. The Commander-in-Chief approved them, promised all possible help and agreed to give him the Canadian Corps for the operation. It was still not possible to fix the date for it because of the demands of the armies near Ypres.

Early in October a decision on the operation could be delayed no longer. The Canadian Corps was put under command of Third Army, but thirty-six hours later was ordered north to Passchendaele. On the 15th Haig again went through Byng's plans with him and arranged for other troops to take part. 'I promised before the operation is launched to concentrate a reserve, if possible Cavan's 14th Corps, including the Guards.'[8] Seven divisions, three brigades of tanks and the entire Cavalry Corps would be available for the attack. On 26 October Byng briefed his Corps commanders on the plan of battle.

It is as well to remember that the operation was still seen as a diversion, subsidiary to the operations in Flanders.

The characteristics of a 'diversion' were well understood in the Army. In this context it meant an attack of sufficient power and tactical importance to attract enemy reserves and even to draw away some of his troops from the primary front in the north. Anything less would not 'divert' the enemy. Byng makes the point clear in a lecture on the battle which he gave to Canadian officers on 26 February, 1918.

It followed, as Byng also pointed out, that 'to achieve any success at all . . . the battle should be going on in the North.'

As he saw it, there were three possibilities of creating a diversion. The first would have an unlimited objective – to break through the

177

enemy lines and cut their communications north and north-east of Cambrai; the second, to take and hold the Hindenburg Support Line; the third, to carry out a major raid to destroy enemy troops and equipment.

Since the tactics he was to employ had never been used before, there was an element of the experiment in the operation. If they proved to be as successful as Byng hoped, the first option, the unlimited objective, would be possible. If not, they would probably result in the capture of the Hindenburg Support Line. At worst, the requirements of the third option would be met.

Boldness, surprise and speed – the watchwords of the attack – are not inspired by equivocal orders. There was no hint in those of Third Army that anything less was contemplated than the seizure of Cambrai, Bourlon Wood and the crossings over the Sensée River, some six miles to the north, together with the destruction of the German divisions holding the line between the river and Havrincourt.

The operation would be divided into three stages. In the first, seven divisions of the 3rd and 4th Corps, with three brigades of tanks, would break through the German prepared defences (the Hindenburg Line), capture the crossings over the St Quentin Canal at Masnières and Marcoing, and gap the Masnières-Beaurevoir line to the east. Then the Cavalry Corps would pass through the infantry, advance around the east side of Cambrai and seize the crossings of the Sensée. At the same time 4th Corps would capture Bourlon Wood. In the third phase, Cambrai and the quadrilateral bounded by the St Quentin Canal, the Sensée River and the Canal du Nord would be cleared and the German divisions in the area to the west of the quadrilateral would be destroyed.

3rd Corps was ordered to establish defences to protect the southern flank of the penetration along the Gonnelieu-Bonavis-Crèvecoeur Ridge and to widen the breach by raiding towards Walincourt, five miles to the south-east. After taking Bourlon Wood on the first day, 4th Corps was to attack the rear of the enemy facing 6th and 17th Corps. 5th Corps, with its three divisions initially in reserve, would be prepared to advance north and north-east to exploit as far as the River Sensée, relieve the cavalry thereon and seize the heights beyond.

The concept was bold and, as with that for the attack on Vimy Ridge, its success depended on meticulous preparation. Again Byng was to surprise those who had no experience of his drive and attention to detail. Every aspect of the operation was analysed, and its problems isolated. Then, until solutions were found, Byng encouraged, prompted and sometimes drove his staff and subordinate commanders. The operation of tanks was one of the first subjects to take his attention.

178

The tanks of November, 1917, differed only in detail from those first used on the Somme, the most significant being that the armour was now thick enough to keep out armour-piercing bullets. To those familiar with modern versions, the first sight of a Mark IV Tank leaves an impression of immense size and awkwardness. At best its top speed was less than four miles per hour; crossing a battlefield, it scarcely seemed to be moving. There were two types, similar in every way except for their armament. The Mark IV Male tank was armed with two six-pounder guns mounted in sponsons on either side of the vehicle, and four Lewis light machine-guns. The Female was equipped with six Lewises, four being mounted in the side sponsons. Inside, the huge engine, with walkways around it, occupied the centre of the compartment. In the bow sat the driver and the commander, who controlled the brakes. Two men operated the gears, and four the armament. The tank, when moving with its engine barely ticking over, was remarkably silent, but at normal operating speed the noise inside was deafening. Communication was by hand signal, often difficult to see in the dim light. There were no ventilating fans, no suspension springs and the visibility through aiming slits and elementary periscopes was limited. The inside temperature often rose to well over 100°F.

The crews were far from invulnerable to enemy fire. The 12 mm of armour plate gave no protection against a direct hit from an artillery shell and when its rivetted joints were hit by rifle or machine-gun bullets, molten metal penetrated. To reduce casualties from the slivers of lead – 'bullet splash' – the crews were equipped with helmets with chain-mail face-masks. Uniforms of crews emerging from battle were often as soaked with blood as they were with sweat.

Based on the number of infantry brigades in the assault, Byng allotted the three tanks brigades. 3rd Corps was given two battalions for each of its three leading divisions, though it retained one company to assist the follow-up division, the 29th, in crossing the St Quentin Canal. In 4th Corps the nine companies of its tank brigade were divided between the two attacking divisions, five to the 51st, four to the 62nd.

The Tank Corps recommended that a reserve of two tank battalions be held to use in later stages of the operation but there were barely enough to ensure the passage of the infantry through the wire. To find two battalions it would have been necessary to remove a division from the assault, dangerously narrowing the frontage.

With the exception of vehicles with special tasks such as supply tanks, all were to be employed in the assault to make paths for the infantry through the enormous belts of wire which protected the Hindenburg positions. Their tracks could each crush a passage about

179

two feet in width. To cross the 12-foot-wide trenches of the system most machines carried a fascine, an enormous bundle of brushwood compressed to a diameter of $4\frac{1}{2}$ feet by chains wound round it and then pulled in opposite directions by two tanks. When a trench too wide to cross was reached, a tank would tip its fascine into it to form a partial bridge over which it and the others would pass.

Detailed drills were prepared to enable infantry to work closely with them. As at Vimy, full-scale sections of the enemy positions were laid out on the ground over which units rehearsed their attacks. Frequently Byng was present at these, sometimes in the company of the Commander-in-Chief.

The elimination from the plan of an artillery bombardment of the German positions implied that there would also be no preliminary destruction of the enemy's batteries. Some would be engaged at zero hour by heavy guns and others by ground attack aircraft, for an unprecedented effort was to be made by the Royal Flying Corps.

Byng's orders to the RFC provided for reconnaissance of the approaches to the battle area, the bombing of enemy airfields and headquarters and the interdiction of the battlefield by attacks on specified railway junctions. As many squadrons as possible were to strafe selected artillery batteries and troops and transport beyond the range of his guns. They make familiar reading to veterans of the Second World War.

To improve cooperation between the Army and the RFC, he established ground liaison sections at the corps squadrons.

There was much justification for the Flying Corps feeling that they were not understood or appreciated by the rest of the army. Many senior officers viewed them with suspicion and regarded their officers as 'not quite top drawer'. Worse, generals seemed to make little effort to learn what aircraft could or could not do to help them.

To what extent Byng was aware of the situation is not known, but when he moved from the Canadian Corps to Third Army, he brought with him an ADC from the Royal Flying Corps – Arthur Brooke, Basil's younger brother. He had become a flight commander in No 6 Squadron, had been wounded and would not be able to fly for some months. He was one of the most promising officers of the RFC and later had a distinguished career in the RAF.

So unusual was his attachment that for months neither the RFC nor the Army would pay him. Fortunately his bank kept him in funds.

Through him Byng learned much about life in RFC squadrons and the attitudes of airmen. There can be little doubt that when he visited them, as he often did, Brooke's presence on his staff would be seen as a sympathetic gesture to the RFC.[9]

180

While Byng's tactics would make it possible to deceive the Germans as to the time of the attack, knowledge of the concentration of a large force on their front would put them on their guard and prompt them to reinforce it. Byng was determined to deny them any clue of what was in prospect. His orders were comprehensive.

Tank Corps officers visiting the area were to come disguised by badges of other arms. When their headquarters opened at Albert, it was to be as a new school for infantry-tank cooperation. False rumours were to be spread and no one was to be told of the intention to attack until it was necessary to do so.

Artillery positions and hides for the tanks were to be carefully reconnoitred and camouflaged before they were occupied. All movement was to be at night and the routine of patrolling, air activity and artillery harrassing fire was to be kept at the level of the past few months. Not a gun would fire from the new positions until zero hour and no fires would be allowed at night.

On the evening of 26 October, following Byng's briefing of his Corps commanders, Haig received orders from the War Office to send troops to Italy whose collapse seemed imminent after their disaster at Caporetto. Two divisions were to go at once. With them went Cavan, under whom Haig had hoped to concentrate a reserve to support Byng. A few days later more divisions and artillery were warned to leave and on 10 November there was a forecast of yet further demands.

In Haig's opinion the Italians could be better helped by renewed attacks in the West. He sent Kiggell to London to beg the Prime Minister that three divisions destined for Italy be left for the battle in which case he was confident of a really big success. Lloyd George replied that he had heard enough prophecies of big successes and insisted that the divisions should go.[10]

On 12 November Haig told his CGS to halt the Ypres offensives, except for bombardments, for another fortnight, but that the Cambrai attack must take place, otherwise the Germans, protected by the Hindenburg Line, could gather enough troops to attack the French.[11]

The strategic aim of the Cambrai offensive had thus been altered from a diversion subsidiary to Haig's northern battles to one which would prevent the Germans from concentrating to attack the French and which might help the Italians.

From the time Byng had first prepared his plans, other significant changes had taken place. In September GHQ had had reserves of fresh troops who could exploit success; now these had been worn out at Passchendaele or sent to Italy. Instead of the fresh and powerful

181

Canadian Corps to spearhead the attack, most of his divisions would be ones which had suffered heavy losses and only recently been restored to strength with inexperienced junior officers and men. As autumn advanced, the hours of daylight were becoming dangerously short for the work which was to be done on the first day. Now the operations at Ypres would almost cease, relaxing the demands on German reserves which were being increased with divisions freed by the collapse of Russia.

None of these facts would prejudice the attack as a diversion, though they might limit its prospects for tactical gains.

During the preparation of the plan Byng had discussed its details on several occasions with the Commander-in-Chief. In its final form it incorporated many of Haig's suggestions, about two of which he was insistent. He considered that possession of Bourlon Wood and the ridge on which it stood would enable the British to dominate the ground beyond and might cause the Germans to abandon their defences almost as far north as Arras. It must be taken on the first day. The outflanking of Cambrai was of secondary importance and should be looked upon as providing flank protection to the Bourlon operation, but at least one cavalry division must be across the St Quentin Canal and through the Masnières-Marcoing gap on Z day.

Because of poor routes forward Byng knew that, for the attack on Bourlon Wood, it would not be possible, in the short time which Haig's strictures allowed, to pass a new division through the troops which had taken the Hindenburg Line. It would have to be captured by the assaulting infantry of 4th Corps. Byng told Haig that he was doubtful that this was realistic because of the inevitable exhaustion which would follow on a sleepless night and the subsequent attack, but the Commander-in-Chief was adamant.

No reserves beyond those already provided for the attack would now be available. Haig told Byng that he would stop the offensive after the first forty-eight hours, or even earlier, if a significant success was not achieved.

There was thus no question in the minds of either Haig or Byng of the attack being pressed home at all costs. If the assault was as successful as they hoped, there was provision for exploitation, but not for a sustained offensive.

On 1 November Haig had informed Pétain of the proposed operation. The French commander was keen to take part by attacking through the gap created by the British and rolling up the German line to the south. In the event the French did not participate in the battle but provision for them to do so resulted in the 29th and 20th Divisions receiving an order more than two hours after zero hour to secure a bridgehead at Crèvecoeur as soon as the second objective was captured.

On the 19th the Commander-in-Chief moved from Montreuil to the GHQ Advanced Operations Centre at Bavincourt (ten miles south-west of Arras) to be closer to Byng at Albert. He remained there until 3 December.

From the outset luck seemed to side with the British. Byng's careful preparations were shrouded by fog and, for ten days before the attack, no German air reconnaissance was possible.

On 18 November the enemy learned from prisoners taken in a raid on the 36th Division that an attack was in preparation in the Havrincourt area and their observers detected some unusual activity on the British side, but they took little action. Their 54th Division's troops were placed on alert but no special measures were taken by the 20th Landwehr Division on the right or the 9th Reserve Division on the left.

The Cambrai sector was defended by the 13th Corps (usually referred to as the 'Caudry Group') commanded by Gen Freiherr von Watter – by coincidence the same commander who had attacked the Canadians at Mount Sorrel in June, 1916. That battle had seen Byng's first corps attack. Now Watter was to meet the first assault launched by Byng as an army commander. His corps was part of Gen von der Marwitz's Second Army, the left formation of Rupprecht's Army Group.

On 18 November Rupprecht had told OHL, 'The British having failed in Flanders, partial attacks may be expected on other parts of the Front.'

Next day, unknown to the British, the 107th Division from Russia began to arrive in Cambrai, preparatory to relieving the 20th Landwehr on the 25th.

As night fell on 19 November the Army began to form up for battle. Tanks crawled out of their hiding places and, with engines barely ticking over, crept towards their forming-up line, 1,000 yards from the enemy. Progress was slow but so silent that from 200 yards it was impossible to hear them. Tapes laid on the ground guided both them and the infantry to their meeting places.

Three divisions of the Cavalry Corps began to move forward shortly after midnight and had arrived in their assembly areas about dawn. Two of them, the 2nd and 5th, would wait there ready to break out across the St Quentin Canal; the 1st would be under the command of 4th Corps.

About 4 am German artillery began firing on the Havrincourt front and there were fears that the assembly of troops had been detected. But by 5.30 all was quiet. Seven divisions, 1003 guns, 324 tanks and more than 300 aircraft were about to be launched at the enemy.

Battle of Cambrai – November, 1917
Tanks and Aircraft

Tank Corps

Three brigades of three battalions each of 36 tanks (MK IV) – total	324
Operational spares – 6 with each battalion	54
Supply tanks	54
Tanks with wire pulling grapnels to work with cavalry	32
Bridge carriers, to follow cavalry	2
Wireless carriers	9
Telephone cable carriers	1
	476 tanks

Royal Flying Corps

Six corps squadrons	125
Seven fighter squadrons	134
One fighter reconnaissance squadron	18
Two flights, day bombers	12
	289 aircraft

Additional on Z day, one GHQ squadron and an unspecified number of fighter squadrons from First Army.

While they waited, chilled by the cold mist of the late November night, an unfamiliar feeling of suspense gripped the soldiers of the Third Army. By this time in other battles the earth would be shaking with the violence of a bombardment, its noise driving coherent thought from the brain. But now all was silence. Everyone knew the importance of secrecy and the price of discovery. As the long minutes passed, the risk of that diminished and allowed thoughts to dwell on the novelty of the plan. Would the new methods really work or would the battle in front of Cambrai be another bloody shambles?

Few of the infantry had ever been so well briefed and rehearsed for a battle. Having seen what the tanks could do, they were confident, but their feelings could hardly match the optimism and excitement of the men of the Tank Corps.

For the first time they would be entering a battle in which theirs was a decisive role. Inspired by their commander, they knew that they would succeed. The day before he had sent them this special order:

1. Tomorrow the Tank Corps will have the chance for which it has been waiting for many months – to operate on good going in the van of the battle.
2. All that hard work and ingenuity can achieve has been done in the way of preparation.
3. It remains for unit commanders and for tank crews to complete the work by judgement and pluck in the battle itself.

4. In the light of past experience I leave the good name of the Corps with great confidence in their hands.
5. I propose leading the attack of the Centre division.

Hugh Elles

B G

Commanding Tank Corps

19 Nov. 1917

Riding in a tank close to Elles would be Basil Brooke, sent by Byng to bring him an early first-hand report – the first use of a personal liaison officer by an army commander in an armoured battle.[12]

It was still dark when, at 6.10 am, the engines of the tanks roared into life and they began to advance. Few Germans heard them amid the noise of British aircraft flying low over the lines. For ten minutes the ungainly vehicles clattered forward. As they crossed the front-line trenches, followed by the infantry, the first light of dawn began to glow and at the same moment, with a deafening roar, the thousand guns of the Army's artillery opened fire. Even where the Germans thought an attack might be coming, none had imagined the violence and precision of this storm of fire or the fear which grew in the face of the inexorable advance of the monsters looming up through the smoke and mist.

Some brave men stayed to fight but most of the defenders of the outpost zone surrendered or fled. Along the whole front the advance went on with scarcely a check through the two trenches of the German front-line system. In most cases the enemy's defensive barrages were weak and fell behind the advancing British. Strongpoints which had not been shelled held out briefly until the infantry and tanks could organize an attack, but first objectives were reached on time. There, after a short pause, the advance resumed across the 'Battle Zone' towards the wire and trench lines of the Hindenburg Support position. There were delays in Havrincourt and Ribécourt, but by 11.30 3rd and 4th Corps had captured the entire outpost and battle zones and were beginning to over-run the battery positions in their rear – except at Flesquières.

Major-Gen G. M. Harper's 51st (Highland) Division had been given the task of advancing north-east between Ribécourt and Havrincourt to the road between Marcoing and Graincourt. From their start line in front of Trescault the ground sloped down behind the German front system to the misnamed Grand Ravine, then rose again to a crest line which lay across their line of advance. Beyond it on the reverse slope were the two trenches of the Hindenburg Support system.

The two leading brigades, Seaforths, Argylls, Black Watch and

185

Gordons, had reached their first objective, high on the slope across the Grand Ravine, with comparatively few casualties. On the left they had encountered some particularly cool German riflemen and machine-gunners who had taken cover until the foremost tanks had passed and had then opened fire on the advancing infantry. But these were soon bombed out of their positions.

The garrison of Flesquières came from the German 54th Division – about three battalions of infantry and two machine-gun companies. Close behind the village and the trenches of the support system were batteries of the division's field artillery regiment. The strength of the Hindenburg fortifications was enhanced by their location on the reverse slope, and by the robust buildings of the village and its château. But the true strength of any position is in its defenders and those of Flesquières were unique. Their divisional commander bore the same name as the Corps commander, Freiherr von Watter. From the first appearance of tanks at Flers-Courcelette, he had studied methods of combating them. His gunners were taught that, when tanks approached, they should haul their guns from their emplacements and engage them over open sights. During Nivelle's offensive in April their tactics and gunnery had defeated French tanks, and they were confident they could repeat their success.

Twenty-six tanks of E Battalion and ten of D Battalion of the Tank Corps were leading as four fresh battalions of Highlanders began to advance toward the second objective. On their right a Nieuport Scout came in low to silence a German machine-gun.

As the tanks reached the crest they were engaged at close range by the German gunners. Every tank leading the right-hand battalion was hit, some bursting into flames. The wire in front of the front trench remained uncut and, within minutes, the infantry were suffering heavy casualties from rifle and machine-gun fire.

To the left the tanks and infantry broke through the wire covering the first trench before the tanks came in view of the German guns. Soon more were ablaze. Not one penetrated the wire covering the second trench. Supported by fire from immobilized tanks, the Highlanders tried desperately to gain a foothold in Flesquières, but were driven back by the machine-guns of its determined defenders.

By 10.45 the 51st Division had been stopped, yet to observers in the rear the opposite seemed true. From across the Grand Ravine troops could be seen entering that part of the front trench which was in sight and prisoners were soon being brought back. It was over the crest and out of view that disaster had struck the tanks.

Setbacks in battle cast their peculiar spell of self-deception and error far to the rear and flanks. Gen Harper telephoned 4th Corps headquarters at about 11 am to report that Flesquières was taken and that 'the road from Trescault to that place was fit for cavalry'.[13]

4th Corps repeated the information to the 1st Cavalry Division (through HQ Cavalry Corps – there was no direct telephone line) with the instruction to 'push forward' through the second objective. The message added that they as yet had no information on the Ribécourt road.

Yet it was by the Ribécourt road that Major-Gen R. L. Mullens had been ordered to direct his 1st Cavalry Division towards Marcoing. Before reaching that town, they were to swing to the left around the east of Nine Wood, move up both sides of the St Quentin Canal, sweep around the villages of Noyelles, Cantaing and Fontaine and help the 51st Division to capture them. They were then to attack Bourlon village in cooperation with the 62nd Division.

Both Mullens and Kavanagh, GOC Cavalry Corps, interpreted the message as meaning 1st Cavalry Division was to advance via Flesquières, not Ribécourt, which was not what Woollcombe of 4th Corps had intended.

Mullens ordered his leading brigade, the 2nd, to move forward through Flesquières. Neither its commander nor the CO of the leading regiment were hard-driving, determined cavalry leaders, as events were now to prove. Delays mounted as they found it impossible to pass the village, wasted time in wondering what to do and eventually moved their axis of advance to the Ribécourt road. It was not until 2.15 that the brigade began to pass south of that village.

Only half an hour earlier had the commander of the 4th Corps learned that Flesquières had not been taken. The tanks which almost everywhere had had such success in leading the attack had also played havoc with communications. With a four-foot fascine adding to their height, they had destroyed poled telephone lines and their supply sledges had ripped up those laid on the ground. Mist and rain obscured visual signals. Runners and liaison officers were too slow.

The reports reaching Byng at his headquarters at Albert were of unblemished success, although his intelligence staff had received an unconfirmed report of the presence of two new divisions in the Cambrai area.

At noon Byng heard from 4th Corps that the second objective had been taken, that cavalry had crossed the old British front line at 11.15 and that the attack was progressing well. Reports from 3rd Corps were just as satisfactory and the Cavalry reported that they were advancing.

But during the afternoon, 4th Corps failed to take Flesquières while the leading troops of 1st Cavalry Division under its command ran into opposition. With darkness fell the last opportunity for them to outflank Bourlon on 20 November.

The opportunity for the full strength of the division to take part had passed much earlier by default, for its commander had never ordered its other two brigades to move forward from their concentration areas behind the old British line at Trescault and Metz. And no orders were given to the tank company allotted to support them, who were waiting near Marcoing, already briefed on the plan of advance and eager to take part.

On the right 3rd Corps' advance had gone well and by noon the 20th Division had battalions with tanks in Marcoing and Les Rues Vertes. At the former the bridge was intact but, at the latter, that over the Canal to Masnières had been damaged and when a tank attempted to cross the structure collapsed.

The 29th Division now advanced with the intention of crossing the Canal and breaching the Masnières – Beaurevoir line. Two battalions were soon across at Masnières, but the village was strongly held and progress was slow. A third battalion, 2nd Hampshires, probing to the east, found a lock in the Canal and began moving across the gates in single file under rifle and machine-gun fire. On the left the Royal Newfoundland Battalion had crossed west of the village and advanced up the spur toward Rumilly until they came in view of the Masnières – Beaurevoir line which appeared to be fully manned.

Meanwhile the 5th Cavalry Division, followed by the 2nd, was arriving at Marcoing and Les Rues Vertes. Leading on the right-hand route was the Canadian Cavalry Brigade. At 2 pm its commander, Brig-Gen J. E. B. Seely, met the brigadier of 88th Brigade who believed that his battalions with tanks already held Masnières. Seely ordered his leading regiment, the Fort Garry Horse, to cross and continue the advance.

As the Canadians rode in across the river bridge on the main street they could see that, beyond it, the one over the Canal was broken and that there were still enemy in Masnières. Looking for another crossing, the Garrys found the twin locks over the gates of which the Hampshires were filing. Projecting upstream from the island between the locks was a wooden pier. Tearing it up, they constructed a bridge suitable for horses and at 3.30 began to cross. At 4 pm B Squadron had assembled on the far side and set out through a gap cut in the enemy wire.

Capt Campbell, the squadron leader, was killed by machine-gun fire as they passed through and command passed to Lt Harcus Strachan, who led his troops at the gallop north toward Rumilly.

Shortly after 3 pm Major-Gen W. H. Greenly, commanding the

2nd Cavalry Division, rode into Les Rues Vertes and conferred with Seely and Brig-Gen Nelson of the 88th Brigade. Given the state of the crossings at Masnières and the few hours of daylight left, the prospects of a large-scale cavalry action seemed too unpromising to proceed. He ordered Seely to halt the advance and recall the men who were already over the Canal.

Neither Gen Nelson nor his brigade major, who should have known of its existence, told the cavalry of a wooden road bridge a mile to the south-east which led to Mon Plaisir farm.

Today that bridge has gone, but an elderly farmer who lived in the farm during the First World War told the author that it had not been removed until the autumn of 1918. 'It was a strong bridge and used to take heavy wagons.'

Lt-Col R. W. Patterson, commanding the Fort Garry Horse, crossed the makeshift bridge at the locks and rode after his squadron. Unable to find them himself, he sent mounted orderlies to recall them, but they failed.

South-east of Rumilly B Squadron was hotly engaged. Having come to a heavy camouflaged road and cut their way through, they saw a German field battery of four guns to their front. They charged, riding down or sabreing the gunners. Beyond, a body of infantry appeared and again Strachan and his men charged. The infantry broke and fled and the squadron continued toward Rumilly under fire. Some 1,200 yards east of the town they occupied a sunken road and remained there until after dark. Only five horses were unwounded and the squadron was reduced to less than fifty men. When it was obvious that they were not to be supported, Strachan ordered the horses to be stampeded and withdrew his men toward the original crossing place. Four separate bodies of German troops were encountered on the way back and were attacked and dispersed. Forty survivors, with eleven of their prisoners, eventually returned across the Canal.

On its left-hand route the 5th Cavalry Division was led by the 7th Dragoon Guards. When their leading squadron crossed the St Quentin Canal at Marcoing at 2 pm they were stopped by heavy machine-gun fire.

In an attempt to find another crossing, a second squadron of the 7th was sent north to Noyelles. Moving through the infantry holding Nine Wood, they galloped through the village, completely demoralizing the garrison by the surprise and speed of their advance. Securing some twenty-five prisoners, they went on towards Cambrai. The main bridge over river and canal had been destroyed, but they found and secured a crossing of wooden trestle bridges. Patrols discovered the enemy to be well entrenched across the Canal. Later the squadron was joined by infantry and, as darkness fell, they were ordered to withdraw and rejoin their regiment.

During the afternoon, on the left flank of the Army's attack, the 186th Brigade, commanded by Brig-Gen R. B. Bradford VC (aged 25, the youngest general in the British Army), had advanced up the east side of the Canal du Nord, clearing the trenches of the Hindenburg Support system. By nightfall they had crossed the Bapaume –Cambrai road, were in contact on their left with the 36th (Ulster) Division, who had cleared the west side of the Canal, and held Graincourt. From there the line of the 62nd Division ran south to join the 51st, halted in the Hindenburg position before Flesquières. From the right of the Highland Division the 6th Division's line ran forward to Premy Chapel where the 29th carried it on to Nine Wood and Noyelles and across the St Quentin Canal to Masnières. East of the village it crossed again to the western side. Before Crèvecoeur the line turned once more to the south, the 20th and 12th Divisions holding it along Bonavis Ridge to join the front line occupied before the attack at Gonnelieu.

On the flanks of the 3rd and 4th Corps Byng had used every available means to pin the Germans to their front and deceive them as to the area and size of the main assault. Bombardment, smoke screens, dummy tanks and local attacks were employed along his front, from the boundary with the French to that with the First Army north-east of Arras.

The Germans later acknowledged their complete surprise and their confusion and feeling of helplessness in the face of the initial assault, but they reacted with characteristic speed. By 8 am Ludendorff had learned by telephone as much as Second Army could tell him and had ordered three divisions from the north and south to converge on Cambrai. Closer to the scene, Crown Prince Rupprecht and his subordinate commanders despatched individual battalions by road and rail to the battle area. None came into action on the 20th but the door was beginning to close on the Third Army's attack.

That night it rained. Bourlon Wood and its ridge had not been taken nor had a division of cavalry crossed the St Quentin Canal. No gap existed between Marcoing and Masnières, but east, between that village and Crèvecoeur, unknown to the British, the defences of the Masnières – Beaurevoir line were still unmanned.

To Byng there were few options open. He could halt the operation and, having taken Flesquières, be content with holding the Hindenburg Support position, or he could continue with the original plan. It was just possible that a quick attack would take the Bourlon Ridge and open a gap for the cavalry to cross the St Quentin Canal before German reinforcements began to arrive in strength. He recommended the latter course when Haig visited him at his headquarters at 4.30 pm. The Commander-in-Chief approved, emphasizing that Bourlon Ridge should remain the main objective.

That evening orders were issued to 3rd Corps to open a gap for the cavalry between Marcoing and Crèvecoeur, to 4th Corps to take Flesquières before morning and to take Bourlon Ridge as soon as possible. The Cavalry Corps were to be prepared to carry out their original orders, as were 5th Corps, who were warned that they would not be required before noon next day.

Rain, mud and darkness made the reorganization for continuing the attack a slow and difficult process. Communications were tenuous at best, exact locations of units were not known and the divisional headquarters had little knowledge of the condition of their forward troops.

Before dawn the 51st Division discovered that Flesquières had been abandoned by the enemy. By 4 pm the 51st and 62nd Divisions had captured Cantaing, Fontaine and Anneux and tanks had penetrated into Bourlon Wood, which was heavily defended.

On the right flank no progress had been made at Marcoing and very little at Masnières. Crèvecoeur had not been taken.

By 5.15 pm the Commander-in-Chief was aware of the situation. He instructed Byng to make no further attempts to push the Cavalry Corps across the St Quentin Canal, but to make a major effort to capture Bourlon Ridge. It seemed so close. Possession of it would menace the German defences and communications to the north and north-west as far as the Sensée River; and it commanded the western approaches to Cambrai. The value of the prize was obvious to both sides.

It would not be long before German reinforcements would be on the scene in force. GHQ Intelligence reckoned, however, that for the moment the enemy was inclined to retire and that the fresh troops who had already arrived were insufficient to do more than replace his casualties. The three divisions of the 5th Corps had not yet been committed and the War Office had telegraphed approval for the retention of two divisions which had been destined for Italy. Furthermore 4th Corps could not simply halt and stay where it was, under close observation from the Ridge. Either it must take Bourlon or withdraw to a defensible position on the Flesquières Ridge.

Believing that the most effective help he could give his weakened Allies was to continue engaging the Germans in battle, Haig made up his mind that the attacks should go on. In doing so he committed the Third Army to the kind of battle which in the past Byng had tried so consistently to avoid.

191

Later that evening Byng telephoned orders to Woollcombe. The new attack should take place on 23 November when the 40th Division and tanks would be available. It should be preceded by a bombardment. While any opportunity to advance on the 22nd should be taken, the risk of heavy casualties was to be avoided.

Byng's orders to 3rd Corps were to select and prepare a strong defensive line overlooking the Canal crossings, as the ground beyond it might prove untenable in the face of a strong counterattack. Bridges should be prepared for demolition.

At nightfall on the first day of the battle, exhausted though they were, the men of the Tank Corps realized the success they had achieved. Hugh Elles had led the attack in the centre, standing in the roof hatch of 'Hilda' from which was flying a large Tank Corps flag. In front of Ribecourt his tank was ditched in the Hindenburg Line. He climbed out and was later seen walking along the trench pointing out targets for other tanks with his walking stick. Later he returned on foot to his headquarters. Fuller said that he came in elated, and well he might have been.

To the Intelligence staff at GHQ it was apparent from German wireless messages, intercepted during the first two days of the battle, that they were confused both as to the strength and direction of the British offensive. To keep them in the dark as long as possible, all press messages were held up. It was not until the morning of the 22nd that the world learned of the Third Army's success. For three years the British people had received little but depressing news of the War. Ypres, Loos, the Somme, Passchendaele – the names spoke of courage, sacrifice, sorrow and frustration, gains measured in yards, casualties by the hundred thousand. Even the Canadian triumph at Vimy had little impact on the British people, for it was but part of the Arras offensive, which had cost 159,000 casualties for a gain of a few miles.

Now there was success. On 20 November the Third Army had broken through the strongest defences on the Western Front, had advanced nearly five miles, capturing more than 4,000 prisoners and many guns for the cost of some 4,000 casualties. By the next evening the number of prisoners had almost doubled. The victory showed at last that skill and inventiveness could win battles and held out a hope that the War might yet be won.

Headlines in the papers spoke of 'The Greatest British Victory of the War', 'Great Battle for Cambrai', 'A Surprise for the Germans', 'Byng Strikes on the Right'.

On the 23rd church bells throughout the country rang a victory peal and Julian Byng became, in an instant, the hero of the Allies.

On 22 November the *Yorkshire Post* reported interviews with the first British wounded back in England from Cambrai:

> They speak with enthusiasm of the leadership of Sir Julian Byng, whom they described as one of the most popular of our Army commanders at the Front. One man of the West Riding Regiment declared that for days before the attack, Sir Julian had lived among the men who were to take part in it, inspiring them with his own confidence of success and impressing on them the fact that, in all that mattered, they were more than superior to the enemy.

The American Press, not content with the limitations of prose, broke into a rash of verse. The following was offered by *The Daily Kentucky New Era*:

Byng!
He is kin to Biff and Bang,
To Wallop, Whop and Wham!
And he smashed the Kaiser's fang,
Gosh Ding:
Oh, he's made the heavens sunny; He's the man for all our money,
Not a Hun but he's a honey,
General Byng!

Even the gentlemen's clubs in New York joined in the effusion of praise. The following was taken from the notice board of 'The Lambs' at 130 West 44th Street:

Cheer Boys Cheer
We sing,
Of Byng,
The Britisher who won his charge,
Without artillery or barrage,
With no attempt at camouflage,
With steady ranks, with sturdy 'tanks'
      He's gained the world's undying thanks.
His prowess flashes o'er the main
While Hohenzollern writhes with pain.
Onward in your victorious swing,
We drink to you, brave warrior Byng!
                Edward I. Kidder.

President Poincaré of France sent his congratulations to the King. The King sent his to the Army, followed by a personal message to Byng himself. A file at Third Army headquarters contained the congratulations of French, Canadian and Australian generals and every British army commander, except Hubert Gough.

A message which particularly appealed to Byng came from his old school:

> Eton filio gratulatur magister informatur –
> Alington

The former 'scug' replied:

> Etonae gratias matri almae ago floreat
> Etona. Pereant barbari – Byng.[14]

The words of praise and the events to which they referred had, by the third day, become history. The battle was now to be renewed on terms quite different from those which had obtained when the well-trained teams of tanks and infantry had been launched at the Hindenburg position two days earlier.

Ominously, German artillery fire from guns of all calibres was heavy on the 4th Corps front. During the morning German counterattacks succeeded in taking Fontaine and other forward positions. On the extreme left Tadpole Copse was taken by the British 56th Division, but elsewhere there were no gains.

At 5 pm Haig called on Byng at Albert. He was satisfied with the arrangements which were in hand for the major effort next day, but went on to say that every day's delay would make it harder to get Bourlon, and, in view of the need to send further resources to Italy, he 'could not continue a wasting fight'. He had with him a message from London approving of the exploitation of the success which had been achieved, but cautioning him to be prepared for further demands from Italy and on the 'very unsatisfactory manpower position'. The lack of replacements for the casualties already suffered that year had become one of Haig's greatest anxieties.

The attacks by 4th Corps next morning everywhere ran into more opposition than was expected. Desperate attempts by the 51st Division, supported by tanks, failed to re-take Fontaine. The 40th Division, operating with tanks for the first time, took Bourlon Wood, but were frustrated in their attempts to take the village. The 36th and 56th Divisions were able to make only limited advances.

In the air, too, the Germans had increased their efforts. Daily their attacks against the infantry had increased in face of mounting losses by the RFC. On the 23rd Third Army was allotted four fighter squadrons for close support of the infantry. Enemy batteries holding up tanks were silenced and strong points neutralized, but thirty percent of the British aircraft involved were lost.

Throughout the day the information received at Third Army headquarters indicated that a considerable success had been achieved. At 2.05 pm Byng told Woollcombe that, if fresh troops were needed to tip the scale, he might use the 1st Cavalry Division dismounted and that another cavalry division would be provided to take its place. At 2.30 he told Kavanagh that the latest reports from the RFC indicated that Bourlon Wood had been captured. He should get in touch personally with Woollcombe to concert measures in case an opportunity for cavalry action presented itself. He then ordered the Guards Division to move to 4th Corps to relieve the 51st and the Cavalry Corps to bring the 2nd Cavalry Division closer to the scene of the battle.

At 7 pm 4th Corps reported 'RFC certain we hold Fontaine and Bourlon village', which was not the case.

Haig, too, was concerned that the securing of the Bourlon Ridge should not be prejudiced through lack of troops and at 8 pm told Byng that he should use dismounted cavalry 'in any numbers' for the purpose.

To safeguard what had been won at such cost Byng later that evening advised Woollcombe to relieve the leading brigades of the 40th Division if they had suffered heavy casualties, and added that he should have no compunction in asking for more troops if he felt they were needed.

During the day the Army's strength had been increased by the arrival of the 2nd and 47th Divisions which had originally been destined for Italy.

Next morning, 24 November, 4th Corps' endeavours to advance further were frustrated by heavy German attacks on Bourlon Wood. By nightfall, the battered British battalions still held it but three companies which had penetrated beyond Bourlon village had been cut off.

4th Corps again failed to take the village on 25th November and an effort to clear the northern fringe of the Wood clashed with a German attack. There was little progress and the Germans were repulsed with difficulty.

Until the shoulders of Bourlon Ridge (the extensions of it on either flank of the Wood) had been taken the Germans would enjoy the significant advantage of direct observation over the positions of the British artillery. To Haig it seemed that the 4th Corps had had ample resources and opportunity to secure them. He recommended that Byng take personal control of the operation and secure the important

195

features of the Ridge without delay. In spite of the strength of the German counterattack, he still thought that there might be opportunities for local exploitation by mounted troops and that the enemy might withdraw.[15]

Reports from 4th Corps during the evening made it clear that nothing but a major effort would secure the objectives set by the Commander-in-Chief. Byng ordered 3rd Corps to take over the right of 4th Corps' front, including Cantaing. Then, placing the 2nd Division under his command, he ordered Woollcombe to capture, not later than Tuesday, 27 November, the villages of Fontaine and Bourlon and the northern slopes of the ridge beyond them and Bourlon Wood.

The next day was devoted to planning and preparation for the attack. During the morning Byng met Woollcombe and Generals Fielding and Braithwaite of the Guards and 62nd Divisions. Fielding had earlier handed Woollcombe a paper containing his objections to the plan he had been given for the attack on Fontaine. The village was particularly well defended – his advance would be exposed to artillery fire from three sides. On the objective, the frontage of the Guards Division would be increased by over a mile and he had only six fresh battalions for the whole operation. In his view it was essential to assault the high ground north of Rumilly (east of the St Quentin Canal) in conjunction with the attack on Bourlon Ridge if the latter were to be secured. If this were not possible, it would be better to withdraw from the low ground and be content with a main line of defence based on the Flesquières Ridge.

Fielding's objections could not be dismissed lightly. Woollcombe deferred making a decision and the matter was placed before Byng.

The Third Army's resources were far too stretched to launch an attack across the St Quentin Canal towards the hills north of Rumilly. The 47th Division, now behind Bapaume, was the last reinforcement which Byng could expect. And the time for offensive action had almost run out. Retire to the Flesquières Ridge? The Commander-in-Chief's verbal orders to Byng followed by a written directive were clear. The Bourlon position must be taken tomorrow.

Byng decided that the attack must take place as planned. Woollcombe's ADC later remembered Fielding saying to his Corps Commander, 'We shall do our best, sir, but you ask a lot of us.'[16]

Later Haig joined the conference. To him the plan for the 27th offered every chance of achieving his object of capturing and holding 'the best line for the winter'. Fielding told him that he was satisfied that he would be able to gain his objectives.[17]

Next day the Guards suffered heavy casualties in their attack on

Fontaine. While they succeeded in taking their objective beyond the village, their numbers were too few to hold it. German counterattacks swept them away. The 62nd Division could make no progress in Bourlon village. In the afternoon, when Byng learned of the failure of the attack, he ordered Woollcombe to cease his offensive as the resources of Third Army were exhausted. 4th Corps was to consolidate its positions, to prepare a defensive line on the Flesquières Ridge, then construct an intermediate line covering Graincourt. The 47th and 59th Divisions could relieve the Guards and 62nd, which would remain in reserve under 4th Corps' command. The tanks would be withdrawn.

On learning of Byng's instructions, Haig gave his approval. The British attack at Cambrai which had begun with such brilliant success had now ended in frustration. The highest part of Bourlon Ridge, with its wood, had been taken, but the Germans could look down from its shoulders on the British gun areas on the plain below. Haig had his desired observation over the enemy-held areas to the north, but the Germans were unlikely to concede such a dangerous advantage without further fighting. The indecisive result on 27 November, which cost so much, augured yet more casualties and hardships for the troops of the Third Army.

For the past few days the Army's attention had been concentrated on the area between Cantaing and Tadpole Copse, a mile west of Moeuvres, where it was striving to advance. Much of its heavy artillery was concentrated to support the attack and was ready to meet an enemy counterstroke which now was expected. 4th Corps lost no time in carrying out the reliefs which would give it three fresh divisions in the line.

Apart from that short critical section, Third Army's front was thinly held. Covering, as it did, some forty miles and with seven corps under command, intimate supervision was difficult for the army commander and his staff.

The operation, beginning on 20 November, had created a salient some nine miles in width and four miles deep, which was not easy to defend. While its northern flank was made reasonably secure by the strong forces of 4th Corps, the remainder, covered by 3rd Corps, was less well protected. Immediately on the right of 4th Corps, the 6th and 29th Divisions held the face of the salient. The latter was confronted by strong enemy defences and had the St Quentin Canal in its immediate rear. Its positions were overlooked from the enemy's side. Joining it, the 20th and 12th Divisions held the line of the Bonavis Ridge back to the junction with 7th Corps at the head of the Banteux ravine. Here, the right boundary of the attack on 20 November, the line ran to the south along the old British front line, and was held by the 55th Division, commanded by Major-Gen H. S. Jeudwine.

From the positions on Bonavis Ridge it was not possible to see the St Quentin Canal and, though attempts were made to establish posts to observe the crossings, they did not succeed in the face of strong German resistance. The reported destruction by the enemy of all bridges between Crèvecoeur and Banteux led Byng and Pulteney of 3rd Corps to believe that physical possession of the crossings of the Canal was not important. It suggested also that there was no immediate threat from this area.

Sir Thomas Snow, commanding 7th Corps on the right, was of a different mind. Both he and Jeudwine were worried that German moves opposite their thinly-held front presaged an attack. Of particular concern was the Banteux ravine which marked their left boundary with 3rd Corps. Running up from the Canal at the town of that name, it provided a covered line of approach to the villages of Gonnelieu and Gouzeaucourt at the base of the salient. Both were on the main supply route of 3rd Corps and about them were grouped much of its artillery, whose task was to support the divisions at the face of the salient and to engage the enemy guns beyond.

Knowing that Third Army needed all its resources for the Bourlon attacks, Snow did not ask for reinforcements but did what he could to improve the defences of the Banteux ravine. It was little enough, but included positioning twelve machine-gun posts to cover it. With that done, he told Haig, who visited him, that he was reasonably happy with the situation.[18] About 25 November he warned his two divisional commanders to be prepared for a German attack on the 29th or 30th, centred on the ravine. On the 28th and 29th there were reports of enemy movement toward Cambrai from the north and north-east, of a higher level of road movement and of artillery registration against 7th Corps. GHQ Intelligence insisted that German losses in Flanders and the Cambrai battle had been so heavy that a major counteroffensive was unlikely. However, an attack could be expected on the Bourlon front and they considered Third Army capable of dealing with it. Since 7th Corps was holding the original British frontline system, there was little cause for anxiety there.

On 28 November Snow asked for help. At 7 pm his senior staff officer, Brig-Gen J. T. Burnett-Stuart, spoke to Major-Gen Louis Vaughan, MGGS Third Army, who recorded the conversation:

BGGS 7 Corps rang up regarding unusual enemy activity opposite their front. GOC 55 Division thinks enemy is going to attack. Discussed question and agreed that an attack from north and south was a good and likely operation from enemy point of view. 7 Corps are in touch with 3rd Corps about it and are on the alert. Told 7 Corps we would arrange to keep Guards handy to help if required. Cavalry also could move up if wanted. 61st Division coming down on 30th.

The nearest reserve thus was the Guards Division around Havrincourt Wood.

The three corps on the right of Third Army now expected the enemy blow to fall at any time. The imminence of an attack on Bourlon was obvious and the divisions of 4th Corps were working desperately to prepare their defences, while the enemy's artillery was becoming more and more active. In 3rd Corps Brig-Gen C. G. Fuller, the BGGS, visited every brigade commander to warn of the need for vigilance. There was no question of the state of alert in 7th Corps, whose commander presumably was happy about the prospects of a battle, since he had not asked that his defences be directly reinforced.

The eyes of Haig, GHQ, Byng and the Third Army staff remained fixed on the most sensitive point of the front – Bourlon Ridge, which is exactly what Ludendorff hoped and predicted.

From early in the morning of 20 November the Germans had begun to move divisions to the Cambrai area. At first they were used piecemeal to patch up their disintegrating defences. When it became apparent that the British offensive was not to be sustained with the overwhelming force with which it had been launched, the German commanders began a more deliberate reorganization of their forces. Two new Corps were formed. Opposite the British 7th Corps the 'Busigny Group' (Gen von Kathen) took over the southern part of the Caudry Group's line and to the north the Lewarde Group (Gen Albrecht) took over the northern half of the Arras Group's frontage. On 24 November Marwitz issued orders for an offensive to be delivered at an early date by the Second Army. On the 27th Ludendorff decided on an attack to roll up the British salient toward the north. That evening Rupprecht ordered Second Army:

1. Attack on 30 November
2. Main blow by eastern groups, direction Metz, capturing Flesquières and Havrincourt Wood from the south in order to take the British in flank and rear.
3. Arras Group attack after Eastern Group's attack had begun, with all available forces from west of Bourlon Wood toward south. Arras Group to begin artillery fire and demonstrations as early as possible to pin down enemy forces on its front.
4. Fresh divisions will be available for exploitation.

On the 28th von Moser began the Arras Group's preparations by firing 16,000 rounds of gas shell into Bourlon Wood.

In all fourteen divisions were about to attack the Third Army. Rupprecht expected that, as a minimum, they should recapture the Hindenburg front system.

Morning stand-to on 30 November had been in progress for half an hour when, at 6 am, a few German guns began to fire on the front of the 55th Division of 7th Corps. Gradually more joined in, but by the time observers realized that the bombardment was a prelude to an assault, telephone lines to the rear had been cut and many machine-guns and their crews had been destroyed. Darkness and mist, which lay thick in the low ground and along the course of the St Quentin Canal, concealed the concentration of German troops from the RFC. Patrols sent forward on the fronts of the 3rd and 7th Corps detected no sign of forward movement by the enemy.

At 7.05 am the first SOS signals were seen along the front of the 55th Division. British guns promptly opened fire but did little to impede the enemy. Small groups of Germans armed with light machine-guns and flame-throwers advanced towards the gaps between the British defended posts. Low flying aircraft, in far greater numbers than hitherto had been seen, bombed and machine-gunned the British defences, causing casualties and distracting the defenders as the assault swept between their positions, which were then attacked from the flanks and rear.

At first the attack appeared to be concentrated on the 55th Division, but by 8 o'clock it had broken upon the defenders of Bonavis Ridge. Calls for artillery fire brought little response, for already many of the heavy batteries and some of the field guns were being over-run or were firing over open sights at German battle groups which had advanced up the Banteux ravine. The machine-gunners placed by Snow to cover it did not open fire because of retreating British troops between them and the enemy. Many were captured without firing a shot.

At 9 o'clock the 29th Division came under attack at Masnières and a massive enemy force moved against the divisions holding the Bourlon front.

From dawn the Germans had been firing gas and high explosive shells at the British batteries and into Bourlon Wood, drawing an immediate artillery response. At 8.50 am they opened a fierce bombardment of the front positions west of Bourlon and large bodies of troops could be seen assembling and moving south to the attack. Terrible execution was wreaked by the British artillery and machine-guns. German batteries attempting to move into action in the open were destroyed and, as the attacking infantry drew nearer, one battery of eight machine-guns on their flank fired 70,000 rounds into them. Yet the Germans pressed on. Desperate fighting took place on the fronts of the 47th, 2nd and 56th Divisions. The British fought it out where they stood, some companies until every man was killed or wounded. Penetrations were driven out by counterattack, only to have the enemy renew his assaults.

While the northern side of the salient was holding, to the south the situation was serious as the Busigny and Caudry Groups drove through the British positions. Shortly after 8 am fifty-eight heavy and field guns were lost with the capture of Villers Guislain. The forward positions of the 55th, 12th and 20th Divisions were overrun, complete companies were captured and bewildered stragglers and transport began moving to the rear. The first intimation which some headquarters had of the seriousness of the situation was when they came under attack from German infantry.

To Jeudwine it was soon apparent that his whole front was in a critical state. Hastily he deployed his small reserves which moved into blocking positions or counterattacked, and by late morning the German advance was brought to a halt. At 9 am Gen Snow, having moved two battalions from his right-hand division to support Jeudwine, for the first time asked Third Army for reinforcements.

Although undoubtedly surprised by the weight of the attack against 7th and 3rd Corps, Byng reacted with commendable speed. Two of the divisions which he had in reserve, the Guards and 62nd, were centrally located at the base of the salient – there was no room for them inside – positioned where they could intervene either in the north or south. Behind them, some twenty miles away, were the two divisions of 5th Corps, while another, the 61st, was moving down to join them. The 2nd Cavalry Division was concentrating about Fins, while the remainder of the Cavalry Corps lay some ten miles behind the right of the 7th Corps' front, where they were preparing to relieve the right-hand division of that formation.

At 9 am, when Snow asked for reinforcement, Byng despatched the 5th Cavalry Division, followed by the Guards, in the belief that the blow had fallen, in the main, on Jeudwine. Shortly afterwards, when he learned of the serious situation on the right of 3rd Corps, he shifted the Guards to them, put the 2nd Cavalry Division under their command and ordered all available tanks of the 1st and 2nd Tank Brigades refitting near Havrincourt to their support. He then ordered Kavanagh to take both the 4th and 5th Cavalry Divisions to the help of 7th Corps. Shortly after noon the first of these reserves was in action.

By 11.25, little more than an hour after GHQ had learned of the situation in 3rd Corps, they informed Third Army of the arrival during the next two days of three divisions and a considerable force of artillery. Later Byng learned that the French had arranged for a corps of two divisions to come under his orders on 2 December, and that two of their cavalry divisions near Péronne would remain there for the present.

He ordered the 51st Division, refitting west of Albert, forward to Bapaume, recalled the 36th Division which was moving to First Army and sent the 61st south from 17th Corps to replace the Guards in army reserve. None of these could enter battle before the next day.

Byng's chief anxiety was the situation of 3rd Corps and the left of the 7th, but it seemed possible that Gonnelieu might be recovered. At 4 pm 4th Corps reported that they had beaten off all attacks and had taken the precaution of establishing a second position.

It was certain that next day the Germans would resume their attack toward Metz. To forestall it Byng ordered 3rd and 7th Corps, with the Cavalry Corps cooperating, to deliver a counterattack. With all his resources stretched to the uttermost, there was little that Snow could do but lend artillery support. At dawn next morning the Cavalry Corps advanced on Villers Guislain and Gauche Wood. They made little progress. On the left, however, the Guards Division, assisted by cavalry and tanks, attacked in the direction of Gauche Wood and Gonnelieu. By 8.30 am both the Wood and the Ridge had been taken, but on the left flank the advance was blocked in Gonnelieu by a large force of Germans preparing to attack.

While the counterattack had not taken all its objectives, it had been completely successful in achieving Byng's purpose of forestalling a further advance on Metz. The attack of more than two German divisions had been stopped. Farther to the left the enemy made little progress against 3rd Corps but without reinforcements it was impossible to maintain the 86th Brigade across the St Quentin Canal in Masnières. That night they were withdrawn, leaving the 87th Brigade holding the bend in the Canal covering Marcoing.

During 1 December 5th Corps headquarters relieved that of 4th Corps, responsibility for the Bourlon–Moeuvres front passing from Woollcombe to Lt-Gen Sir Edward Fanshawe at 6 pm. Although there was fighting on both sides of the Canal du Nord that day, the Germans made no progress.

By that evening it had become apparent to Marwitz that the attack had 'run itself out'.

Third Army now was approaching exhaustion and the divisions which were coming to relieve those in the line were themselves worn thin by the arduous fighting which had taken place during 1917. The ebb and flow of battle had left the British defences and communications in such a state that a supreme effort would be needed by all arms and services of the Army to restore them.

With the Third Army now on the defensive and with further German attacks being likely the salient from Marcoing to Bourlon had become a liability. On 2 December Haig instructed Byng to select a good winter line and make arrangements for withdrawal to it.

On the 3rd Byng told Haig that he had selected a rear line which corresponded generally with the Hindenburg Support system and included the defences of Flesquières. Haig ordered the withdrawal to it to commence without delay.

Beginning during the night of 4th December, the withdrawal to the main line of resistance for the winter was complete by the morning of the 7th. Putting to use the experience they had gained in Gallipoli, Byng and Fanshawe planned it meticulously. It surprised the Germans as completely, if not as unpleasantly, as the attack of 20 November.

Although another ten days were to pass before British Intelligence was confident that the Germans would not renew their attacks, the Battle of Cambrai had ended on 7 December. The grisly score sheet showed that to the Germans' twenty divisions, the British had employed fifteen, plus four of cavalry. They had lost 44,000 casualties to the Germans' 53,000, 158 guns to the Germans' 145. The British gains in the Flesquières salient had been balanced by an equivalent loss of ground in the south.

During the battle it became apparent to Byng that several of his subordinate commanders and their staffs were unprepared and insufficiently flexible in mind and method for the transition from static to open warfare.

The first and most obvious manifestation of this was in the operations of the cavalry, both in 4th Corps and in the abortive crossing of the St Quentin Canal.

Because there was no major success by the British cavalry in the First World War, military historians are inclined to discount its potential by quoting an American general who said that no cavalry charge is possible until the last machine-gun has been removed from the battlefield. Byng's plans for Cambrai envisaged no cavalry charge and, far from confronting enemy machine-guns, called for his mounted troops to adhere to another American maxim – 'to go where they ain't'. In the First World War there were few, if any, machine-guns to be found behind the front. Formation headquarters, artillery batteries and supply installations were only lightly defended. The 7th Dragoon Guards and the Fort Garry Horse had shown that they could be destroyed. Had panic set in among these troops, whose every instinct is to avoid combat, the effect would have spread far beyond the Cambrai sector. Certainly the tasks given to the cavalry were within their capability – to move through undefended country and then to fight dismounted, supported by their own artillery and machine-guns as they had at Ypres.

Even in the best of circumstances, with an enemy like the Germans, gaps in the line through which cavalry can pass were likely to be short-lived. To take advantage of them, the cavalry had to 'tread on the heels of the infantry', and communication and liaison between them needed to be close.

That the Cavalry Corps did not cross the St Quentin Canal on zero day was probably attributable more to the unexpected manning of the Masnières – Beaurevoir Line by German troops from Russia and the lateness of the season than it was to any failure on their part. Even so, in the deliberation of their move forward, there was no evidence of a burning desire to thrust ahead and their liaison with the leading infantry was far from satisfactory.

In the leaders of the 1st Cavalry Division in 4th Corps the lack of the aggressive cavalry spirit was even more obvious. With the Corps Commander they share the responsibility for the failure of their division to sweep around Fontaine and Bourlon before the enemy could organize his defences. For a week before the battle both Mullens, its commander, and Woollcombe knew that the division would come under command of 4th Corps for the battle, yet apparently they only had one meeting beforehand. Mullens was not present when Woollcombe discussed the operation with his divisional commanders. On Woollcombe's order Mullens opened his headquarters at Equancourt[19] but no direct telephone line to HQ 4th Corps was installed. When he received an ambiguous order to advance which cried out for clarification, Mullens, without consulting Woollcombe, despatched a brigade by the wrong route and omitted to order his other brigades to move forward.

In his frustration at the slow progress of the cavalry, it seemed to Woollcombe that there was nothing he could do but appeal to Byng to order them to advance.[20]

Kavanagh's Cavalry Corps were GHQ troops and were thus directly responsible to Haig. As early as 22 November Byng and Haig had discussed the unsatisfactory handling of cavalry in 4th Corps and the Commander-in-Chief asked a senior cavalry officer to investigate. On 30 November, his hand-written report was received by Haig.[21] A house cleaning was due in the cavalry but it would have to wait until the situation on the front had become quiet.

But it was not only in that arm that there had been failures in coordination, in aggressiveness and in perception of the needs of the tactical situations which developed in the battle. With the exception of Fanshawe, each of the corps commanders showed signs of the weariness of age and the strains of three years of war. Byng decided that they must be replaced by younger men.

Pulteney, Snow and Woollcombe never commanded troops in battle again. 3rd and 4th Corps headquarters by now were in reserve. Snow returned to England on 2 January, Pulteney handed over command as his Corps went back into the line on the 24th and Woollcombe, the oldest corps commander on the Western Front, was replaced early in March.

On 15 January Kavanagh spoke to Haig about changes in the Cavalry Corps. He asked that Mullens be replaced by McAndrew, who had written the critical report on the 1st Cavalry Division. Haig agreed in principle. On 19 March he informed Kavanagh that he, too, would return to England. Two days later the great German offensive began. Kavanagh and Mullens redeemed themselves in the subsequent operations and remained with their commands until the end of the War.

Following the reverses of 30 November, the Press in England reflected the public's disappointment, the deeper because hopes had been raised so high by earlier success. Accounts of the fighting told of the German attack being a complete surprise. The dramatic counterattack of the Guards at Gouzeaucourt attracted far more attention than the successful defence of the Bourlon – Moeuvres flank of the salient, which had been a remarkable achievement. The need to withdraw to the Flesquières line was clearly not understood.

On 5 December the War Cabinet demanded an immediate and full report from Haig on the reasons for the German success of the 30th.

Both Haig and Byng were appalled at the gains made by the Germans against 3rd and 7th Corps and needed no urging from London to look for the causes. How could the Germans have driven through the defences of three divisions in less than an hour and yet had been completely defeated by 4th Corps? Neither of them had seen anything to compare with it at Ypres in 1914 or 1915 – the last occasion on which the Germans had attacked the British in strength.

Much heavy weather has been made of the fact that the Third Army did not send out 'a warning order' that a German attack was about to take place, as if it were some obligatory ritual. It was not necessary. The whole Army knew that an attack was likely. 4th and 7th Corps were at the highest state of alert and every brigade commander in 3rd Corps had been warned personally by the BGGS of the Corps of its imminent likelihood. The War Diary of HQ Third Army for 29 November noted that 'Special arrangements were made this day by 3 and 7 Corps to meet a possible hostile counterattack'. Surprise could not be used as an excuse for failure. How was it then that complete companies were overrun, having scarcely fired a shot? They were, of course, surprised. Yet, having been warned that an attack was likely, they should not have been. Their surprise could only be attributed to the fact they had not known how to avoid it, in other words to lack of experience and training.

On 17 December, in a telephoned report to Haig, Byng said that the German attack was not a surprise, that his reserves were well placed to meet it and that the reverse could be attributed to the lack of training of junior officers, NCOs and men. The staunchness of some machine-gunners left much to be desired.

Reports of machine-gun crews retiring prematurely and of guns being abandoned without firing were disturbing. His opinion of the cause was, again, lack of training and discipline.

The defence of the Bourlon front by 4th Corps in the face of equally heavy assault seemed to confirm his views. The success of the 47th, 2nd and 56th Divisions, which had paid special attention to training, was attributed in large measure to their skill at shooting with rifle and Lewis gun, the staunchness of small detachments and the initiative of junior NCOs and men.

Sadly for Byng, his views were transmitted to the Cabinet. Twisted, they became public knowledge and Byng was accused of blaming the troops, not their commanders, for the reverse at Cambrai. Nothing could have been further from the truth. If his views implied criticism, it was levelled not at his men, who by no stretch of the imagination could be held answerable for their state of training, but at those responsible for a situation where a man could find himself in the front line in less than two months after he had first put on the King's uniform, where men were made section leaders and platoon sergeants simply because they happened to survive and where junior officers, commissioned after the most rudimentary training in the routines of trench warfare, found themselves, as a result of casualties, commanding companies in the far more demanding conditions of open warfare. The guilty ones were the War Office and the War Cabinet.

In reply to subsequent questions by the CIGS, Byng said that he and subordinate commanders were satisfied that sufficient troops had been available 'in view of the situation as a whole'. He refused to attach blame to any of his commanders. Haig used Byng's report as a basis for his own, commenting that risks had to be taken at some points on the front in order to be strong at others. But those taken at Cambrai had not been unwarranted, for 'the enemy should not have succeeded in penetrating any part of our defence'. He concluded by saying that the ultimate blame must rest upon his own shoulders. It was he who had decided to continue the attack upon Bourlon after the first forty-eight hours. The fighting which followed and the extension of the line had thrown such an extra strain upon the troops that they had been unable to resist as they would have done had they been fresher.

Haig's reports were analysed by experts at the War Office, who agreed with Byng's comments on the machine-gunners and the inadequate state of training, and added that they sensed 'a certain lack of efficiency in subordinate leadership'. The War Cabinet then asked for the views of an independent and respected military authority Gen J. C. Smuts. He said that in his view 'no one down to and including corp commanders was to blame' but thought that some brigade and regimental commanders might have been partly responsible, but there was no evidence to that effect. He agreed that many of the troops had been unequal to their task and that the training of junior officers and NCOs demanded immediate attention.

The matter did not end there. Manpower was probably Haig's chief concern at this stage of the war. For some time he had been drawing to the attention of the CIGS and the War Cabinet the worrying state of the Army, its units under strength, the inadequate flow of reinforcements and the poor state of training of the young men who were coming to France for the first time. Byng's report on Cambrai, unpalatable though it may have been, reinforced the arguments he had been using with higher authorities in Britain. He now felt it necessary to clarify the question beyond all doubt so that the War Cabinet would at last take action.

After talking to AG & CGS I appointed a Court of Enquiry into the action of certain Divisions* on 30 Nov. . . . The Court is to state as definitely as poss. what actually took place, the orders given, and results of same. Gen Hamilton Gordon (Pres) McCracken (GOC 13 Corps) and Wilkinson (50 Div – senior of all div genls) members.
  *55 Div (Jeudwine) 12 (Scott) 20 (D Smith) 29 (de Lisle)[22]

The Court confirmed Byng's original report and contributed, as an appendix, a special note on the proper organization of the battle training of divisions, suggesting in principle the adoption of the practices which Byng had instituted in the Canadian Corps.

But the false impression that Byng had 'blamed the troops' and exonerated senior commanders persisted, was repeated in the Official History in 1948 and is remembered by some to this day. Certainly he did not blame his corps commanders publicly, but he

207

replaced every one of them who commanded troops in the battle. Lloyd-George repeated the calumny in his War Memoirs and said that Byng had bungled the advance.

It is simply not a done thing in the Army for a commander to blame his men. To a man so devoted to his troops and their welfare, the unjust accusation was doubly bitter. Seeing his words so misinterpreted, Byng took great care in future to avoid making any comment on the conduct of the war which could possibly become public knowledge or be twisted by politicians, military or civilian. After his talk to Canadian officers in February, 1918, on the subject of Cambrai, he refused to be drawn again, even in private conversation, into discussions of the war.

So strongly did Byng impress his views on publicity on his staff that they continued to be guided by it after his death. Lt-Gen Sir Louis Vaughan, KCB, KBE, DSO, his MGGS, wrote the following in the *Army Quarterly*:[23]

> Byng himself never had any use for post-mortems. He considered controversy after the event to be valueless. His sense of loyalty was so great that he himself never attributed blame to those who, in his opinion, had done their best nor, as far as it lay in his power to do so, would he allow others to impart that blame. He always maintained that true history, when written, would reveal all the facts, from which those who had the knowledge to do so could draw their own conclusions. So averse was he from all controversy after the event that he would never enter into it himself and discouraged all associated with him from taking part in it. This is the reason why the Third Army in France is the only War Army of which no private history has been published. *In view of his wishes, it may suffice to say* that Byng's conception of the battle of Cambrai was brilliant, provided that it could have been put into execution at a suitable time with sufficient reserves to exploit the success. No blame can be attached to Byng for the fact that he was forced to mount the operation (certainly for very adequate reasons) at an unsuitable time with practically no reserves; nor for the fact that he was ordered to continue the operation with his inadequate forces even though the initial attack had not achieved complete success.

Unfortunately the controversy drew attention away from the more significant results of the battle.

It had been conceived as a diversion from Passchendaele and an experiment with tanks. It developed to the point where it offered the possibility of a spectacular local success. But its prospects then began to deteriorate. The strong Canadian Corps which was to have led it was diverted to Flanders and the strength of almost every division in the Army was wasted in the north. Then, too late in the year, when days were too short and the Flanders offensive had foundered, Haig saw a need for the British to keep attacking to prevent disaster in Italy or on the French front. He sought to retain three divisions from going to Italy so that the attack could be better exploited, but Lloyd George would not be persuaded. Nevertheless he decided to go ahead.

As Byng told officers of the Canadian Corps:

> In spite of having to send troops to Italy, in spite of not getting ahead in the north as much as he wanted, in spite of only being able to give us divisions which had been over the top a great many times, he had determined to carry out the operation. That is a decision to which only history will do justice. Still, I think it was a remarkably fine one.

Later, he continued:

> In order to achieve any success at all, it seemed there were two absolute essentials. One was that the battle should be going on in the North. . . . The second . . . was absolute secrecy.[24]

The Passchendaele offensive ended one week before the attack at Cambrai began. Of the fifteen divisions which reinforced the Germans between 20 and 30 November, six came from Flanders.

The concept of the operation was much admired by the Germans. Hindenburg wrote:

> With the Battle of Cambrai, the English High Command had departed from what I might call the routine methods which hitherto they had always followed. Higher strategy seemed to have come into its own on this occasion. The pinning down of our main forces in Flanders and on the French front was to be used to facilitate a great surprise blow at Cambrai.[25]

Lt-Col Wetzell, the head of the operations section at Ludendorff's headquarters, said, 'In what a different situation should we not have found ourselves if the blow had taken place simultaneously with the great Flanders attack?'[26] Ludendorff himself later said:

> The English Commander did not exploit his great initial success, or we should not have been able to limit the extent of the gap. If he had done so, what would have been the judgement on (our) Italian campaign?[27]

Before 20 November the Germans had been able to reinforce von Below in Italy at will. During the following two weeks they sent him no reinforcements and the Italians were able to establish themselves on the River Piave without help from the Allies.

Turning from strategy to tactics, Byng felt that by 20 November the odds were against the cavalry crossing the St Quentin Canal.

After describing the preparations and the initial stages of the attack, he spoke of the 29th Division's objective of capturing the Masnières – Beaurevoir line.

> If that division failed to capture it that day, it was useless for the cavalry to go through. . . . If we took Masnières and Marcoing by 1 o'clock the cavalry could get through. As a matter of fact, we captured Marcoing at 12.50 pm and Masnières at 2.30 pm but the obvious solution was that this attack should have been carried out in the summer, when the hours of daylight are long and not in the winter, as we had to do it. . . . It seems doubtful whether, with the time at our disposal, we could have advanced so rapidly that the cavalry would have been able to go through on zero day, even if everything had gone in our favour.[28]

Byng's lecture described the Battle of Cambrai from its inception to its end, its results and the lessons which could be drawn from it. It was the last recorded comment which he made on the subject, although, years later, when he was Governor-General of Canada, he did speak to Major-Gen J. F. C. Fuller of the part which the tanks had played. Yet the British official history of the battle, published in 1948, thirteen years after Byng's death, appears to have taken little account of what he had to say about it. For example:

> Himself a cavalry man, the commander of the Third Army showed remarkably little appreciation of the conditions essential for successful cavalry action. Only by an advance upon a broad front are speed and freedom of movement possible to mounted troops; yet the British cavalry – after negotiating the narrow defiles which had been cleared for it through the captured Hindenburg defences – was confronted by the deep, steep-sided St Quentin Canal, where the passage was to be made at a very limited number of crossings. As these crossings were obstinately defended by the enemy, the check was complete.[29]

Yet, when the cavalry reached the Canal, their 'advance' had not yet begun. They were moving up behind the 29th Division whose task it was to open a way for them to advance. Had it not been for the intervention of a German division from Russia, which arrived in Cambrai the night before the battle, the crossings of the Canal would have been secured. Byng knew that at best it would be a race against time to secure the conditions for a break-out. What would have been said if he had not tried? This is only the first of a number of inadequately thought-out criticisms of Byng in the Official History. It is almost as if the historians were going out of their way to conjure up failures for which they could blame Byng.

Yet why would they do this, at the risk of making themselves appear foolish? One can only speculate. Byng declined to wash off in public the mud which had been thrown at him over 'blaming the troops'. By 1948 it had hardened and he was dead. Perhaps too, the memory of the post-war struggle for mechanization of the cavalry (which, incidentally, Byng favoured) was too fresh for them to view any contemplated use of horsed cavalry objectively.

In the First World War no other mobile force of any significance existed but the cavalry. Tanks were too few in number, too slow, too unreliable mechanically, and too short in range. In combination though, the two arms were the inadequate precursors of the heavy tank of the breakthrough battle and the lighter tank of exploitation. The one crucial element they lacked was radio communication.

It is from the attempt to exploit their potential in combination that the Battle of Cambrai derives its particular significance. It marked a turning point in concepts of warfare. After due credit is paid to the gunners who developed the techniques of 'silent registration', to the imaginative officers of the Tank Corps and to the skill and bravery of the infantry, it was Byng who gathered the instruments into an orchestra. The meticulous planning, the secret concentration and concealment of an overwhelming force of guns and armour, the interdiction of the battlefield and engagement of ground targets by the air force, the deceptive measures, including simulated attacks and dummy tanks, spread over a front of thirty miles to diffuse the enemy's attentions, the plan for a break-out by a mobile force, and above all, surprise, were brought together in a single operation by Byng. All the elements of *Blitzkrieg* were there, including the concept of *'schwerpunkt und aufrollen'*, the overwhelming thrust on a narrow front followed by the rolling up of the enemy's defences. Only once in the First World War were there enough tanks to repeat the pattern which Byng had designed – 8 August, 1918, 'the Black Day of the German Army'.

Cambrai also saw innovations by the Germans which were to have an effect on warfare of the future. Field guns were used effectively against tanks and were the precursors of the anti-tank gun. They even used anti-aircraft guns as they later did the '88'[30]. At first, their infantry were cowed by the tanks, but they soon lost their fear and British tank crew commanders later reported occasions when German infantry were clinging onto the barrels of their guns, attempting to fire through the aiming slits. Later they achieved a notable success by their use of the tactics of infiltration against 3rd and 7th Corps, which they later perfected for their offensive in the spring of 1918.

At Cambrai both British and Germans had found the means of penetrating the other's defences. In future, as the war moved into a

211

more open phase, the gain or loss of ground would lose the significance it had had during the first years of the conflict.

Sensing this, officers in France deplored both the premature celebrations of the 'victory of Cambrai' in England and, later, the over-reaction to the loss of ground in the German counterattack.

Chapter 11
Ten Days in March

THE FIRST FEW days of 1918 found Byng at home, where he had arrived two days after Christmas for a short period of leave. By 7 January he was back in France to deal with his share of the problems which had been thrust upon the commanders of the British Expeditionary Force.

He allowed the repercussions of the Battle of Cambrai to take little of his time, painful though unjust criticisms were. The results of the Court of Inquiry which had assembled at Hesdin on 21 January to look into the later stages of the battle were of interest in so far as they drew attention to weaknesses in tactics and training. There was in any case little time for looking back, for pressing problems demanded his attention.

In January the War Cabinet made decisions which drastically affected the fortunes of the Armies in France. In the face of protests from Haig and the War Office, they agreed to the British taking over the French front to a point well south of the River Oise. They declined to provide the reinforcements needed to replace the casualties which the Armies had suffered and ordered that the composition of the divisions on the Western Front be reduced from twelve infantry battalions each to nine.

Facing the Allies was a German force, growing in numbers as divisions freed by the collapse of Russia moved to the Western Front. From the beginning of the year their strength opposite the British increased and, particularly against Third Army, they became far more aggressive than they had been before. That an attack was coming before significant American forces could arrive in France next summer was obvious to all. Before the extension of their eighty-mile front, Haig's armies faced approximately the same number of German first line divisions as did the French. The British now would hold 130 miles of line, an extension of over sixty percent with no increase in strength, despite the fact that the French army was numerically stronger.

The reorganization of divisions was not simply a matter of doing away with three infantry battalions in each. It would have been folly to disband effective units while sparing others which were weak. Of the latter, some divisions had as many as six, others had none. There were many moves of units between divisions and it took some time for them to become accustomed to the operational and administrative procedures of their new formations.

In the meantime work had to go on on the defences which, in particular on the right half of the Third Army area and on the front taken over from the French, were very weak. In Third Army the reorganization of divisions was completed on 27 February.

With inadequate forces to secure his whole front, Haig had allotted more divisions to the Armies in northern France and Belgium, where a short German advance would reach the Channel ports, than he had in the south where there was much more room for manoeuvre behind the British line. Thus Gough's Fifth Army on the British right held a front of forty-two miles with twelve divisions and three cavalry divisions. Byng, on his left, held the twenty-eight miles from Gouzeaucourt to Gavrelle (six miles north-east of Arras) with fourteen divisions, ten of which were in the line, four in reserve.

Fanshawe's 5th Corps still held the Flesquières (or Cambrai) salient on the right. Of its five divisions, two were in reserve, one being at the disposal of Army Headquarters. In accordance with Haig's instructions, the salient was to be held as a false front in sufficient strength to deal with hostile raids and to force the enemy to disclose his intentions in the case of heavy attack. If seriously attacked, its garrison was to fall back to the defences constructed across its base.[1]

On its left were the 4th, 6th and 17th Corps, each of three divisions. Those of the 6th Corps were all in the line. The other two Corps each had a division in reserve. Behind the centre of his front, east of Bapaume, Byng had three battalions of tanks, while a fourth was on the left, south-east of Arras.

The defences of the Armies of the BEF were arranged in depth. A forward zone, consisting of three lines of mutually supporting posts, was protected by belts of wire. Its object was to delay the advance of the enemy and oblige him to deploy a considerable force to breach its defences. Behind it the 'battle zone' was also organized in three defensive lines, or systems. Here, it was envisaged, the main battle would take place. Further to the rear there was a third defensive zone, but in the Third and Fifth Armies there had been neither the time nor the labour available to construct it. Through most of its length it had only been marked out on the ground and was protected by a single belt of wire. It was known in both Armies as the 'green line'. In the infantry brigades who were manning the defences, about one-third of the troops

214

were in the forward zone, the remainder being divided between the battle zone and a reserve held in rear.

The Germans were now known to have tanks. To counter them the Third Army's defences included a few anti-tank mines and anti-tank guns deployed in the forward zone.

For some twenty miles behind the British front the countryside had been devastated by the Germans when they withdrew in 1917 to the Hindenburg fortifications. The larger towns like Péronne and Bapaume had been completely gutted. Of some villages the only indication was a sign in English saying 'Here stood . . .' followed by the name. Having been utterly ruined by the Germans, the remaining stone and brick had been used by the British to repair the shell-torn roads. All that remained of trees and orchards were three or four feet of trunks, standing dead and bare. The ground, pitted with shell craters, was intersected by old trenches. Wire entanglements stretched for miles. Only the principal roads had been rebuilt – cross-country movement, even on foot, was slow and exhausting. The state of the country, while unsuitable for the defence, was bound to slow an attack.

Following the collapse of Russia, the first months of 1918 offered the German armies what might well be their last opportunity of winning the war in the field. For the first time since early 1916 they would have sufficient strength to launch a major offensive against the Allies. Ludendorff's staff produced detailed plans for a succession of attacks on the British and French fronts. The first, against the British Third and Fifth Armies, would be launched in March by the German Second, Seventeenth and Eighteenth Armies. Codenamed 'Michael', the attack would be carried out by seventy-four divisions, supported by 65,000 guns, 3,500 trench mortars and several hundred aircraft. The Eighteenth and Second Armies were massed opposite Gough, while the Seventeenth, commanded by Gen Otto von Below, prepared to assault Byng's six centre divisions.

The task of the Eighteenth Army in the south was to drive west and south-west to the River Somme and the Crozat Canal. There they would be in position to prevent the French coming to the assistance of the British. The Second and Seventeenth would drive westward to the line Péronne – Bapaume. They believed that, in reaching these objectives, they would break the British front. The two right-hand armies would then wheel to the right and begin rolling up the British line to the north while the Eighteenth protected their southern flank. Simultaneously a second offensive, codenamed 'Mars', would be launched toward Arras, later followed by a third offensive in northern France and Belgium. As their first tactical objective, the two northern armies were to cut off the British in the Flesquières salient.

The intelligence staffs of the BEF were well aware of the location of the German concentrations on their front and Haig had predicted accurately where the blow would fall. This had been reported to the Cabinet in London, yet they seemed to prefer the French view which was that the main attack would be against their defences in Champagne. Never had the British line been held with so few men and guns to the mile. With part of his force absent in Italy, Haig only had an immediate reserve of eight divisions, two behind each of his four armies.

On 26 February the intelligence section of GHQ reported signs of German preparations for an attack along the front between Havrincourt and Croisilles. From then until the offensive began, reports from the RFC and from prisoners and deserters painted a picture of a German build-up along the fronts of the Third and Fifth Armies. By 10 March it was known that three armies stood opposite them where previously there had been only the Second commanded by Marwitz. Further, the commanders of the new formations were Hutier and Below, two of Germany's most successful attacking generals. During the night of the 19th a prisoner and a Polish deserter picked up by the Third Army told of the advanced state of preparations for the attack, that no tanks were present, and that they had been issued with a new type of gas mask. Lt-Col A. R. C. Sanders, Byng's GSO1 Intelligence, advised that the offensive would begin on the 20th or 21st.

In the preceding few weeks there had been little enemy patrolling or other activity along the front. But between the 10th and 16th the enemy shelled the Flesquières Salient heavily with gas. Practically the whole of the 2nd Division holding the right half of the Salient was affected and more than 3,000 men died or had to be evacuated. The 63rd (Royal Naval) Division on the left did not suffer so widely but had 2,580 casualties. During the nights 19/20 and 20/21 March the 47th Division relieved the 2nd.

As night fell on the 20th, cold and damp, a ground mist rose, making the darkness even more impenetrable. On the front of the 4th and 6th Corps patrols found that many gaps had been cut in the enemy wire, but any attempt to penetrate them met with strong resistance. Prisoners captured during the night indicated that an attack was imminent.

Shortly after 4.30 am a terrific bombardment broke out all along the British front and each Corps ordered battle stations to be manned. At first the shelling seemed to be concentrated on artillery and machine-gun emplacements, gas being included to force troops to don their respirators. Divisional headquarters, telephone exchanges and railway junctions were hit and within a short time most of the deeply buried signal cables connecting the forward troops with the headquarters in the rear had been cut.

At 6.15 Byng reported to GHQ that the bombardment had started, but there was no other information. With cables cut, pigeons gassed, movement by runners slow and difficult over the shell-swept ground, and with fog severely hampering the use of aircraft, commanders were unable to learn what was going on on their front. It was not until shortly after 11 am that Third Army learned of the advance of the enemy infantry. At almost the same time they heard from Fifth Army that they were under attack all along their front.

Only later did Byng and his staff learn some of the details of the battle. Two hours after it had begun the Germans switched their bombardment to the trenches of the forward zone and then at 9.40 am their infantry had advanced. Led by groups of specially trained 'storm troops', they worked forward between the British strongpoints to objectives in their rear. So dense was the morning fog that they could not be seen until they were within ten yards range. Defenders of positions in the rear hesitated to open fire on the figures looming through the mist, uncertain if they were friend or foe. The artillery, attempting to fire on likely enemy forming-up places, could not see their aiming stakes. Shortly after 10 o'clock the fog began to lift along the Third Army front, but dust and the smoke of bursting shells continued to obscure the battlefield.

In the Third Army only the 17th Corps on the left was not under direct attack by infantry. Of most immediate concern to Byng was the situation of the 5th Corps holding the Flesquières Salient. About this Haig's instructions had been explicit. In the case of heavy attack the Corps should withdraw to the battle zone across its base. Now, while attacks were taking place on it, they could not be described as heavy. The Salient had earlier been heavily shelled with mustard gas. The forward area had been drenched with the fuming liquid, which would cause casualties to friend and foe alike. This seemed to indicate that the Germans had no intention of occupying the Salient for at least two or three days, when the gas would have dispersed. Byng went forward during the afternoon to visit Fanshawe and see the situation for himself.

German attacks during the morning had succeeded in entering the front line of each of the three divisions in the Salient, but had been driven out by counterattack. Later attempts by the enemy to advance had been repulsed with heavy casualties. As the day drew on no further attacks were made and the enemy's fire diminished, which appeared to confirm that the attacks were really large-scale raids and hence were not 'serious'. Though the garrison had suffered severely from mustard gas, there was no apparent reason why they could not maintain their position.

217

The scale and violence of the attacks against 4th and 6th Corps, defending the line north of the Salient, were of a different order. So heavy had been the artillery bombardment and so swift the advance of the storm troops through the fog that most of the troops in the front lines were killed outright, buried by the bombardment or taken prisoner. With nineteen divisions concentrating their attack on the frontage of little more than four of the British, a penetration of the front was inevitable. In places whole battalions were wiped out. At the outset the enemy were screened from view, but, as the fog dispersed during the morning, the British artillery and machine-guns began to see and hit their targets, slowing the attack as it progressed into the battle zone. Counterattacks won back, for a time, some of the ground which had been lost, but inexorably the German advance ground into the British defences. When night fell the 4th and 6th Corps between the Bapaume – Cambrai road and Fontaine-les-Croisilles had been forced back to the rear of the battle zone. To the north, on the flank of the German attack, only a small part of the forward zone on the extreme right of the 3rd Division had been given up. To the south, in the Flesquières Salient, no ground of importance had been lost, but the 47th and 63rd Divisions which held it had lost 3,000 casualties from gas and many who remained on duty could scarcely talk and were continually vomiting. In the four divisions which bore the brunt of the German assault casualties had been very serious and many guns and machine-guns had been lost. Three of the five divisions in reserve had been committed to prevent a complete breakthrough.

With most of his Forward Zone lost and the enemy driving into the battle zone, Lt-Gen Harper of 4th Corps had sent two brigades of his corps reserve, the 25th Division, to reinforce the 51st and 6th Divisions and Byng had placed the 19th Division under his command. The three divisions of the 6th Corps were all in the line. The front of the two nearest 4th Corps had been penetrated and, about noon, Lt-Gen Haldane requested the help of the 40th Division of the GHQ reserve. Byng had already obtained permission for its use and it was soon on the move.

As the fog began to disperse, the Royal Flying Corps took to the air to look for ground targets. In addition to directing the fire of the artillery, they inflicted many casualties on the enemy by low-flying machine-gun and bombing attacks.

It was not an easy day for the Germans, for, as one of their accounts put it, 'Zero day had proved to Below's Army that its opponent, the British Third Army, was not unprepared for the attack.'

When Byng returned to his headquarters from 5th Corps he found that the position in the Flesquières Salient was becoming hazardous. The heavy attacks which the Germans had mounted on either side of it pointed to the fact that they intended to pinch it out. Its retention as 'a false front' as ordained by GHQ might well result in it becoming an enormous trap. He decided that the troops must be brought back, at least from the apex.

Byng first considered an immediate retirement to the battle zone, but the positions there were weak, with few dugouts. Forward of it, some 4,000 yards behind the forward zone, lay an intermediate line. It had been part of the old Hindenburg defences, but had been rewired on the enemy side. Its deep trenches and dugouts offered much more protection and better fields of fire and had the advantage of flanking the German line of advance against 4th Corps.

With the help of their reserves, there was a reasonable chance that 4th and 6th Corps could maintain their positions on the morrow. To add to their strength, GHQ had sent the 41st Division to Bapaume behind 6th Corps and had ordered the 31st Division and several brigades of heavy artillery to join the Third Army next day. On the right, except for the capture of one strongpoint, the enemy had made no impression whatever against the defences of the 9th Division of the Fifth Army. Accordingly, late in the afternoon, Byng obtained Haig's permission to move 5th Corps back to the intermediate line, the movement to be complete by 6 o'clock next morning. Later that night Byng received a copy of Fifth Army's report on their situation at 11 pm. It indicated that there had been losses of ground, particularly in the south, and penetrations of their battle zone. But it showed that the British line was continuous and that the enemy had been scarcely more successful there than against Third Army. In this Gough's report was misleading and gave the impression that the Fifth Army was in a better position to continue the fight next day than actually was the case. In particular, it induced Byng to believe that a further withdrawal from the Flesquières Salient was not necessary.

By 6 am on 22 March 5th Corps had completed their withdrawal from the apex of the Flesquières Salient. During the day they beat off several German attacks, unaware that most of them were designed to hold the British in the Salient. At Hermies, which the enemy meant to take, the German losses were very heavy and by nightfall the dead lay in heaps before the wire.

Soon after daylight the Germans renewed their attacks on 4th and 6th Corps. Eight divisions sought to overwhelm the depleted British brigades, yet they made little progress. But, as the day wore on, Byng's uneasiness at the situation grew. There was a limit to how long the hard-pressed troops could hold their positions in the face of such odds.

In the early afternoon Byng learned that the situation in Fifth Army had deteriorated and that its 9th Division would be withdrawing to the Green Line, leaving his right flank unguarded. With the likelihood of a further penetration of 4th Corps front growing by the hour, it was evident that the 5th Corps must be brought out of the Flesquières Salient to prevent it being cut off. At 1.15 pm he issued orders for them to withdraw to the battle zone during that night. He also instructed Fanshawe to create a reserve of at least two brigades in the south of his area ready to occupy the Green Line near the boundary in either the Third or Fifth Army areas to secure their junction.

Until about 3 pm the enemy made little progress against the 4th and 6th Corps but then weight of numbers told. At Vaulx-Vraucourt they achieved a break in the British defences and began to widen the opening. Across a six-mile gap between Beaumetz and Mory nothing seemed likely to block their entry into Bapaume.

Further withdrawals were now inevitable. Byng concluded that, if the Germans continued to push back the line south of Arras, it would be necessary to withdraw the right of the 17th Corps in order to keep in touch. This would mean abandoning Monchy-le-Preux, a major prize for the enemy. From it the British had observation over the German lines as far east as Cambrai. Any enemy gun, for miles around, could not fire without its position being spotted from Monchy. On the other hand, its possession by the Germans would give them a new security in their rear areas and a great advantage in developing operations against Arras. During the afternoon Byng informed Haig of the possibility.

At 6.30 pm Gough arrived at Albert to ask Byng for help in securing the junction of the Third and Fifth Armies. The withdrawal of his 9th Division had the effect of increasing the southern flank of the Flesquières Salient by 8,000 yards and there was no immediate prospect of halting the enemy's advance. Byng immediately ordered Fanshawe to move a brigade to his right flank and, instead of withdrawing to the front of the battle zone as instructed at 1.15 pm, to retire his right and right centre even further to the rear. Already the reserves of the 47th Division and the Corps cavalry regiment had been used to extend the 5th Corps line and now Fanshawe sent 99th Brigade of 2nd Division to extend his flank further.

The following telephone message (obviously of particular significance to Byng for it is the only one to be found in the voluminous scrapbooks kept by Evelyn) came from Lt-Col John Dill of the operations Section at GHQ at 8.50 pm 22 March:

Fifth Army situation very critical. Enemy has broken through third system at following points: K32b (north of Havrincourt), Q29 (Poeuilly), Beauvois, Heudicourt and Vaux. Enemy cavalry and guns coming through Beauvois and Vaux. Fifth Army have no troops to fill the gaps and will try to hold a line from Péronne southwards. 7th Corps front intact as yet, but will probably have to conform to rest of line soon.

At almost the same time Lt-Gen Haldane reported that, because of the penetration on the right of the 6th Corps, he was being obliged to draw back his left. The withdrawal of the 17th Corps and the abandonment of Monchy-le-Preux which Byng had already authorized now became inevitable.

At midnight Byng learned that Fins, deep in the 7th Corps area, near the Army boundary, had been taken. This was a serious threat to the garrison of the Flesquières Salient. Within another few minutes came an order from GHQ:

Third Army will keep in touch with left of Fifth Army and be prepared in case of necessity to conform and withdraw to general line Tortille River – Croisilles.

Except for 5th Corps and the right of the 4th, the Third Army was already on that line and, near Croisilles, was to the west of it.

By this time the front of the 4th and 6th Corps was more stable. Byng had sent the Guards Division to the assistance of the much weakened 6th Corps, following it later with the newly arrived 31st Division. Counterattacks, some with tanks, had closed the gap before Bapaume but the line had been driven back about two miles and the right and left wings of the Army would have to conform. At 12 am on 23 March Byng issued a third order to 5th Corps to withdraw, this time to the Green Line. The 4th would fall back with it and, as this would shorten his front, Lt-Gen Harper was instructed to take over 3,500 yards of the 6th corps front providing further relief to that hard-pressed formation. Later, at 2 am, Byng instructed his Corps commanders to begin work on the 'Red' Line, three to five thousand yards behind the Green. Designed as the rear position of the rear zone, it had been surveyed but none of its defences had been prepared.

The rearward movements during the night took place with little interference from the enemy. So heavy had the German losses been in their attacks, particularly on 4th and 6th Corps, that they were forced to change their plans. While Crown Prince Rupprecht ordered the Second and Seventeenth Armies to continue their advance with the object of capturing the Flesquières Salient, he did not think that they would achieve anything like the results which had been obtained against the Fifth Army. It might indeed be necessary to shift the weight of attack to the north. He instructed the Seventeenth Army to make

221

preparations for the 'Mars' attack on either side of the Scarpe near Arras. For the first time Byng's 17th Corps would then be directly engaged.

During the same night an event took place on the Fifth Army front which was to have a profound effect on the operations of the next few days and create an appalling risk to Fanshawe's 5th Corps. Gough had indicated to his corps commanders that in the event of 'serious hostile attacks' they were to fight 'rearguard actions back to the forward line of Rear Zone [Green Line] and if necessary to rear line of Rear Zone,' (in 18th Corps, the River Somme). It was left to corps commanders to decide if an attack was serious and to act independently, reporting their actions to army headquarters. In the south the 18th Corps withdrew to the Green Line during the afternoon, but Lt-Gen Sir Ivor Maxse, the corps commander, had already decided that his troops could not possibly hold any position between it and the River Somme to the west. At 12.30 pm he ordered his divisions to continue their withdrawal during the night 22/23 March. By next morning they were on the west bank of the Somme, leaving a huge gap between them and the 19th Corps to the north. Neither it nor the 7th Corps were prepared for such an extensive withdrawal and the strain of maintaining touch with their more nimble-footed comrades while hanging on to the right of Third Army proved to be too great.

During 23 March the Germans launched heavy attacks against 4th Corps which were repulsed, both sides losing heavily. The withdrawal of that Corps' right flank went ahead and by nightfall it was on the Green Line. To the north the 6th Corps, in counterattacks, took back some of the ground which they had lost near Mory. Beyond them the 17th had completed their move back from Monchy-le-Preux and were hard at work improving their positions. His northern corps gave Byng little cause for concern during the day. His chief worries were over the extrication of the 5th Corps from the Flesquières Salient and in keeping touch with the Fifth Army on his right.

With both of its neighbours forced back, 5th Corps was still in a salient and the jaws of the enemy pincers were beginning to close. It was imperative that it should move back with all speed but the condition of the ground and communications meant that at best the pace would be slow. Signal lines were almost totally destroyed and, forward of divisional headquarters, orders were mainly carried by messengers on foot.

Sir Edward Fanshawe, it will be recalled, was one of Byng's divisional commanders during the successful withdrawal from Suvla. Perhaps the memory of that meticulously planned operation formed the pattern for his actions that night, for he seems to have been less influenced by the need for haste than the demands of careful preparation.

He received Byng's order to withdraw at 1.30 am on 23 March, but not until $2\frac{1}{2}$ hours later did his warning order arrive at the headquarters of his divisions with an enquiry as to when they would be able to move. In order to give time for forward troops to be warned, it was decided that main bodies could not begin to retire until 10 o'clock in the morning and that rearguards should hold the forward positions until 1 pm. The operation order for the withdrawal was not issued by Corps HQ until 7.20 am.

The Green Line was to be held from the right by the 47th, 63rd and 2nd Divisions, while the 17th was to go into reserve in the southern sector of the Red Line, two miles in rear, thus placing two divisions, the 47th and 17th, close to the boundary with Fifth Army. In that formation the 7th Corps had instructed its left division, the 9th, not to withdraw from the Green Line between Nurlu and the army boundary until such time as 5th Corps was ready to retire, but the precipitate withdrawal of 18th Corps in the south compelled the 7th to fall back. By early evening on 23 March heavy attacks had prevented the rearguards of the 9th Division holding the Nurlu Line.

The 17th and 63rd Divisions retired on schedule, but the 47th, on the right, was less fortunate. Enemy probes against its right were successful in finding a gap between its flank and the 99th Brigade which formed the link with Fifth Army. Pressing in from the south and south-east, they succeeded in driving the 47th to the north-west, off its line of retirement. The effect was to widen the gap between the Third and Fifth Armies. By 6 pm it had grown to three miles.

During the afternoon Fanshawe, anxious about his right flank, had ordered the 47th Division to occupy a line which would secure the army boundary near Manancourt, relieving any troops of the 9th Division and 99 Brigade who were in Third Army area. The order was too late and, because of its northward retirement, the Division could not comply.

At 5 o'clock the following order to Third and Fifth Armies was telephoned from GHQ:

Fifth Army will hold the line of the Somme river at all costs. There must be no withdrawal from this line. It is of the greatest importance that the Fifth Army should effect a junction with the French on their right without delay. The Third and Fifth Armies must keep in closest touch in order to secure their junction and must mutually assist each other in maintaining Péronne as a pivot.

As this order was being received, Gough arrived at Byng's headquarters where the two commanders decided on new measures to ensure

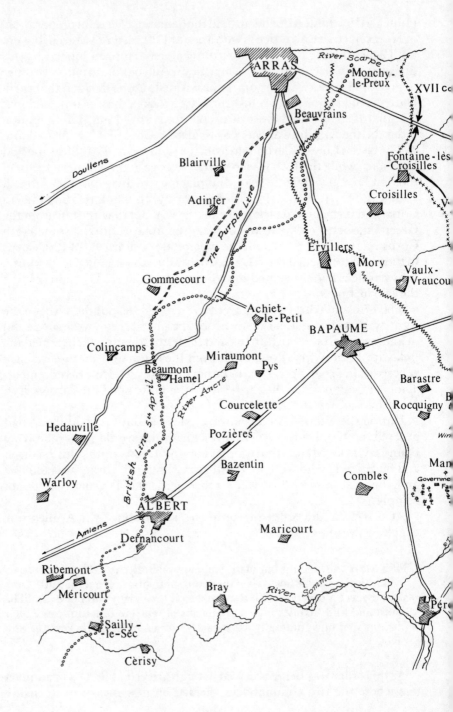

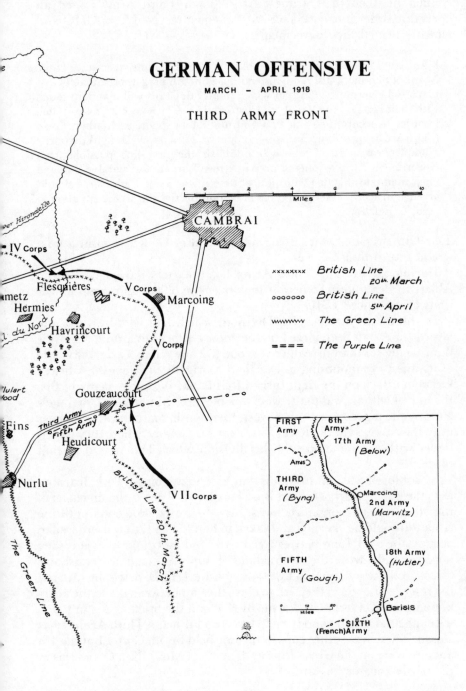

GERMAN OFFENSIVE

MARCH — APRIL 1918

THIRD ARMY FRONT

Miles

CAMBRAI

IV Corps

Flesquières

metz
Hermies

du Nord

Havrincourt

V Corps

Marcoing

V Corps

Gouzeaucourt

Third Army

Fifth Army

Fins

Heudicourt

Nurlu

British Line 20th March

VII Corps

The Green Line

ver Hirondelle

'lulart
lood

xxxxxxxx	British Line 20th March
ooooooo	British Line 5th April
wwwwwww	The Green Line
====	The Purple Line

FIRST Army   6th Army

17th Army (Below)

Arras

THIRD Army (Byng)

Marcoing
2nd Army (Marwitz)

18th Army (Hutier)

FIFTH Army (Gough)

Barisis

Miles

SIXTH (French) Army

contact between their armies. At 7.20 pm Third Army issued an operation order in compliance with one just received from GHQ and which reflected their agreement:

Fifth Army has been ordered to hold the line of Somme river at all costs. North of Somme, Fifth Army intend hold line running approximately due north to Government Farm at which point 5th Corps will maintain touch with them. It is essential that 5th Corps and 7th Corps keep in closest touch in order to secure their junction and mutually support each other. Fresh troops are being sent up probably tonight by Fifth Army along Maricourt – Combles road. 5th Corps will establish the best line possible from Government Farm to join our present Green Line at most suitable spot and must maintain this line with utmost determination. . . . 5th Corps should arrange to keep a reserve in echelon behind his right to secure situation at point of junction.

The 99th Brigade, which Byng had loaned to Gough to form a link, would return to 5th Corps.

During the evening Third Army headquarters moved back from Albert to Beauquesne where it took over the offices and communications of Advanced GHQ.

In the meantime the 47th Division, which had withdrawn to the Green Line, had been forced by the enemy attacks to form a defensive flank facing south from Vallulart Wood to Four Winds Farm, the whole of its infantry amounting to less than a brigade in strength. A heavy German attack on the right turned that flank. With the enemy in Bus the line of withdrawal to the west was blocked. Major-Gen Gorringe's left brigade moved north, then west, then south, marching by compass until they arrived at the River Line near Rocquigny, where they joined forces with the remainder of the division which had retired to that place.

So confused was the situation that at 2.30 am on the 24th, learning that the enemy had occupied Bus, Fanshawe ordered the divisions of the 5th Corps to reorganize and secure their own protection until the situation could be clarified and taken in hand. The 17th was ordered to occupy the Red Line between Barastre and Rocquigny, where they joined hands with the 47th about 6 am. As soon as Fanshawe discovered the location and the state of the 47th Division, he ordered the reserve brigade of the 17th to close the gap between it and the army boundary at Government Farm. By 8.30 am the brigade was in touch with the 9th Division and the gap between Fifth and Third Armies was closed. There were other gaps in the line held by 5th Corps, but the 4th and 6th were on the Green Line and, north of Mory, 17th Corps was in the battle zone or forward of it.

Many of the troops later remembered its third night, that of 23/24 March, as the worst of the battle. Near to exhaustion and still suffering from the effects of gas shelling in the Flesquières Salient, they stumbled through the dark with no landmarks to guide them, expecting at any moment to meet the enemy who were attacking almost behind their front.

On 24 March GHQ issued orders for a further defensive line to be prepared, which generally followed the front held by the British prior to 1 July, 1916. In the Third Army sector it would run from Dernancourt, just south of Albert, along the River Ancre, north to Gommecourt, then north-eastwards to join the defences of Arras. Byng arranged for work to begin on this new 'Purple' Line and informed his corps commanders that it had not yet been decided whether future retirements would be to the north-west, to cover the Channel ports, or westwards to keep in line with the French. That question was at the time occupying the minds of the British and French commanders-in-chiefs.

Pétain told Haig that he was placing two armies – some eleven divisions – under Gen Fayolle on the British right, but could do no more because he expected at any moment the enemy would attack him in Champagne. He suggested that, to ensure touch being kept, Fayolle should be given command of all British troops south of Péronne. Haig agreed and ordered that this should take place at 11 pm on 24 March. While this relief to the British was welcome, it was obvious that, so long as Pétain was in command of the French, little further assistance would be available.

Later Haig arranged with the commanders of the First and Second Armies to form a force of six divisions under command of Lt-Gen Morland of 10th Corps as a GHQ reserve located west of Arras, available for counterattack. That evening he had supper with Byng and noted, 'All at Third Army are in good heart.' He cautioned Byng to hold on with his left at all costs to the right of First Army near Arras.[2]

It is now time to look at the battle from the German point of view. It had not gone according to plan. On their right, progress of the Seventeenth Army and the northern wing of the Second Army had been slow and disappointing. Against Gough, the left wing of the Second Army had made good progress, while, further south, the Eighteenth Army's success had been spectacular. They had crossed the Somme and the Crozat Canal and little seemed to stand in the way of a further advance. On the morning of 23 March Ludendorff received a report that the Seventeenth Army had captured Monchy-le-Preux by attack, whereas it had been evacuated deliberately by 17th Corps without fighting. There were air reports of the roads behind the British front being crowded with columns hurrying to the rear. The First

227

Quartermaster General concluded that the British were beaten. He now ordered the Eighteenth Army on the left to advance to the south-west against the French, the Second Army to continue its drive to the west and the Seventeenth Army to the north-west. The object now was to separate the Allied armies, drive the British into the sea and defeat the French. It meant a considerable shifting of the weight of the attack to the left.

It was evident that, as in 1914, the Germans had concluded that, because the Allies retreated, they were beaten. Yet the advancing German divisions were finding their task far from easy. Except in the south, their casualties had been heavy and it was not only the stubborn resistance of the British which slowed their progress. When in 1917 they had retired to the Hindenburg positions, they had devastated the country. Keeping direction in that bleak landscape was as awkward for them as for the retiring British; moving their guns forward was so difficult that their infantry soon passed beyond the range of artillery support. Assured that they had achieved victory, their weary troops kept running into stubborn British defences. Their advance became more cautious as their morale subsided from the peak to which it had been brought before the attack.

During the morning of 24 March the Germans renewed their attacks on the right of the Third Army. A powerful thrust succeeded in driving back Gough's left-hand corps and again contact was broken with the Fifth Army.

With difficulty the 2nd Division fought its way back to the Red Line, where it joined the 17th and 47th, while the 63rd retired behind them to reorganize. Outflanking the line to the south and forcing their way through gaps in the tenuous line, by noon the Germans were closing in on the battered brigades and threatening to defeat them in detail. At one point they succeeded in bringing up four guns to enfilade the 17th Division's line and began to knock out its machine-guns one by one, while low-flying aircraft strafed the infantry. Fanshawe sent orders to his divisions for a further retirement but before action could be taken on them, Byng intervened. At 3.45 pm he ordered 4th and 5th Corps to swing back their line so that the right of the Army would be at Bazentin.

While the retirement would straighten the front, it involved abandoning Bapaume and the Péronne – Bapaume – Arras road, the main lateral route behind the Army's front.

By nightfall the 5th Corps, exhausted and disorganized, had succeeded in shaking off the enemy and had established themselves on a new line. Constantly fighting off German attacks, Harper's 4th Corps moved back to join the 5th, while to their north the right of the 6th Corps conformed. By midnight the 5th Corps lay with its right flank seventeen miles west of the original front line, but from there the depth of the ground which had been given up diminished until near the boundary of the 17th Corps it was negligible.

As a result of the agreement between Haig and Pétain reached earlier in the day, the 7th Corps and Cavalry Corps would come under Byng's command at 4 am on the 25th and he would be responsible for the front as far south as the Somme. At about the same time Gough and the remainder of the Fifth Army would come under the command of Gen Fayolle. The Third Army would then be covering a front of twenty-seven miles with five corps, while, behind them, the 3rd, 4th and 5th Australian Divisions and the 12th, 62nd and New Zealand Divisions were concentrating. No matter how shaken some of the troops had been by the German attack and the arduous withdrawal, none of them believed they had been beaten. From their commander down, the Third Army was confident now that they could maintain their front.

At 8 pm Haig visited Third Army HQ to discuss future operations. He instructed Byng at all costs to cling with his left to the First Army near Arras and, that if he was forced to give way, he should do so by drawing back his right to the old British defence system whose trenches ran from Arras to the south. He intended to concentrate all possible reserves by thinning the line in the north, so that he would be able to strike a blow southward if the enemy's advance approached Amiens. No firm plan could, however, be made until it was learned what the French intended to do in the Fifth Army area south of the Somme. Lt-Gen Lawrence, Haig's CGS, had arranged to meet the Commander-in-Chief at Byng's headquarters following a visit to Generals Gough and Fayolle. The French general had told him that he expected to receive no more troops until the 28th. As Haig left Byng's headquarters, the strategic outlook was far from promising.

Haig was not diverted by Pétain's growing pessimism from the plan of operations which he had outlined to Byng. He assumed that the French Government would order their army to maintain touch with the British by sending strong forces to cover Amiens. During the afternoon of the 25th he confirmed his instruction that Third Army should move back to the old British front line Bray-sur-Somme – Albert – Beaumont Hamel – Gommecourt – Arras. He placed the 4th Australian Division under Byng's command, to be followed next day by their 3rd. First Army was directed to concentrate all available troops on its southern flank, prepared to assist the Third Army by attacking south and south-east of Arras.

The Cavalry Corps had been placed under Third Army on the previous evening, but, because of the critical situation in Fifth Army, it was not yet possible to extricate its divisions which were in action. The

12th and New Zealand divisions had now arrived and were in army reserve.

During the 25th the 7th Corps, on the right, now under Byng's command, held its position in the face of strong enemy attacks. Five German divisions attempted to break through the 35th Division, which drove out every penetration by counterattack. On its left the exhausted and depleted divisions of the 5th Corps fell back slowly. By 2 pm its thin line, in places with many gaps, ran from the right of 7th Corps to Pozières, Courcelette and Pys (the scene of the first Canadian battles on the Somme) with its field artillery still in close support. Believing that the British were on the run, the enemy now pushed forward their infantry in mass, without artillery, and in so doing suffered the heaviest casualties of the March fighting. But numbers told. The divisions of the 5th Corps were gradually forced back and by nightfall were close to the River Ancre.

Further to the left 4th Corps was attacked by no fewer than fifteen German divisions – the left half of the German Seventeenth Army. In their own words, the enemy formed 'a battering ram' of six divisions which drove against the right of the 4th Corps and succeeded in forcing it in a north-westerly direction. By 5 pm, with their right flank at Pys, the Corps was facing south-east instead of east as they had been in the morning. When Byng placed two fresh divisions, the 42nd and the 62nd, under his command during the day, Harper sent them to hold positions from near Achiet-le-Petit to Ervillers. By nightfall his other exhausted formations had retired beyond them to the west.

At 6 pm on 25 March Byng telephoned orders to his Corps commanders to retire that night to the line prescribed earlier by GHQ: Bray-sur-Somme, Albert, thence along the River Ancre to Beaumont Hamel, Gommecourt and Arras. While confusion inevitably would result from carrying out such a retirement at night by tired troops who were in contact with the enemy, he believed it to be essential to bring the Army back as quickly as possible from its present unorganized and indefensible line to a position where cohesion could be restored. For the weary troops of the Third Army it meant another night of stumbling, in a darkness made worse by a storm of hail and sleet, through a barren landscape lit only by the fires of burning dumps and airfields.

By morning the new line had been occupied through most of its length. Where possible it was held by relatively fresh formations, behind which the more exhausted divisions were withdrawn. There were gaps which would be filled during the morning of the 26th, but the future course of operations was hard to predict. The addition of the fresh New Zealand and Australian divisions greatly restored the strength of the Third Army, but the immense pressure which the

Germans had brought against the right flank made a further retirement seem likely.

Early in the morning of the 26th a warning order for a further withdrawal was telephoned to the corps commanders and was confirmed in writing at 2.20 am. It began:

Every effort must be made to check the enemy's advance by disputing ground. It is to be distinctly understood that no retirement is to take place unless the tactical situation imperatively demands it. In case of our line being forced further back, the line will pivot on 17 Corps, and fall back fighting in a north-westerly direction to the line Beaurains [three miles behind the right of the 17th Corps] – Blaireville – Adinfer – Gommecourt – Colincamps –Hedauville – Warloy [nine miles north-west of Bray-sur-Somme]. Cavalry Corps will protect the right flank falling back toward the general line Amiens – Doullens.

Late the previous afternoon Byng had received notice to attend a conference at 11 am at the Hotel de Ville at Doullens to discuss future operations with Haig and other army commanders. Horne and Plumer of First and Second Armies were there, but Gough, being under the command of Gen Fayolle, was not invited. Byng reported that he was satisfied with the situation of the Third Army. On the southern flank the enemy was very tired and no real fighting was taking place; friend and foe alike were dead beat; further north the enemy was trying to press on, but Third Army was holding its own.

Haig then said that the present object must be to cling to the ground now held in order to gain time for the French to arrive and render help; the covering of Amiens was of vital importance for the success of the cause; if the enemy pressed forward the line of the Third Army must not be so extended by giving ground as to run the risk of breaking. To prevent this happening, he ordered General Horne (First Army) to pull three Canadian divisions out of the line and place them at some central point behind Third Army.

Immediately following the meeting of army commanders, a conference took place which considerably influenced the future course of the war. Present for France were President Poincaré, Clemenceau, the Premier, Loucheur, the Minister of Munitions, Foch, the Chief of the General Staff and Pétain, the Commander-in-Chief; for Britain, Lord Milner, the Secretary of State of War, Haig, Wilson, the CIGS, and Generals Lawrence and Montgomery. Byng and the other army commanders waited for the outcome.

The most important decision was to give Foch the authority to coordinate the operations of the Allied armies. No longer was the possibility of the Germans driving a wedge between them to be tolerated.

Foch lost no time in assuming control and instructions were soon on the way to Fayolle to support and then relieve the Fifth Army south of the Somme.

As soon as the conference ended Byng telephoned orders to his headquarters that there must be no retirement of the Third Army. Any local withdrawals should be in the general direction east to west, and not to the north-west. In particular, 7th Corps must ensure that its right holds firm on the Somme. The position at Bray was to be maintained with the utmost determination. Unfortunately the withdrawal of the 7th Corps was already under way.

Of all the corps commanders of the Third Army, only Lt-Gen Congreve seems to have misunderstood the intention of the warning order which Byng had issued shortly after midnight. Based on an initial warning which he had received by telephone, he issued an order at 2.15 am to his divisions which began:

> The 7th Corps will fight today on the line Albert – Bray, in order to delay the enemy as long as possible without being so involved as to make retirement impossible. Retirement when made will be to the north of the Ancre which is to be held again as a rearguard position, all bridges being destroyed after the crossing.

The right flank of the new position would be Ribemont on the Ancre, six miles south-west of Albert, with the left being at Albert where it joined 5th Corps.

The retirement began about 2.30 pm. Half an hour later 7th Corps headquarters received a message from Third Army. Referring to the warning order issued earlier, it stated:

> It must be distinctly understood that no voluntary retirement from our present line is intended. Every effort is to be made to maintain our present line.

Congreve immediately tried to halt the withdrawal and restore the line but it had progressed too far to stop. About 7.30 pm Third Army learned of the situation and ordered the Cavalry Corps to cooperate with 7th Corps in holding a line between the Somme and the River Ancre, which they finally established between Sailly-le-Sec and Méricourt. The withdrawal had uncovered the left flank of the Fifth Army at Bray.

Elsewhere the gaps in the Third Army line were filled and everywhere it held firm, despite strong attacks mounted against the 5th, 4th and 6th Corps. The crisis on the front of the Third Army had ended, although the battle was not yet over. South of the Somme, the

232

Fifth Army's front was also beginning to hold. Everything now depended upon the French moving sufficient forces into the line protecting Amiens.

The Germans had failed in their object of breaking through the Third Army and their troops were exhausted. So difficult had it been to advance across the area which they had deliberately devastated in 1917 that ammunition and ration supplies had frequently broken down. Some German infantrymen had been without food for forty-eight hours. Their morale was failing. Casualties, hardships and disappointment all played their part in this, as well, strangely enough, as their capture of British Expeditionary Force canteens. When they saw the stocks of food, cigarettes and drink which they had been denied for years, they realized that the Allies were not being strangled to death by the German blockade. Their disillusionment was complete.

On 26 March Ludendorff showed his displeasure at the lack of progress of the Seventeenth Army against Byng. Commenting on a telephone conversation, Crown Prince Rupprecht said that Ludendorff was 'quite beside himself and dissatisfied with the Chief of Staff, whom he talked of removing from his post'. That evening he issued orders for a new attack to be mounted in the north against the junction of the British Third and First Armies. In the south the Seventh, Eighteenth and Second Armies were to form a barrier to hold back the French while the Germans destroyed the British in the north. Zero day for the new attack would be 28 March.

Soon after first light on the 27th the Germans renewed their attacks on the right and centre of the Third Army. At Dernancourt and Albert 5th Corps lost some ground and the enemy gained two small lodgements on the 4th and 6th Corps' front. In the main the battles were directed by the infantry's brigadiers and there was no need for intervention by Byng.

South of the Somme, where the left of Fifth Army had been exposed by the withdrawal of 7th Corps the day before, the Germans began to cross the river at Cerisy in their rear. As soon as Byng learned of this development he sent the 1st Cavalry Division south of the river to help Gough restore the situation. News of this reinforcement reached the Fifth Army commander as Major-Gen H. G. Ruggles-Brise, the Military Secretary, arrived to tell him that Rawlinson and HQ of Fourth Army would relieve him and his staff next day.

The crisis in France was not yet over and the Government in London, prompted by Sir Henry Wilson, the CIGS, considered that Gough was responsible for the British retirement which had brought it about. Poor Gough! With great resource he had handled his inadequate forces in the face of an overwhelming attack and, while many of his

233

formations had been cut to ribbons, his line was still intact and the German advance in front of it had been brought to a halt. Haig protested, but to no avail. Even before the battle the Government had wanted him to be replaced.[3] Lloyd George was determined that Gough should go and that was the end of the matter.

On 28 March the Germans for the first time launched a heavy assault against the whole of Byng's front. Twenty-nine divisions, with sixteen more in support, advanced between the Somme and Arleux, north-east of Arras beyond the Scarpe. Their principal effort, codenamed 'Mars', was directed at the junction of the Third and First British Armies. Only here, where they were supported by the immense battering train of the German artillery, did they make any progress. Elsewhere they were stopped in their tracks by the Third Army and on the right, near the Somme, even lost some ground.

They attacked with the greatest bravery, sometimes almost shoulder to shoulder, having been assured that only one more effort was needed to break the British front. Their losses were appalling. Not having the numerical advantage of three or four to one which they enjoyed on 21 March, and with no fog to cover their movements, they failed; by the afternoon the fighting had stopped and was not renewed.

The 'Mars' Attack had struck at the 3rd Division of 6th Corps, the 15th and 4th Divisions of 17th Corps and the 56th Division of the First Army. None had previously been heavily engaged in the March battles. A few days earlier the first two of these divisions had been obliged to withdraw from their forward positions to the battle zone to conform with withdrawals which had taken place further south, but elsewhere the British were manning their original well-organized defensive system. By the end of the day the four divisions had been forced back from their forward positions to the battle zone in rear, the shock of the attack being absorbed in the forward defences. It made no further progress. At no point was it necessary for Byng to intervene in the battle, but shortly after 6 pm, since it might be renewed next day, he placed the 2nd and 1st Canadian Divisions, which were in army reserve, at the disposal of the 6th and 17th Corps.

'Mars', known to the British as 'The First Battle of Arras, 1918', was a significant defensive victory. It lasted less than a day. That evening Ludendorff recognized that so far his operations to crush the British had failed. He ordered that 'Mars' be ended and that, in Flanders, the German Sixth Army should plan to attack in ten days' time across the Rivers Lys in the direction of Hazebrouck.

234

29 March was the quietest day on the Third Army front since the fighting had begun on the 21st. Opposite them the German Seventeenth Army reverted to ordinary trench warfare. A German historian later wrote:

The results of its operations had been far behind expectation; it had failed to 'pinch out' the Cambrai salient; it had failed, in cooperation with the right of the Second Army, to break through the line Bapaume–Arras and was never in a position to wheel north-west to roll up the British line. The result could not but exercise an unfavourable effect on the course of the whole spring offensive.

On the 30th the Germans made some determined but unsuccessful attacks against parts of the Third Army front. They offered fine targets and by the end of the day the British had driven them back and had even improved their own positions. Ludendorff postponed further major operations until 4 April to allow his battered formations time for rest and preparation.

On 5 April, in mist and rain, a bombardment of the whole of Byng's front began at 7 am. The previous night patrols and prisoners had revealed that an attack was about to take place. By dawn all units were alert and ready. A general offensive by the German Second and Seventeenth Armies against the fronts of the 5th and 4th Corps resulted in gains too small to record on the map.

Rupprecht later recorded:

The final result of the day is the unpleasant fact that our offensive has come to a complete stop and its continuation without careful preparations promises no success. . . . In the evening Ludendorff ordered the attacks to be stopped; they were only to be continued where an improvement of the local situation demanded it.

There were now increasing signs that Ludendorff intended to make his next effort farther north on the front of the First and Second Armies. It was likely that the southern arm of his attack would have as its object the capture of Vimy Ridge, by turning its flanks from Arras and from Lens. At the same time he would probably attack north of the La Bassée Canal against the front held by the Portuguese. In order to better coordinate the defence of Vimy Ridge Haig transferred the 17th Corps from Third to First Army and moved Byng's left boundary south of Arras.

As the British intelligence staff predicted, the next offensive did fall on First and Second Armies and, when it was halted, the Germans turned their attention away from the British and began to prepare for a major effort against the French in May.

For Byng and the Third Army the battle was over, but, as they worked to restore the Army's fighting strength and build its defences, a controversy began to boil over the great March retreat. For three years the British had been attacking the enemy, gaining at most a few miles of useless ground. Now the Germans had driven almost forty miles in a week. The Press and Parliament demanded explanations.

At the Allied Conference at Doullens Pétain had said of the British Fifth Army, 'Alas, it no longer really exists; it is broken,' and went on to compare Gough's troops disparagingly with the Italians after Caporetto. His remarks were simply not true but they inevitably played their part in the decision to replace Gough.

While the Fifth Army had suffered grievous losses and had retreated a long way, and while there had been many scenes of disorganized troops and transport hurrying to the rear, giving the impression of a fleeing army, the fighting troops had battled on. On the day that Gough was relieved he had two corps in action before Amiens and had forced the enemy to halt. His soldiery did not consider themselves in any way defeated. They and their commander were resentful of any suggestion that they had been. It was not long before others began to speak in their favour and to point out all the factors which had contributed to the long retreat.

The partisanship which stemmed from the unjust treatment of Gough has, as Liddell Hart has pointed out, caused the British Official History of the War to be written with a bias in favour of Gough and Haig. The one-sided explanations and accusations had gained a long start by the time it was published in 1935. Sadly it and other military works which have followed its lead too closely have done less than justice to Byng and the Third Army.

Byng himself refused to be drawn into the controversy. He had good reason to be wary of doing so after the misrepresentations of his words after Cambrai.

His only recorded comments are contained in letters to Blumenfeld. On 10 April he wrote:

I hope people are not going to judge Goughy hastily, also that he is not going to make an ass of himself by chattering.
Whatever else happens, we must keep DH [Douglas Haig] where he is.

All too soon he heard reports of Gough's outspokenness. He wrote 'Am afraid Goughy is talking too much. He had better keep quiet.'[4]

After the war, when a spate of officers' memoirs were published, often filled with self-justification and criticisms of one general or another, Byng made it obvious to his friends that he considered that they did more harm than good.

There is at first a temptation to draw comparisons between the conduct of the battles of March, 1918, in the Third and Fifth Armies, but close examination reveals that in this there is little to be gained. So many of the factors which affected the outcome differed between the two armies – length of front, state of preparation of defences, enemy objectives, availability of reserves and so on. Further, it is not always apparent if the responsibility for certain practices or dispositions lay with the army commander concerned or with the Commander-in-Chief.

Two aspects of the defensive posture of Third Army which later were criticized were not of Byng's doing. The defensive system of three zones with its manning procedures followed a directive from Haig's headquarters. It involved one third of the infantry's being in the forward zone, the remainder being divided between those in rear. On 21 March the troops in the forward zone were practically wiped out by the bombardment and initial German assault. The loss of so much of the Army's infantry strength significantly weakened its powers of resistance. But it is easy to be wise after the event. No one on the Allied side had experienced a bombardment of such intensity before and the German infiltration tactics seen here for the first time were never to be so successful again.

The second aspect was the retention of the Flesquières salient after the Battle of Cambrai. Haig knew that ultimately the war could only be won by attacking the enemy, and the salient posed a threat both to the communications centre of Cambrai and the German defences to the north. Plainly it was desirable to retain it for those reasons alone. He was not going to give it up gratuitously, but equally was not prepared to defend it to the death. His orders to Byng reflected this.

Having said that these two bases of the Third Army's defensive plan were imposed on Byng, there is no reason to suppose that he did not agree with them.

When night fell after the first day of the battle Byng saw that retention of the Flesquières salient until it was directly attacked might result in it being pinched out by the enemy. He as yet had no reports which suggested that the Germans had made any real progress in this way, but he ordered the troops in the apex to withdraw to the Intermediate Position. It was not until the afternoon of the second day that he learned that the threat through Fifth Army's front was far greater than had been reported. He immediately ordered 5th Corps out of the salient.

At that point he and Gough were mutually responsible for securing the junction of their Armies but the progress of the Germans on his front made it necessary for Gough to ask Byng for help. This he provided and ordered a further withdrawal of 5th Corps to secure the link. But then the unforeseen and precipitate withdrawal of 18th Corps in the south stretched Fifth Army to breaking point. It was then that GHQ made Byng responsible for keeping contact with Gough.

For the next two days Byng's principal concern was the extrication of 5th Corps while keeping his army intact. Fanshawe, who had been carefully briefed by Haig personally on how to conduct the battle in the salient,[5] knew that it might have to be abandoned. Evidently his contingency plan for doing so was inadequate and, when Byng ordered him to withdraw, he took so long in planning and implementing the operation that his Corps was in danger of being cut off. Like the corps commanders at Cambrai, he lacked the flexibility of mind needed in fast-moving operations. Byng asked that he be found a job at home. On 25 April Haig agreed and replaced him with Major-Gen C. D. Shute, the commander of the 32nd Division.[6]

Even in the most anxious days of the withdrawal, Byng never lost his sense of humour. Early in the battle Major-Gen J. H. Davidson, head of the Operations Section, GHQ, was visiting him at Albert. Every few minutes messages were brought in with news of the retreat of another division. Then came a report from Fanshawe that he was retiring to take up a new position in the rear because his flank was in the air. Byng grinned ruefully at Davidson: 'Have you ever heard of an admiral of my name?'[7]

More than once, as at Gallipoli, he referred half humorously to his unfortunate uncle, revealing that the shade of Admiral Byng was nagging at him during the retreat and spurring his determination to halt the enemy offensive.

The gap which opened between the Third and Fifth Armies on 22 March was not finally closed until 7th Corps came under Byng's command on the 24th. It was created by the left of Fifth Army being pulled back to keep contact with its right. Byng might have kept pace with it, had he been given earlier warning of the true state of affairs in Fifth Army on 21 March and consequently abandoned the Flesquières salient earlier. He probably could have secured the junction if 18th Corps had not made the task well-nigh impossible or if a reserve division could have been sent to that flank. But his only reserves were needed to prevent the enemy breaking through on the fronts of the 4th and 6th Corps and from achieving what was their main strategic aim, the rolling up of the British front towards the Channel ports. In that key area he had taken a firm grip early in the battle and, by the night of the second day, had forced the German High Command to doubt if they would succeed against the centre of Third Army. Withdrawing to keep aligned with the Fifth Army, Byng ensured that any gaps in his line were quickly closed. When at last Gough halted before Amiens and the Germans made a final desperate attempt to break Byng's line, they suffered some of the heaviest losses of the war and gained not one of their objectives.

Chapter 12

The Victory Campaign

FRUSTRATED IN THEIR attempt to break through the Third Army, the Germans turned their full force on the British and Belgians in Flanders. By the end of April, when they were finally halted, the Allied line was near the breaking point close to the outskirts of Ypres and Hazebrouck.

For most of the month of May an uneasy quiet existed along the Allied front as commanders sought to divine the sector where Ludendorff would strike again. Only the Americans correctly predicted that it would be between Rheims and Montdidier.

On 27 May the blow fell. In six weeks the Germans drove forward to the Marne, but for them time was running out. So strong were they still that, during this last offensive, they were able to contemplate a further attack against the British in Flanders, who watched warily as preparations for it went ahead. But the build-up of American forces in Europe was now becoming a curb to German freedom of action, and a further cause for disquiet was the appearance of British and American troops to bolster the French, reflecting the new unity of command of the Allied forces under Foch.

As the German advance progressed, the Allied 'General-in-Chief' watched carefully for signs of weariness in the enemy armies. Their reserves of men, material and morale had been almost entirely used up in the attacks of the past four months. When the enemy finally reached the point of exhaustion, Foch intended to launch a full-scale counteroffensive with the aim of inflicting a decisive defeat. On 17 July the Germans halted and on the next day the French, with British and American divisions in their command, turned to the attack. In two weeks the enemy were driven back from the Marne to the rivers Aisne and Vesle.

On 24 July Foch conferred with the commanders-in-chief of the armies of the three Allied nations, Haig, Pétain and Pershing. As a first step in the development of offensives against the Germans, he planned to secure from enemy interference the lateral railways essential for moving troops from one part of the front to another. He proposed then to clear the northern coal-producing areas, important to France's war effort, and drive the enemy from the neighbourhood of Calais and Dunkirk. Following these moves, he contemplated convergent attacks by all the Allied armies. Gen Weygand, Foch's chief of staff, later confirmed that Foch never envisaged a breakthrough of the German front or a vast envelopment. Rather he intended that, when an attack showed signs of slowing down, he would widen its front on both wings, stretching the enemy armies to the utmost so that nowhere would their line be strong enough to hold.

Foch gave no indication during the summer of 1918 that he foresaw that the war would end that year. As a result of his policy, everywhere the Germans would be given time to prepare successive defensive lines to which they could withdraw.

The situation in which Byng and the other commanders of Britain's five field armies found themselves offered little scope for tactical innovation and less for strategic brilliance. Commanding the most warworthy and potent fighting formations on the Allied side, they were about to be directed to make a frontal assault on the most heavily fortified section of the German front. And yet there were few if any alternatives to the course of action chosen for them.

The experience of moving French troops into a British zone and vice versa, except in an emergency, had not proved to be successful. If the Allied Armies were to attack in the near future, it must be in the national sector in which they were now located. Unfortunately for the British, the German defences on their front were backed by several rows of well prepared positions, including the formidable Hindenburg positions.

Haig's first task would be to drive the Germans back from Amiens, at the junction of the French and British armies, to prevent further interference with traffic through that important railway centre.

In the early spring of 1918 Byng was able at last to introduce into Third Army the training methods which were so successful in the Canadian Corps. At Fort Mahon Plage, on the Channel coast south of Le Touquet, he organized three schools of instruction – weapon training, tactics for captains and lieutenants, and a commanding officers' school.

On 15 May Haig visited them for the first time. He came again on the 24th to watch twelve battalion commanders carrying out an advanced guard scheme with forty-eight young officers of the tactical school, each CO working with a syndicate of four. So impressed was he that he ordered the other armies of the BEF to set up similar schools.[1]

241

Another visitor to Third Army was Lloyd George. Byng was not impressed. 'Yes, I had the PM in all his beauty for an hour. He wants his hair cut.'[2]

During this time the Third Army front was only relatively quiet. In addition to constant patrolling, some minor operations were carried out to improve local positions and there was much shelling by the enemy with both high explosive and gas. At first Byng's main preoccupation was with restoring the strength of his battered divisions and their defences, but never far from his mind was the knowledge that eventually he must attack.

An immediate problem for Byng was the state of his infantry battalions. Fifty percent of their soldiers were eighteen- and nineteen-year-old boys. They had been well trained in Britain (but not in open warfare), their discipline was good and they were keen and physically fit. If their first action was a success, they would do well, but a bloody reverse could break their morale. Most of their officers were young, inexperienced second-lieutenants.

Fortunately, by comparison the artillery was highly efficient.

For the initial attacks of Third Army, Byng decided to confine the advance of his troops to objectives which were within artillery range. To limit the number of casualties in individual battalions, fresh divisions would pass through the assaulting formations at intermediate objectives. The tactical formations used by the infantry were altered to ensure that the few experienced officers who remained in each unit would control them. Despite the limited time for preparation, most of the infantry were given training in operating with tanks.

On 8 August Rawlinson's Fourth Army began the British offensive at Amiens. So violent and successful were the attacks of its Canadian and Australian Corps that Ludendorff referred to it later as the 'Black Day of the German Army'. To take advantage of their progress, on the 10th Haig ordered Byng to carry out raids and minor operations along his whole front from Albert to Arras and, if practicable, push advanced guards in the general direction of Bapaume.

Rawlinson, however, was unable to exploit fully the successes of the 8th and by the 11th his advance had halted on the western edge of the area devastated in the Somme battles. Haig now decided to shift the main weight of his attack farther north. He instructed Byng to be ready, as soon as reinforcements reached him, to mount a full-scale attack in the direction of Bapaume with the object of outflanking the enemy's present battlefront.

Byng's three corps, reinforced by four infantry divisions, two cavalry divisions, five battalions of tanks and additional artillery, were to break into the enemy's position on a four-mile front, seven miles south of Arras. They would then drive southwards toward Péronne in order to outflank the enemy forces facing the Fourth Army.

Early in the morning of 14 August reports began to come in to Third Army headquarters of enemy withdrawals and by 11.45 they were able to report to GHQ that the German Seventeenth Army was falling back on a six-mile front between the Ancre and Bucquoy. The frontline divisions immediately followed, harrying them with artillery fire and offensive patrols, and Byng ordered his corps to push forward advanced guards with vigour. By the morning of the 15th these had entered Beaumont Hamel and Serre and were probing into the outskirts of Beaucourt and Bucquoy. Haig ordered Byng to begin his attack toward Bapaume without waiting for his promised reinforcements to arrive. The five battalions of tanks were essential, however, and it was agreed that the attack could not begin before 21 August.

Once again the Third Army was to cross the area devastated by the Germans in their retirement in 1917. On the right 5th Corps would first have to cross the Ancre. The banks of the river had been broken and the fields alongside were a marsh covered by a tangle of trees and branches, laced together with barbed wire. Their orders were to attempt to push fighting patrols across, and, next to 4th Corps where the going was somewhat better, to take Beaucourt and advance to the Amiens–Arras railway. Should they meet serious resistance, neither of the leading divisions was to be committed to a costly attack.

Beyond the river the advance of 5th Corps would take them through the old battlefields of the Somme–Thiepval, Pozières, Courcelette, Flers and Guedecourt. So broken was the ground that tanks could not be used and progress would probably be slow. Northwards, the going was better. It was in this area that Byng directed the 4th and 6th Corps to mount the main effort. The five battalions of tanks would be divided between them.

Directly supporting the operation would be the 3rd Brigade, Royal Air Force, whose strength had been increased to ten squadrons, two of which were American. One squadron was attached to each corps to attack ground targets and a fourth was allotted to the Tank Corps for low flying attacks on anti-tank guns.

Crucial to the success of Byng's plan would be the 1400 guns of his artillery.

On 19 August Haig visited Byng and told him that he thought his plan was too limited. It provided for an advance of only six thousand yards in the centre, whereas the aim should be to break through the enemy's front, to push on quickly to prevent roads and bridges being destroyed, and to seize Bapaume as soon as possible. Intelligence reports on the state of the German Army lent strength to Haig's view.

Byng believed that it was more important to give his young soldiers a successful first battle than to gain a day in the advance to Bapaume. Not only would they learn much and their chances of survival increase, they would begin to acquire the habit of winning which is so important in a sustained offensive. There was a long road ahead to victory.

The plan remained unchanged.

The Third Army's attack began at 4.55 am on 21 August. A dense fog had settled over the battle area, screening the advancing infantry from the view of the machine-gunners who were the backbone of the German defences. Both the 6th Corps on the left and 4th took their first objectives from Moyenneville to Beaucourt with surprisingly few casualties.

On the right the Amiens–Arras railway, which was the second objective, lay some $2\frac{1}{2}$ miles further forward and it was necessary to move artillery after the initial assault to bring it within range. By this time the fog had lifted, enabling the enemy to spot the advancing batteries. Shelling and air attacks caused many casualties, especially to their horses, and they did not reach their new positions in time to support the infantry. Some tanks which reached the railway came within close range of enemy guns and were knocked out.

A fresh enemy division counterattacked on the 4th Corps front and at the end of the day its attacking divisions were halted short of the railway. On the left 6th Corps had crossed the line which there had marked the enemy's main position. On the right 5th Corps took Beaucourt and advanced to the railway line. Further south, only small parties managed to get across the Ancre and these, by morning, were in Grandcourt and Thiepval Wood.

During the afternoon, when the difficulty of crossing the Ancre by large forces became apparent, Byng ordered 5th Corps to halt the advance of the 38th Division on the right until the Fourth Army had taken Albert, which they expected to do next day. The division could then pass through the town, outflanking the obstacle.

In its initial attack the Third Army had gained considerable ground and taken some 1500 prisoners. Exploitation by tanks and cavalry beyond the infantry objectives proved to be impossible in the

244

face of determined enemy resistance. The advent of open warfare was still far away.

No break had been achieved in the enemy defences and Byng decided to halt the offensive for a day while his guns were brought forward and his divisions reorganized for another attack. The troops had suffered much from the heat of a blistering August day and would benefit from the rest. When told of the decision, Haig expressed the wish that the attack be resumed without delay.[3]

During the evening, Byng ordered Haldane, commanding 6th Corps, to extend the frontage of the attack on 23 August to the north in order to secure ground from which to launch a further advance, giving him three new divisions with tanks, and extra artillery for the purpose.

Next day, when Haig learned that Byng had not moved, he issued an order for the advance to be resumed,[4] followed by a telegram addressed to all his army commanders. He ordered them to impress on their subordinates that the enemy were weakened and disorganized. Now was the time to press the attack to advance even when flanks were exposed, to reinforce success. 'Risks which a month ago would have been criminal to incur, ought now to be incurred as a duty.'[4]

Obviously more was required than the preliminary operation which Byng had ordered Haldane to conduct.

Confronting 4th Corps in the centre of the Army was a well-prepared enemy position between Irles and Achiet-le-Grand which could not be taken by frontal attack without a heavy cost in casualties. Byng decided to turn its flanks. 5th Corps would bypass the Thiepval heights and drive north-east towards Pys, while 6th Corps, in addition to extending its left, would take Gomiecourt which lies two miles to the north of Achiet-le-Grand and dominates that village. The flanking movements would take place during the night 22/23 August and bring enfilade fire on the Irles – Achiet-le-Grand positions while 4th Corps advanced against them.

Preparations were speedily completed. 6th Corps captured Gomiecourt and some 400 prisoners by 5 am, while the 4th secured its right flank by taking the high ground at Beauregard Dovecot which overlooked it, thus lessening the need for 5th Corps to take Pys. Their main attack was launched at 11 am and by noon the enemy main position, except at Irles, had been captured. The remainder was taken before nightfall.

It was a day of success. Third Army, attacking an enemy stronger in numbers, had taken considerable ground and more than five thousand prisoners. Haig noted in his diary that Byng was 'very pleased with the results of today after yesterday's halt and thinks he did right to halt for a day.'[5]

Consideration for his troops was always an important factor in the operations which Byng planned, but no general can allow sympathy for the undoubted hardships and hazards borne by his soldiers to limit the demands which he makes upon them. He intended to give the enemy no rest and ordered the advance to continue that night towards objectives eight miles to the East.

5th Corps on the right now faced the task of capturing the German bastions which had held out so long during the Somme battles of 1916. To avoid the swamps of the Ancre valley, Lt-Gen C. D. Shute, its commander, planned convergent attacks from the north and south of the flooded area to outflank Thiepval and Grandcourt with a zero hour of 1 am.

To the north, just inside the 4th Corps boundary, the town of Miraumont was still holding out, blocking the advance of that Corps' right. If 5th Corps could take the high ground south-east of the town, it would be possible to cut off the village and prevent the withdrawal of the garrison and the destruction of the bridges over the Ancre. Byng decided to risk a bold stroke by sending a brigade by night to break through to the high ground which lay three thousand yards beyond the known line of the enemy.

The 64th Brigade of 21st Division was selected for the task. Moving off before midnight, they rushed the enemy posts which barred their route and by early morning reached their objective, where they came under heavy fire from all sides. Each of the battalions was strongly counterattacked and the brigade commander was badly wounded. Ignoring calls to surrender by the Germans, the men from Yorkshire and Durham held their ground.

In the meantime the 42nd Division of 4th Corps had been unable to get across the Ancre at Miraumont during the night, but, with the light of morning, when the German defences came under the fire of 64th Brigade above them, resistance weakened. For several hours fighting went on in the town before it fell, leaving 540 prisoners, a battery of 5.9-inch howitzers and some 4.2-inch guns in British hands. At noon firing on the front of 64th Brigade ceased and the enemy withdrew from the area.

During the first five days of the battle Byng's original thirteen divisions had not been reinforced, while the Germans had thrown in eleven fresh divisions to support the eight which had originally held their front. The Third Army was gaining steadily in self-confidence and Byng's subordinate commanders were learning that they could trust their troops in the more complicated tactics of envelopment.

On the left the 6th Corps was now approaching the Hindenburg position which ran from north-west to south-east across the front. On 25th August Byng ordered Lt-Gen Sir Charles Fergusson of 17th Corps to take over command of the two divisions on the extreme left, which would be the first to close up to the formidable defences, and to begin the considerable preparations which would be needed for a direct assault. Further to the south it would be several days before the right flank of Third Army arrived at the Hindenburg Line.

Rawlinson's Fourth Army had been advancing in step with Byng on the right. Now, on 26 August, the British offensive was extended to the north as the Canadian Corps attacked south-east from Arras between the Third Army boundary and the River Scarpe.

By nightfall they had taken Monchy-le-Preux and had forced the Germans to decide on a retirement, not only on the Arras – Somme front but in Flanders as well. 17th Corps now joined the Canadian advance south-eastwards astride the Hindenburg front position, but the defences were strong and progress was bitterly contested. Elsewhere the divisions of Third Army advanced steadily eastward. There was heavy fighting at key points such as Bapaume which the Germans had been determined to hold but, wherever possible, Byng directed that centres of resistance be encircled or by-passed.

From the village of Quéant in the Third Army sector, running north across the Rivers Sensée and Scarpe, a defensive position of great strength lay across the paths of the 17th and Canadian Corps. Known to the Germans as the Wotan Line, it was called the Drocourt – Quéant (or D – Q) line by the British. On 29 August Haig ordered the First Army to break it and exploit through Bourlon Wood to the outskirts of Cambrai. Third Army was to assist the operation while holding the enemy down by attacks across its whole front. The advance would take 17th Corps through the maze of defences which marked the junction of the Hindenburg and D–Q systems. As evidence that the task would be difficult, a fresh German division attacked the village of Bullecourt on 30 August, driving back the 167th Brigade with heavy casualties.

On 1 September the 17th and Canadian Corps advanced to within assaulting distance of the D–Q line, while, on the right of Third Army, 5th Corps had almost shaken itself free of the old Somme battlefields. Further south, in one of their most memorable actions of the war, the Australian Corps captured Péronne and Mont St Quentin, turning the German line along the Somme.

Next morning, in a brilliantly conceived operation, Arthur Currie's Canadians burst through the D–Q line at every point where they attacked it and established themselves well beyond. Taking advantage of their success, 17th Corps advanced and occupied the villages of Quéant and Pronville.

Shortly after 2 pm that day Ludendorff recognized the inevitable consequences of the breaking of the D–Q position. He ordered his armies to retire behind the Sensée, the Canal du Nord and, farther south, to the Hindenburg position, beginning that night. Next morning the Third Army discovered that the Germans had gone. Air reconnaissance revealed the extent of their retirement and Byng ordered the 5th, 4th and 6th Corps to 'pursue the enemy with properly constituted advanced guards of all arms', while 17th Corps moved forward to the Canal du Nord. In the next few days Third Army followed up the retreating Germans, crossed the Canal du Nord south of Havrincourt and closed up to the Hindenburg position.

On 8 September Haig asked his army commanders for their views on the prospects of future operations. Byng answered that in his opinion the enemy was fighting to gain time – to resuscitate his demoralized divisions, to recuperate and to make preparations either for an offensive or for a better thought-out retirement than the one which was being imposed upon him. His divisions therefore had been told to hold on as long as possible and to counterstrike, a policy which gained time but which was wasteful in men. The enemy's main stand opposite Third Army would no doubt be on the Hindenburg position. His next solid defensive line would be the St Quentin Canal. Beyond this no strong defence line was ready. The enemy would therefore try to hold a position west of St Quentin – Cambrai – Douai as long as possible.

Byng considered that the general state of the enemy's troops was poor. Many would surrender if they dared and many had fought extremely badly. Every division as it arrived fought well for a couple of days, and then became demoralized by the never-ceasing action forced upon it. This demoralization of the enemy would not last unless he was constantly attacked and harassed and therefore continuous offensive action must be the role of the British armies.

Byng proposed that an attack should be carried out as soon as possible to get astride the Hindenburg Front System by striking east of the Canal du Nord. If this succeeded, he hoped that it would be exploited by an advance of the First Army. Later a decision either to attack the line of the St Quentin Canal or to turn it would depend to a great extent on the condition of the enemy troops at the time.

As the Third Army moved up to the Hindenburg position the stout resistance of the enemy bore out Byng's forecast that here he would attempt finally to stop the British advance. Only a well-planned and coordinated 'set-piece' attack could penetrate the enemy line and,

248

before that could take place, its outlying defences must be driven in and observation obtained over it.

At 5.25 am on 12 September Byng launched three divisions to capture the Trescault and Havrincourt spurs which ran parallel to the front, ground which included the villages of those names and the Grand Ravine, which featured in the Battle of Cambrai, 1917. After hard fighting, the New Zealand and 37th Divisions on the right cleared the enemy defences and, after beating off several counter-attacks, held Havrincourt Wood and Trescault.

On their left the 62nd Division drove the Germans from Havrincourt and from the Hindenburg Front System to the north and south of it. Then the enemy counterattacked. A violent bombardment was followed by a determined infantry assault, supported by low-flying aircraft. The attacking troops were beaten off by rifle and machine-gun fire, while artillery prevented their supporting troops from moving forward. There were signs of further counterattacks to come as the weary troops of the 62nd set about consolidating their positions.

The importance of Havrincourt to the defence of the Hindenburg position was obvious to Byng and he expected that the enemy would make a major attempt to retake it. He brought forward the fresh 3rd Division to relieve the 62nd and arrange for reserves to be ready to support them from both 4th and 6th Corps.

The German High Command had made it clear to Marwitz, commanding the Second Army, that Havrincourt must be recaptured. Two fresh divisions, the 6th and 20th, Brandenburgers and Hanoverians, were selected for the operation. They were among the best and proudest in the German Army, with a tradition of success in the attack, which stemmed from the Franco-Prussian War when, together in the 3rd and 10th Corps, they drove Bazaine's army from the heights at Vionville.[6]

Supported by two additional divisions, they attacked on 18 September with the object of recovering both Havrincourt and Moeuvres to the north. A heavy bombardment, including consider-able amounts of gas, battered the British positions and communica-tion trenches for more than an hour, followed by bombing and strafing attacks by large numbers of aircraft. Close behind their supporting fire, the German infantry succeeded in overwhelming some frontline posts and, north of Havrincourt, reached the line of the support trench and began to bomb their way along it. But, before they could secure a hold on the position, Byng's well-placed reserves blocked their advance, then cleared them out of the trenches. By midnight the whole line was reestablished.

After the war Byng was to say that 18 September was one of the most significant days in the history of the Third Army. The Brandenburgers and Hanoverians had been soundly beaten at Havrincourt and the heart was out of the enemy thereafter.[7]

There was more immediate evidence of how serious the defeat was regarded by the Germans. For the failure of his counterattack von der Marwitz, one of the most senior and experienced of their generals, was removed from the command of his army.

Earlier that day 5th Corps on the right attacked in conjunction with Fourth Army and reached Gouzeaucourt and Villers Guislain and, by the evening of 26 September, the Third Army with the First and Fourth was in position to attack the Hindenburg Line. At 10.30 pm the preliminary bombardment began.

Haig had ordered Third Army to operate in the direction of the general line Le Cateau–Solesmes, its first task being to secure the passages over the St Quentin Canal. Facing it was the right wing of the German Second Army and the left of the Seventeenth, their junction being near Havrincourt. Their forward defences were in the Hindenburg Line backed by the Hindenburg Support. Behind these a maze of trenches covered the ground back to and beyond the St Quentin Canal. Rumilly, which overlooked the bend between Masnières and Marcoing, was particularly strongly held.

On the left 17 Corps began their advance by crossing the Canal du Nord. Only partially constructed, it was dry in this area and much of the Army to the south were already over it.

It was a 'sticky' day for the three attacking corps. The left-hand division of 17th Corps was slow in passing through the divisions which led the attack and next morning was three thousand yards behind the right of the Canadians who had taken Bourlon Wood. While both 6th and 4th Corps made some progress, they did not reach their objectives for the day. Their progress might have been better if the timings of their attacks had been better coordinated by the staff of Third Army. Despite that, all had made an advance through well-planned defences which would have been seen as a great victory in 1916.

On the 28th progress was better and Byng told Haig that the enemy was showing signs of cracking.[8] The Army advanced distances varying from 2,000 yards on the right to 5,000 on the left. It cleared the trench system between Marquion and Cantaing, and part of the Hindenburg Support system. Between Marcoing and the Army left boundary, it reached the St Quentin Canal and south of Cambrai secured small bridgeheads over it. Next day 6th and 17th Corps were across the Canal on their whole front. That night the enemy facing 4th and 5th Corps on the right withdrew to the eastern bank but patrols found that any attempt to cross was met by heavy fire.

The Germans were determined to hold Cambrai and its outer defences. For a week the Third Army worked slowly forward, taking Rumilly and Crèvecoeur. Then, on 5 October, being outflanked by the advance of the Fourth Army, the enemy opposite Byng's right pulled back from the St Quentin Canal to the Beaurevoir Line, three miles to the east.

With all his Army across the Canal, Byng directed his corps to advance toward the River Selle where the Germans were hastily occupying the new defences of the so-called Herman Line. On the 8th the 63rd (Royal Naval) Division of 17th Corps took Niergnies, overlooking Cambrai from the south, whereupon the Germans ordered its garrison to withdraw.

In order to keep in touch with his advancing divisions, Byng had moved from his spartan headquarters to a train of ramshackle carriages and goods trucks which was the despair of some of his staff. By 21 October it had moved to Masnières, four miles south of Cambrai.[9]

The country ahead was untouched by war and there was no sign of trenches or wire. Against the rearguards of machine-guns and artillery, Byng's four corps moved forward to the River Selle which they found was well defended by the Herman Line beyond. Some small bridgeheads were secured but attempts to reach the high ground which overlooked the river valley were beaten back. Another set-piece attack would be necessary and each day's delay gave the enemy more time to develop his defences. Large amounts of ammunition would be needed, yet the railways to bring it forward had not been rebuilt as far as Cambrai. Damage to roads and bridges behind the front further slowed the accumulation of supplies. It would be several days, at the least, before an attack could begin.

On 17 October Haig ordered his army commanders to be ready to launch a general attack from positions on the east bank of the Selle on or about the 21st with the object of securing the line of the Sambre Canal, the western edge of the Forest of Mormal and northwards to the Schelde.

Most of the Third Army were still on the west bank of the river and, even where it had been crossed, the bridgeheads were shallow. In order that his assaulting divisions should have a favourable jumping-off line, Byng ordered them to cross the river before the general advance and secure the high ground two miles beyond it. With only seven divisions attacking six of the Germans, who had three more in close support, numbers were not in Byng's favour. Depending on surprise, he dispensed with a preliminary bombardment. Zero hour was to be at 2 am on the 20th when the moon would be full.

Operations were now complicated by large numbers of French civilians in the battle area. In the little towns of Solesmes and St Python, which were heavily defended by the Germans, their presence was particularly awkward to the advance of 6th Corps. To minimize the danger to them, Byng ordered that the full artillery barrage should pass by either side of the built-up areas while firing over them should be confined to shrapnel and machine-gun bullets from which civilians could take cover in their cellars. Enemy resistance was strong and took a heavy toll, especially among the Royal Engineers bridging the river. It was night before Third Army was established on the high ground beyond the Selle, ready to attack on 23 October with the First and Fourth Armies on its flanks.

Again Byng decided to attack at night and zero hour was set for 2 am. Progress was relatively easy and in the next thirty-six hours his corps reached the ridge of high ground which runs from Englefontaine at the north-west corner of the Forest of Mormal, to Ghissignies, Ruesnes and Quérénaing. There the Army was to dig in and rest until the supply situation was more satisfactory.

Rest and sleep for the troops were now essential. Since August they had been in action almost constantly, much of the time at night. Casualties had been heavy in the BEF. For the three months of August, September and October, in the infantry and cavalry of the British, Canadian, Australian and New Zealand divisions, losses amounted to 300,000 out of a fighting strength of 1,200,000. (The total strength was 1,800,000). Reinforcements had been available, though, and most of the casualties had been replaced.

By 27 October, having followed up a local withdrawal by the enemy on the left, Third Army rested on a line running from Englefontaine west of Le Quesnoy and along the River Rhonelle over which it had secured bridgeheads. Both sides dug in while preparations began for a further offensive.

On the left of Third Army Valenciennes was taken by the Canadians and the stage was set for another advance of the British armies, the Fourth to Avesnes, the Third to Maubeuge and the First to Mons. It would begin on 4 November.

Byng gave his Army, as an intermediate objective, the long straight road which runs through Pont-sur-Sambre and Bavai (the Bavai Road) which he expected would be reached on the 5th. In the path of 4th Corps lay the ancient fortress of Le Quesnoy, which he ordered to be surrounded but not stormed.

The town was ringed by two ramparts separated by a dry ditch into which projected the bastions of the inner fortifications. The New Zealand Division which faced it planned to detach a brigade to surround the town and its fortifications, while the remainder, having by-passed it, advanced with 4th Corps. The investing brigade would ascertain whether the Germans were still in occupation and, if so, invite them to surrender.

The first stage of the operations was accomplished with little resistance except from the town itself. A platoon succeeded in crossing the outer ramparts, but was pinned down by machine-gun fire from the inner walls. Prisoners were sent to recommend surrender, backed by a formal request to do so dropped from an aircraft. It was refused.

About 4 pm the 4th New Zealand Rifle Battalion put down a mortar concentration on the western ramparts and soon afterwards an intrepid party succeeded in scaling the walls by a single ladder. The rest of the battalion followed, while some 2nd Rifles got into the town by the road bridge which was only partially destroyed. Soon they were advancing through the streets and found the German troops only too willing to surrender. Using the tactics of the Middle Ages, the New Zealanders had captured the fortress without destroying the town or injuring its inhabitants.

In Le Quesnoy and during their advance beyond it the New Zealand Division captured over 2450 prisoners and more than 100 guns. It was a remarkable achievement, even for this outstanding division.

The remainder of Third Army met with indifferent opposition and, by the evening of 5 November, had reached the Bavai road. It now seemed that the enemy were retreating all along the front and orders were given to continue the pursuit, but next day progress suddenly slowed.

The Seventeenth Army, facing Byng, had been ordered to hold on as long as possible to gain time for the German armies farther north to escape. Heavy rains made the bad roads of the area even worse and delayed the delivery of bridging material needed by the Third Army to cross the River Sambre and other minor streams, the crossing areas of which were defended by small but determined rearguards and were under incessant shell fire.

Added to Byng's problems was the task of feeding the French people liberated by his Army. The British had undertaken to provide for them for four days, after which the civil authorities were to take on the task, but in fact no French supply train or motor transport arrived until after the Armistice. To provide food the battalions of Third Army regularly gave up twenty-five to thirty percent of their rations, some units voluntarily going on half rations and, at their own expense, buying everything available in their canteens, especially for the children.

Next day, 7 November, the enemy shelling of the Sambre valley abruptly ceased and the Army continued toward Maubeuge, the frontier fortress whose loss with 30,000 troops had struck a cruel blow to French morale in 1914. The end was now in sight. German plenipotentiaries arrived in the Allied lines that evening and were taken by train to the Forest of Compiègne to seek an armistice from Marshal Foch.

Byng had ordered the Army to advance to the Avesnes-Maubeuge road on 8 November, but after learning that armistice terms had been offered to the Germans, he had instructed his corps commanders to confine operations to pushing forward patrols, following up the retreating enemy, or manoeuvring him out of position.

Despite this restriction, good progress was made. On the right 5th Corps reached the Army objective, and on the left 19th Division cleared a party of Germans from Marlborough's old battlefield of Malplaquet. During the late evening 2nd Guards Brigade detailed 3rd Battalion Grenadier Guards to move on Maubeuge in an attempt to rush its defences. It was a pitch dark night and, apart from a few stray shots, they encountered no opposition. By 2 am the citadel of the old fortress was in their hands.

Before dawn the enemy was in full retreat. A cavalry squadron and two troops of cyclists moved in advance of the infantry of each division but they made no contact with the enemy until the afternoon. By that time the infantry had reached the Avesnes – Maubeuge road and were establishing a line of observation beyond it over the River Soire.

Byng now ordered Haldane of 6th Corps to form an Army advanced guard to keep touch with the enemy, while the other three corps stood fast.

When the cavalry and cyclists went forward on 10 November they found village after village clear of the enemy. It was dusk when they finally found him entrenched near the Beamont – Rouveroy – Mons road. Next morning 6th Corps were pushing forward their infantry outposts and cyclist patrols when a message ordering hostilities to cease at 11 am was received. There was barely time for it to reach the forward troops before the guns along the front fell silent.

Byng was quick to acknowledge what his men had achieved.

SPECIAL ORDER OF THE DAY
– By –
GENERAL HON SIR J. H. G. BYNG, K.C.B., K.C.M.G., M.V.O., COMMANDING THIRD ARMY

11–11–18

To all Ranks of the Third Army

The operations of the last three months have forced the enemy to sue for an armistice as a prelude to peace.

Your share in the consummation of this achievement is one that fills me with pride and admiration.

Since August 21st you have won eighteen decisive battles, you have driven the enemy back over sixty miles of country and you have captured 67,000 prisoners and 800 guns.

That is your record, gained by your ceaseless enterprise, your indomitable courage and your loyal support to your leaders.

Eleven Divisions in the four Corps (Guards 2nd 3rd and 62nd, 5th 37th 42nd and New Zealand, 17th 21st and 38th) have been continuously in action since the beginning of the advance and have borne the brunt of the operations. Other Divisions have joined and left, each one adding fresh lustre to its history.

To all ranks, to all Corps and formations, to all administrative and transport units, I tender my thanks. May your pride in your achievements be as great as mine in the recollection of having commanded the Army in which you served.

> J. BYNG, General
> Commanding Third Army.

For the last hundred days of the war the British armies had borne the main weight of the Allied strategy. That they were able to do so speaks for their remarkable resilience in recovering from the heavy losses they suffered in March and April. The morale of the troops increased as that of the enemy declined. Weary as they were toward the end, their determination to win grew as they came to see what the French population in the occupied areas had suffered at the hands of the Germans.

The price of victory was high. Between 21 August and 11 November 115,429 officers and men of the Third Army had been killed, wounded or were missing.[10]

For Byng the operations of the last three months were the culmination of his military career, yet there was about them something anticlimactic. His was the largest of Britain's five field armies and he controlled its operations with the sureness of touch which four years of active operations had given him. Its successes reflected both his meticulous planning and a personal flair in which was combined an

255

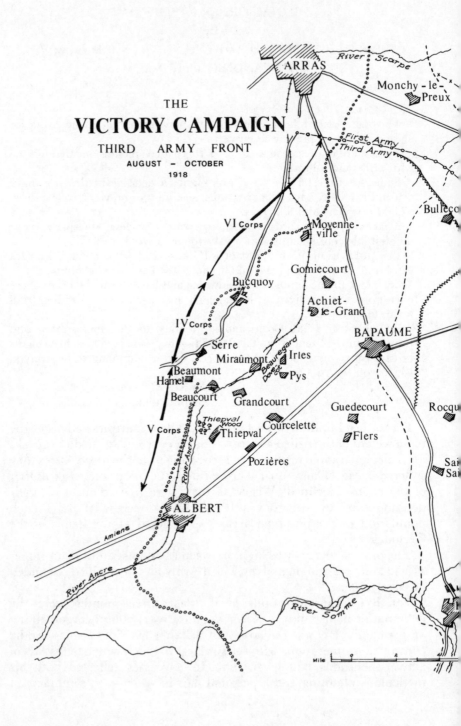

THE

VICTORY CAMPAIGN

THIRD ARMY FRONT

AUGUST – OCTOBER
1918

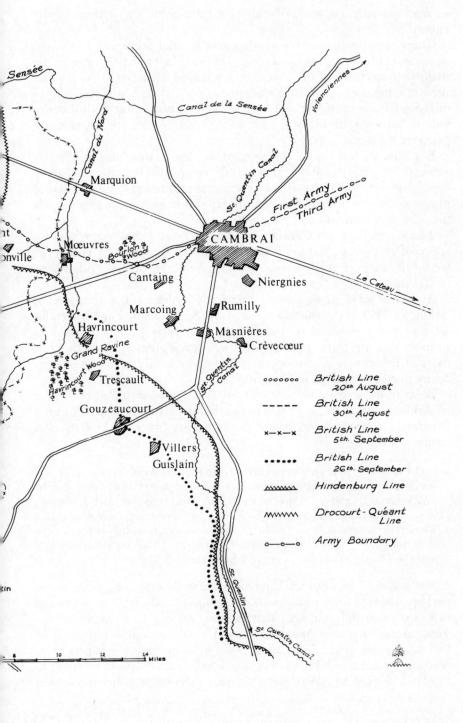

Sensée

Canal de la Sensée

Canal du Nord

Valenciennes

St. Quentin Canal

Marquion

First Army
Third Army

CAMBRAI

Mœuvres

Bourlon Wood

...onville

...t

Cantaing

Niergnies

Marcoing

Rumilly

Le Cateau

Havrincourt

Masnières

Grand Ravine

Crèvecœur

Havrincourt Wood

Trescault

St. Quentin Canal

Gouzeaucourt

Villers
Guislain

○○○○○○○   *British Line*
             20ᵗʰ August

– – – – –   *British Line*
             30ᵗʰ August

x — x — x   *British Line*
             5ᵗʰ. September

● ● ● ● ● ●   *British Line*
             26ᵗʰ. September

ʌʌʌʌʌʌ   *Hindenburg Line*

MMMMM   *Drocourt - Quéant*
             Line

○—○—○   *Army Boundary*

St. Quentin Canal

...tin

6   10   12   14 Miles

instinct for surprise and a faculty for forecasting the actions of the enemy.

There was an inexorable quality to the final advance, as though nothing could stop the four corps of the Third Army. From the deliberate restraint of the first attack north of Albert, its soldiers and their commanders grew in confidence and skill. Such was the quality of Byng's leadership – he wore an aura of success – that he imbued a will to succeed in his generals which resulted in an unrelenting pressure on the enemy.

But the advance was trammelled by the restrictions of Foch's strategy of deliberation. There was no possibility for an army commander to bring about large-scale envelopments or outflanking manoeuvres which might have brought earlier and more spectacular disaster to the enemy.

There had been no Cannae, no Waterloo, and now there was no surge of elation at Victory. Byng's soldiers, like those of Henry V, were but warriors for the working day. Now that it was ended they would rather forget than cheer.

At a meeting of Army Commanders at Cambrai in the afternoon of Armistice Day Haig announced that the Second and Fourth Armies were to move forward to the Rhine. The others would remain in France and Belgium pending further developments. For Byng it marked the end of active operations, but he would remain with his Army until it returned to Britain.

Later in the month his wife crossed to Belgium with Princess Alice of Athlone to be present when the King of the Belgians entered Brussels. Byng refused to attend. Some twenty-five years later Evelyn wrote:

> His hatred of pageants even extended to this immortal moment. He just sat tight in his own headquarters. Not only did he refuse to come but he was extremely angry at my having gone and I got an awful wigging afterwards just as I did over the La Panne visit. However, neither scolding affected me much, because by then I was no longer as foolish as I had been in India when I missed the Curzon Durbar; for I had learnt not to give him the chance of vetoing a thing I had set my heart on.[11]

Her account does not tell the whole story. Written long afterwards, perhaps she had forgotten that the rule against officers' wives coming to France and Belgium was strictly enforced and had prevented her from taking a job near Montreuil in 1915. No commander in the BEF had been more punctilious than Byng in denying himself privileges which were not available to his men. The five short leaves he spent in England during the War were no more than the entitlement of a private. His spartan headquarters and his smashing of the windows in his shelter in Gallipoli showed that he wished to live as much like his men as was practicable and that he cared what they thought of him. While Evelyn accompanied Princess Alice in an official capacity as a lady-in-waiting on the visits to La Panne and Brussels, she did so more for her own pleasure and interest than as a duty. She could easily have declined to go and by doing so would have avoided the possibility of misunderstandings in the BEF about her presence in the theatre of war.

'Not to give him a chance of vetoing a thing I had set my heart on,' she had not told Byng beforehand that she intended to go to Brussels. When he returned to Thorpe-le-Soken on the 6.40 pm train on 27 November she was not waiting on the platform. A cheering crowd greeted him as he emerged from the station and a torch-light procession escorted him to Thorpe Hall. The grounds of the house were lit by fairy lights and an illuminated crown shone above the front entrance. As he arrived a huge bonfire was beginning to flare up in the park. The happy, cheering villagers ignored the cold and 'there was festivity inside the Maid's Head and the Crown such as was not seen since the war began.'[12] But Evelyn was not at the door to greet him: she was still in Belgium. It was not the kind of homecoming a soldier should expect. Small wonder that Byng was put out with his wilful wife!

A few days later he was back with the Third Army.

About 15 December he learned that he was to return to England with Haig and the other army commanders for an official reception in London. When it had first been proposed Lloyd George objected. He was annoyed with the Commander-in-Chief who had refused to accept any honours or reward for his services until the government committed themselves to making provision for disabled officers and men. Effectively Haig had blocked the granting of any awards to the country's naval, military and civilian wartime leaders. The delay was embarrassing and would become politically disastrous if the reason were made public. The Prime Minister's petty objection to the reception was removed when the King said that, if the Government would not arrange it, he would receive the commanders himself.

They crossed to Dover on 19 December and, about noon, arrived at Charing Cross where they were greeted by the Duke of Connaught, the Cabinet and the Army Council. Byng shared an open carriage with Plumer for the drive via Pall Mall to Buckingham Palace for lunch.

As they passed the Athenaeum, to which they both belonged, the two army commanders laughed and waved enthusiastically toward the Club. Inside, members felt honoured by their attention and waved back, unaware that the generals were responding to the Club's chambermaids dancing on the upper balcony. Seeing the remarkable behaviour of the bishops and learned academics who were their fellow members, Byng and Plumer nearly collapsed with laughter, resulting in yet more effusive waving from the Club. Seldom can the members of that august establishment have presented such a cheerful picture to the public.

On 28 January, 1919, Byng was summoned urgently to GHQ by Haig who told him that he wanted him to go to Calais where there was a 'strike or something of the kind'. When Byng arrived at the port he discovered that troops of the Railway Operating Department, the Ordnance and Service Corps and the Women's Auxiliary Services employed in the base had been on strike for nearly three weeks. To complicate matters some five thousand troops of different regiments had returned to Calais from leave two days earlier and, taking advantage of the strike, had mutinied, turned all officers out of the camp and formed a 'Soviet'.

It took Byng little time to discover that the strikers and the mutineers were poles apart in their aims and objects. The men and women who had refused to work had had much provocation. Weeks after the end of the war they were working seven days a week, living in intolerable quarters and had good reason to believe that a continuing shortage of rations was due to corruption in the Quartermaster's stores. When one of them grumbled about conditions, he was arrested, charged with sedition and sent to the military prison at Boulogne. Next day the men refused to work until he was released and their grievances righted. The Base Commandant refused to listen to them, whereupon the strikers threatened to go to Boulogne and free the man themselves. The Commandant then promised to obtain his release by telephone. Until he had, the men refused to allow any of their officers and NCOs to leave camp without a written permit.

Byng met and talked with the ringleaders among the base troops and became convinced that their complaints were legitimate. He told them plainly that they had gone too far, but that he could sympathize with them and proposed to do something about conditions in the base. He then summoned the heads of the Services at GHQ whose troops were among the strikers and made plain what he thought of the lack of leadership and interest in their men's welfare which were at the root of the trouble. He told them that he would try to persuade the men to resume work in return for a pledge to see to their complaints. There would be no disciplinary action or reprisals against them.

The strikers were reasonable men. Byng promised that their grievances would be attended to and by 6 am next day all had returned to work. There was no further trouble. One of their leaders, Mr B. G. A. Cannell, later explained the reason: 'He kept his word.'[13]

The mutiny was another matter and Byng saw that it could best be overcome by a display of overwhelming force. He summoned reinforcements and by the morning of 30 January had disposed two infantry brigades of the 35th Division with sixty machine-guns around the mutineers' camp. At a signal the 104th Brigade, led by Brig-Gen Sandilands, marched into the camp with bayonets fixed. He called out to the men he saw, 'Fall in those who wish to return to their units.' About 2000 at once picked up their packs and were moved out. The Brigade continued its way through the huge camp, collecting the surrendering mutineers and driving the hard core into a corner. Their leader, a sergeant in the Scottish Rifles, called to his men to 'stand fast and stand united'. He was at once arrested, as were two other NCOs.

There remained some 200 men who refused to surrender unless their leaders were released. They asked to send 'a deputation to meet with the General'. Byng had no intention of treating with mutineers and replied, 'I have heard of Field-Marshals in the Army, of Generals, Colonels, Captains, Sergeants and Privates, but I have never heard of a deputation. Surrender unconditionally in half an hour or bear the consequences.' The men gave in. Most asked for a second chance and were released.[14]

For several days the mutineers had had little food. After they had been given a hot meal, Byng warned them against being so foolish again and sent them back to their units in the forward areas.[15]

The four ringleaders who had fomented the trouble were tried by court martial and sent to prison.

Shortly afterwards Byng returned to England, his future in the Army uncertain. For some weeks he was employed at the War Office as president of a committee on the reorganization of the Royal Regiment of Artillery.[16] On 12 March Winston Churchill, now the Secretary of State for War, offered him the appointment of Commander-in-Chief of Southern Command, but Byng asked permission to decline to make way for some younger and more junior officer who might otherwise not be employed.[17]

On 19 July he appeared in the Victory Parade in London. Followed by a Life Guardsman carrying his Army Commander's

261

flag, he rode behind Haig through miles of streets lined with cheering crowds to salute the King in front of the Palace. When he dismounted in Hyde Park his last duty as a soldier on the active list had been completed.

Chapter 13
The Byng Millions

BYNG WAS NOW 57. As a full general he could look forward to another ten years of service until superannuation, but having turned down Southern Command, he had shown that the routine of peacetime service held no attractions for him. Indeed, he had intended to retire to Thorpe after his service in Egypt was completed, and now, following the strain of the years of war, he would be content to do so. But the Treasury were far from happy at the prospect of paying a pension to a general as young as he. For the present he must remain on the active list.

But what to do with all the officers who had risen to high rank in a much contracted peacetime army was only one among many of the problems facing the War Office and the Government. Another was the disposal of the accumulated profits of the Army and Navy canteens during the war. These amounted to about seven million pounds (worth at least ten times that amount in the money of the 1980's). It was a subject about which emotions could be raised very quickly, the nub of the problem being that this vast amount of money represented profits made from purchases by the men of the Forces out of their own pay. Plainly the disposal of the United Services Fund, as it was called, would not be a simple matter and was fraught with political hazards.

Obviously the Fund must be managed by someone in whom the ex-servicemen had confidence, of undoubted integrity, strength of character and with the experience of administering large projects. On 19 July, 1919, the day of the Victory Parade in London, the Government offered the chairmanship of the Fund to Byng. It was a daunting prospect, but affecting as it did the welfare of his former soldiers, he felt that he could not refuse. He accepted on two conditions. One was that the Fund should be absolutely free from Government control and should be set up as an independent organization. Consequently it would be impossible for him, as a soldier, to run it, so they must accept his resignation from the Army. The second condition

263

was that in all the operations of the Fund there must be complete publicity. In his view, the money belonged to the ex-service officers and men and they must know what was being done with it.[1]

In his words, 'No sticky-fingered individual will ever touch one pound of the seven million which we are distributing among the serving and ex-serving soldiers.' All the work would be done by volunteers, the only salaried staff being one secretary and two clerks.

Within a few days he had established offices at 38 Parliament Street, in London, where visitors would find him working at an army issue 'table, 6 foot, folding' in a room bare of rugs and other furniture, which he shared with Pat Hodgson, from his old staff at Third Army, who had volunteered to help. Former privates knocking on the door were often astonished to find it opened by the former Army Commander himself.

But the immense task of helping the ex-servicemen, their wives, widows and orphans, as well as welfare work within the peacetime services, could not be handled in detail from a small office in London. From the outset Byng sought to work through philanthropic organizations and clubs, in particular the Federation of Discharged and Demobilized Soldiers and Sailors, and the Comrades of the Great War. He was concerned that while they, and other smaller associations, were doing much to help ex-servicemen, they were rival organizations and were working at cross-purposes. Early in August, 1919, he said, 'It seems to us that if we could get those associations to amalgamate into one big organization, we should be doing a very big work for the benefit of the ex-servicemen. . . . We could support it very strongly financially and we could help in many other respects.' His concept was to result in the formation of The Royal British Legion.

In so far as the families and widows of wartime servicemen were concerned, he believed in supporting that uniquely British organization, the Soldiers', Sailors' and Airmen's Families Association, whose volunteers covered the whole country and could reach directly the individual in need.

To the public the Fund became known as the 'Byng Millions'. Within the first four months he received applications from individuals and associations which amounted to £240,000,000. Even the seven million pounds promised was not available at once. Over two million represented surplus stock on hand in the canteens, which, if dumped on the market, would realize nothing like that sum of money. Inevitably there were criticisms and complaints but few could find fault with the principle which he established for spending the money, which was 'to support any scheme which has for its object the collective benefit of the ex-service community'.[2]

One of his first problems was with the Government itself over the conditions under which he accepted the chairmanship of the Fund. On 30 October he became quite short with the Secretary of State for War, his former galloper:

My dear Winston,
I am sorry to say I shall have to resign my position on this Fund unless 1) I am gazetted out, 2) the money is transferred to our account.
A month ago I mentioned to you that these were my two difficulties in dealing with the men and that suspicions were growing in consequence of the non-fulfilment of the promise.

Yours sincerely,
J. Byng.

Furious over the effect which Churchill's failure to honour the agreement was having, he took no chances that the situation would be allowed to continue. Having signed the letter, he called at Buckingham Palace. Next day Churchill received a letter from Lord Stamfordham. It began:

The King is much concerned to learn that there is every reason to fear that Byng will resign his post as head of the United Services Fund on the grounds . . .

and ended

the King wishes you to find satisfactory *modus operandi* by which Byng's services may be secured both now and in the future.

A hurried note from the War Office to the Treasury pointed out that Byng was eligible for half-pay of £3.5.0 per day – £1186 per year – or for retired pay of £1175 per year. He was placed on retired pay on 7 November.

In August, with the other commanders of Britain's wartime armies, Byng was elevated to the peerage and awarded a grant of £30,000. He chose as his title Baron Byng of Vimy and Thorpe-le-Soken and announced that he intended to devote part of his grant to building a club for demobilized soldiers in his village.[3]

Other honours came his way. From Canada there was a commission as Honorary General in the Canadian Militia,[4] from Cambridge an honorary degree of doctor of law and from the War Office, a trophy of war, a German 135-mm gun and carriage[5] to be positioned by the gates of Thorpe Hall.

In the years immediately following the war there were many public engagements for a retired general. Almost every village in Britain erected a memorial to those who had died in the war, and Byng unveiled several, particularly in his own area of East Anglia – Little Clacton, Halstead, Thorpe-le-Soken. These ceremonies, attended by the whole population of the villages, most of whom had suffered personal loss, were deeply moving.

There were so many invitations to speak that, at the anniversary dinner of the Royal Geographical Society in 1920, Byng commented that, not only had they heard the toast of the army replied to about five times a night since the Armistice, but they also suffered from the fact that several distinguished generals had written their memoirs. He was inclined to paraphrase Scripture and say

The rest of the Acts of Douglas Haig and his Army, and how he took his soldiers to the land flowing with plum and apple, are they not written in the Chronicles of our literary generals?[6]

Byng enjoyed once more having time for the society of the writers and artists who were his friends. He had a knack for amusing them with absurd stories, particularly about the over-dignified. One day in the cloakroom of the Athenaeum he said to the Archbishop of Canterbury, 'Have you noticed that since we elected the last three Bishops to this Club three pairs of nail scissors have disappeared from the lavatory?'[7] An indication of how the members of the Club regarded him was seen when a number of them, including Sir Reginald Blomfield RA, Sir Henry Newbolt CH, Dr W. H. D. Rowse and Sir Owen Seaman, the editor of *Punch*, wished to give a dinner for André Maurois in January, 1921, they chose Byng for their chairman.[8]

In 1920 Evelyn persuaded Byng to visit his battlefields and to show her the place whose name they both now bore. Standing on the summit of Mont St Eloi, he showed her the strategic value of Vimy, then climbed the ridge itself to gaze down on Lens and the flat country beyond. Nothing had been touched on the Ridge. It was littered with broken rifles and all the wreckage of war. Bullrushes grew in the shell holes, the silence broken only by the song of birds. Near Hellfire Corner, on the Ypres – Menin road, they found his old dugout, strangely untouched, saw his old headquarters under the shadow of the church at Albert, where the Virgin's statue had hung precariously for so long. There were stirrings of life in the rubble which had been the villages of the Somme, so ruined that even the curés were not certain of the precise spot where their churches had stood. Bourlon Wood brought a reminder of the disappointments of Cambrai and they made a pilgrimage to Monchy-le-Preux where the 10th Hussars had suffered heavily in taking the town in 1917. He never returned to northern France or Belgium again.[9]

In the spring of 1920 Major Henry Willis-O'Connor DSO, who had been Currie's ADC throughout the war, was a guest at Thorpe. One morning *The Times* reported that Byng had been appointed Governor-General of Canada. Byng knew nothing about it and thought there must be some mistake. Jokingly he suggested to Willis-O'Connor that, if anything came of it, he should become his ADC. In the same spirit O'Connor accepted.

The source of the story was a 'group of influential Canadians' who had recommended to the King that Byng succeed the Duke of Devonshire. It was not until a year later that the Colonial Office, having found that he would be willing to serve, put forward his name. To their surprise the Canadian Government were not enthusiastic. Weeks went by while other names were considered. Eventually in June, during a visit of Prime Minister Sir Arthur Meighen to England, the decision was reached. Byng would be Canada's next Governor-General and would arrive in Ottawa early in August.

The appointment met with the approval of the Press in England and Canada, but nothing they said matched the enthusiasm of the veterans of the Canadian Corps. Most of their telegrams of congratulations were formal and respectful, but Major-Gen Sir Edward Morrison, Byng's artillery commander at Vimy, expressed their real sentiments when he cabled 'Oh frabjus day!'.[10]

Despite the obvious satisfaction of the public, there were politicians in Ottawa who viewed Byng's appointment with misgivings. The flowering of national spirit which began at Vimy and continued until the end of the war had been inspired by the unbroken successes of the splendid Canadian Corps. As the commander who shaped it and led it to its first major victory, Julian Byng's popularity was unparalleled. In the words of Gen McNaughton, 'The Canadians literally adored Byng.' Arthur Currie, who succeeded to its command, was not regarded with the same warmth of affection, but his men would contend that he was without doubt the best general on the Western Front. Canadian politicians had no experience of popular soldiers and were apprehensive that they might turn their popularity to political advantage. So abject was this fear of 'the man on horseback' that when Currie, returning from the War, arrived in Halifax in August, 1919, no one met him when he stepped ashore. Eventually an official arrived to escort him and his wife to a drab little civic ceremony. When it was over one of his former officers came forward, saluted and said, 'Welcome home, Sir'. For a moment he lost his self-control. His eyes moistened and his lips trembled as he placed a hand on the officer's shoulder and

267

hooked two fingers of the other in his Sam Browne belt, then quietly shook him for a moment, saying not a word. His reception in Ottawa was an even more pointed rebuff. No publicity was given to his arrival and he was greeted officially on Parliament Hill by a cold and non-committal speech given by a junior cabinet minister. The Prime Minister was out of town.

In 1921 militarism was a bogey of many in official life in Ottawa. The presence, as the Sovereign's representative, of the most popular commander of Canada's wartime army would remind people of the spirit and unity of the Canadian Corps, and of what it had accomplished under his leadership. By contrast, the war years in Canada had been fraught with controversy – conscription, the intrigues of Sam Hughes, profit-eering. With the men now home and, in many cases, discontented, they feared that the Corps might become a political force, comprised of its former members and their families, and the focus of their aspirations.

For his part the future Governor-General had only vague ideas of what his new post entailed. Ceremonial held no terrors for him, nor for that matter, much attraction – but he had no experience and only slight knowledge of constitutional practices. King George attempted to reassure him that, with his well-known common sense and due regard for the advice of his ministers, he would find that he could do the job well and would enjoy it. He remarked that, 'You will be just like a king in your kingdom.' Byng instinctively drew back from that prospect.

'Oh no, Sir,' he grinned. 'More likely I shall just be Byng in my Byngdom.'

'I daresay you're right, Bungo,' commented his Sovereign.

One of his first tasks was to select his new household. Capt Oswald Balfour, the military secretary, and Arthur Sladen, the private secretary, now with the Duke of Devonshire, would remain, and the Comptroller would be Lt-Col Humphrey Snow. It remained to choose his ADCs and a lady-in-waiting for Evelyn. In the past governor-generals' households had formed a small English enclave in Ottawa, insulated by convention and the rather artificial society of the capital from the main stream of Canadian life. Byng was determined that this situation should not continue. Remembering his lighthearted conversation with Willis-O'Connor, he sent him a cable inviting him to become his principal ADC. For another he chose Major Georges Vanier of the Royal 22^e Regiment. Pat Hodgson agreed to come as a secretary and Capt the Hon William Jolliffe, Capt the Hon Francis Erskine and Lord William Montagu-Scott would be his other ADCs. Miss Rachel Walpole, the librarian at the Athenaeum, became Evelyn's lady-in-waiting.

Before their departure for Canada Winston Churchill, now Secretary of State for the Colonies, gave a dinner for his old commanding officer.

Already one of the most controversial politicians of modern times, he was used to criticism, but as he remarked to Evelyn, 'I don't think anybody ever cursed me as heartily as Bungo did in the Light Horse days.'

On 2 August Byng received from Churchill his commission as Governor-General and Commander-in-Chief of the Dominion of Canada[11] and from the King the Grand Cross of the Order of St Michael and St George. Next day, as the Byngs prepared to sail, a message arrived from the Royal Yacht *Victoria and Albert*:

The Queen and I wish you both Godspeed and all good luck in Canada – George RI[12]

Chapter 14
Canada

THE CANADIAN PACIFIC liner *Empress of France* made a near-record crossing from Liverpool bringing the Byngs to Quebec almost half a day before their scheduled arrival. The Under-Secretary of State came aboard to greet them unofficially and discuss the arrangements for the next day. He suggested an incognito landing for a game of golf, but Byng refused.

The official reception began at 10.30 the next morning, 11 August, with the arrival on board of the Prime Minister who paid his respects and returned ashore. Fifteen minutes later, the Government steamer *Lady Grey*, dressed with every flag in its signal locker, came alongside to take the Byngs and their suite to the King's Wharf. As they moved toward the ancient town a battery at the Citadel began to fire a nineteen-gun salute. Waiting to greet them were most of the Dominion and Quebec cabinets, resplendent in the dark blue and gold lace of their court uniforms.

After inspecting a guard of honour of the Royal 22^e Regiment, the viceregal party were taken in three open carriages, escorted by a mounted escort of the Royal Canadian Dragoons, through the winding streets, lined with cheering crowds, to the Parliament Buildings of the Province of Quebec where Byng would be installed as Governor-General.

It was a solemn and impressive ceremony. Preceded by ADCs and the heads of the armed services (they had not yet become 'chiefs of staff'), Lord and Lady Byng moved in procession to the Legislative Council Chamber, where they were awaited by the members of the Federal and Quebec cabinets, all in full dress, and the judges of the Supreme Court in their robes, standing on either side of the long council table.

While Byng stood on a dais at the end of the room, his military secretary read out his Commission from the King as Governor-General. The Clerk of the Privy Council brought forward a bible, bowed and handed it to the senior puisne judge of the Supreme Court. Byng then stepped down from the dais, received the bible and, precisely at noon, took his oath of office. The Secretary of State then handed him the Great Seal of the Dominion of Canada. He returned it, saying' 'I hand you the Great Seal of Canada for safekeeping.' The Under-Secretary of State then read the proclamation of Byng as Governor-General and invited him to sign it, whereupon it was sealed and the band played 'God Save the King'. The wife of the Prime Minister of Quebec presented a bouquet to Lady Byng, addresses of welcome from the Province of Quebec and the City were read, to both of which Byng replied.

On leaving Parliament there was another guard to be inspected, this time from the Royal Rifles of Canada. Then, in their carriages again, they drove by way of the Grand Allée and the St Louis Gate to the Citadel, the Governor-General's residence in Quebec. There was only a brief rest before an official luncheon given by the Government of Canada, at which there were further speeches. In the evening the Lieutenant-Governor of the Province gave a dinner at Spencerwood, his official residence, from which the Byngs drove directly to the railway station, to be met by yet another guard of honour, before boarding the viceregal train at 10.30 pm for Ottawa.

So much for 'Byng and his Byngdom'! If he had any illusions that he might bring a less formal style to the position of Governor-General, they probably bore some cracks after his first few hours in office. But it was not of ceremonial that he was thinking when he said to Arthur Meighen that day, 'I've never done anything like this you know, and I expect I'll make mistakes.'

When he arrived in Ottawa next afternoon the streets were filled with happy, cheering crowds, come to see the man who had led the Canadians at Vimy. On Parliament Hill were thousands of his old soldiers and members of the public. Byng spent some happy minutes walking amongst them in the sweltering humidity of the August afternoon, until dark patches of perspiration soaked through his scarlet tunic and the rim of his cocked hat became limp.

Addresses of welcome were presented by the City of Ottawa and by the Great War Veterans Association, to which he replied. Then, with a mounted escort of the Royal Canadian Mounted Police, the Byngs were driven along the route which would soon become familiar, to Rideau Hall.

Their home for the next five years had originally been a regency villa built for a wealthy contractor named Thomas MacKay. In 1864 when the Government of Canada was preparing to move from Quebec to the new capital of Ottawa, there was no residence for the Governor.

271

Until something suitable could be built they leased Rideau Hall and some eighty acres of the MacKay estate as a temporary residence and began to enlarge it. By 1921, despite the addition of its handsome front, imposing entrance hall and reception rooms, it had more of the atmosphere of a comfortable country house than a palace. Set in its wooded park, with no views of the city and with its own stables and outbuildings, the illusion was enhanced. In earlier years, some governors and more particularly their families, came to regard it as a refuge from the unfinished roughness of the new capital, with its muddy streets and often ramshackle buildings. The home of the head of state in Canada is not known to the people as is, say, Buckingham Palace. There is no square outside where people can gather at times of national celebration or crisis, nor is there any visible sign such as a flag flying from the roof to show the people of the capital that the Governor-General is with them.

For many Canadians the location of Rideau Hall contributed to an impression of aloofness on the part of its residents. There was no way for the people to come to the Governor; he must come to them.

To make his contact with the people even more difficult, there was an instruction from the Colonial Office that the Governor-General could accept hospitality only from cabinet ministers and privy councillors, from members of the nobility (of whom there were very few in Canada) and from members of the diplomatic corps. Since this latter consisted only of the papal nuncio, and the current cabinet ministers rarely entertained, there were real barriers in the way of the Byngs developing friendships in Ottawa.

Even as the War had shattered the equilibrium of international relations, so, when Byng came to Canada, was its groundswell shaking the constitutional and political structures of the Empire. Canada had gone to war automatically on Britain's declaration, although the extent of her contribution had been decided by her own Parliament. At its end she had been a signatory of the Peace Treaty in her own right. By no means all British politicians and officials were aware of the significance of this and continued to assume that they might speak for Canada in matters of foreign affairs.

To be fair, opinion in the country was divided on the subject. Canada had no experienced foreign service and many doubted the ability of their political leaders to deal with international affairs. They would prefer to leave them to the British whom they were inclined to support in any event. This was not so much a reflection of a colonial mentality as evidence of the modesty and unpretentiousness of Canadians which so often surprises their friends.

28. The Governor-General of Canada and his Household after an opening of Parliament. Front row—Eva Sandford, Lord and Lady Byng, Arthur Sladen. Pat Hodgson is third from left in back row, Willis O'Connor third from right.

29. Georges and Pauline Vanier. (*Public Archives Canada*)

30. The Prince of Wales and MacKenzie King in Ottawa 1924. *(Public Archives Canada)*

31. Rideau Hall – residence of the Governor-General. *(Public Archives Canada)*

32. SS *Distributor* on which Byng sailed down the Mackenzie River to the Arctic – 1925. *(Public Archives Canada)*

33. A relaxed Byng on the farm of E. B. Little in Manitoba. Byng is in the middle, holding his hat.

34. The Chief Commissioner of the Metropolitan Police. *(Sport and General Press Agency)*

35. Byng arriving at Scotland Yard from which he could not retire. *(Public Archives Canada)*

36. Field-Marshal The Viscount Byng of Vimy – P. A. de Laszlo. *(National Portrait Gallery)*

37. Evelyn, Viscountess Byng of Vimy – P. A. de Laszlo *(Courtauld Institute of Art)*

A growing number, however, had come to recognize the realities of nationhood and realized that, imperfect though their chosen instruments might be, they must act independently in Canada's interests. It was not just the emotive subjects of peace and war, of loyalty and patriotism that were involved. It was trade and tariffs and the price of wheat and fish.

Understandably, the mood for independence was strongest in French Canada, but nowhere was it an issue which absorbed the minds of the populace. Most Canadians were far more concerned with the problems of earning a living in the uncertain conditions which existed after the War.

Within the country the two-party system was breaking down. Feeding on the discontent of the farmers, a new party, the Progressives, had grown in strength and, after the election of 1921, held the balance of power between the Liberals and Conservatives. Within each there was dissension. Regardless of party, politicians from the western provinces were influenced by the interests of the farmers, those from the east by the needs of industry, from the Maritimes by fish and coal and steel. Free trade, tariffs and freight rates were issues which divided parties on sectional lines, while the natural north-to-south communications of the continent tended to attract the regions of Canada to the neighbouring part of the United States.

In the circumstances the role of the Governor-General had grown in importance. Unlike today, he not only performed the constitutional functions of the sovereign in Canada, but was the representative of the British Government. Byng recognized that this would lead to difficulties and soon began to press for a change. In the meantime he would only act as a channel of communication between governments and would do nothing to press the views of British ministers on their Canadian counterparts. As he was to stress again and again, 'I will not act as their ambassador.'[1]

Byng was well aware of the conflicting interests which divided Canadians. Influenced by them, the Corps in Belgium had been more a collection of rival battalions in 1916 than the mutually loyal and cohesive force which he welded together. It seemed to him that the enormous potential of the country would never be realized by her people until they subordinated their local interests for the common good. Within the limits of his office, he was determined to work for national unity.

Few Canadians would argue with the course which he had set himself and, until the fifth year of his term as governor, there was no complaint about his performance of his constitutional role. After the election which took place within months of arrival no party held an

273

absolute majority in the House of Commons and no party had a broad representation of members from across the country. At any time a change in political groupings could involve the Governor-General in a change of government and even in the exercise of the residual powers of his office.

Byng readily admitted to his Canadian ministers his lack of experience of political and constitutional matters, where it might not have occurred to a civilian to do so. It would be strange indeed, and out of character, if Byng had not read everything available on these subjects as they pertain to Canada. Who then would have been better prepared to exercise the functions of the office than this widely experienced and intellectual soldier? A colonial administrator, a politician, a judge, a civil servant – each suffers from at least some theoretical disadvantage which renders him less than ideal for the job. Particularly in the exercise of his residual powers, it is unlikely that anyone other than the sovereign would have had the experience to prepare him for the task.

In the first few weeks after his arrival Byng had long conversations with Arthur Meighen, the Conservative Prime Minister, and his senior ministers. Already he was familiar with Canadian history and was eager to learn as much as he could of the problems of government. To discover the Opposition viewpoint he invited its leader, William Lyon Mackenzie King, to come to Government House for a private chat.

At this early stage in his term of office it is doubtful if Byng was aware of the bitterness and animosities which characterized Canadian politics. Probably he would only have been amused by the entry in Mackenzie King's diary about the Byngs' arrival in Ottawa. The Liberal leader's impression of them had been good:

> The note of youth and vigour and absence of side was noticeable in Lord Byng and of naturalness and pleasantness in Lady Byng, a refreshing contrast to the heaviness of the Duke of Devonshire and the formal exclusiveness of the Duchess. I feel sure both Lord and Lady Byng are going to be most popular and acceptable.

Later Meighen introduced him to the Governor-General as Leader of His Majesty's Opposition, adding, 'Who will be your Prime Minister in all probability one of these days.'

> I was so taken by surprise (at) such an admission from Meighen. His Ex. said, 'Mr King, I have been waiting to shake you by the hand and I am glad to meet you.' With respect to Meighen's remark which followed

274

this greeting, he said, 'That was a fine spirit,' or something to that effect, to which I replied, 'It is characteristic'. The words were not what I had intended, but it seemed to me the one rejoinder needed the other.

Later that day King called on Lady Laurier, the widow of the former Liberal leader.

In speaking of Lady Borden's action of putting her next to Lady Byng, I said, 'She had herself known what it meant to be in the second row'.
  'Oh,' Lady L said, 'it was because she didn't want Mrs Meighen next. It takes a woman to know a woman's mind.' [Meighen had replaced Borden as leader of the Conservatives.]

It was characteristic of King to record these trivia and of Canadian politicians and their wives never to relax their partisanship.

King called on the Governor-General at noon, on Friday, 2 September.

He greeted me in a most natural and informal and hearty manner, taking my hand in his two hands and saying he just wanted to shake me by the hands and have a word or two. . . . He opened the conversation by asking me if my grandfather was the Mackenzie of the Papineau-Mackenzie rebellion.

King confirmed this and they discussed the outcome and the subsequent report by Lord Durham.

Then he said, 'Mr King, I want to put myself in your hands. I have only one object that is to be of what service I can. I have no axe to grind, only to do what I can where opportunity offers. I shall be glad to have you speak very freely. As to being a constitutional governor, I understand that there will be little difficulty to keep on right lines. As to party politics, they are easily understood. I suppose the old parties are here much as they are in England. The one wants a little more liberty, the other a little more law. There are Liberals who are conservative, and Conservatives who are liberal. With the Farmers one can understand it is the tariff.' I said I should welcome a chance to tell him a few things on this score – give him the Lib'l point of view. He spoke of unemployment: need to cope with the situation at once. Spoke of his plan with returned men, a democratic self-governing organization, he had ear-marked part of money for Canada before leaving England – sd. he would be glad to talk at any time. I told him I might speak too frankly, without tact etc. He replied that that was what he wanted. I spoke of help it was to have Lord Grey to talk with. The interview had very gratifying effect: I felt the confidence I needed.[2]

275

Byng and Mackenzie King were to play important roles in each other's lives and their relationship was to affect significantly the development of constitutional government in Canda and the Commonwealth. To the extent that King's diary can be believed, it had now begun with a misunderstanding.

If we accept that King's record is accurate, he seems to have misinterpreted Byng's meaning. When the Governor-General said, 'I want to put myself in your hands', he was in effect asking for a full and frank response. He had probably said much the same thing to other prominent figures, whom he had already seen. His remark that 'I suppose the old parties are here, much as they are in England' was an obvious attempt to draw out King on the subject. At the Staff College it is known as 'the simple boy approach'. From this interview stemmed King's belief that he was developing a special and exclusive friendship with Byng and that the Governor was completely naive in a political sense.

It would nonetheless seem to have been improper for Byng to say 'Mr King, I want to put myself in your hands' in speaking to the Leader of the Opposition and one wonders if he really could have done so. This raises the question of the use of Mackenzie King's diaries as evidence. It is unlikely that in a record written up hours later he could be completely accurate in recording Byng's words. Other examples show that King had a tendency to take from a conversation what he wanted to hear. His attitude to people was influenced to an almost unnatural degree, not just by their attitude to him, but to his colleagues, his enemies, and even to non-controversial subjects which interested him. In this case there is no doubt that he wanted to develop a favourable relationship with Byng and was keen to detect signs of his approbation. Remembering that Byng had been having a series of interviews with political figures in which he was seeking information about their departments or policies, it is likely that the purpose of the meeting with King was to find out at first hand what were the policies of the Liberal party and their views on the present situation in the country. Is it not then also likely that he would say to King, 'I know nothing of these details – I am in your hands, you must tell me?'

On 19 September, 1921, King wrote to Violet Markham, whose friendship with him had begun sixteen years earlier:

> I cannot tell you how pleased I am with him as a man and how certain I am that his administration will prove worthy of the best that has preceded it. I took an immense liking to him from the moment we met and, in each conversation I had since, I have felt a sense of oneness in aim and point of

276

view, which is really quite remarkable. If by any chance I should come to be his advisor in the near future, I shall expect that the association will be one of the happiest and best in my life.

King's desire to establish good relations with Byng and his inner need for approbation from one whom he respected seemed to have been fulfilled. Like so many, he was warmed by Byng's friendliness and by his genuine interest in him and his opinion. John Buchan opined that Byng talked to every man as if he were a blood relation.[3] Unfortunately Mackenzie King believed that Byng's capacity for friendship was more like his own, limited and exclusive.

At the end of his first six weeks in Ottawa Byng wrote to Buchan:

> We have settled down – myself as governor general, i.e., a governor who doesn't govern and a general who cannot generalize and my better half as governess general.

Having learned something of the machinery of government and met its leading personalities, he was eager to see more of the country and its people.

During the next month the Byng visited Toronto and Quebec, then returned to Ottawa to avoid becoming involved in the federal election campaign. From Quebec they brought back with them two nieces, newly arrived from England, the Ladies Elizabeth and Mary Byng, daughters of the Earl of Strafford, who they thought would help attract young people to social events centred on Government House. The people of the capital cities of Canada's two largest provinces had welcomed the Governor-General enthusiastically and in both cities Byng had been delighted to meet and talk to veterans of the Canadian Corps. At almost every turn, he heard a popular song 'Lord Byng Canada Welcomes You' by Jules Brazil of Montreal. It was played in '*tempo di marcia*'. Its enthusiastic tune outshone its words which were little, if any, better than the poems addressed to him after Cambrai.

> Who is the man we all admir'd in time of war,
> Who is the man that we were proud to be fighting for,
> And who is the man who led us on the Victory,
> Yes, who is the man that Canada's mighty glad to see?
>
> It's you, Lord Byng,
> And Canada greets you with a hearty cheer,
> Like they did in London town,
> When the Strand they marched us down,
> They shouted out this welcome, 'See the Byng Boys are here';
> So, now we sing,

277

For Canada's heart goes out to you;
You had Byng Boys over there,
Now you have them ev'rywhere,
Lord Byng, Canada welcomes you!

Defeat for the Conservatives in the election of 1921 was almost inevitable. Arthur Meighen, their leader, had drafted the conscription laws during the War for which Quebec would never forgive him at the polls. He was almost as unpopular in the West where his advocacy of protective tariffs led the farmers to believe him to favour their continued exploitation for the benefit of the industries of the East. During the campaign Mackenzie King confined himself to abuse rather than issues and let the momentum of their unpopularity carry the Government to defeat. The Liberals took every seat in Quebec, Nova Scotia and Prince Edward Island. The Progressives, the union of the farm parties, triumphed in the prairies and established themselves in the Tory heartland of Ontario. The Liberals, with just short of an absolute majority, would be the largest group in the Commons and Mackenzie King would be the new Prime Minister. But, because of the approach of Christmas and the time involved in travel between Ottawa and outlying constituencies, it would not be possible for him to take office until 29 December. In the meantime the Conservative Government remained in power.

Meighen had himself lost his seat and thus would be unable to lead the shattered remnants of his party in the House when it assembled in January unless he could first win a place. This would require one of his party to vacate a seat. The usual procedure would be for the chosen member to resign, whereupon a writ would be issued for a by-election.

It seemed likely to Meighen that the new Prime Minister would use his power to delay the issue of the writ for six months and he would miss an entire session of Parliament. Furthermore, no newly elected member could resign until the elapse of a period during which his election could be contested by petition, in this case 20 January at the earliest.

There was, however, another course open for which there was a precedent. In England the Stewardship of the Chiltern Hundreds exists as an office of the Crown for the purpose of enabling the immediate creation of a vacancy when needed in the House of Commons. In Canada, where no such position exists, the procedure is to appoint the member concerned to a paid position in the civil service.

Two days before the change of government Meighen obtained Byng's approval for the appointment of Mr A. C. Casselman, the member for Grenville, Ontario, to a post in the Department of Soldier's Civil Re-establishment from which he resigned next day. At the same time a writ was issued for a by-election in Grenville to take place on 26 January.

278

Mackenzie King indignantly informed the press that Meighen had been guilty of a violation of constitutional procedure; whether or not his action could be defended on technical or legal grounds, it was morally indefensible.

While no contemporary record is available of their conversation, years later Meighen said that the Governor-General had given him no reason to believe that he had any reservation about the Casselman appointment.[4] Byng confirmed that he had not done so when Mackenzie King came to be sworn in as Prime Minister.

Probably because of the indignation he had expressed about it, Byng told him that, during the few weeks which followed the election, Meighen or his ministers had come to him with some eight or nine important matters or appointments which he was unwilling to approve. In each case he had requested them not to ask for consent, which constitutionally he would be obliged to give. The one exception had been the Casselman appointment, which, as it affected Meighen personally and violated no constitutional principle, he did not question.[5]

Effectively the Governor-General had dissuaded Ministers of the Crown from actions which, if not unconstitutional, were, in the circumstances and in his opinion, unethical.

By approving the Casselman appointment Byng had conferred a measure of political advantage on Meighen. King did not criticize him for doing so but contended that Meighen had been wrong in recommending it. Whether or not that was so, he, the Governor-General's advisor, had expressed moral outrage over an action with which Byng was associated. It is not surprising that in future the Governor-General would be cautious about approving any act which might unfairly influence a political situation. Was it really necessary for him to agree to everything recommended by his first minister, no matter how questionable?

From their conversation King certainly took away the impression that Byng felt bound constitutionally to approve any recommendation of his Prime Minister. He seemed unaware that his criticism of the Casselman appointment might have planted a reservation in the mind of the Governor-General.

On Monday, 2 January, 1922, Byng held his first New Year's levée. The custom dates back to colonial days when worthy citizens took the first opportunity in the New Year to pay their respects to the Governor. In Ottawa calls were also made on other dignitaries and at the officers' messes of military units, all of whom kept open house at different times of the day. Strong drink featured at them all. Beginning at 9 am, probably after a traditional New Year's Eve party, it was possible for a

279

strong head to make as many as a dozen calls before 5 o'clock. It was considered bad form to be in an obvious state of intoxication when presented to the Governor-General at noon.

King joined the members of Byng's staff and watched the proceedings.

> There were over seven hundred 'callers', most of them civil servants. I confess they seemed to me for the most part far from alert or 'progressive'.

Later Byng told him of his broken elbow and said that it pained him a little in shaking hands.[6]

A month later he attended a dance which the Byngs gave for the ministers of the Government and their wives:

> Took her Excellency into supper. Find it a little difficult to talk to her, mostly because of lack of subjects and interests in common. She has not had the training or background of the wives of previous GG's but is most pleasant and unconventional. His Ex. is very retiring and a little standoffish and shy, a feeling I can well appreciate as I feel it in myself.[7]

The Byngs had been doing a lot of entertaining. Admiral of the Fleet Lord Beatty and Marshal Foch had paid official visits and there had been a series of dinners for prominent citizens, the first being for a doughty Calgarian, Sir James Lougheed. Byng was beginning to acquire a feel for the possibilities, as well as the limitations, of his office. He told the Prime Minister that he would like in particular to help the youth of the country. He was interested in the Boy Scouts, the YMCA and other movements and hoped he would not object. In his view it was time to stop talking publicly about the War and to strive to get back to normal peacetime conditions in thought as well as in actions.[8]

Early in December Byng had accepted a suggestion by Arthur Currie that he tour Montreal with him and that city's Director of Social Service. 'That subject, and education, interest me more than any others.'[9] There would be repercussions.

Currie was now the Principal of McGill University and, as a newcomer to Montreal, was shocked to discover that within blocks of his home, people lived in abject poverty and squalor. No Canadian should have to live in such appalling conditions, but the situation had a singularly unpalatable aspect. These were French Canadian poor living within sight of some of the wealthiest English Canadians in the country.

Poor Currie had never seen anything like the slums which he and Byng visited. He had to rush from one building to vomit in the street. It brought back to Byng the anger and sympathy which had been awakened in his survey of the slums of London with Lord Rowton almost forty years earlier.[10]

On 24 February Byng addressed the Women's Canadian Club at the Windsor Hotel. He spoke of the need for a civic conscience, saying:

I want to rub three little pinpricks into this Montreal conscience.

The first twinge is the question of your slums. . . . We in the old country have them, and plenty of them, much worse than you have, but they are very old and they are deep-seated and we over there do not quite see daylight for getting rid of them. But in Montreal you have some new slums and that is just the first little twinge of conscience. Why have you new slums?

I think you probably know that in 1920, 192 children died out of a thousand, also that some of those slums are converted stables, and the manure smells rise through the flooring. You probably know that there is a woman in Montreal who has had twenty-one children, of whom eighteen died. I think it is right just to bring this up at this time, for is not that a little twinge on the Montreal conscience?

The second one is, do you give your children much in the way of playgrounds? You have the most glorious playground for children up the hill, but you don't take them up there until they are dead; then you take them up to the most lovely cemetery I have ever seen. I am not quite certain that some of the children in the murky atmosphere between St Catherine's Street and the river do not sometimes look up there at that happy Utopia, knowing that they will not go until they are dead.

The third little twinge was felt when my wife and I went last Sunday for a walk up that splendid old mountain and saw hundreds of people enjoying themselves. We saw thirty-four horses, some ridden, some driven, and seven were dead lame. Hundreds of Montreal citizens were enjoying themselves every minute of that afternoon, while seven horses were hating every second of it.[11]

Not everyone in the audience liked being spoken to in this way and when the speech was reported in the Press there were criticisms that the Governor-General was interfering in a political matter. It was not so much that Byng had hit at an unpleasant truth, he had implied a lack of conscience in the City of Montreal, the Province of Quebec and the landlords, among whom were French and English Canadians and the Roman Catholic Church.

In the end it did him no harm, and it even spurred on to some extent the eventual eradication of the slums, for surprisingly few Montrealers of wealth and influence were aware of the squalor which existed near the slopes of Mount Royal.

Back in the capital the Byngs had further opportunities to see and wonder at the foibles of its society. In 1922 Ottawa was still a small

281

provincial town on to which had been grafted the apparatus of government – parliament, public servants and the buildings to house them. The diplomatic corps was practically non-existent and there was little of the financial, commercial, artistic and academic activity which give their flavour to the life of a major capital. There was about Ottawa far more of the unfinished, ingenuous atmosphere of a young country than could be sensed in more sophisticated Montreal and Toronto.

Socially, members of parliament and government officials counted for far less than did certain 'acceptable' families who had lived in the city for many years. They had seen governor-generals come and go and felt that they possessed proprietorial rights which opened the doors of Government House and placed them in a superior position from which they could view the activities of newcomers such as the Byngs. The rest of society, as in other specially-built capital cities, was composed of gifted men and the women they had married when they were very young.

Being a local boy, Willis-O'Connor, the senior ADC, was regarded as a rather harum-scarum upstart by the Old Guard. Instinctively they disapproved of any Canadian influence other than their own in the social affairs of Government House, but they did feel that they could speak frankly to him. It was made plain that, in their view, for a newly created baron to replace two successive dukes as governor-general implied an affront and augured a distinct lowering of tone at Rideau Hall. And they did not approve of its doors being opened any wider than they had been in the past.

'Tell me, Willis, who is that *person*?'

'I haven't the slightest idea,' he answered, 'but I'm sure she is one of His Majesty's loyal subjects.'[12]

Byng viewed the social scene in Ottawa as more amusing than important. He met many more interesting and influential people at functions in Montreal and Toronto. He was happy to provide the hospitality which was expected of him but insisted that no artificial exclusiveness should restrict guest lists to the safe and the dull.

Etiquette set fairly rigid bounds to the routine of drawing rooms, when debutantes were presented, and to garden parties and state dinners. Young people now began to be invited to Rideau Hall and, while the niceties were observed, the atmosphere became distinctly more relaxed and friendly.

It took Byng some time to become accustomed to the deference which ladies paid to him. One of them recalled that, after dinner, as their hostess led them from the dining room, each dropped a curtsey to the Governor-General which he acknowledged with a little wave of a hand, which happened to be holding a napkin. On reaching the drawing room Evelyn remarked:

'I must remember to tell Julian not to flick us out of the room.'[13]

While it is difficult to judge the importance of much of their entertaining, one innovation of Byng's did prove of value. Soon after his arrival he began holding lunches and dinners for small groups of members of parliament of all parties, ministers and officials. From them he learned much about the country's problems and the operation of the government. Some of his guests he later invited to play golf and a few of the friendships which began in this way endured for the rest of his life.[14]

In its relationship to the Governor-General his household was not unlike a wartime army commander's personal staff, with the exception that wives were present. The unmarried members lived in Rideau Hall and had most of their meals with the Byngs. Under the influence of their warmth and friendliness, they came to regard themselves as more than just his 'official' family. While they observed the courtesies due to the Governor-General, there was an easy familiarity in their relationships with him.

Evelyn Byng made no secret that she enjoyed ceremonials and pageantry and on state occasions could be an awesomely dignified figure. Willis-O'Connor wrote that

All those who ever saw Her Excellency will remember how handsome she was in what today is called 'a sultry sort of way'. She liked to wear her beautiful tiara, inherited from her Greek grandmother.

Yet, while in some ways more 'viceregal' than her husband, she would not allow the household to address her by the royal 'Ma'am'. They protested that they must be able to call her something other than 'Lady Byng' and it was agreed that, to them, she would be 'Memsahib', as she had been when a colonel's wife in India. Though there was about her none of the aloofness which characterized some other chatelaines of Rideau Hall, she was not a 'comfortable' mistress of the household. She had a spectacular temper and, in the privacy of her home, was apt to give it rein, startling everyone nearby with the range of her profanity. But it was not long before the household noticed that these outbursts never took place when Byng was present.[15]

During their five years in Ottawa there were several changes in the household, particularly among the military ADCs who could only be spared from their regiments for a year or two. One of the first to leave was Georges Vanier who was sent as one of the two Canadian students to the Staff College at Camberley. (The other was Major H. D. G.

Crerar who would command the First Canadian Army in the Second World War.) In the autumn of 1921 Vanier had married Pauline Archer, daughter of a Montreal judge, and they lived in Rideau Cottage in the grounds of Government House. On their first entrance into Byng's study he placed his hands on their shoulders and said, 'Now you're members of the family'. Mme Vanier recalled that what might have seemed a rather hollow remark had such a ring of sincerity that 'I was just bowled over – anyone who met him came under his spell. You could immediately sense his goodness, his integrity, his attractiveness.'[16]

Georges was then 34. A barrister when war began, he served with the 22nd French Canadian Battalion, had been much decorated and badly wounded. His enquiring intelligence and idealism appealed to Byng and they soon became firm friends.

Byng knew that the Vaniers would not have an easy time in England and did his best to smooth their path and prepare them for it. Before they left Byng asked Pauline to come into his study to tell her something of what she might expect in England.

I was a simple Canadian girl with no experience and I think perhaps he recognized that. It sounded like such a different life that I was appalled and, at the end of our chat, I couldn't help bursting into tears of apprehension. He took me in his arms like a daughter and gave me a good hug. Then, when I'd dried my eyes, he led me back into the drawing room and laughed as he said, 'Look what she's done to my shirt front!'

Byng arranged for his much-loved sister, Margaret Boscawen, to meet the Vaniers when they arrived in London, and for his nephew, the Earl of Strafford, to invite them to stay for a few days of Wrotham.

At Camberley the Vaniers moved into a small house where no one paid them the least attention. At the Staff College new students tend to be very much on their best behaviour and, being English, they retire behind a façade of well-mannered reserve. No one wants to make the first move, particularly with colonials who may not know the rules.

Byng suspected that this might happen and had written to Field-Marshal the Earl of Cavan, the CIGS, now his nephew by marriage. On a visit to the College, he enquired of the Vaniers how they were settling down. Georges wrote to thank Byng and drew the following response:

My dear George,
    Thank your for yours of 15 Dec[r].
    I am not surprised at the C.I.G.S. offering his kind services at getting you a cook – and it is not altogether due to Pauline's 'way with the male'.

Remember he is now my nephew and thus full of avuncular respect. So if at any time you are desirous of undeserved promotion or unauthorized indulgence, a line enclosing cheque to me will probably produce anything from a Field-Marshal's Baton for yourself to another reinforced pyramidical knitting-needle for your wife.

All the same, Fatty Cavan is a good creature and is becoming a most satisfactory nephew. . . .

You are now probably just starting and all smelling round each other and growling like a lot of dogs – but that stage will soon pass and you will begin to like the fellows in your term – in fact it is hopeless if you don't – and then all will go well. The senior term will probably patronize you a bit, but let them; you will get your own back next year and it is great fun being told about things you probably already know.

You will be shown all the photographs of the 'has-beens' including my term in 1893–4. You will notice we all wore ferocious moustaches in those days – (it was before the Beaver Epoch). I think it helped to win the war, at least something must have done so, and why not ferocious moustaches?

Your professors will be summing you up but not so much as you will be summing them up. They will ask you seemingly innocent questions such as 'Can one use a mashie in the middle of a Canadian winter?' This will really be meant to know if you consider that 'surprise is the handmaid of victory' – but you will find it all out for yourself, and I have told you all I know.

Servants' ball last night. Whirled Mrs Tanner's sylph-like form till we both dropped, she by loss of breath, me by loss of manpower. The night watchman, with lighted lantern complete, came to see if anyone was about (there were four hundred people about) but he made the discovery, entered it in his report, and then appeared with lighted lantern complete and danced the whole night through.

We all go to Montreal tomorrow. We are doing practically 0 in the way of entertaining – but I give two dinners (a) to French Canadians carefully selected by Father-in-law – the dinner to be altogether French Canadian and I feel that in some way or other I shall be expected to produce the word 'accueil' – but I am getting jolly cunning and am quite prepared with 'bienvenu' for all occasions, having practised it while shaving. (b) English Canadians – the Railways, the Banks and the University will furnish their quotas and we shall all say Montreal is the hub of hubs and day by day in every way it gets hubbier and hubbier.

Patrick, [Hodgson], muttering to himself and frothing at the mouth, has left this morning to warm the beds and ice the champagne or vice versa for our arrival – so we may expect him with Mayor Martin and the General (whose name I always forget,) to greet us.

Good luck to you both.

Yours ever
B of V.[17]

The attention paid to them by the CIGS opened a few more doors for the Vaniers in Camberley, but Byng did not believe in half measures.

An introduction from him resulted in Lord Stamfordham asking them to luncheon at Windsor. Then on 22 May they were invited to dine with the King and Queen at Aldershot. General Ironside, the Commandant of the College, was also there and soon all Camberley took another look at the quaint colonials and found them charming.

Byng's easing of their way in England was only the beginning of his influence on their lives. Later he persuaded Vanier to leave the Army for the young Canadian diplomatic service, where he served with great distinction eventually himself becoming Governor-General of Canada. In speaking of their friendship Madame Vanier said, 'Georges had a filial devotion to Bungo. We owed everything to him – our entire career.'[18]

During their first winter in Ottawa the Byngs decided that they should learn to skate. A professional was engaged but Evelyn never progressed beyond pushing a chair across the ice. The Governor-General was more persistent. In time he could make an uncertain circuit of the rink, but, after a particularly heavy fall, he muttered that this dog was too old for new tricks and gave it up.

The cold weather was indirectly the cause of Byng giving a rare display of temper and petulance. He had given orders that the radiators in his bedroom should be permanently shut off. On one particularly bitter night, when the temperature in his room was well below freezing, Evelyn had a fire lit in the grate. He was late coming down for dinner and his face was like a thundercloud. When she asked what had kept him upstairs, he said, 'Putting out that darned fire you lit.' He had poured jugs of water on it until it was awash and the acrid smell of extinguished coals filled the room. Evelyn recalled, 'I wasn't spoken to for several days after that as he pondered over his 'wrongs'. Anything that he thought was 'soft' had that effect on him, and, poor dear, he really was quite unreasonable in these matters.'

While the Byngs gave up trying to learn to skate, they fell in love with hockey. The Ottawa Senators were one of the best teams in the National Hockey League and Evelyn, particularly, seldom missed a game when they were playing at home. Later she presented the trophy which bears her name for the cleanest player in the League.

As a young officer Byng had never been part of the popular social scene and after marriage had only attended dances under protest. Now they were part of his life. In the capital and in other Canadian cities the Governor-General was the host or guest of honour at several each year. Watching from a dais at the end of the room or wandering among the guests, he felt that he was a dampener on the fun of the party. He must learn to dance.

With Pat Hodgson playing the piano, Evelyn and his nieces pushed and pulled him about the floor until he had mastered the waltz. But there was a drawback. He was committed to 'duty dances' with the wives of important officials and they were by no means all expert performers. One evening he was heard to complain to Willis-O'Connor, 'I'm discouraged. I've got corns and I'm a pretty poor dancer, but, dash it all, even Nijinsky couldn't dance if a woman stood on both his feet at once.'[19]

With the coming of spring the Byngs set out to see more of Canada and its people. To most of them he was the hero of Vimy. That they liked what they saw is reflected in this typical description in the *Stratford Herald* of 19 April:

> The Baron is a fine figure of a man, dressed with democratic plainness, he stands out among his fellows. Of commanding height, the erect carriage of the soldier and the cool poise of the cultured British gentleman, Lord Byng bears the stamp of a big man, mentally and physically and, withal, a very human personality. During the reading of his address in reply to the civic welcome, he donned glasses – not fussy ones either, but plain specs., if you please – a little touch which somehow got home to the people. His Ex. reads well. His is the true English voice, softly resonant and always pleasing to the ear. The similarity of his tone to that of the Prince of Wales is notable. Above all Baron Byng has the handgrip which both men and women love – firm and real.

Veterans of the Canadian Corps were in the forefront of every reception and led the cheers for their old commander. On Saturday, 8 April, Byng attended a Vimy dinner with a group of them in Toronto and they left him in no doubt as to the importance of the battle to Canada. A telegram he received on 12 May showed that his part in that victory was remembered by another old friend: 'I have just spent the night at Vimy and my thoughts were with you. George RI'.

During his five years in Canada Byng travelled more widely than any previous Governor-General and was seen by more of the people. His four tours of the West were marathon affairs lasting two or three months each. Eastern Canada being more accessible, visits there involved shorter absences from Ottawa. The viceregal train enabled him to visit the smaller towns and cities, which, in the days of air travel, tend to be bypassed by Governors. Often he used the steamer services which operated on the Great Lakes and on the coasts of the Maritime provinces and British Columbia. Memsahib and her secretary, Pat Hodgson, and two or three ADCs made up the official party. The train consisted of the two antiquated wooden viceregal carriages, sleeping and dining cars for staff and guests and a baggage van. In the West particularly, it was often parked for a day or two on a siding miles from the nearest town, to allow for rest in complete privacy.

In the main visits to cities were well stage-managed and tended to be formal. Often worried local officials seemed to be trying to insulate the Governor-General from direct contact with people whose manners might not be as dignified as their own. He caused them no little anguish for he genuinely enjoyed meeting people. In Bowness Park, in Calgary, for example, he stopped his car to speak to a veteran wearing medals and spent long minutes happily comparing the boating facilities there with those in Hyde Park in London, while his aides despaired of keeping to their schedule.

In his speeches he attempted to counter the divisive influences which bedevilled the country by appealing to the spirit which had united the Canadian Corps. To an audience of veterans the appeal was direct:

I am among my old friends now – those old friends of mine of 1916/17. I do not know that I have a greater affection for anything on earth than I have for that old Corps. . . .

Gentlemen, have you ever considered for a moment what a democracy that force was? What a democracy that Corps was from the moment it left these shores until the moment it came back. I have seen, and you have seen, millionaires filling sandbags. I have seen a newspaper boy commanding a battalion. I have seen the sinking of all questions of east and west, of capital and labour, and employee and employer. I have seen differences all sunk in that great idealism of 'What did Canada send us here for?'

Canada said 'Go to it boys'. That was the old notice put up and those are the words which sunk deeply into the Corps and myself. Those were the words for the time being which obliterated all those small questions (are they small? I don't know) which agitate some of our minds today.

Would it not be possible to get back to that stage that the Canadian Corps reached when it sunk all those differences into one idealism. Is not the making and the future of Canada as great a thing as what we fought for? I think it is. I think possibly, Gentlemen, you here see eye to eye with me that there is a good to be obtained by trying to revive that old idealism we had in France.[20]

He knew that the problem was far from simple, that barriers separated the regions of Canada, its races, religions and, sad for a young country, its social classes.

To a business men's club, he was apt to quote Ruskin:

There is another thing which appeals in addition to the ethics of Rotary. You come across every class of society, you know the rich and the poor, you know the good and the bad. I want to read you something from Ruskin, something he has said on this subject, which you will all agree with.

He went on to say:

There is an idle poor and idle rich. There are busy poor and busy rich. Many a beggar is as lazy as if he had ten thousand a year, and many a man of large fortune is busier than his errandboy.

So that, in a large view, the difference between workers and idlers as between knaves and honest men runs through the heart and innermost nature of men of all ranks.

There is a working class strong and happy amongst both rich and poor. There is an idle class weak and miserable among both rich and poor and the worst of the misunderstandings arising between the two orders come from the unlucky fact that the good of one class habitually contemplate the bad of the other. If the busy rich people watched and rebuked the idle rich people all would be well among them, and if the busy poor people watched and rebuked the idle poor people, all would be right among them. But each looks at the faults of the other. A hard-working man of property is particularly offended by an idle beggar and an orderly but poor workman is naturally intolerant of the licentious luxury of the rich.[21]

His message could be summed up in his charge to the Canadian Club of Edmonton –

Be as big, with minds as large and souls as great as the land in which you live.[22]

Other audiences were impressed by his erudition and the depth of thinking behind his words. 'Diplomacy and Strategy in their Relation to War' is not an unexpected title for a speech by a general, but its content reflected a considerable knowledge of the history of the last three hundred years and included a summary of ideas put forward for international peace organizations from those of Grotius in 1625 to the Holy Alliance of 1815, with some apt comments on the League of Nations, then in its infancy.

To a learned audience in the Maritimes he spoke on 'Cromwell and the Constitution', showing a knowledge of the fundamentals of parliamentary democracy which would have surprised those politicians who later assumed that constitutional problems were beyond the understanding of a soldier. In most of his speeches he included a plea for every citizen to work for a united Canada and in this he paraphrased the dying William Pitt: 'In the war Canada helped herself by her energy. She must now help the world by her example.'[23]

Byng did his best to meet reasonable requests to speak. He knew it was expected of him but had no illusion that what he said would be long remembered. He believed that he could do far more good and could learn more himself by talking personally to as many people as possible.

One or two speeches in an area were enough and he would not be bullied into making more. One particularly importunate company got this:

> Gentlemen, I thank you very much for the way in which you have responded to the toast of my health, but I believe that a Governor-General should be an obvious person. Obvious, according to the dictionary means 'Goes without saying'. Therefore I am going without saying.

Then he sat down.[24]

For Byng the most enjoyable feature of the tours were his visits to rural areas, where in 1922 the largest part of the population lived. The programme at many cities allowed time for him to drive out into the country, accompanied only by a local official of the Soldiers' Settlement Board, to tour farms in the area.

In September, 1922, Byng called on Ellis Little and his wife on their farm forty miles east of Saskatoon. They had bought 160 acres through the Soldiers' Settlement Board and, together with Little's aged father, who owned a like acreage, farmed 320 acres as a unit under the supervision of the Board. They found Byng's interest in their operation far from casual.

Later the Littles remembered, not the honour of having been visited by the Governor-General, but 'that he took time out from his usual duties to call on a returned soldier's farm in order to try and further a project he appeared deeply interested in, that of improving the life of orphaned boys by getting them settled on farms where they would receive training to fit them to take up such a life at a later date.' At the time the Littles were having difficulty in earning a living out of their farm and felt that they could not take on the responsibility for an orphan. The visit gave them genuine pleasure and they treasure two snapshots taken at the time. They show Byng's lean figure, relaxed in a tweed suit, cap tilted forward to shade his eyes, leaning against a wall, pipe in hand, and grinning. Little, his wife and father appear much more at ease than the three watching officials, hatted and business-suited.[25]

Earlier that summer, when his train was parked on a siding some ten miles from Medicine Hat, Byng took a walk by himself. Out of sight of the train, he met an old farmer and stopped to chat with him about crops, the probable price of wheat next fall and the prospects of rain that evening. Byng suggested tea and asked him to come over to his train, explaining casually that he was the Governor-General. The farmer was obviously surprised and pleased, but said that he didn't think that he should come because his wife was at home alone and he didn't like to leave her for such a long time without any one else in the house.

Immediately Byng suggested that the old man go home, collect his wife and bring her around to the train for a cup of tea with Lady Byng and himself. Delighted with the suggestion, the farmer whipped up his horses and in a short time he and his equally delighted wife were chatting informally with the Byngs and other members of their party.

Not unnaturally, as a horseman, Byng was fascinated by his visit to the E P and Bar U Ranches near Calgary and by the cowboy sports at the Stampede. In Banff he rode every morning shortly after sun-up with Mr Stronach, the Superintendent of the Park.

Evelyn told of another encounter Byng had when their train was parked in a remote siding to spend the night before a reception in a neighbouring town.

As he strode over the prairie there wasn't another soul in sight except an elderly farmer in an equally elderly buggy who stopped and they began to talk. Gathering that the man on foot was a stranger, the farmer said, 'Guess you've come in for the Governor-General's visit in town tomorrow?'

My husband said he had and the farmer asked whether he knew 'old Byng' to which Julian answered 'Yes'.

'Umph,' grunted the farmer, 'what's the old bugger like?'

'Oh, not so bad on the whole.'

'High hat?'

'I don't think so, but why not come and see for yourself at the reception?'

A grunt from the old man. Then, grudgingly, as he moved on, 'Well I guess I may as well go and see the old son of a bitch. My lad served under him and said he was a damn good fighter.'

Next day at the reception he duly appeared, and when he came up, rather taken aback, to shake hands with us, Julian said 'Well, is the old bugger so bad after all?' They had a good laugh over it and the farmer slapped him hard on the shoulder, for Julian had made a firm friend.

In the August of their first western tour the Byngs sailed from Victoria to Prince Rupert, through the Wrangell Narrows to Juneau in Alaska where they dined with the American governor. From there they went on to Skagway where they boarded the train to Whitehorse, in the Yukon Territory, following much the same path by the Chillcoot Pass, Deadhorse Gulch and Bennet Lake as the prospectors during the Gold Rush of '98. From Whitehorse they travelled in a flat-bottomed sternwheeler 'down north' to Dawson. Though its glamour had faded with its lawlessness, there was still much of the atmosphere of the frontier about the place and its people.

The ball which the town gave for them was like none other they were to see in Canada. Evelyn danced with sourdoughs and the Mounted Police, some of whom had ridden in hundreds of miles for the occasion, and Byng pre-empted one of his ADCs to dance with the prettiest girl in the room.

One trip which occasioned some controversy took place in the summer of 1923. Planning for a visit to the Maritimes had been completed when a serious strike broke out in Sydney, Nova Scotia. The situation had got so far out of hand that troops had been sent in to support the police. The Federal Government advised Byng not to visit the city. He had, however, accepted invitations there and felt that to renegue would do considerable harm. He informed the department concerned that he would be visiting Sydney. Possibly in a further effort to dissuade him, they said that, if he were determined to do so, Her Excellency could not, of course, accompany him. He replied that that depended entirely on what she decided, which, when asked, was that she would go. Byng insisted that he would have no police protection during the visit.

They arrived in Sydney on a hot summer's day to find a huge cheering crowd. The strikers were in complete control of the town and it was their leaders who cleared a way through the laughing, shouting crowd so that the Byngs could drive to the town hall for the official receptions, speeches and lunch. In the afternoon they were taken around the steel mill by its manager who seemed ill at ease in the presence of the crowds of strikers and their families, who gave no sign of the bitterness which had prevailed until then. The workers then asked if the Byngs would be their guests at a reception in the public gardens that night, an invitation they accepted, much to the dismay of the officials who were accompanying them. Evelyn wrote:

> But it was, they decided, our funeral, not theirs – if there was to be a funeral at all. I shall never forget that reception of thousands, mostly ex-soldiers and their wives and families, of whom not one of them would have allowed anything to harm us. How many handshakes we gave and received that night I never knew – but our hands and arms ached by the time we were escorted back to the train.

There they found that, since there were no police, the strikers had formed a bodyguard to protect them.

Byng's assessment of the situation had been far more accurate than that of officials in Ottawa. The people of Sydney felt that the whole power of industry and government was ranged against them and that they were friendless and alone. Had they seen a bodyguard of police protecting the Governor-General, they would have felt that he too did not trust them. In the circumstances the absence of protection did much more than avert ill-will. It was welcomed by the people as a positive gesture of faith on the part of the sovereign's representative.

The Byngs were shocked by the wretched conditions in which many of the workers lived and by the complete lack of social services in the area. Their concern was obvious. When they left next day the same crowds cheered them on their way, singing 'Will ye no come back again?' They had not stopped the strike, but their visit had reduced tension and bitterness which blighted the efforts of those who tried to do so.

Byng's train had barely left the station when reports reached Ottawa to the effect that he had promised that the troops sent to Sydney in aid of the civil power would be withdrawn, which the Prime Minister, Mackenzie King, complained was an unconstitutional interference in the affairs of the country by the Governor-General.[26]

Byng delighted in some of the bizarre incidents which took place on their tours, usually the result of people wanting to welcome him with the dignity due to his position. Sometimes they over-reached themselves.

Two towns, separated by a mile in distance and an ocean of rivalry, refused to have a joint reception for the Byngs, making it necessary for them to travel from one to the other. Both claimed the privilege of providing the Governor-General's transportation, but eventually came to an uneasy compromise. There was no denying that an antiquated landau which belonged to one of the towns was the most suitable vehicle. It would be drawn by four horses, two from each town, with their two drivers seated on the box, each driving his own team. Headed by a band and groups of ex-servicemen, the procession set off in the summer sunshine. Behind the carriage came Boy Scouts and Girl Guides, and the city fathers in their cars. Soon Byng could see that a violent argument was taking place between the two drivers. Suddenly the carriage came to a halt, causing the procession behind to telescope, while the band and ex-servicemen marched briskly ahead. Having steadied his team, one of the coachmen leaned over the side of the carriage, loosed a stream a tobacco juice onto the road, then whipped up the horses into a smart trot. If he had spat while they were on the move the Byngs would have received his wad full in the face. His consideration for his passengers resulted in the rear of the procession having to double to keep up and contributed nothing to the friendship of the two towns.

In August, 1924, the Byngs and their entourage spent three weeks in the Okanagan Valley and toured the Lakes on the steamer *Nasookin*. On 5 August they were on deck for some time, dressed in their best, waiting to arrive at a small settlement on the dot of 3 pm. When the time drew near the captain sounded a loud blast on his siren to warn the inhabitants of their approach. As they rounded a promontory, instead of the crowd they expected, there was one old man, sitting on a log, smoking his pipe, while a few dogs barked at the interlopers. When an ADC went ashore and asked where everyone was, he jerked his pipe over his shoulder and said that they were all off fighting a forest fire. In short order the viceregal party changed into old clothes and went ashore for a walk, where Evelyn dragooned the ADCs into finding new specimens for the rock garden she was building at Government House.

The following report later appeared in the local paper:

A few citizens welcomed their Excellencies on arrival in an informal way and there were many settlers and veterans along the valley who were disappointed in being deprived of the pleasure on account of forest fires raging in the vicinity of Gerrard on which they were engaged.

The evening was spent in walking through the groves and gathering rare wild flower seeds, which are called weeds here, fishing, rowing, etc, and they seemed to enjoy the quiet, free and easy life of the Lardeau country and the few who had the pleasure of meeting their Excellencies trust that sometime they may come again.[27]

Travels in rural Quebec had a flavour of their own. The little towns with their large solid churches and brightly painted houses, choirs of well-starched schoolgirls escorted by their nuns, and their obsession with baseball and hockey differed markedly from the villages of Ontario and dramatically from those of the West. Byng's genuine interest in their lives and problems drew a warm response, particularly from the farmers. Fortunately he spoke serviceable French, far more than did the average English-speaking Canadian and he worked hard with Georges Vanier to improve it. They had a standing joke over his pronunciation of 'acceuil' which figured in almost every speech. In 1924 the Montreal Gazette reported 'His Excellency's growing mastery of the French accent charmed the people and some old timers were loud in saying that he spoke better French than did Lord Grey, who was a fluent linguist.'[28] Evelyn was completely bilingual.

In Ottawa Byng kept fairly closely to a routine schedule. Except in very cold weather, he liked to ride before breakfast, which was at 8.30. At 10 he conferred with his staff and an hour later received ministers or other visitors. Lunch was at 1 pm. In the afternoons he played golf, or, if that was not practical, went for a walk or a ride. For his walks about Ottawa he enjoyed wearing old, comfortable clothes. His favourite hat was so frayed that its brim had to be trimmed with scissors and he frequently wore a pair of white rubber boots presented to him by a miner in the Yukon. In this battered gear he explored much of Ottawa and boasted of finding a shortcut into town through a succession of backyards. Willis-O'Connor warned him that he might be arrested at the instance of some indignant housewife thinking he was a common trespasser. His ADCs took it by turn to accompany him and all went as far as they could in persuading him to turn out in something less shabby. Pat Hodgson summoned up courage on a Western tour and dropped one of Byng's more disgraceful jackets out of a train window.

By contrast, in uniform he was perfection and insisted on an equally high standard in his staff.

One morning, Willis-O'Connor was summoned to see Byng in his room.

> He was in bed, looking rather miserable and the quiet smile was almost non-existent.
>
> 'Are you ill, Sir?' I asked in some concern.
>
> 'A touch of lumbago,' he replied, trying to smile. 'At least that's what we'll call it for the benefit of the household.'
>
> More disturbed than ever, I asked what really was the matter and then he did muster the old delightful puckish grin.
>
> 'Yesterday,' he explained, 'I fell off my horse and this morning I ache in every inch of me. I'm positive there are no bones broken, but bed seems indicated and officially, you understand, I am suffering from a touch of lumbago.'
>
> The truth never leaked out as far as I know.[29]

In 1924 the colonelcy of Byng's old regiment, the 10th Hussars, would become vacant and the King had his Private Secretary remind the War Office of his views:

> Please remember His Majesty wishes Lord Byng to succeed Lord Downe as Colonel of the Xth Hussars . . . of course he would give up the Colonelcy of the 3rd.[30]

The appointment was announced on 28 February to the great delight of the Regiment and of Byng.

Later that year Evelyn returned to spend the summer in England, taking Rachel Walpole and Pat Hodgson with her. After three years in Canada Miss Walpole was returning to a life of books. Hodgson was to find her replacement. Already he knew who he would like that to be.

Eva Sandford had all the qualities needed for the role of secretary and lady-in-waiting. Now in her late twenties, she was an experienced secretary and had served for two years as a nurse in France during the War. She had the poise both of maturity and of an impeccable social background – she was a cousin of three dukes – slim, attractive and good-natured. Like so many young women of her generation, she had lost a fiancé in the War. Having no money of her own, she had become a secretary and had just finished a difficult year in Kenya as companion to a woman who had suffered in a difficult divorce case. Pat Hodgson, who had known her since childhood, arranged to meet her at his mother's house and found her happy to take the job.

She went to Thorpe to meet Lady Byng, they approved of each other and sailed back to Canada together in July, on the Canadian Pacific liner *Montclair*. She expected that her appointment in the Byng household would be for the two remaining years of their stay in Canada. It was to last for life.[31]

The highlight of the 1924 autumn season in Ottawa was the visit of the Prince of Wales in October. From Byng's point of view the visit was anything but a success. One evening a dance was given at Rideau Hall and considerable pains were taken to see that the guests were young and interesting. Anticipating a crashingly dull time, the Prince asked Eva Sandford if he might use her small sitting room as an escape, to which she agreed. In the event he found the company a good deal more interesting than he expected and spent most of the evening with one particularly attractive woman. Both were missed for a time and were later seen emerging from Eva's sitting room. Unfortunately they were observed by far more than just the Governor-General's household.

Next day he told Byng that, following dinner that night, he would like to go to a dance at the Country Club. Byng was aware that by now most of Ottawa knew of the attention that the Prince was paying to a married woman and would be only too ready to blow up any indiscretion into a scandal. Byng advised him that, as the dance would last until 3 am, he should stay to the end and then come back direct to Government House and not go to any private home. The Prince agreed, but, knowing his reputation, Byng was not confident that he would do so. To close one loophole, he asked the president of the Country Club to make sure that the dance did in fact continue until 3 am.

In the event the Prince broke his word. He went to the house of the woman he had monopolized at Rideau Hall and did not return until very late indeed. Byng was furious. The Prince had compromised himself and serious damage to the reputation of the monarchy might result. His promise to him had been broken and in flouting the authority of the Governor-General he had technically disobeyed the King.

Next morning Byng sent for the Prince, who was leaving that day, and told him that he was not to come back to Canada so long as he remained Governor-General. He said that when his term of office was up and he returned to England, he would tell him frankly if he thought that he should ever return. The Prince was inclined to be resentful and asked if he might come back on an official visit. Byng said, 'No'.

It was not the first time that he had had to deal with young officers who misbehaved, but he did not enjoy it. Obviously the King had to be told, but, rather than write to him, Byng explained the situation to their mutual and trusted friend, John Buchan, who saw the King after his return to England in November.[32]

The Prince of Wales did not return to Canada until 1927, when he caused Lord Willingdon, Byng's successor, some anxious moments. His behaviour in Ottawa was probably no worse than it was in London, but it was far more indiscreet. In England peccadilloes of princes tend to be shielded by a loyal circle of friends from a society which is, in any case, tolerant and sophisticated. In Ottawa, as indeed elsewhere in Canada, there was a strain of puritanism which had almost ceased to exist in the 'old country'. People whom the Prince was likely to meet there were far more easily shocked and were a good deal less tolerant of personal foibles.

While the opinion of 'society', in the sense that it means 'people of influence', could not be ignored, some of its members made themselves more than a little ridiculous in relation to Government House. Usually this arose from manoeuvring to obtain an invitation to a ball or garden party. By some, to be asked to a smaller affair was regarded as a social coup which earned a few steps up the Ludo Ladder in the social game in which they regarded everyone else as competitors. Most people in Ottawa sensibly had nothing to do with the competition, but to some it was deadly serious. They provided much amusement to the Household and to Byng.

Unknown to anyone except his assistant secretary, Fred Pereira, Byng wrote a musical comedy which he called 'Oriental Ottawa', using popular melodies and a few original tunes composed by Pereira's wife. Its characters all bore the names of streets in the village of Rockcliffe, in which Rideau Hall is located – many streets in Ottawa are named after its prominent families. The cast was drawn from the staff of Government House and their friends and was performed in front of a carefully selected audience.

Needless to say the cast enjoyed it even more than the audience, particularly since they knew of the incidents on which some of the numbers were based. Eva Sandford had cause to remember one which she sang which had been inspired by a woman who was so curious about activities in Government House that she bought a telescope to watch the driveway. It became:

> If you wonder what goes on behind the gate
> As you're walking by the Rideau Hall estate
> Buy yourself a pair of binoculars

At this point in the song, at the dress rehearsal, she felt a snap and her harem pants fell down and she heard the shrill voice of her maid shriek, 'There, I knew it. She never could wear elastic!'

Byng took no part in the performance and it was months before the name of the author was discovered.[33]

In July, 1925, Byng set out from Edmonton on a month-long journey to the Arctic Ocean at the mouth of the MacKenzie River. Accompanied only by Pat Hodgson and his valet, Bristowe, he went by special train to Grande Prairie in northern Alberta. From there he was driven in an open touring car by an old comrade of the South African Light Horse, a Mr Howell, to Peace River, sharing the car much of the way with clouds of grasshoppers. For the next week they travelled on the stern-wheeler *D. A. Thomas* down the Peace to Vermilion Chutes where they were delayed by low water. Eventually they portaged to a point below the rapids where they were picked up by a motor launch. Two days later they arrived at Fort Fitzgerald and drove the sixteen miles to Fort Smith in order to avoid another set of rapids. There they boarded the S.S. *Distributor*, another stern-wheeler, and were joined by Major W. A. Steel of the Royal Canadian Corps of Signals, who had installed a radio on the ship. There were eighty-four people aboard, of whom forty-one were saloon passengers. A freight scow was pushed at the bow. Ten days after leaving Peace River they arrived at Fort Resolution on Great Slave Lake. Here Byng disembarked and visited a large Indian boarding school, run by a Roman Catholic Mission, where his health was proposed by the sisters in fresh cow's milk, considered a great delicacy in the north country.

Great Slave Lake is an immense body of water and offers a real obstacle to transportation in the MacKenzie Basin. Boats which are large enough to be economical, and of draught shallow enough to operate on the rivers, do not have hulls capable of withstanding the rough weather which is often met on the lake. Steamers frequently were delayed for days, waiting for suitable weather to cross its western end, and even then it was often necessary to run for shelter from sudden squalls. On leaving Fort Resolution the *Distributor* had to wait for twenty-four hours at Burnt Island for the wind to drop before going on to the entrance to the MacKenzie River.

For five days they steamed down the river, stopping to visit trading posts of the Hudson's Bay Company, Indian settlements, Mounted Police posts and missionaries. Near Fort Norman they visited the oil well of the Imperial Oil Company then producing about eighty barrels per day. Having passed Fort Good Hope on 29 July, they crossed the Arctic Circle and on the 31st, after a brief visit to Fort McPherson, came to Aklavik.

Byng was disappointed to find that the Eskimos, whom he had been looking forward to meeting, had left the town after the arrival of the first freight boat in June for their summer hunting areas along the Arctic shore. The weather was very warm, the temperature being in the mid 80's, yet away from the river frozen ground was to be found eight inches below the surface.

Canon Edward Hester, the head of the Anglican Mission, suggested that Byng travel by motor boat to Kittigazuit on the Arctic, where he was sure they would find Eskimos. About a hundred miles from Aklavik they ran into heavy fog and were forced to depend on the sharp ears of Oliver, an Eskimo, who was piloting the boat. He navigated along the coast for the last thirty miles by the sound of the waves lapping on the beach.

At 7 am on 2 August they arrived at Kittigazuit where they were welcomed by the Eskimo chief, William Maglaluik, a tall, finely built man with a great personality. Immediately he learned Byng's identity, he organized a reception breakfast in his tent. He did not think it right that the Governor-General should sit on the floor, so he had his wife take the cover off her sewing machine and this, spread with a skin, was the Governor-General's throne. A dead seal was dragged in for Pat Hodgson to sit on, this being the height of Eskimo politeness. Breakfast of hot and cold fish, bread and tea, was spread on the floor, the fish being eaten off tin plates with fingers and tea being served by dipping mugs into a large open pot.

After the meal, in an atmosphere a bit smokey from the fire, a sort of durbar took place. The chief made a speech of welcome and Byng told of the King and how interested he was in his Eskimo subjects. He said that he himself would write to the King to tell him of their loyalty and the welcome they had given him. The idea that the King was a person who could actually be written to seemed to impress them more than anything else.

Byng was impressed by the appearance of the Eskimos, who were physically superior to the Indians whom they despised. They were cleaner and their tents more sanitary. Even at that time their boats had petrol engines, for the Eskimos have a natural aptitude as engineers. One of their more endearing qualities was their obvious fondness for children – their name for them was 'noogiduks'.

The party arrived back at Aklavik at 6 am on 3 August, well satisfied with their trip, but very tired, as the 24-foot boat did not provide much space for exercise or rest. Almost immediately they boarded the *Distributor* and sailed up the MacKenzie. On the 11th they arrived at Fort Fitzgerald on the Slave River, then digressed from their outward route by crossing Lake Athabasca to Chipewayan. Home of the Roman

Catholic and Anglican bishops, it had been a trading post since 1780 and was the oldest settlement in the north. Next day they arrived at McMurray where Byng talked to geologists about the development of the production of oil from the tar sands. Later that evening his steamer arrived at Waterways where he, Hodgson and Bristowe boarded a train which took them back to Edmonton.

Byng had travelled over 4,000 miles, farther than from Halifax to Vancouver. To most people in Canada the far north was a distant frontier land in which they had little interest. Byng's journey to the Arctic was the first by a Governor-General, or indeed, any prominent figure from the government in Ottawa. It served notice that the long process of bringing the north into the mainstream of Canadian life had begun.[34]

Pat Hodgson returned to England at the end of the year to become Private Secretary and Comptroller to the Duke of York, the future King George VI, giving rise to rumours that the Prince would replace Byng as Governor-General. In February, when he was invested with the CMG, the King told him that he had heard some disquieting rumours about Byng's shabby clothes and 'expressed his views on that subject with emphasis'. Hodgson assured him that the stories were exaggerated.[35]

Chapter 15
King and Constitution

FOR ALMOST THE entire period of Byng's governor-generalship, his prime minister was William Lyon Mackenzie King, the leader of the Liberals, and their relationship was central to the performance of his constitutional duties as the Sovereign's representative.

King was forty-seven years of age in 1922 when his party came to power. With four degrees from Toronto and Harvard Universities, he had become Deputy Minister of Labour when only twenty-five, had won an enviable reputation as a conciliator in industrial disputes and joined Laurier's government in 1909 as minister of his department. Two years later an election brought ruin to the Liberals and King lost his seat in Parliament. He was then invited to become head of the Department of Industrial Relations of the Rockefeller Foundation in the USA, became a friend of John D. Rockefeller Jr and did much to keep American mines and factories operating during the War. At its end, he had the opportunity of remaining in the States with the substantial annual salary of $30,000 or returning to politics in Canada.

In 1919 Laurier died, King replaced him as leader of the Liberals and won a seat in the Commons.

So much for his curriculum vitae. While it says much for his intelligence, his skill as a negotiator and his political acumen, the driving forces in his character are not so easily discerned.

His grandfather, William Lyon Mackenzie, had been the first mayor of Toronto and led the abortive rebellion of 1837 in Upper Canada. His mother had taken as her husband John King, a lawyer who proved to be unsuccessful both in his profession and as head of his family. She suffered much on account of her father and from the weakness of her husband. Understandably she caused her children to believe that their first loyalty was to her and the family. King took the responsibility seriously. More than once he cleared his father's debts and always looked to his mother for inspiration and guidance, even after her death. He never married.

At one time he had considered the ministry as a career and religion was to comfort, inspire and cause him much anguish. He came to believe that he had been specially chosen for his role in life and, as his diaries show, visions and dreams often supported him in times of crisis and controversy. It is not an exaggeration to say that he viewed his task as being to give the Canadian people the benefits of the enlightened policies of the Liberals while protecting them from the Tories who he regarded as venal and self-seeking and whose main concern was to impose policies which would further only their own selfish interests.

His friendships were not with contemporaries. Most of those were rivals, in or out of his own party, subordinate to him in government, or had nothing in common with him. He had several women friends, usually older than himself, his relationships with them probably being platonic. (He had associations of another kind with women as well.) But throughout his life he sought the friendship of men whose position, character, intellect and outlook he could respect. It was as if he was looking for a figure to whom he could give the admiration he had never felt for his own father. In turn, Sir William Mulock, Lord Grey and Sir Wilfrid Laurier had filled this need. Now he had found another in Lord Byng.

The Governor-General was, through his position and achievements, worthy of respect and was in no sense a potential rival. He was frank and open in his manner, gave every evidence of being friendly to King, took a serious and intelligent interest in what he had to say and gave him sensible advice which he often took. Furthermore, the breadth of his knowledge was wide and, in the case of religion, was at least the equal of King's.

More than once he supported King on questions where he disagreed with the British government. In 1922, when Lloyd George wanted the Dominions to help the British fight, if necessary, to keep the Turks out of Constantinople, the 'Chanak Affair', King had refused to send a contingent without first consulting Parliament. It was an ill-advised move on the part of Britain. Byng was touring in the West at the time and decided not to hasten his return to avoid speculation in the Press that the situation was worse than it was. When he returned, he approved the course which King had chosen.[1]

In 1924 the growth of isolationism in the United States was resulting in a similar development in Canada. When the question arose of who should control the Suez Canal and who should maintain order in Egypt, the Government was inclined to express no interest. Byng persuaded King that Canada did have a direct interest in keeping the Canal open but that the internal situation in Egypt was in no way a matter for Canada – 'it was not us that laid that egg'. King pressed Byng's view on his cabinet and they agreed to support the position that the Canal should be kept open to the shipping of all nations.[2]

In domestic policy, too, Byng was sympathetic to King's views. He counselled the need to reduce the cost of living, even if it involved a fight with the Manufacturers' Association. Because of lower costs in the United States and the danger of increased migration there from Canada, he was prepared to say in a speech from the throne that, even if the budget were not balanced for a year or two, prices must be kept down.[3] A position more radically different from traditional Tory thinking of those days would be difficult to imagine and would have shocked many Liberals.

On another occasion he spoke to King of the need for a 'big' policy for the development of natural resources and agriculture, for obtaining markets for Canadian products and for immigration. He believed the young men of the country were looking for leadership and were eager for a large and imaginative approach. 'Get a large policy; don't be afraid of it being too large.' King commented:

> Lord Byng is truly anxious to be of real help and is most kindly and generously disposed towards myself. He said, being detached and looking on, he could see what the young men were thinking, feeling and saying. He is right about the need for a large, constructive policy. I must get down to this side of my work and that soon.[4]

So much in tune did their views seem to King that he was lulled into looking on Byng as a helpful colleague and mentor rather than as the embodiment of a separate and independent constituent of the apparatus of Government.

The Byngs returned from the West to Rideau Hall on the morning of 4 September, 1925, and the Prime Minister came to report. King told the Governor-General that he was glad to see him back; he had missed him and been lonely without him.

An election was in the offing and Byng plainly hoped that, whatever party came to power, it would be broadly representative and able to unify the country. He suggested to King that he should spend a good deal of time in the West and should take with him a good young French Canadian who would talk 'Canada'.

According to King's diary the Governor-General agreed that, if no party had a clear majority, he should be given a chance to meet parliament as the Prime Minister. Perhaps King raised the subject simply to clarify it, because the choice in that situation would be his. He did, however, assure the Governor-General that he would not

303

attempt to do so unless he were sure of his ground. He then told Byng that he had decided on dissolution for the next day.

Another subject which they discussed on that occasion was the Canadian flag, which officially was the Union Jack. Byng thought something more distinctive was needed – perhaps one with the Union flag in the upper corner and a national emblem in the fly. He was becoming a Canadian nationalist.[5]

A week later Byng again told Mackenzie King that he would like him to come to him after the election with a following from the West that would make Canada a united country. He had no illusions about the outcome, though, and predicted it remarkably accurately. On 24 October, five days before the election, he wrote to John Buchan:

> The result of our election is difficult to foresee. Meighen will probably have the largest party which would be larger if he were more popular but I am doubtful if he will beat King if the latter unites the Liberals and Progressives under one banner.

In the event, in a house of 245 members, 116 would be Conservatives, 101 Liberals and 28 would come from the Progressives and other groups.

The Liberal Government had held just short of a majority of the seats in the House before the election and had appealed to the voters to give them a clear mandate. They had been disappointed and now could only govern with the consent of the Progressives. Several members of the cabinet, including the Prime Minister himself, had lost their seats. Discounting the ten seats added to Parliament by redistribution, King had lost 15 seats whilst Meighen gained 66.[6]

Characteristically Mackenzie King refused to interpret the result as meaning that he and his Government had been rejected by the people. In his view the voters had been offered a chance to give their support to Meighen and had declined. He drew encouragement from a strange source. His diary for 30 October records:

Before going to the office received in the morning mail (mailed Kingston 28th) from Mrs Bleaney [a fortune teller] a very remarkable letter – the interpretation of the dream I sent her. It is simply astounding how it spoke of the present elections, of seeming defeat, of the party being in a stronger position a little later on, of a clear way ahead after these troublesome times, of the time it would take for people to understand, of great spiritual power to come later on, of the nearness of dear Mother, it was all like a great revelation, and the more wonderful in that she said I would have a remarkable dream and asked me to send it to her to interpret. I cannot but believe dear Mother is very near to me and is sending me the light and

304

leading in this way. Very remarkable, too, in this connection was reference to Mrs Col Foster in the dream. I saw no reference to her in the interpretation, I was wondering what that significance was. As I came in from the office I found Col Foster's card on the card tray at the door, he had been here to call. Surely surely the loved ones are very near me at this time – think of this and the letter regarding the figure appearing with the eyes bandaged, – It is all truly wonderful.

Perhaps it was as well that the Governor-General was unaware of his Prime Minister's unconventional advisers. When they met later that day, Friday afternoon, King was inclined to continue as Prime Minister but, when Byng pointed out the disadvantages, he agreed that it would be wiser not to do so. He met the Cabinet on Monday and later reported to Byng that they insisted that he should not resign and that consequently he must continue until Parliament decided that he should not carry on the Government.[7]

Byng then said to him, 'Well, in that event you must not at any time ask for a dissolution unless Mr Meighen is first given a chance to show whether or not he is able to govern.' King said he was pleased to agree.[8]

While there is no mention of this arrangement in the King diaries, Byng not only told the Hon Charles Murphy of it but also Georges Vanier.[9] His official report said, 'We were both agreed that all alternative forms of Government should be tried before resorting to another election.'[10]

One of Byng's concerns was that until Parliament met a Government led by a prime minister who had lost his place in the House would continue to administer the country's affairs. The only course open to Byng was to insist that King call the House of Commons to meet at the earliest possible moment and to make him understand that no political appointments (senators, judges etc.) could be made in the interim, and no contracts be let for new public works.[11]

The tone of their discussions which took place between 30 October and 4 November became very frank and at one point King said to Byng that

It was strange that Governors coming out from Britain seemed almost invariably to side with the Tory party in Canada. I did not think he intended to but that wd be the impression created, it wd be bad for the Imperial connections. He stressed the idea that he was a sort of 'umpire' in situations. I opposed the idea strongly urging that as Govr. Genl. he was not entitled to have views, but to accept or reject advice of his ministers.[12]

To the extent that his diary can be believed, King had shown that not only could he be forthright in expressing his advice to the Governor-General, he could be almost insulting.

Later, however, he wrote:

> Lord Byng has certainly tried to be fair and just and has been fair and just. The natural Tory could not helping (sic) asserting itself in the feeling that the Govt. shld resign and let the Tories come in, but this, I truly believe, was meant as much, if not more in my own interest, than from any love of or desire to help Meighen – I do not think he likes Meighen.

and

> I begin to see where care must be exercised in choice of G.G. – that a man with large experience in prlty life the best for Gov. – Byng has acted well – but we have been dangerously near a serious situation.[13]

King was now becoming more sensitive than even he usually was to imagined slights by the occupants of Rideau Hall and much quicker to criticize. He thought that the Byngs should have invited the Japanese Ambassador to London, who was visiting Ottawa, to stay at Government House, that they should not have been away when a British West Indies trade delegation were in town, and that they 'never lose a chance to get out of some social function or obligation.'[14] Of 19 November, he wrote:

> Tonight I had Mr and Mrs King [a Senator] & Murdock and his wife to dinner – we went to a hockey match after. It was in reply to a request from Her Ex. to lend my patronage. I spoke to Their Excellencies during the first and second intermission. I felt they not only might but should have asked me to come into their box. After all I am the prime minister of the Country, and His Ex. is a visiting governor. The fact that at the moment there is a difficult situation only makes me the more indignant that they had not the courtesy to recognize the situation as meriting a little graciousness – The box was full of a lot of people from England who adopt a sort of superior air towards those of us who are in Canada – I confess to a certain feeling of genuine indignation at the action of their excellencies tonight – Toryism – (one word illegible) –[15]

By now the nerve ends of Mackenzie King's sensibilities were exposed. Parliament had not yet met and Byng had not altered his view that it would have been wiser for King to have resigned. King returned to the subject following a meeting with the Governor-General on 30 November.

> On the way out I mentioned I was sure I was right in the step I had taken in

306

meeting prlt. – that our own forces, and the Progressives who had been, not an opposition, but allied with Govt. & cooperating with us this last prlt. & to whom something was also owing would never have forgiven me if I had turned over to a common political enemy the reins of office, when apparent he was not in the position to control the H. of C., that I believed they intended to cooperate with us now – His Ex. listened & simply said 'of course, I do not agree' – there was nothing gracious in his manner, it was that Tory air of superior knowledge and station which makes a man with red blood in his veins feel a deep resentment, 'the tranquil consciousness of effortless superiority' of which Asquith spoke – I confess I felt as I came away real indignation at an attitude which if it means and spells anything means and spells 'colonialism' for Canada. Lord Byng had a chance to help end that. His attitude has made me for one feel quite differently than I did, and to realize that in our dominion if we are to have self-government we shall have to have it in its entirety without anyone 'sent out' by England to 'umpire' our behaviour. This is the most difficult and unpleasant trying of the situations I see ahead. We can only pray it will work itself out by a natural and peaceful evolution.[16]

His growing resentment was praying on King's mind and affecting his dreams:

I had an unpleasant dream about Govt. House, & oddly enough at noon Sladen came to say His Ex. hoped I wd go down anytime, that he was not asking me, that I might feel rested etc. It was all kindly meant. I opened out to Sladen a bit, on the cool kind of reception given me by their Ex. – at the rink the night of the Hockey. I said I had felt distinctly hurt at treatment, that I thought His Ex. owed it to me as Prime Minister when I went to his box to shew me some courtesy, of shaking hands, or inviting me to sit for a moment in his box. I sd I wd never have gone but for [Her] Ex. writing me to lend patronage. I had made up my mind not to go again. I spoke, too, of the putting off of the drawing room & state dinner as being in a way reflections on the Govt. – that these things wd be misconstrued in England etc. He told me the drawing room wd be held on Saturday, but State dinner later on account of Her Ex's dance. – This is all wrong and I shall tell His Ex. so if he asks me. Why shld a birthday party precede a State function?[17]

Evelyn Byng did not care for Mackenzie King and, try as she might, she could not conceal completely her attitude towards him. Later she claimed that she had never trusted him and had warned her husband to be on his guard. Over the past two months King had been at his most self-righteous in returning again and again to the subject of his right to meet the House, in an endeavour, presumably, to convert Byng to his views. Byng rarely showed any sign of impatience with him and did his best to maintain a friendly feeling

307

for the Prime Minister, for if their relationship was wrecked inevitably the country would suffer.[18] But the strain was beginning to tell.

On 12 December, King

> went to dinner at Govt. House. It was a trying sort of ordeal. Two new aides, neither of whom I knew by name and who had more or less all the superior ways of the young English bloods who come out, seated next Miss Sanford (sic) who I do not care for, & to left of Her Ex. who looked very tired and worn. There was no pleasant or conving (sic) conversation, – chit chat of a critical character.[19]

Eva Sanford's account was illuminating:

> During dinner Mr King asked me in the most sympathetic way if I had enjoyed my first year in Ottawa, if I found time to get out on my own, if I had made any friends here and so on. Suddenly I was horrified to feel a pinch on my thigh. A short time later, it was followed by another. Instinctively I raised my right foot and kicked downward hard with my high heel against his leg. There was a sort of moan as I turned my back on him. For the rest of dinner I ignored him and talked only to the man on my left.
>
> Next day Lord Byng summoned me and said 'Now, young lady, I must speak to you about your conduct at dinner last night. You really cannot treat Mr King the way you did. You most pointedly turned your back on him. It's your job to be polite to guests in this house, particularly to my prime minister.' Lady Byng was very firm about it too, and I blurted out what had happened. If I had thought about it, I wouldn't have said a word for who would believe such a thing about the Prime Minister? Fortunately, Lady Byng did believe me. I've never seen her in such a rage! She went straight to Lord Byng and said she'd never have that man under her roof again.
>
> Of course that was impossible but Lady Byng did her best to avoid Mackenzie King in future. Whenever he came to see the Governor-General, she'd say to me 'Here he comes – let's go to ground!'
>
> Willis-O'Connor, the senior ADC, had also spoken to me in much the same way as Lord Byng and I told him what had happened. He was horrified.

Now the story was out. On 11 January Evelyn's birthday was celebrated with a fancy dress ball. A rather short round figure in a clown's costume asked Eva Sandford to dance. No sooner were they on the floor than she felt a pinch. Quickly she drew away and heard people nearby laughing. It was then she realized that she was dancing not with Mackenzie King but with one of her friends. The story became the joke of the season in Ottawa.[20]

The Prime Minister had been to the ball:

An attractive affair, but not the kind of thing I care for at this time. I took Her Ex. into supper. Went as a Courtier in Geo III's time. Stayed till end of Ball about 3 am, which was a mistake. I should have left at midnight. I seem never to be able to control my own will, and to be carried away against my real purpose strive as I may.[21]

How improbable King's behaviour must have seemed at the time! The story of his relationships with women and the extent of his sexual proclivities only became widely known with the publication in 1976 of *A Very Double Life – the Private World of Mackenzie King* by C. P. Stacey and the release of his diaries to the public about the same time. By then Eva Sandford was dead.

A few days after the dinner incident, Byng ended a Christmas letter to John Buchan:

John, my friend, I have had difficulties of a political nature and could write you volumes on the subject – but perhaps better not. If you ever go to see Stamfordham, he will probably tell you the story as he knows the whole of it.

The situation of my Prime Minister was eloquently described by Jeremiah XXXVIII 22 Thy familiar friends have set thee on and have prevailed over thee: now that thy feet have sunk in the mire, they are turned away back.

So far things have gone all right but there are rocks ahead when Parliament meets.

Good luck, dear John

Yours ever
Julian[22]

To his friend Arthur Currie he wrote:

I have rather avoided seeking a confabulation of late with you though goodness knows I wanted to unbosom myself badly, especially to a friend, but I was afraid of compromising people so I bottled myself up so that no one else would have a share in the decisions I had to make. It has not been easy, nor have the politicians made it easier. But it has gone fairly well up to now.[23]

It required no great experience of the ways of parliament to realize that the forthcoming session would be engaged with constant wrangling as the Liberals sought to retain power, the Conservatives to bring them down and the Progressives to make what they could from the situation. Byng was worried that, by indulging in partisanship, Parliament would have neither the time nor the will to do anything about the many problems facing the country. Perhaps it was his soldier's instinct which made him want to bring the warring factions together to work for country, not for party. Unless they did, Parliament

309

would be impotent and another election more bitter than the last would be inevitable.

On 24 January Byng called on King at Laurier House and proposed that he should see Meighen with a view to the two leaders reaching an agreement for carrying on the work of Parliament in the interests of Canada. It was perhaps naive of him to expect either politician to agree but there was little doubt that their unrelenting partisanship was making for disunity in the country and for disenchantment with parliament among the voters.

King commented:

> On what lines cld a policy be worked out between Meighen & myself? This is really old country interference, tho' I was careful not to so state it. I know Lord Byng means well, but it is the point of view that we are incapable of managing our own affairs. With any knowledge of politics Lord Byng wd never make a suggestion of the kind. A Governor- General in Canada breathes a tory atmosphere.
>
> The most difficult part of the conversation was telling His Ex. that I did not think he shld concern himself about any arrangement – that it was an old- country and old-time point of view of Govr. Genl., that it was the tory attitude etc. etc. – all of which it is, tho' he resents the thought and honestly resents it.[24]

King was at that time by no means the constitutional expert he imagined himself to be. For all the good qualities which he recognized in Byng, he could not free his mind from the suspicion that the Governor-General was impelled by an unconscious attitude of superiority. Yet it is clear that Byng considered that his duty lay to the King and the Canadian people and to no one else. He acted for the sovereign in the capacity of the King of Canada.

Mackenzie King had not yet progressed far enough in his thinking to recognize this. He remained the colonial politician suspicious of Whitehall. In his mind the Sovereign was the 'King of England' and it followed that Byng, as his representative, personified the colonial power, standing aloof from and somewhat superior to the Government of Canada. That the Sovereign was the King of Canada, concerned with its people and their problems and involved in governing the country (through the Governor-General) as he was in England, was a concept which Mackenzie King did not yet accept. Yet he was prepared to support the concept of a sovereign of Canada as far as foreign treaties were concerned.

To him Byng's suggestion of cooperation with Meighen could only be construed as interference. To the extent that it failed to further his political aims, it was a Tory proposal.

But there was much on which the Governor-General and his adviser agreed. Byng supported King against the British Government over the Locarno Treaty as he had over the Chanak Affair in 1922, the Halibut Treaty in 1923 and the peace treaty with Turkey. On 8 February he surprised and pleased the Prime Minister: 'He said the word Empire was a mistake, we were sister nations not an Empire.' They agreed, too, against the wishes of Baldwin and Amery, on Lord and Lady Willingdon for the next residents of Rideau Hall.[25]

Up to this time much of King's edginess and Byng's disquiet arose from the fact that the Prime Minister, having lost his seat in the election, was not a member of Parliament. The situation eased somewhat on 16 February when he won a by-election in Prince Albert, Saskatchewan, and established once more the legitimacy of his position.

Next day King learned of a suggestion by a senior Conservative politician that Meighen would be prepared to make an arrangement with him for the business of the parliamentary session in return for an agreement to an election in June. Immediately King connected the proposal with that made by Byng and concluded that it had been put in the Governor-General's mind by his wife who had received it from her friend R. B. Bennett, a leading Conservative. He was indignant, disappointed and hurt.[26] Again his diary contained criticisms of the Byngs. They should have entertained a visiting Liberal politician from Britain[27] and he thought it 'disgraceful that the Byngs do not seem to have been in anyway at home' to Mr Oswald Mosley and his first wife, Lady Cynthia, daughter of Lord Curzon. The future fascist leader was then a member of the Labour party in Britain. 'I like both Mosley and Lady C immensely. I shall be surprised if some day he is not Prime Minister of England.'[28]

Throughout his five years in Canada Byng was careful not to take an undue interest in the Armed Forces, which might give the impression that he was a 'militarist', but his abiding affection for the Canadian Corps which he had commanded and for the men who served in it was apparent to all. Within weeks of his arrival in Canada he attended a huge gathering of veterans at the Canadian National Exhibition in Toronto. So warm was their welcome that he had difficulty controlling his emotions. In the other major centres Byng's reception by veterans was the same and in all his tours across the country he devoted time both to see his old soldiers and to enquire after their welfare. More than any, the occasions which gave him pleasure were the annual dinners on Vimy Day. The first had

311

been in Toronto in 1922. In the four succeeding years it was at Government House in Ottawa. Of these the last was the most memorable.

On the evening of 9 April, 1926, by arranging them carefully, tables had been fitted in to seat 200. It had taken over five hours to arrange the flowers and the room was aglow with spring colours. The guests, many of whom had come hundreds of miles to be present, were in a curiously ambivalent mood. They were excited and happy as they had been at the previous dinners, but they were also gloomy; this annual reunion of veterans would be the last of its kind. Old Bungo was going back to England soon and the Canadian Corps would lose sight of its most cherished personality.

The veterans were nearly all civilians now; there had never been many regulars among the Canadian officers of the First World War. When hostilities ended, they had taken up again the careers they had set aside in 1914. A roll-call of Byng's guests would have sounded like a reading from a Canadian 'Who's Who', for the nation's wartime military leaders now had important peacetime responsibilities. They published newspapers, headed great businesses, occupied the Bench, supervised hospitals, were prominent academics and sat in Parliament.

Joining Arthur Currie and divisional, brigade and battalion commanders of the Canadian Corps were Basil Brooke, now launched on a political career in Northern Ireland and Edmund Ironside who would be Chief of the Imperial General Staff on the outbreak of the next war.

Evelyn recalled:

> It was a riotous night, for they were all young again in spirit, as the pipers marched up and down the passages . . . a glorious reunion between officers who seldom met at any other time throughout the year.

On this last Vimy night she came in 'like a child for the dessert'. There were presentations to be made. Pipe Major John Gillies, Seaforth Highlanders of Canada, handed Byng a Gaelic motto on parchment that was a gift from all the Highland regiments of Canada and Lady Byng received a specially commissioned portrait of her husband painted by Ernest Fosbery, RCA. Then Arthur Currie rose to speak but had difficulty finishing his speech, so upset was he at the prospect of Byng's departure. Finally he turned to him and said that the veterans wished him to accept a gift 'in memory of other days and as a small mark of our deep affection.' It was a motor car.

Byng could say little more than his thanks.

The *Ottawa Journal* reported that 'The cheering resounded, the pipers

312

tuned up with renewed vigour and all the party marched out with General Byng to the front door of Government House where the limousine was waiting in a special portico.' It was no ordinary car – a seven passenger, 75 horse-power McLaughlin-Buick. It carried a silver beaver, clutching a maple leaf, on the bonnet. The workmen who had built it, many of them veterans, had asked that they be allowed to do it without pay as their contribution, but the fund had been so over-subscribed that the offer was declined. It was undoubtedly one of the best Buicks ever made, for much love had been lavished on every part of it. The *Journal* said quite simply that it was 'the finest motor car that has so far been made in Canada'.

After that there was a final drink in the racquets room while old stories were told again and a few songs were sung. Currie said, 'The Vimy days are part of our lives, and shall not vanish from the tablets of our remembrance this side of the grave.'

The annual dinner of the Press Club took place on the following night. Byng was the guest of honour and both the Prime Minister and the Leader of the Opposition were to speak. Traditionally it was not a serious occasion; it was a sort of parliamentary hazing with everyone, especially the leaders of the parties, being the butt of jokes and songs. Mackenzie King dreaded the occasions, which he found rather coarse for his taste. Tonight when he spoke there were no ill-mannered interruptions of his speech for he confined his remarks to appreciation of Lord Byng. In the warmest terms he spoke of the affection and regard in which Byng was held by members of the government and press as well as by officers of the Canadian Corps who had expressed their feelings on the previous night. He compared Byng's actions at Vimy with those during his sojourn in Canada, the making for unity in the country as he had in the Forces, 'the nine provinces going up the hill together with one idea and one ideal'. He spoke of his talks with the Governor-General concerning Canada and the Empire and endorsed his belief in the imperial ties as 'a common sovereign and a common love of traditions, of ideas and aspirations and of the association with the old land'. He concluded that the remembrance that they would have of him was 'the portrait in heart and mind of an English gentleman with the wealth of meaning implied in those words'.

Charpentier, the president of the Parliamentary Press Gallery, spoke warmly of the regard which the Press had for Lord Byng and the usually somewhat cynical journalists sang a song to him to the tune of Land of Hope and Glory, its last verse:

Fade away your titles,
Gone your gay plumed hat,

Byng you're so damned human,
We'll remember that.

The following evening the Prime Minister came to dine at Rideau
Hall. The euphoria of Vimy night, followed by the warmth and
friendliness of the Press Club dinner and the unreserved praise which
King had poured on him, had softened Byng and even 'Her Ex.'
toward the Prime Minister. The long talk which followed was
agreeable and King felt that much had been done to restore the old
relationship between the Governor and himself.[29]

For the first five months of the parliamentary session Mackenzie
King had retained power with the grudging support of the
Progressives. In February a breach with them had been narrowly
averted by establishing a Special Committee to investigate allegations
of corruption and incompetence in the Customs Department. Another
condition of their support was the turning over to Alberta of its
natural resources, control of which had been retained by the federal
government when the province was formed. King had agreed that the
enabling legislation would be passed during the session but had
postponed its consideration while a section of the agreement was
tested in the courts.

In June King's fragile structure of support was shaken when a
Conservative moved that the Government had lost the confidence of
the House by failing to transfer Alberta's resources. Though the
Progressives supported him in defeating the motion, King appreciated
that the strain of doing so was becoming too much for them.

Shortly thereafter the report of the Special Committee on the
Customs Department was presented to the House. It proved that
corruption was widespread in the service, but it was not specifically
critical of the Government or of Boivin, the minister concerned.
Scenting blood, H. H. Stevens, a Conservative, proposed an
amendment to the report which would fix a measure of responsibility
on the Government. It constituted a motion of censure which, if
passed, would compel the Government to resign.

J. S. Woodsworth, one of the two Labour members of the House,
worried lest defeat of the Government would delay the passage of old
age pensions legislation, proposed an amendment to the Conservative
amendment which would set up a Royal Commission to investigate
the Customs and remove criticism of the minister. His motion,
supported by the full force of the Government, was defeated.

A Progressive member, W. F. Fansher, then proposed, probably
with Meighen's connivance, that Woodsworth's idea of a Royal

314

Commission be combined with the original Conservative amendment. The Speaker ruled the motion out of order and, on division, the House over-ruled the Speaker by two votes. Again the Government was out-voted.

To rally Progressive support King now offered to give Alberta its natural resources. So far, while two motions which they supported had been lost, no motion proposed by the Government had been involved. Technically, they had not been defeated. But King and his supporters were nearing exhaustion and time was needed to rest and think. He persuaded a member of the Progressive party to move that the House adjourn. After debate, this third Government-supported motion was defeated by a single vote.

King was desperate for time but, under the rules, some business would have to be recorded before a second adjournment motion could be considered. Incredibly, he announced that he would accept Fansher's critical amendment. A motion to adjourn was carried by one vote.

The Prime Minister knew there was a little hope of avoiding censure, which would mean going to the people as a defeated and discredited administration. If by some chance the Liberals were to survive the motion, it would be virtually impossible for them to complete their programme for the session. He decided to seek dissolution.

To bystanders, of whom one of the most interested was Byng, the House had presented an appalling picture. For four days and nights the debate had gone on with standards of parliamentary conduct diminishing by the hour. Shouts and insults echoed in the chamber, neither side conceding an inch for sickness or even bereavement.[30]

King called on the Governor-General on Saturday afternoon, 26 June. The day before, he had seen Byng and told him of the progress of the debate and of the motions before the House. Now he reviewed further developments and said that he thought that neither he nor Meighen would be able to carry on. Dissolution was the only practicable course.

Byng reminded him of their agreement after the election that if King met the House and subsequently was unable to carry on, Meighen should be given a chance to form a government. He was not prepared to agree to dissolution and hoped that King would not request it.[31]

In anticipation of such a response, King had come armed with volumes of Hansard and other documents to support his case. He found that the Governor-General also was well prepared. (Indeed he had been advised by some of Canada's best legal minds.[32]) Byng agreed that dissolution had not been refused in Britain for 100 years and had not been refused to a Prime Minister in Canada since Confederation. But neither was there a precedent for the present situation.[33]

In this Byng was correct. No Prime Minister had ever asked the Sovereign or a governor-general for dissolution to avoid a vote of censure in the House. It would be akin to a prisoner in the dock asking the judge to dismiss the jury before a verdict had been reached and to place the trial before a higher court.

The power of the crown to refuse dissolution unquestionably exists. That it has so seldom been invoked is a comment on the good sense of ministers in recognizing the realities of political situations and in not pressing improper proposals to the point of inevitable rebuff.

Byng pointed out that King had insisted in November that he should be allowed to meet Parliament so it could decide on his right to govern. In fact, if not in theory, the recent votes in the House had constituted a defeat in that King admitted that he could carry on effective government no longer. Parliament had decided against him.[34] Now, in accordance with their earlier agreement, the party with the largest number of seats in the House must be given the chance to govern.

King threatened that to refuse him dissolution, and then to give it to a political opponent, would result in it becoming an issue in an election campaign and would work great injury on the Crown, the Empire and on Byng personally. When he saw that he could not shake the Governor's determination, he urged Byng to seek advice from the British Government before making a decision. He claimed that it was out of the love, affection and regard he held for Byng and to save him from a very serious error as well as to maintain a great constitutional principle that he advised him to take this course.[35] How King could have regarded any British advice, had it been offered, as other than interference in Canada's internal affairs is hard to imagine. It is a measure of his desperation to retain power that he should have proposed that Byng obtain it.

Byng flatly refused. He told King that to do so would be liable to jeopardize the relationship of the Dominion to the old country whereas an incompetent or unwise act of a governor-general could involve only himself.[36]

The discussion went on for hours. On Sunday King returned to harangue the Governor-General, who would not be moved in his conviction that he had the right to withhold dissolution and that in the present circumstances he should exercise it. He said that three alternatives were open to the Prime Minister:

One was to ask him to call for Mr Meighen and let Meighen demonstrate what he could do, the second was to ask for dissolution, which he earnestly hoped I would not do and which he would refuse if I did. The third was to go on in parliament and continue there remaining in office unless defeated, in which event I would then be obliged to ask him to send for Mr Meighen.

Again and again King went over his arguments and preached about the rights of the people, of his love for Canada and for the Empire. Byng was tired:

His Excellency seemed to get a little impatient as I brought out these points and said that nothing that I could say could influence his mind, and that it was painful to go over the ground again. I replied that I was not trying to influence him beyond what I felt it my duty, as his adviser and adviser to the Crown to do.

Still King pressed his case upon the unmoving Governor-General. As he was leaving, some time later, he again suggested that the British Government be asked for guidance and again Byng refused.[37]

Finally on Monday afternoon, after another lengthy session, King formally asked for dissolution and, when Byng refused, he handed him his resignation:

Your Excellency having declined to accept my advice to place your signature to the Order-in-Council with reference to a dissolution of parliament, which I have placed before you today, I hereby tender to Your Excellency my resignation as Prime Minister of Canada.

Your Excellency will recall that in our recent conversations relative to dissolution I have on each occasion suggested to Your Excellency, as I have again urged this morning, that having regard to the possible very serious consequences of a refusal of the advice of your First Minister to dissolve parliament, you should, before definitely deciding on this step, cable the Secretary of State for the Dominions asking the British Government, from whom you have come to Canada under instructions, what, in the opinion of the Secretary of State for the Dominions, your course should be in the event of the Prime Minister presenting you with an Order-in-Council having reference to a dissolution.

As a refusal by a Governor-General to accept the advice of a Prime Minister is a serious step at any time, and most serious under existing conditions in all parts of the British Empire today, there will be raised, I fear, by the refusal on Your Excellency's part to accept the advice tendered a grave constitutional question without precedent in the history of Great Britain for a century and in the history of Canada since Confederation.

If there is anything which, having regard to my responsibilities as Prime Minister, I can even yet do to avert such a deplorable and possibly far-reaching crisis I shall be glad so to do, and shall be pleased to have my resignation withheld at Your Excellency's request pending the time it may be necessary for Your Excellency to communicate with the Secretary of State for the Dominions.

Next day the Governor-General replied:

I must acknowledge on paper, with many thanks, the receipt of your letter handed to me at our meeting yesterday.

In trying to condense all that has passed between us during the last week, it seems to my mind that there is really only one point at issue.

You advise me 'that as, in your opinion, Mr Meighen is unable to govern the country, there should be another Election with the present machinery to enable the people to decide'. My contention is that Mr Meighen has not been given a chance of trying to govern, or saying that he cannot do so, and that all reasonable expedients should be tried before resorting to another Election.

Permit me to say once more that, before deciding on my constitutional course on this matter, I gave the subject the most fairminded and painstaking consideration which it was in my power to apply.

I can only add how sincerely I regret the severence of our official companionship, and how gratefully I acknowledge the help of your counsel and co-operation.

With warmest wishes.[38]

Having called for Meighen who agreed to form a government, Byng first wrote to King George,[39] then next day telegraphed the main parts of that letter to L. S. Amery, the Secretary of State for Dominion Affairs:

As already telegraphed, Mr Mackenzie King asked me to grant him dissolution. I refused. Thereupon he resigned and I asked Mr Meighen to form a Government, which has been done.

Now this constitutional or unconstitutional act of mine seems to resolve itself into these salient features. A Governor-General has the absolute right of granting dissolution or refusing it. The refusal is a very dangerous decision, it embodies the rejection of the advice of the accredited Minister, which is the bed-rock of Constitutional Government. Therefore nine times out of ten a Governor-General should take the Prime Minister's advice on this as on other matters. But if the advice offered is considered by the Governor-General to be wrong and unfair, and not for the welfare of the people, it behoves him to act in what he considers the best interests of the country.

This is naturally the point of view I have taken and expressed it in my reply to Mr King (text of which is being telegraphed later).

You will notice that the letter in question is an acknowledgement of a letter from Mr King (text of which is also being telegraphed later) appealing

318

that I should consult the Government in London. While recognizing to the full the help that this might afford me, I flatly refused, telling Mr King that to ask advice from London, where the conditions of Canada were not as well known as they were to me, was to put the British Government in the unfortunate position of having to offer solution which might give people out here the feeling of a participation in their politics, which is to be strongly deprecated.

There seemed to me to be one person, and one alone, who was responsible for the decision and that was myself. I should feel that the relationship of the Dominion to the Old Country would be liable to be seriously jeopardized by involving the Home Government; whereas the incompetent and unwise action of a Governor-General can only involve himself.

I am glad to say that to the end I was able to maintain a friendly feeling with my late Prime Minister. Had it been otherwise, I should have offered my resignation at once. This point of view has been uppermost in my mind ever since he determined on retaining the reins of office (against my private advice) last November. It has not been always easy but it was imperative that a Governor-General and a Prime Minister could not allow a divergent view-point to wreck their relationship without the greatest detriment to the country.

Mr King, whose bitterness was very marked Monday, will probably take a very vitriolic line against myself – that seems only natural. But I have to wait the verdict of history to prove my having adopted a wrong course and this I do with an easy conscience that, right or wrong, I have acted in the interests of Canada, and have implicated no one else in my decision.

I would only add that at our last three interviews I appealed to Mr King not to put the Governor-General in the position of having to make a controversial decision. He refused and it appeared that I could do no more.

To this he received the following secret and personal reply:

I have read with the greatest interest your secret telegram of June 30th and your correspondence with Mr Mackenzie King. I am sorry that it should have fallen to your lot to have to deal with so difficult and delicate situation. I cannot, of course, express any opinion on your action but I can state that I unreservedly concur in the view which you took of the suggestion that you should refer to me before deciding on the request for a dissolution. The matter is clearly one concerning the internal affairs of Canada, in which Ministers here could not take it upon themselves to intervene, and I may say that if you had referred to me, I could only have replied on lines similar to the statement which I made in the House of Commons on March 15th with regard to the political situation in New South Wales, viz., that in my view it would not be proper for the Secretary of State to issue instructions to the Governor with regard to the exercise of his constitutional duties.[40]

King's action placed Byng in a particularly invidious position. When

319

a Prime Minister offers his resignation he customarily agrees to withhold it until the Governor-General is able to offer the government to someone else. If no one feels able to govern, he may then persuade the incumbent to carry on or may dissolve parliament.

In this case, if Meighen were to refuse to attempt the formation of a government, Byng would have no alternative but to recall King, who probably would only accept on condition that he was immediately granted dissolution.

King apparently believed that Meighen would be so eager to become prime minister once more that his acceptance of the office could be assumed. It now appears that, had he granted the Governor-General this last courtesy, he might yet have gained the dissolution he desired. Certainly at least two prominent Conservatives, for purely political reasons, advised their leader against trying to form an administration. But both Meighen and Sir Robert Borden, the former leader of the Conservatives, agreed that the attempt must be made. To refuse would leave Byng in the position of having to consent to Mackenzie King avoiding a motion of censure by granting dissolution. Byng might well have to resign.

Meighen was aware of the difficulties before him when Byng asked if he could form a government. He said that he would need to consider the situation before committing himself.

'Meighen's apparent hesitancy seemed to trouble His Excellency, for as they were parting he said "I feel justified in saying to you that I think my position should be considered." Concerning this remark, Meighen wrote many years later:

> I had no doubt in my own mind what he meant. He meant to indicate that he had acted constitutionally in discharge of his duty, and that a refusal on my part would be, in some places anyway, regarded as a rebuke to him. In that I think he was right. I was quite certain at the time . . . that a refusal on my part would have been proclaimed at once as a rebuke to Lord Byng, and the more I thought of the subject, the more I was convinced that it would be a rebuke he did not merit. That was a consideration I did not think I had any right to ignore.'[41]

The Meighen administration did not last long. During the afternoon of 29 June the censure motion against the late government, its leader and the Minister of Customs was passed, but on 2 July the new government was defeated in the House. Meighen reported the circumstances to the Governor-General and recommended dissolution.

Byng was now in an even more unenviable position. No matter what he did, one party or other would vilify him and he would have to sit silent on the sidelines during the election campaign, listening to half-truths and lies about his conduct, his judgement and his attitude to Canada. The issue, however, was clear cut. Byng granted Meighen's request.

Predictably Mackenzie King and the Liberals made the constitutional crisis one of the main issues of the election. King spoke bitterly of the Governor-General's partiality for Meighen in granting him dissolution with the attendant control of the election machinery, when only four days earlier he had denied it to him. Upon the Conservative defeat in the House, Byng should have sent once more for him and granted him dissolution. He, who had been undefeated in the House, had been denied dissolution. Meighen, who had been defeated in the House, had been granted it.

In fact Byng had behaved with complete impartiality. He refused King's advice to dissolve Parliament when to do so would prevent it voting on a motion censuring the government and before it was known whether the largest party in the House was prepared to form a government. He accepted Meighen's advice which was to dissolve Parliament after it had been shown that neither party could govern. Had he refused Meighen's advice and sent once more for King, he would have been recalling a Prime Minister who had tendered him unconstitutional advice and whose ministry had been formally censured by the House of Commons.

Dr Eugene Forsey, the eminent constitutional expert, commented that had Mackenzie King 'simply resigned without asking for dissolution, and if Mr Meighen had taken office in these circumstances and, after being sustained for a time, been defeated, his right to dissolution would have been incontestable. To suggest that Mr King could deprive him of that right by making a prior unconstitutional request for dissolution is once again to place the whole Constitution at the mercy of any Prime Minister's caprice, or lack of scruple, or ignorance of constitutional usage.'[42]

Byng had planned to return to England later in the summer, but now, feeling that that would be unfair to his successor, he decided to remain in Canada a few more weeks until the election was over and the new government was safely installed in office.

After the dissolution of Parliament, Byng received many letters of support from old friends. To Arthur Currie he replied:

I want to tell you the whole story but I had better wait till we meet. I begged Mr King not to put the King's Representative in the position of having to make a controversial decision and offered him two ways out of it. He refused and then told me(1) I was ruining the constitution (2) Breaking up the

321

Empire (3) Putting Canada back in a colonial status. I replied that he put me in the position of being either (1) an inefficient and unconstitutional Govr Genl or (2) a moral coward – and that I chose the former and left the verdict to history.

But there! there! 'Nuff said' – I will tell you the whole story when we meet –

I don't think I let Canada down, or the Corps or my friends.[43]

His letter of 16 July to John Buchan was couched in much the same terms. Evelyn saw no point in being diplomatic to such an old friend and wrote to him on the 21st:

My dear John,

Julian shewed me your nice letter to him, and I am SO glad you wrote, as we really have had a far far more hellish time than any of you at home can realize or believe. How much J. will have told you in his reply I don't know, but I hope enough to show you both what a scurvy cad M. K. is and always has been. You were both so 'entiche' with him at Ottawa, that you never saw through him, as with more intimate knowledge one did oneself. Now he has come out in his true colours, as totally regardless of Empire, Crown, and everything but his own 'place in the sun'. As for his treatment of J. all through that recent period it was disgusting beyond all words. For three solid days he came up and insulted, bullied, threatened him, with everything he could think of, in the hopes of bringing an utterly upright man of honour to his own despicable depths of moral degradation.

Power is his watchword – the power of M. K. – and there is not one other thing in the whole world that counts in his sight. A true Judas Iscariot, he tried to betray J. in the House with lying protestations of a sham affection that had NEVER really existed, and which was only an incidental handle to him for attempting his own advancement. That he should have dared behave as he did, even I, who always despised and knew him, hardly expected, and God knows I expected a goodish deal of filth, once his power was in danger.[44]

In August the Byngs stayed at Point-au-Pic on Murray Bay, next door to Judge Archer, Pauline Vanier's father. Three or four mornings each week Georges came over to walk with Byng down to the shore, or along the Boulevard or towards the plateau which stands above it. They talked of many things but always the conversation came back to the constitutional crisis which had begun to haunt Byng. He told Vanier:

It seems to me that when Mr Mackenzie King came to ask for dissolution, there were only two courses open to him – to resign or to fight it out in the House. The courageous course was to fight it out and to stand or fall by the verdict of Parliament. The proper jury, it seems to me, to decide on a

322

question is the one which has heard the evidence; and Parliament in this case had the right, I believe, to pronounce its verdict. That is my idea of Government of the people, by the people and for the people. If dissolution can be obtained each time a PM fears an adverse vote in the House, it is the negation of Parliament's authority; Parliament represents the people – Parliament should judge. Mr King had always said in the past 'Let Parliament decide' and now when Parliament was to be given an opportunity to decide, he asked for a dissolution, thus seeking to deprive Parliament of its prerogatives and casting the issue into the confusion of a general election.

But some may say – even granting that Parliament should normally be allowed to pronounce on a matter that has been thrashed out before it – should not the Governor-General accept the advice of the Prime Minister, the mouthpiece of the people? What did Mr King represent? A discredited minority – a minority which three times had been defeated in the House – a minority over whose head a vote of censure was hanging. How can Mr King say that he represented the people when he had been beaten three times, and if he represented the people, why should he fear the verdict of Parliament which is the voice of the people? If Mr King, who represented a minority, a discredited minority, had been given a chance to govern, why should not the man who represented the numerically greatest party be given a chance to govern before throwing the country anew into the throes of a general election.

I have often asked myself – is there anything I should have thought of that I did not think of? And frankly I don't think there is. It is the hardest thing I have done for Canada.[45]

On other days Pauline would accompany Byng on his walks, but then he would say little and his long silences were broken only by the occasional deep sigh. 'He was a very troubled man, very tired and depressed.'[46] It was during this summer that the first signs of the heart trouble which later afflicted him were detected.

The election took place on 14 September and the Byngs were back in Rideau Hall to await the results. Not unexpectedly, King and the Liberals won.

A week later, before Meighen resigned, Byng asked Mackenzie King to come to Rideau Hall to see him. He received him courteously. Byng particularly wanted to clear the air with him before they were forced to meet in public and it is plain from King's diary that their discussion, though entirely civil, was somewhat strained. As he was leaving Government House King mentioned to the ADC on duty that he intended to be present at a farewell dinner for His Excellency that evening. He was told that the Governor-General 'was counting on my being present and would have felt it keenly were I not to attend. Lord William Scott remarked that none of the young ladies would be present.

I hardly knew to whom he had reference, unless it was to Her Excellency's Secretary.'[47] The barb in Scott's remark had found its target as surely as had Eva's high heel.

On Saturday, 25 September King brought his Ministers to be sworn in. It was the last audience which Byng gave as Governor-General. On Monday morning, accompanied by the Prime Minister, he laid a stone for the altar in the Memorial Chamber of the Peace Tower at the Parliament Buildings and in the afternoon departed on the viceregal train for Quebec.

Thousands of people lined the streets of Ottawa to cheer the Byngs on their way. With difficulty a space was kept open at the station for the Governor-General to inspect the guard of honour of his Foot Guards. The concourse was filled with people and many found their way on to the platform.

The formal farewells were said and scarcely heard. Then official Ottawa, joined and jostled by ordinary citizens, filed past the Byngs to shake their hands and bid them godspeed. An old lady stumbled on the gravel ballast of the tracks and a huge Cameron Highlander lifted her onto the platform in front of Lord Byng. He took her hand and bent over to speak to her and for a few moments they laughed together to the exclusion of everyone else.

Eventually Byng managed to climb on to the train and stood on the rear platform, biting his lower lip hard to control his emotions. As the train pulled away he raised his arms high as if he wished to embrace the whole crowd, then waved them gently to and fro until he could see the station no more.

To mark his departure from Quebec, Mackenzie King did no more than protocol required. To represent the Canadian Government he sent two minor cabinet ministers who were residents of Quebec to say farewell. The crowds, large and enthusiastic, included hundreds of ex-servicemen, and there was nothing lacking in the way of military ceremonial. But the Governmental snub was obvious. Among Byng's friends who were there were Arthur Currie and Georges Vanier. Later Pauline Vanier spoke of the day:

It was interminable. That morning, we all spent at Spencerwood and stayed for a depressing lunch made worse by the presence of the two dreary and embarrassed ministers of the Federal Government. Bungo was exhausted and when he sailed there were tears in his eyes, not just of sadness at parting, but of real grief. He was a broken man.[48]

324

Chapter 16
Metropolitan Police

WHETHER OR NOT Pauline Vanier was accurate in describing Byng as a broken man when he left Canada, he was undoubtedly worn out and suffering from the strain of his recent ordeal. During the summer he had suffered chest pains and a feeling of lassitude, presaging a heart condition. He wanted nothing more than to escape to the refuge of Thorpe and intended to do so as soon as he was free from obligations in London which included a speech at a Canada Club dinner on 18 October.

In the meantime he became involved in another sort of controversy, one which appealed to his sense of humour. In June he had been elevated from the rank of baron to viscount and had declined to pay the fees levelled by the College of Heralds. He failed to see why it should cost him anything to accept an honour given for service to his country – indeed Lords Oxford, Balfour, Birkenhead, Haig, Jellicoe and Beatty had had their fees remitted on the same grounds.[1] Eventually so had he.

Willis-O'Connor, by now an even closer friend of the Byngs, had been upset by their departure from Ottawa and had agreed only reluctantly to remain on the staff of the new Governor-General, Lord Willingdon. Byng wrote to cheer him up:

Dear old Wilkie,
    This is indeed the 'coals of fire' epistle as you owe one already, but I thought I would just write. There is nothing to say as you will find out when you peruse this.
    I went to the Station to meet Mackenzie King – 'beau geste' of perfection – he fell into my arms and produced a Niagara of gush – 'how noble' – 'how thoughtful' – 'he would ever remember it'.
    There was a considerable crowd, the most prominent being Vincent and Alice (Massey) bellying with the prospect of favours to come.
    Then we had the Canada Club dinner, my speech may be said to have been an unqualified success owing to the enthusiastic applause of WLMK who cheered every utterance. It ran something like this.

325

Self 'Your Royal Highness'
WLMK 'Hear, Hear'
Self 'Mr Chairman'
WLMK 'Tres Bien, Hoch, Hoch'
Self 'My Lords'
WLMK 'Attaboy, "Buno oratorio" (italian)'
Self 'And Gentlemen'
WLMK 'Banzai' – 'Perfectly fine' (Clap, Clap, Clap) and so on to the end.

Then I had to go to see the Garter King at Arms about this new title. He began by asking me what name I wanted to take. I naturally said 'What names have you this morning?' He thought this frivolous and the Garter nearly fell off his Arms. He then said I might keep my old one. To this I urged that that course was perfectly satisfactory as I could spell it, having as a boy written it frequently on the walls of a lavatory and as an old man having signed thousands of Orders in Council, so we left it at that.

My wife has taken to gardening!!! M'yes, I don't think.

What you saw in Canada is fleabite to what is going on now. The ordinary traveller mayn't walk anywhere because it is sown with Canadian bulbs or nuts or seeds or cuttings. It is quite a rest to get on the high road and dodge the charabancs.

Talk about the whole damn forest – that was an arid desert to our place.

(This is a damn lie!! You know I never did get the damn forest because you were far too lazy – you old Mutt).

The above was written by my wife. You probably can't read it. When are you coming to see us?

'If they ask us – To Damascus
You could stay a while'.

Dear old Wilks – how I miss you all.[2]

Evidently Mackenzie King really had enjoyed his evening with the Canada Club. Founded in 1812 and the oldest dining club in London, its guest list was impressive. King had agreeable conversations with the Prince of Wales, Winston Churchill and the Duke of Connaught and rated Lord Byng's speech as 'distinctly good'.[3]

On 22 October the Byngs returned at last to Thorpe-le-Soken. The station had been decorated with flags and the villagers and ex-servicemen of the district joined in their welcome with a torchlight procession, firework displays and bonfires.[4]

Two years earlier Evelyn had arranged for their house to be redecorated and the for its staff accommodation to be gutted and rearranged so that the servants would have comfortable rooms overlooking the gardens. When she and Julian arrived, they were well pleased with the result. Canadian materials had been widely used and efficient central heating and modern bathrooms installed. With its

326

grey-toned, natural-grained hemlock panelling, light colours and wide windows, it resembled the handsome residences of Westmount and Rockcliffe. Already Canadian maples, poplars, cedars and firs had been planted in the grounds and Evelyn had brought crates of cuttings, seeds and bulbs for her by now impressive garden.

Energetic and intelligent, with no children to confine her activities, Evelyn had developed her own interests, especially during the War. For her there was much to do. She soon found herself back in her former role of a leading figure in community and county affairs and the development of her gardens became almost an obsession.

There were no such local interests for Julian. After a few weeks at Thorpe Byng began to feel restive. For the first time since he joined the army, he was without employment and he groped for some way in which he could be of use. About one thing he was clear, he did not intend to write his memoirs. When it was suggested that he do so, he commented, 'The trouble is that when soldiers write their memoirs, they always abuse someone and, for my part, there isn't a soul I want to abuse.'[5]

In their indignation about his treatment over the constitutional crisis, his friends in Canada persisted in trying to put the record straight. Early in 1927 Arthur Currie wrote:

You have probably observed that the Prime Minister has denied in the most emphatic manner that there was any agreement, implied or otherwise, between yourself and him that he should not seek a dissolution of the Parliament after the election of 1925. You know I do not think it is right that he should . . . get away with what he is doing in the matter of the events of last June. I know you won't say anything because you feel that no good can come of it, and you object to having your name bandied about in the heat of political contention. I daresay you are right, but there are a great many of your friends who would like to put the people right if you would allow them to do so.

Byng replied:

Politics spoil so many of people's best efforts at reconciliation, comprehension, sympathy and compromise. Once a question gets into Parliament, any form of 'get together' becomes impossible.

For your private ear alone, I give you one instance. The new Trades Union Bill has been a good deal in people's minds and it is foreseen that the debates will become the bitterest, most acrimonious and harmful. It was suggested that a real meeting of employers and union representatives should be arranged and I was asked whether I would accept the chairmanship. I replied that I would, if the terms of the Bill were not published before we had finished. Once they were known, the Conservatives

327

would be dreadnought protagonists and the Labour would commit themselves to an unstinted 'anti' campaign and nothing would come of any effort on our part. This has now taken place and we have got to witness an unpleasant period. . . .

No, Arthur, I think I was Cardinal Wiseman not to make any statement re the King – Byng episode. In the first place, I am too fond of Canada to do a bad turn to her representative government. In the second place, what good would it have done? The Canadian Conservatives would have made some capital out of it, if they knew the truth – but are they fit to govern? Look through the list of names in Meighen's eleven-day governing and say if you would like them back?

King of course lied about the agreement, but I suppose he had to. The first thing he said when I spoke to him about it was, 'The time for all we said last November is over' and, 'A new situation has arisen'. M'yes. Well, that's that.

The great effort I have always had in mind was not to be peevish, hence my civilities to King when he was in London, and never writing about it except to you. I have nothing to regret and am really quite happy in the retrospect as I don't think I did Canada any harm. If I thought I had I should be miserable. It was forced on me, as you know, and I had to try and not let the Canadian down.[6]

The proposal that he should become involved in the Trade Union Bill was only the first indication that the British Government had not forgotten him. He later told Willis-O'Connor:

They have been offering me jobs lately, one was an idea of going to Kenya to arrange the native difficulties with Tanganyika, but it did not mature owing to the fact that I was not a politician. The next was to go to India . . . to regularize and standardize the position of rajahs. I refused as the committee, and the work, did not appeal to me so much as ferreting rabbits and grubbing roots which I do now.[7]

During the war Byng had been accustomed to spending long periods alone, thinking through the problems with which he was faced. This habit of solitude was continued in Canada where most evenings he would escape from the gossip of the household to the privacy of his study. At times he would ask one of his staff to accompany him and they would sit quietly as he smoked his pipe, sometimes reading, sometimes chatting, at others having deep discussions on a book or some philosophical subject which interested him. Not all members of his household had the wit, learning or sensitivity to his moods to act the role of restful companion to the Governor-General. Willis-O'Connor, Georges Vanier, Eva Sandford and Pat Hodgson did. Young enough to be his children, yet mature enough for real friendship, they became

328

utterly devoted to him and he to them. Most of his ADCs had been regular soldiers, who remained only for a year to two. But a surprising number, if not so close to Byng as these four, remained his friends until the end of his life – Sandy Urquhart, Tommy Erskine, Lord Hylton, Oswald Balfour and Lord William Scott.

In the last year in Canada Hodgson and Vanier departed and, with O'Connor being married, Eva was his most frequent companion. She returned with the Byngs to England and agreed to stay with them, nominally as their secretary, in fact as a member of the family.

Hodgson was now Comptroller to the Duke and Duchess of York. Vanier was commanding the Royal 22e Regiment in Quebec and Willis-O'Connor had remained with Lord Willingdon. Byng sensed that his morale was suffering under the new régime at Rideau Hall.

Willingdon had been Governor of Bombay and Madras, and his wife in particular appeared to expect in Canada the protocol and the deference which they had found in India. (On arrival she had expressed disappointment at finding there was no Government House band!) She was a strong influence on her husband and initially led him to adopt an attitude of aloofness which affected his staff and was apparent to the people of the country. Gossip in Ottawa, which found its way to England, was that the Willingdons were snobs. Plainly they did not appreciate the effect of their too formal conduct on the sensitivities of Canadians. Byng knew how valuable Willis-O'Connor's unique knowledge and experience could be to the Governor-General and wrote to Willingdon to suggest that he have confidential talks with him about Canada.[8] By now the staff at Government House had developed a resentment toward the changed atmosphere and became even more resistant to the changes which are inevitable when a new governor-general takes office. Byng continued to write to O'Connor, persuading him not to resign. His ministrations appear to have worked, for a better relationship developed between the Willingdons and their staff and they left Canada without doing quite so much damage to the office of governor-general as was feared.[9]

It had not taken Byng long to discover that Georges Vanier was no ordinary ADC. That he was older, held a law degree, was much decorated for bravery, was French Canadian and was married to a beautiful and intelligent woman obviously set him apart from the young Guards officers who were his colleagues. But there was more – a breadth of vision, a depth of character and an incisive intelligence which could carry him to positions of real importance in the country's affairs.

Each had found the other able and willing to discuss thoughts and ideas which went far beyond the bounds of conventional subjects of conversation. Both were idealists and were able to explore with each

329

other wide ranges of philosophy and the depth of their own beliefs. Such an association is rare and both treasured it.

A year after the Byngs left Canada, Georges and Pauline came to England for a month's holiday and spent some time at Thorpe. One day while walking over the fields Byng said, 'George, I have been putting down lately what I think of myself, what I know about myself. I find it very interesting and right to put on paper my views on what I am, why I act, and what I shall become.'

'Now's the time to do it sir.'

'Yes, before I die.'

'I didn't mean that, I meant now that you have the leisure. Later you will be busy doing something for the good of man and of your country. I for one hope that you will be engaged on some other and great work.'

'What work?'

'I don't know: but there are many things you could do better than most men.'

'I don't know – there has been some talk of offering me South Africa, but I don't think I would take it. I have had the best, Canada. If you like, after tea, I shall show you what I have written about myself. I have never shown it to a living person.'

The paper was entitled 'Know Thyself' and Vanier spent some hours reading it. In it Byng had written about his personal beliefs and what he had learned about life and men. In his diary Vanier recorded what he said about immortality:

A great number of people have tried to prove immortality to me. They have not succeeded and I am rather pleased that they have not succeeded. I believe in it as implicitly as anyone, but I like the faith in it better than the proof – I want to keep my faith in it and not have it proved.

To Vanier, the devout Roman Catholic, it was 'a gentle and consoling philosophy, very human and at the same time divine, resting upon a very simple faith.'

Vanier was now approaching the end of his term of command of his Regiment and Byng was worried that he might become enmeshed in the restricted structure of the tiny Canadian militia or would try to make a career in law as a civilian. In either his potential for good as a leading figure of French Canada would be lost. To give him some broader experience, he tried to arrange for him to be posted to the War Office in London. Before this could happen, he learned that Vanier had been made military representative on the Canadian Delegation to the League of Nations in Geneva. Byng was delighted.

Vanier's work was largely concerned with disarmament, a subject to which Byng had given much thought and had some strong views:

We all want peace and consider that the League of Nations may be the best channel to reach it. But there is only one royal road to peace and that is friendship – real friendship.

In my opinion friendship never will be obtained by vague talks on disarmament. Talks on disarmament lead to rivalry and rot.

If we establish friendship, disarmament will follow – but friendship will never follow disarmament, as is instanced in the present state of feelings of almost every country.

Friendship is obtained by intercourse, understanding and harmony and not by the half-hearted suggestions of politicians and servicemen.

To my mind, there are many fields for the operations of harmony. Art in all its branches is international. Science is international. Hygiene and health is international. Education is international. These are all unexplored fields. Finally, religion – is not the worship of the same deity more or less international?

Is not the Sermon on the Mount better than the sermons at Ottawa on Parliament Hill and in London on Tower Hill?

The Sermon on the Mount is not a bad code of ethics for any nation and it does not mention disarmament. The words 'love your enemies' seem to me to be better than 'reduce your cruisers'.[10]

He continued, too, to be interested in the progress of the Canada League, whose ideal was national unity. He had left its future in the hands of William Herridge, a brilliant advocate who had broken with Mackenzie King over the constitutional crisis and later became a close adviser to R. B. Bennett and Minister to Washington. Herridge had all the qualities needed for the leadership of such a movement, except the will to take the first step. Byng had left Canada when it was in its formative stages and Herridge's failure to breathe life into it was to cause him much frustration.

While Byng had no employment in the two years following his return from Canada, he had a number of part-time interests. He took his duties as Colonel of the 10th Hussars seriously and he worked with the Canadian High Commissioner on a scheme to encourage suitable settlers to emigrate.[11] He had always been inclined to joke about his poor performance at school, yet he had constantly striven for knowledge and had read widely. After the War he studied economics in relation to 'The Byng Millions', history and constitutional matters associated with Canada, as well as reading widely of other things which interested him. 'His mind was stored with a mass of information on diversified subjects, as far apart as Confucius and Canadian ducks and he would often astonish one by knowledge of a totally unexpected nature.'[12] Not surprisingly he received many invitations to speak, not only on Service occasions, but to learned societies and to dinners such as that of the Royal Literary Fund.[13]

331

While none of these activities was particularly challenging, Byng was not discontented and he came more and more to enjoy his life at Thorpe. It did not long remain undisturbed.

In June, 1928, he received a letter from the Home Secretary, Sir William Joynson-Hicks, asking if he would come to see him to advise on the selection of a new commissioner for the Metropolitan Police. He explained that he was not certain whether it would be wise to appoint a military man or a civilian and asked Byng for suggestions. Byng and Joynson-Hicks had never met.[14]

It was common knowledge that all was not well with the Police. So many of the restraints of an ordered society had been shattered by the War that, in the years which followed, the uninhibited pursuit of pleasure in the West End of London took on a tone of near hysteria. In spite of the General Strike, of mass unemployment and the rising cost of living there was no lack of money to spend on frivolity, but there was about it that forced gaiety which has scented the far-off whiff of disaster. Paper fortunes were piling up, and night clubs, not much different from the speakeasies of New York, proliferated. Every day the press reported the excesses of their customers.

The Police, who had earned the gratitude of the nation for their efficiency and moderation during the General Strike, now faced mounting criticisms for their apparent inability to control a new rowdyism. Stories of lawlessness, of disrespect for the law and even of police corruption filled the columns of the daily papers. For a generation or more the public had regarded the London bobby as a paragon. To them his good-humoured forbearance and incorruptibility were uniquely and characteristically British. It took only a few unconnected cases to make them feel let down.

The police as public servants could do little to defend themselves from the wildly inaccurate charges which were levelled at them. Morale slumped and scapegoats were sought. When his contract expired, Sir William Horwood, the Commissioner, did not ask, as he might have done, to have his term of office extended for the five years which would bring him to the age of 65, and the Home Secretary had the unenviable task of finding a replacement.

Having concluded that none of the Assistant Commissioners of the Force could restore its morale and prestige, he and Stanley Baldwin, the Prime Minister, considered the qualifications of several officers of the Forces, before offering the position to a senior Army officer who refused. They next explored the idea of bringing in a successful businessman of proven organizing ability. The stumbling block here was the salary of £3,000 per year. Finally they decided to ask Byng for advice.

At their meeting, as Joynson-Hicks explained the nature and problems of the post, Byng came to the conclusion that it held no appeal for him. He suggested what qualifications and qualities the Home Secretary should look for in a prospective commissioner, and after about half an hour's discussion, Joynson-Hicks decided that Byng himself was the obvious candidate. He asked him to accept the position. Byng refused[15] and suggested that it be offered to Lt-Gen Sir Warren Hastings Anderson, who had been Horne's MGGS.

The General soon made it clear that he was not interested in giving up his career in the Regular Army for the dubious prospects of the Commissionership of the Metropolitan Police.[16] On obtaining his refusal, Joynson-Hicks appears to have discussed his dilemma with the King, for from several quarters pressure began to be exerted on Byng to take the job. On 19 June John Buchan sent him a wire saying that he hoped he would take the position, and on the same day[17] Lord Stamfordham wrote that the King hoped that he would accept the offer of the post: 'His Majesty feels that you are preeminently fitted for this most responsible position at a time which, without exaggeration, may be regarded as a special moment in the history of the Metropolitan Police Force.'[18]

Byng still refused, giving his reasons in a reply next day:

My dear Stamfordham,
    The Home Secretary sent for me last week and offered me the Commissionership of the Metropolitan Police, and I definitely refused it.
    There are two ways of looking at this action on my part – there is the general aspect and the public service aspect.
    The personal aspect is very soon arrived at. The work as Commissioner holds out no inducement to me and I feel I should dislike it. There would seem to be no possibility of having a free hand and it is almost obvious that it would be impossible to give it. I do not want any appointment, having had the best the world can give.
    So much for the personal which you may quite justifiably say should not weigh against what one conceives to be one's duty to the throne and country.
    The only point worthy of consideration in this respect is that I should be the most suitable person for the job. This point seems rather mitigated by the fact that the Home Secretary has already offered the job to someone else (and I think rightly).
    Without undue criticism, I think it may be said that the Police Force is weak at the top and uneasy at the bottom and is deserving of the very best that we have in the land for their leader – that, I feel, at the age of 65 and not quite eighteen carat in point of physical fitness I am not. A younger, more active and more energetic man seems to me to be obviously the one on whom the selection should rest.
    To undertake this task and to do it badly is to my mind a calamity as is

333

evidenced by previous experience and it would be a lasting unhappiness to me to feel that I have been the cause of any deterioration in the force.

Finally, having put my feelings before you as clearly as I can, it only remains for me to place myself unreservedly in His Majesty's hands, promising my most unstinted loyalty at all times.[19]

Byng had no illusion about the demands of the commissionership and he seriously doubted that he was fit for the job. The warning of a heart condition which he had received in Canada and the length of time it had taken him to recover from influenza last winter indicated to Eva, a trained nurse, that at his age he should not be subjected to undue strain. She pleaded with him not to accept.[20] Evelyn, however, to whom Byng would never admit that he was not well, thought that he needed an intellectual challenge and tried to persuade him to take the position. On learning of his refusal, she wrote to Stamfordham:

My dear Stamfie,

I have been very unhappy and upset over all this police business. J. was away in London *alone*, when the offer was made, and without consulting me, he turned it down. Saturday he came back here, told me what had happened, of which I had had NO knowledge. When he told me I answered that he was acting MOST wrongly in refusing, that though it was not a pleasant job I felt he should take it because of the crucial state of affairs in the Force and because he could do excellent work. I frankly said I was very vexed with him and did my utmost to get him to reconsider the matter. Having done that I haven't again referred to the thing a single time. However Kipling was here for the weekend and HE had a good old go in. What he may have managed to do I have no idea, but he spoke to him like 10 Fathers and as J. is fond of K. and thinks highly of his opinion I can't help hoping some good may come of it IF it isn't too late.

I wanted you and H. M. to know just what had happened as I believe the King was most anxious he should do this job and I would like him to know that I did my best and that what happened in London was done without any consultation with me. As you know J. is not very easy at the present time to handle and I think IF I had been with him things might have gone differently. Anyhow I have done my best, and knowing my man as I do I have merely left it to soak in and shall have another final try when I see an opening. But I am doubtful of success.

Bless you dear old friend

Yours
Evelyn[21]

Next day came another letter from the Home Secretary saying that Hastings Anderson had turned down the position:

Now I am going to make a very firm and even stern appeal to you to help the

334

country at this very difficult juncture. I am authorized by the King and the Prime Minister to say that they both heartily concur in my wish that you should take over the commissionership of the Metropolitan Police.

I have seen the King again since our interview and he tells me that if you still feel diffidence about it, he would like to see you himself before you refuse finally.

I might also tell you, in strict confidence, that I have told Ramsay Macdonald of my proposal, and he received it with enthusiasm.

I think, therefore, that you would find that there would be universal delight and confidence in your appointment.[22]

The pressure was becoming too great to resist, but before accepting, Byng called informally on the King to ensure that he had been made aware of his misgivings. On returning home, he sent his acceptance to Joynson-Hicks and wrote to Buchan —

Beloved John,
  You've won! . . .
  How the shades of my two ancestors Thomas Wentworth (Earl of Strafford) and Admiral Byng must be chuckling to see me following their footsteps to the scaffold and the quarter deck.[23]

Byng made stipulations, however. The appointment was to be for an indeterminate period; if his health got worse, he would retire at once. Further, since he did not want the job, 'I am the most readily sack-able person in the world, so please do not hesitate.' Having suffered at the hands of politicians in the First World War and in Canada, when he was unable to defend himself, the Home Secretary's assurance that Ramsay Macdonald had received the news of his proposed appointment with enthusiasm was important to his acceptance.

On 2 July, when Joynson-Hicks announced in the House of Commons that Byng was to be the new Chief Commissioner of the Metropolitan Police, an Opposition spokesman, George Lansbury, immediately rose to deplore the appointment.[24] That same day the Parliamentary Labour Party conferred on how best to attack it and Ramsay Macdonald characterized as 'absolutely untrue' the report that he or any other member of his party had been consulted about the selection of Lord Byng.[25]

When the appointment was debated a week later, Macdonald pleaded a toothache as his reason for not being present in the House, leaving Philip Snowden to sneer at the Government's 'practice of finding jobs for pensioned army officers'.

'I do not wish to say anything that might seem offensive but men [were] retired because it was found that they had outlived their

335

usefulness and were no longer capable of rendering fully efficient service. . . . However great Lord Byng's ability as a military officer might be (the Labour Party) submitted that his training and his experience and, naturally, the outlook and point of view which he must have developed by long years of military service were not the sort of qualification necessary for the post of Chief Commissioner of the Metropolitan Police.'[26]

The Press reacted to the announcement predictably. The *Daily Herald* sniffed at the appointment with all the distrust of a working man facing the prospect of a police force run by an aristocrat.[27] The *New Statesman* wondered if the reason why Byng had accepted the job, since the pay was so low, might be a desire to become, not just a viscount, but Earl of Hyde Park. The appointment was a 'piece of uncommon stupidity . . . police discipline ought not to be confused with military discipline at all.'[28] Predictably the *Morning Post* was in favour of the appointment as was *The Times*.[29]

Acrimonious wrangling went on for several days. By concentrating on hypothetical questions of discipline and implying that Byng was some sort of drill sergeant, the Press obscured the fact that the problems in the police were not so much those of discipline but of organization, administration and morale. In fairness, though, the police had made little attempt to inform the Press of their work or their internal problems.

Two or three unfortunate cases had caused the Press to suspect that all was not well within the police organization. Now the appointment of Byng, with his immense prestige, to replace a minor figure who had been so much his junior in the Army – a brigadier-general in the military police – inferred that the situation really was serious. Scotland Yard would now be under even closer surveillance.

In October, 1928, before he took office, he heard again from his former Prime Minister. Showing a remarkable insensitivity to Byng's feelings, he asked him to come to France and show him around the battlefields. Byng replied civilly that he had another engagement, which was true.

I am afraid that there was rather more to this invitation than met the eye. He wanted to boost it around Canada that I had rushed over to France to take him for a tour etc. etc. Some Canadians told me that they thought it 'a d——d insult'. I don't agree with that, but I do think it was for political ends that he wished to make it seem that I was courting his friendship. However, I am going to see him for a few minutes in his hotel as he is Canada's Prime Minister and as such deserves my courtesy – but I will not undertake any performance of a public nature where we shall appear in the illustrated press as *personal* friends.

In the same month Evelyn's devoted uncle, Pandeli Ralli, died and left her his house in Belgrave Square, with its contents and a fortune totalling £750,000. In practical terms it meant that the Byngs could have a comfortable house in London where their life would now be centred. Julian commented to Willis-O'Connor, 'I only hope we shall be as happy with this money as we have been without it.'[30]

Ralli's fashionable residence would have been impractical, however, and within three weeks of obtaining it Evelyn had sold it and bought another in a much quieter location – 4 Bryanston Square.

Byng had become philosophical at the prospect of his new position. 'Perhaps one will knock a certain amount of humour out of it and perhaps it will not be as bad as one thinks.'[31]

For their part the Metropolitan Police did not know what to expect. One day, shortly after his appointment was announced, H. M. Howgrave-Graham introduced himself to Byng at the Travellers' Club, explaining that he was the Secretary of Scotland Yard. ' "Oh are you? Why?" he replied. My complete failure to account for the position clearly gave him much enjoyment. He then asked, "Are they a happy family at Scotland Yard?" ' Graham had to admit that that was not the keynote of the Yard at that time. 'We must attend to that,' said Byng. 'It's important.'[32]

Another who met him was Miss Edith Drysdale, the Commissioner's private secretary. When Byng arrived to make his first call on Gen Horwood, well in advance of the hand-over, she was waiting at the lift. She introduced herself and said she would take him to meet the Commissioner. Byng said, 'Before that, I would like to have a word with you in your office.'

Miss Drysdale knew of Eva Sandford and imagined that Byng intended to bring her to Scotland Yard and that she would have to go back to the typing pool, a prospect which she dreaded. Her spirits sank as Byng entered her office, closed the door and leaned against it saying, 'Are you permanent or temporary?'

'I'm a permanent employee, Sir.'

'No, I mean here in this job. Are you temporary and can you be moved?'

Her spirits sank further. 'No, I'm not permanent in that sense.'

'I really just want to know if they can move you.'

She readied herself for what she thought he was about to say, as she replied, 'Yes, they can.'

Byng's eyes twinkled as he replied, 'Well, I don't want that. I want you to promise me that you will stay in this job as long as I remain at the Yard.'

With relief, she agreed.

'Of course I won't hold you to your promise if you don't like it,' he added.[33]

It was a sign that the forthcoming shake-up might not be so violent as expected.

Byng had no intention of becoming involved in the detailed administration of the Force or in its day-to-day operations, leaving those to the heads of its departments. The experience of recent years had left the senior officers of the Police uncertain as to the bounds of their authority and with a sense of frustration in those of them who had tried to bring about improvements in organization and techniques. At the outset Byng saw his chief function as being 'a soothing influence'.

His methods proved to be highly original, often oblique and usually graced with humour. On his first day at work he inspected his new office with Miss Drysdale. Pointing at an array of telephones, he said, 'Take them away.'

'Oh, but you must have a telephone,' she protested.

'What for?' he asked.

'For talking to people, the Home Secretary for instance. He often talks on the telephone.'

'Not on your life,' said Byng. 'I hate telephones. Take them away.'

Edith Drysdale was a good secretary. She persuaded him to keep one in case of real need, concealed the others and arranged with the switchboard that all calls would come to her. None would be put through to the Commissioner without her permission. For some months all went well, then one day Byng opened the door to his secretary's office and said, 'Drysie, that thing went off. I knew it would. Please do something about it.'

Another day there was a call from the Palace, and Byng, for almost the only time, used the telephone.[34]

Byng was, in fact, no more averse to using the telephone than anyone else. But his refusal to do so at the Yard was a practical way of avoiding involvement in detail by forcing the Home Secretary and others outside the Yard to deal directly with the responsible department heads.

No incident demonstrated more clearly to his subordinates that he intended that they should take responsibility and trusted them to do so than his handling of the Commissioner's Annual Report. While addressed to the Home Secretary, it was published as a parliamentary paper and was always scrutinized closely by the Press. In effect, it became the Commissioner's annual report to the public on police matters and contained much that was contentious. It was drafted and redrafted by the staff of Scotland Yard with the thought much in mind of how it would appear in the papers.

The one for 1928 was the first which Byng had seen. He turned over

338

some of its pages, commented to Howgrave-Graham that there seemed to be an awful lot of it, and asked where he should sign. That was the end of a matter to which former commissioners customarily devoted much time and worry. The technique involved some risk to Byng but it had the good effect of making his heads of departments feel that they had his trust and were on their mettle to prove themselves worthy of it.

Byng expected every head of a department to take complete responsibility for it and not to seek his approval for their plans unless it was essential to do so. He was always courteous to them, insisted that they state their proposals or problems in the shortest possible way and dealt with them quickly and effectively. If he thought that an officer should have dealt with a question himself rather than asking him to consider it, he was apt to give a quite ridiculous or impossible answer, his way of saying 'do it yourself'. Usually people left his office smiling, the result of his knack of finding something amusing in most situations. It was not long before he had restored the self-confidence of the senior officers and created a team spirit at their headquarters on the Embankment. Most of them by now had nicknames which he had given them. Admiral Sir Charles Royds, a big cheerful booming sailor who was Deputy Commissioner, he christened 'Old Broadsides'. Like the Army, the Police called him 'Old Bungo'.

Based on his military experience, he had a strong preference for getting about and seeing things for himself, making himself known to his men and looking to their welfare. He visited the Force's 200 police stations and a great many of the rest points where policemen on the beat took their breaks. To the constables, sergeants and inspectors whom he met he seldom spoke of police matters unless there was a specific problem to be dealt with. Howgrave-Graham remembered 'overhearing him one day chatting to a constable in a south London station. Before they had been talking two minutes, he was advising the constable about the education of his boy who was a 'bit of a scholar'. He discussed the question of that boy's future as if it was the one topic in the world that really mattered.'

On another occasion they went into the kitchen of a north London section house 'where we found a neat clean somewhat spherical little cook in a light green over-all, cooking vegetables. Lord Byng talked with her for a few minutes about policemen's food and the size of their appetites.

'A little later, as we sat in the car, he suddenly said with an air of great profundity "Have you observed the influence of environment on personal appearances?"

"Yes, I suppose so. What were you thinking of?"

"That nice little cook," he replied, "didn't you notice her astonishing resemblance to a brussels sprout?" '[35]

Evelyn Byng herself saw the effect of his presence on the Force:

It was interesting to see how quickly the police responded to Julian's friendly approach. The first few weeks, when we walked together from the Bryanston Square house to Scotland Yard, we were met with the regulation salute and the blank official face. Gradually a smile was added to the salute, because we always smiled at them, and very soon we walked through a series of beaming good mornings.[36]

Byng soon found himself back in the saddle – literally. Mounted on Snowball, a superb white police horse, he led the Centennial Parade of the Metropolitan Police in May of 1929 and later escorted the Sovereign at Trooping the Colour and the State Opening of Parliament. Not unnaturally he took a close interest in the Mounted Branch and frequently went for an early morning ride in Hyde Park with Assistant Commissioner Laurie, who commanded it.[37]

As a result of his contacts with the men on the beat and his unannounced visits to police stations, he introduced several changes to make the lot of the policeman somewhat happier. Facilities at rest points were improved and meal breaks and reliefs were made more convenient. A police historian later wrote, 'The devotion he engendered – and it was nothing less – was by no means confined to his immediate entourage. It quickly infected the whole Force.'[38]

In the Police, as in the Army, Byng's personal magnetism, his kindness, consideration, his capacity for friendship and his wit are the qualities which most seem to remember. His competence and efficiency seem to have been taken for granted. There were others who had cause to take a less kindly view of his term as Commissioner.

On almost his first day at Scotland Yard Byng said, 'There is nothing wrong with the machine. It just needs oiling here and there.' It was his way of saying that there were some obvious areas where improvements could quickly be made. Liaison between the Criminal Investigation Department – the detectives – and the uniformed branch was poor at best. Incredibly, it had been the practice to close down the CID at 11 pm and no experienced detectives were on duty for the rest of the night. Policemen's beats were patrolled on a regular schedule and their reliefs took place at fixed times, enabling criminals to plan their operations when there was little danger of interference. While a few cars were ready at Scotland Yard itself to take police to important incidents – the Flying Squad – none were available elsewhere. Promotion was almost entirely by seniority, with the result that the ambitions of intelligent and unusually gifted policemen became frustrated.

340

The problems were not particularly difficult of solution. They existed because, before Byng identified them, no one had recognized that they were problems. The loudly-voiced complaint of the public that 'there is never a policeman about when you want one' was simply viewed as an inevitable expression of frustration which should not be taken too seriously. The situation in the Police was rather like that of the Army at the Somme. It required imagination and drive to break out of the shell of conformity and to make the best use of the resources which were available.

Byng did not impose his own ideas on his department heads, but, having indicated that an improvement was required, told them to find their own solutions. Not all had the imagination or ability to do so and found themselves retired early. By the end of 1928, within two months of his arrival at the Yard, the CID were open for business twenty-four hours a day and were cooperating closely with their uniformed colleagues. The Flying Squad had been increased with detachments at each divisional headquarters. A policy of promotion by merit was introduced, police patrols were operating on new 'random' schedules and a network of police telephone boxes was being set up all over London from which residents could speak directly to the nearest police station (private 'phones were less common at that time).[39]

It was only the beginning. Byng was determined to bring the Police into the 20th Century, yet the financial resources available were decreasing with the decline in national prosperity. Manpower had been relatively cheap and the tendency had been, when necessary to improve police coverage, to hire more men rather than look to technical innovations. The cumbersome organization which resulted, and its ponderous methods, were inadequate for their task. As Byng put it, 'Time is on the side of the criminal. We must give the criminal less time.'

At Police Headquarters he established an information room, similar in function to an Army operations centre, which controlled a fleet of radio-equipped cars. The reporting of crimes was speeded by the expanding system of police telephone boxes and later by the introduction of emergency procedures for private 'phones – the '999 call'. Against considerable opposition, he introduced unmarked police vehicles (known as Q cars after the wartime Q ships).

At the street level he linked the new random beats with cycle and motor patrols.

A serious and increasing drain on police manpower was caused by the burgeoning of London's motor traffic. An indication of the magnitude of the problem is seen in the accident figures for 1931 when 1326 people were killed and 54,300 were injured. As a result of Byng's quest for practical innovations, in that year the first traffic lights were installed in Oxford Street.

There were wrong-doers among the police, but not nearly so many as the public had been led to expect by the Press, who tended to headline the story of a simple disciplinary case, of which there are bound to be some in a force of 20,000 men, 'Another Police Scandal'. A few fairly senior officers were corrupt and there were others whose conduct was, at worst, not up to the standard necessary in a senior police officer. Byng's problem was to eliminate them from the force and to imbue the rest with a pattern of conduct which would be proof against the infection of corruption.

Much investigation and sifting of evidence would be needed, a process which would take months. If the Press reported and speculated on each move that was made, Byng's difficulties would be enormously increased. He asked Lord Riddell, the chairman of the Newspaper Proprietors, for help and Riddell arranged for Byng to be present at a meeting of their Association.

In his simple and forthright manner, Byng explained his problem, said what he was doing about it and made a plea that police matters be reported in a less sensational way. In particular, he asked that disciplinary cases be treated with a sense of proportion and that they should not be featured unless there was justification for doing so. A fairly spirited discussion followed, but it was obvious that Byng had won their sympathy. For more than two years London's newspapers made no reference to such cases in the Metropolitan Police, while Byng implacably rooted out the dishonest men.[40]

A principal source of temptation to misconduct had been the nightclubs of the West End. Some officers had been bribed to overlook breaches of licensing hours and other regulations, and the vice of all sorts which centred around the more sordid ones. A spirit of lawlessness seemed to permeate the area and extended into Hyde Park where it was dangerous to go after dark.

From the outset Byng made it clear that the law was to be enforced and made frequent visits late at night during the next few months to ensure that his orders were being carried out. So unpopular was his attention that there were several threats to his safety and officials insisted that a guard be mounted on 4 Bryanston Square.[41]

On only one occasion did he himself confront wrong-doers as a police officer. He gave orders that on the night of the Oxford-Cambridge boat race all undergraduates who were picked up by the police for disturbing the peace should be brought to Scotland Yard rather than to Bow Street. He waited through the night to see them,

342

realizing how much more lasting an impression a few words from him would make than a ritual fine by a police court.

By the beginning of 1929 public confidence in the police had begun to grow.

There was a tone of near amazement in newspaper reports of dramatic changes at the Yard. The *Evening News* commented that they were certainly not the work of a tired old warrior and the *Sunday Express* reported 'And all this has been done without fussy interference, without speechmaking and with hardly any outward or visible sign that anything has been done at all.'

'A new spirit is permeating all ranks. It is no longer an accepted axiom that black sheep are inevitable in a force of 20,000 men.'[42]

In June, 1929, a Labour Government replaced Baldwin's Conservative administration. Mindful of their resentment at his appointment, Byng immediately called upon the new Home Secretary, J. R. Clynes, and told him that he was quite prepared to resign. Without hesitation Clynes answered that he possessed the complete confidence of the Government and would receive their full support. It was a remarkable testimony from the Party which had so strongly questioned his motives and ability.[43]

Byng's success had not been achieved without cost. Early in May his heart had given him another warning that too much work and strain would result in something more serious. Evelyn was away at the time, spending a few weeks with the Vaniers in Geneva, and it seems that Byng did not tell her about his heart trouble. She had had worries enough in that both her father and her uncle had died in the previous year and her mother was seriously ill. Probably he feared that she would make too much of it and become over-protective. (At least three people who knew them well told the author of Byng's frequent admonition to his wife: 'Don't fuss, Evelyn, don't fuss.')[44] Neither would she be able to disregard the deaths within the past year of Haig and Horne, or that of Rawlinson, three years earlier, all at about the same age as Byng, and the much publicized and worrying illness of the King.

People throughout the Empire were surprised to find how deep was their personal anxiety over the illness of the Sovereign. It had continued for some months. One of the first visitors, other than members of his family, whom he received was Byng, who called on him privately on 20 August. Byng told him that the anxiety of the people must have shown him how much he was loved. The King seemed genuinely puzzled and said that he wondered why this should be? It was a difficult question to answer but Byng was close to the truth when he said, 'Because you didn't go rushing off to the battlefields but stayed at home and saw the War through with your people'.[45]

343

Whenever possible Byng spent his weekends at Thorpe where often there were guests – old friends like Kipling, Basil Brooke and members of Punch's Round Table, and new ones whom he found congenial, such as Sir John Anderson, the Permanent Under Secretary at the Home Office, and Stanley Baldwin. To his delight, Arthur Currie also came for a few days of reminiscence and golf.

Early in November, he organized a shoot with a few friends. It was a bitterly cold day and by the Monday morning when he was due to go back to London, he had a wracking cough and was running a high temperature. Neither Evelyn nor Eva, nor John Anderson, who was with them at the time, were able to prevent his going to the Yard. Dr Cassidy, his own physician, was senior medical officer of the Police. Alerted to Byng's condition by Miss Drysdale, he ordered him home to Bryanston Square, where Byng was annoyed to find a nurse waiting to put him to bed. His cold soon became bronchial pneumonia, a dangerous illness and difficult to treat. It continued for more than two months. His doctors ordered him to convalesce in a warm climate and as soon as he was fit to move, he and Evelyn, with Eva, Orchin his valet, Miss Vaughan, Evelyn's maid, and a nurse boarded the *Carnarvon Castle* for South Africa. A doctor friend of Cassidy's who was making the journey undertook to look after him.

It was blowing hard when they left Southampton and within hours Evelyn, the nurse, Orchin and the doctor were too sea-sick to be of any use. Next morning the weather was worse and when Evelyn managed to drag herself to his cabin she found him sitting up in bed, eating eggs and bacon and chatting to Eva. Within a few days, Byng was able to go on deck and sit in a secluded corner. When his presence on board became known, he received several messages of good will from other passengers, including one 'from an old enemy', Gen Jan Christian Smuts. Later in the voyage he and Byng discovered that they had much more in common than their experiences of the South African War. By the time he arrived in Cape Town, Byng was much stronger, though he was still far from robust.

For the first few days the Byngs stayed with the Athlones at the Governor-General's summer residence, Westbrooke, outside Cape Town, then moved to Vergelegen, the lovely Dutch colonial mansion of Sir Lionel and Lady Phillips. Some five peaceful weeks later Byng, Eva and Orchin went by boat to Port Elizabeth to stay with Dr Rogers, the old MO of the South African Light Horse, at Addo, a tiny settlement on the Sunday River, while Evelyn, with her maid, and a driver made the journey by road.

Rogers had long since given up his surgeon's practice and had become a fruit grower. He and Byng had spent many hours together on the veldt and soon resumed their easy relationship. The relaxed atmosphere of the comfortable farm was ideal for Byng's recovery and he felt a new man when he departed at the beginning of May. Three days before they left Evelyn slipped on the polished tiles of the verandah and broke her right wrist. Though 'Bodge' Rogers set it perfectly, she was far from comfortable on the bumpy train journey back to Cape Town. Never one to grin and bear it, she thought the journey seemed far longer than its two hundred miles and so did the rest of the party. Its nadir came in the dining car where she saw the steward breathing heavily on the knives and forks to polish them as he laid the table. Upon the meal being announced, she declared that she would rather not eat. Both Byng and Eva asked if she were not feeling well and when she confessed the reason they burst out laughing. She was not amused. Timid Miss Vaughan, who had a notoriously weak stomach, overheard the conversation, began to feel queasy and had to retire. It was with much relief that they arrived in Cape Town to be welcomed once more by the Athlones.[46]

Byng was now fit enough to join in the social round and to see old friends, nothing giving him more pleasure than a reunion with veterans of the Light Horse.

He returned to England to a warm welcome from the Police.

Shortly after his return Byng dined at the Palace. He was wearing his General's full-dress uniform and the King asked after dinner why he was not smoking a cigar or cigarette like most of the others. Byng told him that he only smoked a pipe and there was no room for it and a pouch and matches in a full dress tunic. The King beckoned an equerry and told him to 'phone Lord Byng's man and have him bring his pipe and tobacco. In short order, Orchin delivered them by taxi and the King said, 'Next time, Bungo, do find a way to bring them. It makes me feel uncomfortable to see you smokeless'.[47]

There was now speculation in the papers as to whether he would resign from the Police. On 17 June he wrote to Willis-O'Connor:

I went back to work again as soon as I returned, but take it very easy, only being at the office for two hours in the morning, and always resting between tea and dinner. It would have been impossible to chuck it when such pressure was put again upon me, both by the Government and all my friends. Also, if I were to go now, they would ask me who I would recommend as a successor, to which there is only one answer in my opinion, which is 'Get the best soldier you can find, and one who the Army does not want to lose.' Most probably the Government would agree, but they would have a very bad time, especially if Labour were still in, at getting their own

345

people to support them, and it is quite possible they might even have a hostile vote.

So there it is – I have agreed to remain providing I do not get seedy again. I am really quite well except getting a few reminders that my heart is not all it should be.[48]

Byng was trapped. He could not leave the Yard unless his health broke and if he stayed it surely would. Much remained to be done to perfect the organization of the Police and to complete the replacement of the 'passengers' among its senior ranks. Both tasks called for the personal supervision of the Commissioner, in the exercise of which drive, energy and no little ruthlessness would be demanded. It was not a prescription for continued health in a man suffering from a weak heart and emphysema.

Chapter 17

A Friendship

GEORGES VANIER HAD come to London to be near Pauline who was seriously ill in hospital and, when Byng returned from South Africa, was able to spend some time at Bryanston Square and Thorpe. He was not a regular or compulsive diarist, but he recorded his conversations with Byng as if to secure a memory of a friendship which he valued so highly.

His oldest son, Georges, known in the family as Byngsie, was Byng's godson. He was not yet five years old when Vanier brought him to call.

> HE was seated and smoking his pipe. When he saw us, he half got up, a little awkwardly; since he is not (alas) used to children, he was not quite certain what to do. Byngsie went straight over to him, put his arms round his neck, and kissed him affectionately. H. E. was moved and not far from tears.[1]

A few days later he and 'Chopper' Titchfield spent the weekend at Thorpe. There was much discussion of politics and of relationships between the countries of the Empire. They agreed that there should now be a permanent body – a kind of consultative council through which the Dominions could coordinate their interests. Byng hoped that in time all the Dominions would take part and would accept responsibility for their own defence. 'If a Dominion wishes to have a distinct foreign policy, it must be in a position to enforce its policy.' Talk turned to the War at which point Byng became silent. Vanier noted that one could not make him talk about it.[2]

About this time Byng discovered that Georges had suffered badly from the crash of the stock market in New York. Pauline's lengthy and serious illness had been as costly as it was worrying and he was concerned that the Vaniers might be in real financial difficulty. When he learned that Pauline had been released from hospital, he determined to sound her out on the situation and invited her to have tea with him at Bryanston Square. Seated on the floor by his feet, Pauline, whose nerves had suffered with her body, soon reacted to his sympathetic questioning and told more than Georges would have done.

The relief which she felt at being able to talk about her worries was shattered when Evelyn unexpectedly entered and said coldly, 'I wasn't aware that you would be here.' Hurriedly Pauline left.[3]

A few days later, with her anxious parents, she left London to recuperate at St Lunaire in France. Georges came to stay with Byng at Bryanston Square where a conversation took place which showed the sensitivity of the two men and the depth of their friendship.

23rd July. At breakfast. H. E. 'There is something I want to speak to you about. I know you have had a hard time lately. Can I help you? I would like to do something for you . . . and Pauline.'

He seemed a bit embarrassed as he said this, and his tone was very affectionate. I wasn't expecting this offer, and wishing to understand what H. E. was really thinking, I answered: 'May I think about it, Sir, and may I say how much I appreciate the thought?'

Reflections of G. P. V. during the day. Perhaps H. E. thinks that I am momentarily embarrassed and would like to advance me the money to pay Richardson or Cassidy, or both. . . . I can manage, and even manage very well, since the grandfathers are generous . . . the truth is that I can pay everything, and pay it now, but . . . H. E. wants to help me, I know it would please him . . . have I the right to refuse? I decide – no; I shall accept the offer and repay him in a few months' time. I shall speak to him about it tomorrow.

24 July: At breakfast. 'I have thought of what you said yesterday . . . really I can manage very well . . . on the other hand I suppose one should pay these bills as soon as possible . . . Richardson's account is paid.

'How much was it?'

'The operation itself cost about £120 – that is paid – but Cassidy's bill – he was very reasonable in his charges – is not paid yet and it amounts to one hundred guineas.'

Reply: 'Why don't you let me pay that?'

G. P. V.: 'Well, Sir, it would be a great help and I could pay you back in a few months. . . .' (I see that I have struck the wrong note . . . I look at H. E. . . . It's a *gift* that he wants to make me . . . I wait). H. E. hesitates: then: 'Oh George, it's a little douceur I would like to offer you. I have some pennies and I would like to give you some of them.'

I try not to show my surprise . . . what should I reply? 'It is very nice of you, but (I proceed tentatively, he *wants* to help us . . . what should I do or say?) 'Not nice at all – it gives me pleasure . . . I have thought a great deal about this . . . I have wondered whether we are great enough friends – we are great friends aren't we? – to do this – only very great friends could do this without any *arrière pensée*. I would like to pay Cassidy's bill, George.'

348

'Before you go on, I think it only fair to explain the situation to you, Sir. I *can afford* to pay the account. It would be a temporary relief to me . . . but there must not be any false pretences on my part, it will not be a hardship for me to pay . . .'

'False pretences – my dear George! . . . I *want* to help you and perhaps I am putting you in a position of embarrassment . . . of obligation to me? . . . I hope not.'

'There is no one else in the world' (apart from our parents, I meant, and he understood) 'from whom I would accept such a gift.'

'I know that George, I had hoped that . . . George . . .' (But a hundred guineas, no, really that makes no sense I must protest.)

'Perhaps you might pay half of Cassidy's bill . . . it would be a great help . . .'

'No George – the whole of it . . . let me.'

After breakfast I am in my study (Eva's room), and H. E. brings me a cheque for £105. 'Let's hear no more about it, George.'

No man has ever given me such proof of trust and affection – I accept this money with joy – it is the finest and most touching compliment that H. E. could have paid me, and I believe that *in accepting it* I am paying him the finest compliment that one man can pay another – to accept his money, for the medical care given to my wife, *a miracle of friendship*.'

(It was not the only example of Byng's generosity. As a present for his godson Byngsie, instead of a silver mug, he undertook to pay for his education.)

Next day, Friday, they drove to Thorpe for the weekend, speculating inevitably about the prospects in the Canadian General Election which would take place on Monday. Evelyn was away at Buxton, the spa in Derbyshire, for a rest and to try the cure.

26 July 30 – 1030 H. E. 'All right George . . .'

We go to the front door where he tells me to take a heavy stick and hands me also a thistle cutter. (we) walk towards fringe of cart road at point about 15 yards from the road. H. E. says 'We might start here – don't stand too near anyone when cutting the thistles . . . we move slowly away from one another. . . . Occasionally I look up and see H. E. who seems to be taking things easy. A little after 11 (I should say) I look up and see Eva near him – cutting thistle also – I am about 75 yards from them. . . . About 10 minutes later I look up again and see H. E. in a sitting posture . . . then I see him quietly and slowly fall over on his side. Eva sees incident at same moment. I run towards H. E. – Eva already there – we raise him to sitting posture – undo collar, tie, shirt . . . eyes closed, he is quite unconscious, breathing heavily and with difficulty at rather lengthy intervals – I mean about once each second – his colour to me does not seem too bad – he is rather brick-coloured, there is a trickle of saliva from his mouth. He is quite helpless. Eva runs for brandy and for doctor. About four minutes later Orchin arrives with brandy – all the while H. E.'s breathing is the same, heavy, difficult . . .

349

give him a little brandy ... breathing becomes easier, he seems relieved. ... After about five minutes of easier breathing and two or three small doses of brandy, breathing becomes heavier and harsher again. First words H. E. says about 15 to 20 minutes after falling over are: 'I'm absolutely all right' ... 'Yes, Sir, you're all right. ...' Eyes begin to open. 'I'm quite all right.' ... Car arrives in field about 20 minutes after the accident. We (Orchin and others) lift H. E. in and seat him on floor of car. En route to house H. E. opens eyes and says: 'What's happened George?'

It was Byng's first serious heart attack. A local doctor was soon at his side, followed later by his regular physician from London and a nurse. Evelyn and Miss Drysdale, summoned by Eva, returned from Buxton. Byng joked with them all and protested at the fuss.

Next afternoon Vanier had a long chat with Byng who was resting in his study.

I ask him if he has always had the same sense of humour or if it was acquired – as a form of philosophy – modestly he will not admit that he has a sense of humour but rather thinks what he has, he was born with – that it runs in his family.

Yes – he has always been interested in philosophy – 'Do you know, George, the difference between Good and Evil – Is Good what is beneficial to you or is it a process of self-denial? ... will you do something as readily for a person you dislike as for one you like? ... and if you do isn't this an affront to your 'amour propre'? ... When you do something for someone you love, you rather expect an 'augmentation' of love – that the love will be returned – if you do the same thing for someone you dislike, will it make you love that person better (shake of head) and if you do good to someone you dislike isn't it disproving the idea that Good is founded on love? ... Suppose in Geneva you had tickets for an interesting Conference or Meeting would you distribute them as readily to people you like and dislike? (I shake my head meaning no) 'Very well then would it be wrong not to distribute them as readily to people you dislike as to people you like ... you can argue as much as you like about the definition of Good – but you don't get very far – Altruism and Utilitarianism are the great stumbling blocks.'

Later after dinner:

H. E. 'Doctors are a curious lot – some of them at least ... Brockwell is a good chap I suppose and he wants to cure his patients I'm sure. ... But this morning he tried to frighten me ... he told me I had had a close call yesterday and he seemed disappointed when he didn't frighten me into a jelly ... perhaps it was a close thing and that I was near death – perhaps one was dead for just a moment – but each one of us is near death each day. Sometimes several times a day ... some of these doctors have no knowledge of human nature ... they mean well I suppose.'

(G. P. V.) 'A lot of people who mean well won't be in heaven.'

I am angry with Dr B. for attempting to make H. E. understand the attack was more serious than he believed before .... à quoi bon? Some day, of course,

350

dear H. E. will pass out of this life in the painless unconscious way in which he nearly went yesterday . . . but why *try* to take from him the illusion of strength and the wonder of his fortitude?'

Next morning in the paper there were a few preliminary reports about the Canadian General Election. After breakfast the telephone rang and Evelyn was called to hear a cablegram read by the operator in London. A moment's silence was followed by her shriek, 'King's Government completely defeated', and she raced up the stairs toward Byng's room. Georges thought her zeal was somewhat imprudent but understandable; she had waited for this news for a long time.[4]

What romance there had been in Julian and Evelyn's marriage had long since evaporated and she had grown more self-centred and wilful with the years. They were not even particularly good companions, but they continued to respect each other and certainly shared and discussed their mutual interests. Their relationship was based more on consideration than on real warmth. Evelyn was loyal and in her protectiveness toward Julian displayed a passion that was much more Greek than English. She unreservedly rejoiced in Mackenzie King's defeat. To Willis-O'Connor she wrote, 'It's too splendid to feel that the filthy brute is downed at last and SUCH a downing too!!!'[5]

Byng's first comments to Vanier were that R. B. Bennett was an educated gentleman and would be a better and more impressive representative for Canada at the impending Imperial Conference in London than would Mackenzie King. Vanier agreed, saying that he felt King was for himself first, the Liberal party next – then Canada and the Empire.

'You're a funny kind of Liberal, George!'
   G. P. V. 'Before being a Liberal, I am some other things (meaning affection for H. E. and dislike of King and of his methods).[6]

The contrast between Byng's restraint and Evelyn's open delight at King's defeat obscures the fact that they were as one in their attitude to the Canadian political scene – they were neutral. Mackenzie King's repeated accusation that they were biased toward the Tories had served only to add to Byng's sense of hurt and Evelyn's indignation.

There is no doubt that Byng liked Meighen and Bennett personally more than he did King, but he took great pains to conceal the fact. At the same time he thought that Meighen's short-lived cabinet were far less competent than the Liberals they succeeded and he was soon to show that he was not impressed with the men surrounding Bennett. He and Evelyn had made more personal friends among Liberal cabinet ministers than among the Conservatives in Ottawa.

351

It was only natural that, when King attempted to make political capital out of the constitutional crisis, the Conservatives would take the opposite side. Byng could hardly be blamed for that. That the issue was not dead, a letter from Arthur Currie soon revealed:

I have not seen Bill [William Herridge] for the last ten weeks but he has toured the country continuously with Bennett and I am sure has given him a great deal of help. The first thing we know old Bill will be the power behind the throne! Mackenzie King has only himself to blame for the deviation of Bill's allegiance to him, because up to the time of King's differences with you, Bill was his stout supporter. In fact I am quite certain that tens of thousands of men voted against King in this election because it was their first opportunity of expressing their opinion of his actions in 1926.[7]

A few years later Vanier was to owe to Mackenzie King his appointment as ambassador to France and, to his regret, the memory of the injury done to Byng in 1926 remained forever to cloud his gratitude.[8]

By now Byng was looking forward to getting back to work. After seeing him on Friday the doctor told Evelyn that he had said he would return to London on Tuesday.

At lunch Memsahib said, 'You had better go up Wednesday.'
'No, I think I'll go up Tuesday' (determined – chin thrust forward)
'Very well dear.'

He was in high good humour and his sense of the ridiculous soon revived. 'Have you noticed how all nurses have a way of saying "Wash your fac'an'ands . . . only your fac'an'ands.'

At breakfast on Monday, Vanier wrote:

We were, for an English home, *a merry party – there was quite a lot of laughter* in spite of the rain falling on Bank Holiday. Banks, cheques etc. were discussed. Then H. E. told us a charming story about his mother.
'I think Drummonds must miss my mother. She never made out a cheque for any amount except £50 – to save the bank worry and bother. She used to say what a bother it must be for them to receive a cheque for say £4.17.6. No, if she wished to pay an account for this amount she would go to Drummonds herself and draw fifty pounds – nine £5 pound notes, £5 in gold of which 10/–in silver. She would put the money in an old-fashioned purse – I can see it now – with an inside pocket for gold and another pocket for silver and then she would raise her skirts and put everything in a pocket under several petticoats. She would say to the bank clerk, 'Would you like me to wait to see the amount entered in your books?' The bank assured her it wasn't at all necessary. She would then go off in a barouche and pay the a/c herself.

352

Sometimes, if she wished to know what her balance was, she would say to the clerk 'I don't want you to sit down and add up all those figures now but sometime in the course of the week, would you be so kind as to let me know what my balance is?' If she had ever been overdrawn I think she would have cried. She would have thought of the Banker, how very sad for Drummonds.'

When Evelyn remarked, 'I hope the King will send us some grouse from Balmoral. Last year he sent some three or four times,' Byng said 'You know the grouse are not marked with the Royal Coat of Arms – they look like other grouse!'[9]

Chapter 18
Retirement

ON 11 AUGUST, 1930, Byng drove into London, visiting the police stations at Walthamstow and Holloway on the way. Two days later he performed one of the Commissioner's ceremonial duties by saying goodbye to the King on his departure from King's Cross to Scotland. They compared notes about dentistry and the King told the assembled directors of the railway, with some delight, that Byng had had his last tooth out. About more serious matters, His Majesty informed Byng that the partridges were damned bad this year.

Evelyn had by now become quite grand dame-ish, a trait not missed by her childhood friend, Queen Mary, who asked very slowly, bowing as she did so, 'And . . . how . . . is . . . Lady Byng?'

Later in August Canada's new Prime Minister, R. B. Bennett, let it be known publicly that the Government and people would like Byng to return to Canada as Governor-General, in succession to Lord Willingdon. It was kindly meant but Byng's age and health made it impractical. By now it was clear that his position with the Police would be the last he would fill as a public servant.[1]

In late autumn Byng was again ill with bronchitis and Pauline Vanier was once more in hospital in London. Dr Maurice Cassidy attended them both. On 15 November he wrote to Georges about his wife:

The last twenty-four hours she has been upset by hearing from various sources of Lord Byng's bronchitis. There is no need for immediate anxiety about him. He is up and about, but I am not letting him go out for a few days and have advised him to winter abroad, which, of course, will entail resignation from Scotland Yard. This is the more bitter blow in view of the apparent imminence of a General Election, but there seems no hope for it. He took it very well and Lady Byng is in a ferment, taking steps to sell the house, buy a villa or a yacht or a dahabiyeh, etc.!

It is a grim outlook for him, poor old man, and I sometimes almost wish he had not come round that day he was cutting thistles.

At the bottom of the letter was this postscript:

Since dictating the above, I hear that Lady B went out this morning, took a villa at Menton, booked passages for Saturday and let Bryanston Square furnished to the Peruvian Minister at 50 shillings a week. When B heard of this he blew up and he now refuses point blank to resign from Sct. Yard! No doubt he will change his mind in a day or two.[2]

Byng did not change his mind about resigning from the Yard but he did go to the South of France. When Sir Percy Radcliffe, Byng's BGGS at Canadian Corps, learned that he might have to winter on the Riviera, he at once invited the Byngs and Eva to come and stay over Christmas.

In the New Year they moved to a rented villa at Cap Ferrat, where an expedition from Thorpe had arrived to staff the house. In addition to Orchin and Miss Vaughan, who were with the Byngs, the butler, the first kitchenmaid and the first housemaid came by train while the second chauffeur brought one of the cars by road. Evelyn did not wish to trust themselves to uncertain French transport and its erratic drivers.

The weather was good and ideal for walking, which Byng enjoyed. On one expedition by car into the hills, near the Italian border, he took Orchin with him to look for an ancient road used by Caesar's armies. After walking some distance over the hills they came to what appeared to be a wide grass track. Byng prodded at it with his stick and soon uncovered the fitted stones of a Roman road that lay close beneath the surface.[3]

In March Byng again played a part in his protégé's career. His work in Geneva completed, Vanier had returned to Canada where he was considering leaving the government service. It was suggested that he might become the Secretary of the Canadian High Commission in London, but neither he nor Pauline were keen to have another posting in Europe. They asked Byng for advice and he wrote from Cap Ferrat:

I would like to see you in a job where your abilities, knowledge of men and matters, manner and manners etc. would have some scope – in fact where you would have some ideal of life to chew upon. Geneva does not give it, the Royal 22ᵉ does not give it, and beginning again in the Law, which is probably overcrowded, offers at best the academic future that one sees everywhere in that profession. You and Pauline should make a huge success of London, and a huger success of French and English Canadianism in London.[4]

Vanier accepted the London appointment and by doing so moved from the Army to Canada's small foreign service and the path to a brilliant future. He and Pauline acknowledged that, if it had not been for Byng, Vanier would not have made the choice he did.[5]

The Byngs found little in the social life of the Riviera to attract them. They had soon become bored and looked forward to returning home in April, with all the longing of unwilling exiles.

Their return reopened speculation about how long Byng would continue as Commissioner of the Metropolitan Police. Certainly Clynes, the Home Secretary, knew that he could not go on indefinitely, but no one else seemed willing to replace him. He told Stamfordham in January that, even though he was an invalid abroad, Byng was more use to the Government than anyone they could bring in.[6]

Arthur Currie was forthright in saying what he thought. He had been discussing Byng with Bill Herridge.

We . . . both concluded it was high time you gave up being a policeman. I always become annoyed when I think about it. . . . You know as well as I do, however, that governments are heartless: they will willingly let you kill yourself serving them, utter a platitudinous eulogy when you are gone, but promptly forget all about you after that. I do not think it ever was fair to yourself to take on these very arduous duties, and I think you owe it to yourself and to your wife and your friends to get out at once.

I know you will not think it presumptuous on my part to say these things, but I am concerned because I realize that every day you stay there you are shortening your life unnecessarily. May I respectfully suggest that you resign in early autumn, spend the winter in California, and some time next May, return to England through Canada where there are hundreds of thousands of men who would like to welcome you here once more. I do not see why such a visit should be embarrassing to the present Governor-General. You could come as the old Corps Commander and accept welcomes officially from no others than your old comrades. I know it would do them a world of good to see you again, and I believe it would do you just as much good.[7]

On 22 July Byng answered:

I suppose what you say is true and I have made up my mind to leave this show in the autumn. The work I wanted to do will not be finished but that cannot be helped.

He told Currie that, next winter, he and Evelyn would go to the West Indies and California, then return through Canada. The prospect 'thrills me to the marrow'. But he warned that he would have 'to refuse all ideas of making speeches . . . as this seems to worry my heart more than anything.'

By 24 September, when Byng told the senior officers at Scotland Yard that he would shortly be retiring, a new spirit was manifest in the Police. Corruption had been rooted out and public respect was restored. The process of modernization of equipment and methods which he had begun so dramatically in his first two months in office had continued and with it a thorough reorganization had begun.

In the hundred years since Sir Robert Peel had founded the Police the distribution and size of London's population had changed enormously but the police structure had not kept pace. Byng had ordered an extensive re-arrangement of the divisional and sub-divisional areas and the redistribution of men and resources with the aim of achieving both economy and efficiency. The process had been completed on the southern side of the Thames and was beginning in the remainder of the district.

Much remained to be done, particularly in developing the professional skills of the police, when he handed over his responsibilities in October to Marshal of the Royal Air Force Lord Trenchard. But the men and the organization were sound and the way had been charted for the new Commissioner to begin the series of reforms for which he is remembered.

The Times concluded:

Scotland Yard in short, owes what it has gained to a personality. The gain is nothing less than the complete restoration of public confidence in the police force and the force's recovery of confidence in itself. The good which Lord Byng has done will live after him. He has set the police officer of all ranks a professional standard which is valued and is not likely to be lost, and has given an impetus to internal reforms by which London and his successors will profit.[8]

J. M. Barrie, in recent years a frequent guest at Thorpe, said what was on many minds:

My dear Byng,
    It is with something of a pang that one hears of your leaving the police. Not a pang for yourself, for having done what you set out to do, you are doubtless relieved to be able to pass things on to other hands, but we all know it has been so finely done that we fear it may not be so fine by and by. In this world where we slide about, it is certainly good to know that there has been such work done . . . we are all grateful to you.[9]

Punch broke into verse: *Punch to Lord Byng of Vimy*

Great soldier, who on many a stricken field
Undaunted, steadfastness of soul revealed;
Wise governor, unmoved by factions hum
Throughout your aureum quinquennium
Avoiding flights flamboyant or Icarian

357

and though a JULIAN, never a Caesarian –
None of the laurels that you won and wore
For splendid services in Peace and War
Proved in the winning of them quite as hard
as those which crown you when you leave 'The Yard' –
Your irksome duties resolutely done –
Once more the finest Force under the sun
Regenerated by your selfless zeal
And the best bulwark of the Commonweal.
                                  'C. L. G.'
Punch 14 October, 1931

Soon after Byng left the Yard Willis-O'Connor came to stay at Thorpe. In January Lord Willingdon had been translated from Governor-General of Canada to Viceroy of India and he and his wife had been succeeded by the more congenial Bessboroughs. Life had taken on a pleasanter aspect for O'Connor and he was once more his old cheerful self. He offered his help in arranging the trip across Canada next spring. Byng told him that he would like to visit the larger centres, beginning at Victoria. The route could be varied but he particularly wanted to go to Calgary to see an old friend, Julian Snell, (and Mr Reader of the Parks Department, interjected Evelyn), and he must stay with Currie in Montreal. Obviously they would go to Ottawa.

O'Connor began the arrangements as soon as he returned to Canada, consulting where necessary with Evelyn and Eva by post. For his part, Byng began to enjoy his retirement and spent some happy days on his shoot until the time came to sail for Jamaica on a banana boat.

It was their first visit to the island and from the outset they found it much more to their taste than the Riviera. A Captain and Mrs Stewart, friends from the army, owned the delightful Shaw Park Hotel on Cutlass Bay near Ocho Rios. Byng spent most days reading on its cool verandahs and walked in the evenings with Eva or Orchin. On days when there was polo at Knutsford Park near Kingston, he happily went to watch and enjoyed discussing finer points of the game with the players, many of whom were former soldiers.

Early in March, 1932, they sailed through the Panama Canal to Los Angeles where they were to stay for a month at the Hungtingdon Hotel as Pasadena. Another of Byng's former aides in the War, Sandy Urquhart, made the arrangements for their stay and was there to welcome them.

Byng's lifelong interest in the theatre moved him to accept an invitation from George Arliss, the actor, to watch a film being made. He enjoyed meeting Harold Lloyd, had tea with Mae West, and got along famously with Will Rogers who invited him to his ranch. Evelyn spent the last week in California touring with a well-known botanist, collecting seeds and cuttings for the gardens at Thorpe, leaving Eva to accompany Byng to San Francisco where they would meet and sail for Canada.

Eva was now Byng's constant companion. She was intelligent, sympathetic, well-read and a good listener. To their friends it was obvious that she was devoted to Byng.

Curiously, she was one of three intelligent and beautiful women – the others being Mme Georges Vanier and Lady Bigham (Drysie) – who told the author in identical words, 'You couldn't help loving Bungo'. Pauline Vanier added that, had she been in Eva's position, 'I would have been in love with him too.'

While it is impossible to penetrate the bedroom doors of what had become a *ménage à trois*, one can be confident that, though Julian Byng and Eva Sandford loved each other, they were not lovers. Byng's sense of honour, his iron will power and his innate kindness would not have allowed him to compromise Eva or to injure his wife. Neither is there anything to suggest that Eva would have been less fastidious in this respect than he. In other days that would have been enough to say, but there is other evidence.

Sex seems never to have been a significant factor in Byng's life. As a young man he was no womaniser, never went to dances and did not marry until he was forty. For years he and Evelyn had had separate bedrooms. That they had no children was the result of her miscarriages, but it is nonetheless true that of the seven sons of the second Earl of Strafford, only two apparently became fathers. Byng was 62 when Eva joined his staff in Ottawa and from the time he left Canada exhausted his health was far from robust.

For no other reason than that she knew how attractive her husband was, Evelyn was jealous of other women, but never of Eva.[10] It is not conceivable that, if she had had cause to be, she would not soon have known.

The 22nd of April is of special significance in Canadian military history for on that day in 1915 was born the unique reputation which her army gained in the First World War. For the first time poison gas had been used by the Germans and the stubborn bravery of the 1st Canadian Division had saved Ypres and the Channel ports. In the battle the 16th Canadian Scottish of Victoria, British Columbia, and the 10th Canadians (now the Calgary Highlanders), though badly punished by gas, had counterattacked and halted the enemy advance.

Byng could not have chosen a more felicitous day than its anniversary in 1932 for his arrival in Victoria. The welcome he received from veterans was near to rapturous. After a few days there the tour across Canada began and and, to his delight, he was greeted at every station by cheering groups of 'Byng Boys'. What surprised him, though, was the remarkable size of the crowds of non-veterans who came to watch and wish him well. Canadians' newfound pride in their country was rooted in the achievements of their soldiers and, as their commander, Byng was as near to being a national hero as anyone could be. No matter what their view of his part in the constitutional affair of 1926, it was forgotten for the moment. Patriotism was a virtue which transcended politics.

In Ottawa the Cabinet welcomed him. Sir Robert Borden was there, and Mackenzie King. Evelyn stepped down from the car first, to be greeted with a kiss on the cheek by R. B. Bennett, much to the delight of the Press who celebrated this unusual behaviour of the reserved and dignified Prime Minister with a poem entitled 'Osculatory Dick'. King shook hands with Byng, who spoke civilly to him, managed not to catch Evelyn's eye and stayed out of the 'line of vision of Miss Sandford whom I much dislike'.

King felt that the Government had not made enough of his presence and was wounded by 'the lack of anything like chivalry in the Tory nature. . . . This was the moment of moments for Bennett. The fact that Lady Byng and he kissed in public on arrival disclose their common hate not less than their common love.'[11]

To Mackenzie King the disagreement with Byng in 1926 nagged like a sore tooth and he could not leave it alone. His diaries reflect an obsession with regaining Byng's confidence and friendship. Whether this was a subconscious desire for forgiveness for the wrong which he had done him, but would not admit even to himself, or a need to regain the approval of the father-figure which Byng had been, is a psychological question for King's biographers. Its reality resulted in the one disturbing incident of the visit.

After lunch at Rideau Hall on 12 May Lord Bessborough left Byng alone with King who soon began to speak of their disagreement in 1926. Bursting into tears, he told Byng that the whole affair had been due to a misunderstanding. Surprised by the change in attitude and acutely embarrassed by King's emotion, Byng asked on whose part there had been a misunderstanding. King said on both their parts. To this Byng took exception and said that, while he did not expect anyone to broach the subject while he was in Ottawa on an informal and friendly visit, he could not agree that there had been any misunderstanding on his part. He referred to their agreement that King would not ask for dissolution until Meighen had been given the opportunity of forming an administration. King thereupon admitted that there had been such an understanding, but said that it applied only to the first days of the first

360

parliamentary session after the election of 1925. He then added that, anyway, it would have been unconstitutional to have made a contract or agreement such as they were discussing. Byng asked, if that was the case, why did King enter into it. Its constitutionality would depend not on how long the agreement would remain in force but upon the fact of making such a contract. He repeated 'Why make it at all if it was unconstitutional?'

King's tears continued and Byng tried to end the conversation. He told him again that he had not expected to discuss the issue, did not want to and would be content to leave a decision on the matter to history. Still King persisted in trying to justify his position until the exasperated Byng abruptly ended the performance.*

> I left him to find nearly all the others gone, Lady Byng and Miss Sandford alone looking towards Byng and myself. They both shook hands very cordially and Lady Byng even had a sort of kindly smile – but she is a viper and responsible for most of the wrong that has been done – with Bennett back of her.[12]

King could not have done more to alienate Byng. Evelyn wrote later that her husband's disgust was roused, as she never saw it before or since, when King said tearfully that it all had been a misunderstanding. 'This attempt in exculpation revolted Julian's honesty and he said to me bitterly, "Your judgement was right. Mine was quite wrong that time".'[13]

The last few days of the tour were spent in Montreal with Arthur Currie. The two men had much to discuss. They may be forgiven if they had little good to say of politics and politicians. The list of those who

---

*Two accounts exist of this interview. One is in King's diary, the other in a letter dated 17 May, 1932, from Senator Charles Murphy to M. J. Quinn of Toronto. The latter was copied and widely distributed. It created a furore among Byng's friends, in particular C. M. Edwards who criticized Murphy for abusing a confidence. Murphy was one of the Liberal Cabinet Ministers who had become a friend of Byng's and was in the Civic Hospital during the latter's visit to Ottawa. Willis-O'Connor later wrote and told Byng about this new controversy. On 23 September, 1932 he replied:
'I was upset about Charlie Murphy. When I went to see him in Hospital, I found he knew all about the interview at G. H. with Billy King, but he had received a rather exaggerated story which I told him was overdone, and also what had really happened. I did not swear him to secrecy, as perhaps I ought to have done, but of course I never thought that he would broadcast what I looked upon as a private talk – but he did so without telling me and the fat was in the fire.'
In his diary for 12 May, 1932, King confirmed that the agreement had existed but contended that it had expired once Parliament had met. He does not mention the question of its constitutionality, nor his tears.

had injured Byng was long – Lloyd George, Mackenzie King, Philip Snowden, Ramsay Macdonald (the whole Labour party after 1931 would agree with Byng when he referred to the last named as a 'four-flusher').[14] But Currie had been wounded even deeper. Sam Hughes, the Minister of Defence through much of the War, had begun a campaign of vilification against Currie, charging him with wasting lives for the glorification of his own, and after the war, sparked a whispering campaign which worried and sapped the strength of one of the country's most selfless soldiers. It affected the morale of veterans who began to wonder if perhaps their comrades had indeed died in vain. For ten years it went on until it reared its head above ground in an article in an obscure country newspaper. Currie sued for libel in a celebrated trial and won. Across the country the result was seen as a vindication of his generalship.

The appalling reception of Currie on his return from the war had been hurtful enough, and no politician had risen to his defence in the House of Commons when Hughes launched the first of his attacks on his generalship. Robust though he was in mind and body, many believed that the worry over his reputation and that of his Corps shortened his life.

It was the last meeting between the two who had led so brilliantly the most durable and effective formation on the Western Front.

Evelyn Byng, an habitual hyperbolist, later wrote that she and Julian had loathed politicians. A biographer of Mackenzie King wondered, that being so, why Byng accepted the post of Governor-General. Shorn of its implicit sneer, it is an interesting question. The short answer is that, unpleasant though his experience with some of them had been, politicians never destroyed his strong sense of duty to his country. A corollary is that the vocation for service in the officers of the forces is an asset which must be guarded if we are ever to need the likes of Julian Byng and Arthur Currie again.

Early in October Byng received an honour which meant more to him than any of the titles and decorations which he now bore in such numbers. He was promoted to the rank of Field-Marshal.

It was a popular gesture. One paper reported how much satisfaction it had given to ex-servicemen 'of the humble other ranks variety' for the

Third Army Commander on the old western front was perhaps the most genuinely popular of the lot with the men in the trenches. . . . They put great trust in his capacity as a soldier, but most of all liked him for his fine manners. These Lord Byng combined with the oldest imaginable clothes. He used to roam around the lines attired in a wretched old khaki suit with the fewest possible insignia of rank and usually an equally old mackintosh. . . . I once saw Lord Byng show a panicky sergeant how to manage a frightened horse without either cursing or kicking it. This little demonstration was given with calm finesse under intensive shell fire.[15]

Letters of congratulations came from other Field-Marshals, the Duke of Connaught, King Alfonso of Spain, and 'Wullie' Robertson, from Clive Wigram who spoke of the King's pleasure, from a German whom Byng had interned in Egypt, from Kipling and others all over the world. One which gave him particular pleasure was from the Governor of the Royal Hospital at Chelsea.

I was going around the Infirmary yesterday after church – a rather trying proceeding when it happens every week because it is a little difficult to find something new to say to all the old men.

I suddenly saw one Candy, late of the 10th Royal Hussars. 'Well, Candy,' I said, 'do you remember Lord Byng in the 10th?'

'Oh', said Candy. 'Byng, him we used to call Bungo. Of course I do, he was my adjutant.'

'Well,' I said, 'he has become a Field-Marshal. Didn't you see it in the papers?'

'No,' said he.

'Well,' I said, 'he has; he has just been made a Field-Marshal.'

'Bit early for that, isn't it?'

On 10 November he received his baton from the King.

Byng was now completely retired. Though his health was fragile, he was still able to enjoy his shoots, but he could no longer ride. One of his favourite pastimes was to walk through the village, dropping in for a chat with Mr Barton, the saddler, or Mr Abbs, the blacksmith. Often he called at the ex-servicemen's club which he had built with money from the grant he was awarded by Parliament in 1919.

One weekday morning in the autumn of 1932 he noticed that the Club seemed unusually full and asked Harry Tricker, the steward, for the reason. The men, seventeen of them, had no work.

Arriving home, he told Evelyn what he had seen and that he would like to do something to help them through the winter. Within a few days they planned the construction of a new formal walled rose garden, and hired all the unemployed members of the Club to build it. It took them more than four months.

That winter and the next he was able to remain in England, much of the time at Thorpe. He had shed most of his outside responsibilities now, an exception being one which was particularly

363

close to his heart, the Colonelcy of the 10th Hussars. The Regiment was in India, stationed at Lucknow where he had first joined it. It was thirty years since his service with it had ended so abruptly in 1904, yet, as with most old soldiers, he remembered it with a special and private affection. At his last Old Comrades Association dinner in London on 5 June, 1934, he said

> The whole of our regimental life has been a great ideal to us and it is something we treasure in our innermost innards. It is something we think and feel rather than talk about. We think of you gentlemen, you serving Tenth, we think of you all in Lucknow doing what we did fifty, forty, thirty, twenty, ten years ago. You have got us absolutely with you.[16]

He continued to write to his friends but saw less and less of them. As Evelyn watched with dismay the erosion of his strength, she became more and more protective, turning away even such close friends as the Vaniers at the door.

In December, 1934, they sailed to California for the winter, where in February he suffered a mild stroke. For the journey home across the United States, which had to be by the complex southern route, President Roosevelt intervened to arrange for the railway car in which he was travelling to be switched from line to line to avoid the exertion of frequent changes. In Washington he stayed with Bill Herridge and met Roosevelt, but the visit was marred by another attack of bronchitis.

In the spring the Byngs returned to England in time to be present at the Silver Jubilee Service at St Paul's on 6 May, 1935.

On Sunday, 2 June Byng complained of a slight pain in his side. Next day it was worse. The local doctor was summoned and recommended that Dr Cassidy be called from London. In three hours he was there and, when he had examined Byng, sent for a surgeon. It was decided that an operation was required and the household staff, directed by Eva and Orchin, converted a guest room into an emergency theatre. Nurses and equipment arrived and next morning the operation took place under a local anaesthetic. The surgeon found an abdominal blockage which could only be remedied by major procedures which his heart could not withstand. By then the pain was so severe that he was kept under morphia.

Late on Wednesday night, having put a distraught Evelyn to bed, Eva came into his room. The nurse asked if Byng was very religious for he had been saying something that sounded like 'My God, my God'. Eva sat down beside him and took his hand at which he smiled faintly at her and said 'My Pog', his nickname for her. For the rest of the night she sat with him, as she had so often with soldiers in their last hours during the War. Early in the morning he died.[17]

The funeral was on 8 June at the little church of Beaumont-cum-Moze which he and Evelyn attended and it was she who chose Psalm 15 to be sung at the service. His plain oak coffin, covered with a Union Jack, had been brought there from Thorpe on a gun carriage, and eight sergeants of the 5th Royal Inniskilling Dragoon Guards had borne it into the church. The regiments with which he was most closely connected were each represented by two officers – the 10th Royal Hussars, the 3rd Kings Own Hussars, the Suffolk Heavy Brigade Royal Artillery, the 5th (Territorial) Battalion of the Essex Regiment and the Metropolitan Police. No one but the bearer party and artillery drivers wore uniform and there was no military ceremonial. At the service and committal in the churchyard, only the family, representatives of his regiments and public bodies were present. All this was in accordance with Byng's wish for simplicity, set out in his will.

But all along the route from Thorpe to Beaumont, hundreds of ex-servicemen and residents of the district lined the road. The British Legion branches of Thorpe, Clacton, Walton and Frinton had formed a guard of honour at his house and his gamekeepers lined the path into the church.

A week after his death a memorial service filled St Martin-in-the-Fields. Field-Marshal Lord Allenby represented the King. The Duke of Gloucester and the Athlones were there, the Army Council, the Canadian High Commissioner, representatives of the fighting services and the police, and a host of old comrades. Among them were Col Harden of the South African Light Horse, de Rougemont, his CRA in the 3rd Cavalry Division, Kavanagh of the 10th and the Cavalry Corps, Ian Hamilton and Roger Keyes of Gallipoli, Farmar, Burstall, John Dill and Hoare-Nairne of the Canadian Corps, Louis Vaughan, Haldane and Braithwaite of Third Army and Hugh Elles of the Tanks. Among the soldiers sat writers and artists and businessmen, and many of the Canadians who lived in England.

In Canada there were memorial services in Ottawa and Montreal and prayers were said in churches across the country.

Byng might have been surprised that so many gathered to pay tribute to him and give thanks for his life. One can almost hear him say 'Please! – no fuss.'

The obituaries in papers in Britain, Canada and the United States reminded people of the debt they owed to Julian Byng as a soldier, a

365

governor and a wise administrator and for his example of integrity in public life. There were many who would like to have written, as John Buchan had:

My dear Julian, yours is the kind of career which does one good to think about, just as whenever I am depressed about human nature, I think about you yourself.[18]

Epilogue

PAT HODGSON WROTE to Willis-O'Connor after the funeral:

> Evelyn Byng and Eva are wonderfully brave but quite heartbroken. Eva in fact is just a shadow and looks so pathetic that it makes one's heart ache. She has looked after him devotedly for eleven years and now the bottom of everything has dropped out for her. She is going on living here with Evelyn who realizes what Eva has been and is and at present they are very united. Evelyn has her garden to fall back on but Eva will have to remake her life. . . . I am so thankful they accepted my offer to come and help. It was the last thing in a way that I could do for the best friend you and I have ever had.[19]

Except for a period in the Second World War, when Evelyn Byng was in Canada and Eva Sandford was lady-in-waiting to the Duchess of Gloucester, they remained together. Evelyn died in 1949 and Eva was the chief beneficiary in her will. She died in 1974.

Of Byng's friends, John Buchan, followed by the Earl of Athlone and Georges Vanier, became Governor-Generals of Canada. Willis-O'Connor remained at Government House until he retired in 1945.

Basil Brooke, his senior ADC in the War, became Prime Minister of Northern Ireland in 1943 and in 1952 was created Viscount Brookeborough. Brooke's eldest son was Byng's godson and it was his and Evelyn's intention that he would eventually inherit Thorpe and Evelyn's considerable personal estate. He was killed in action in 1943.

Byng's will provided that his Field-Marshal's baton should go to the 10th Hussars and his medals to the Earl of Strafford. There were generous bequests to his servants. His wife was to have the benefit of his estate during her lifetime and on her death, five thousand pounds would go to Basil Brooke, the remainder to Eva Sandford.

In 1940 Evelyn was staying for a weekend with the Athlones at Rideau Hall and to her dismay the Prime Minister, by now again Mackenzie King, came to dinner. While the men sat over their port, she took up her knitting in the drawing room. Just as they returned, she dropped a ball of wool which rolled under the grand piano. At once Mackenzie King was on his knees, joining Evelyn under the piano. At this unique view of their two posteriors the other guests burst into laughter and King and Evelyn rose up smiling at each other. Lord Athlone persuaded her to dance a Highland fling and later told her:

Evelyn, the best thing you ever did was drop that wool.[20]

The strained atmosphere may have been lightened but her reminiscences, published in 1946, showed that she had never in her life forgiven anyone who had harmed her beloved Julian.

References

Abbreviations:

DNB – Dictionary of National Biography
HLRO – House of Lords Record Office
PARC – Public Archives of Canada, Ottawa
PRO – Public Records Office, Kew
RA – Royal Archives, Windsor Castle

The term Official History refers to the volume of the British Official History of the Great War which covers the appropriate area of operations and date.

Chapter 1

1. The Martyrdom of Admiral Byng by Gerald French, 1961
2. Byng family records, Wrotham Park
3. Up the Stream of Time by Viscountess Byng of Vimy, 1946, referred to subsequently as Evelyn Byng memoirs.
4. Edmonton Journal 14 Sep 22
5. The Tenth Royal Hussars by Col R. S. Liddell, 1891

Chapter 2

1. The Egyptian Campaign 1882–1899 by Charles Royle, 1900 and The Tenth Royal Hussars by Liddell
2. The 10th Royal Hussars by Michael Brander, 1969
3. Interview Major R. A. Archer-Shee 7 Feb 72
4. Article 'Byng of Vimy – An Appreciation' – Lt-Gen Sir Louis Vaughan K.C.B., K.B.E., D.S.O. – Army Quarterly Vol. XXXI, Sep 1935 referred to subsequently as 'Army Quarterly Sep 35'
5. Interview RQMS W. N. Willis and 'Rowton Houses' by Michael Sheridan, 1956

6. Army Quarterly, Sep 35
7. 'Ceremonial for the Funeral of H.R.H. Prince Albert Victor'
8. Records – Staff College, Camberley
9. 'Truth' – 27 Oct 32
10. Evelyn Byng memoirs.

Chapter 3

1. Soldiers and Others I have Known by Sir John Adye, p 167
2. Daily Express 9 Jun 26
3. Times History of the War in South Africa, Vol. 3 p 94
4. Montreal Herald 11 Aug 21
5. My Army Life by the Earl of Dundonald, p 102
6. ibid, pp 105–7
7. My Early Life by W. S. Churchill, p 320
8. London to Ladysmith via Pretoria by W. S. Churchill, p 229
9. My Early Life, Churchill, p 332
10. My Army Life, Dundonald, p 147
11. Quoted in 'Goughie' by Anthony Farrar-Hockley, p 58
12. Letter Dundonald to Byng 11 Apr 02 – Byng papers
13. Velvet and Vinegar by Norman Thwaites
14. Trooper R. W. Browne quoted in Wigan Examiner 6 Oct, 1900
15. Letter Trooper R. W. Browne to Byng 20 Apr 00 – Byng papers
16. Letter G. A. Mitchell to Dr W. G. Rogers 10 Nov 36 – Byng papers
17. Memory Hold the Door by John Buchan, p 174
18. Three Years War by C. R. De Wet, p 350

Chapter 4

1. Evelyn Byng memoirs pp 44–47
2. Byng papers
3. ibid
4. Handbook for Visitors to Paris – John Murray, 1900
5. Evelyn Byng memoirs, p 71
6. Telegram from Master of the Household 2 Oct 02 – Byng papers
7. Evelyn Byng memoirs p 77
8. RA
9. Records 10th Hussars, Home Headquarters Royal Hussars, Winchester
10. Letter from Brig-Gen F. A. Whitby DAG Punjab Command, Murree to Byng, 24 Sep 03 – Byng papers
11. Evelyn Byng memoirs, p 72
12. Proceedings of Medical Board, Mhow 22 Feb 04
13. Proceedings of Medical Board, Netheravon House, Salisbury Plain District, 1 Sep 04
14. Evelyn Byng memoirs, p 78

15. East Kent News 20 Aug 05
16. Goughie, Farrar-Hockley pp 75–78
17. Essex Weekly News 30 Sep 11
18. The Times 1 Aug 11
19. Essex Weekly News 12 Aug 11 quoting The Times
20. Byng papers
21. England in Egypt by Lord Milner, p 30
22. Life of Lord Kitchener, by Sir George Arthur, p 333
23. Evelyn Byng memoirs p 87
24. RA Geo V, F259/19
25. African World 10 Jan 14 – Byng papers
26. Evelyn Byng memoirs, p 91
27. ibid, p 98
28. The Near East, Aug 14 – Byng papers

                          Chapter 5

1. A/Q War Diary 3 Cav Div
2. History of the 6th Cavalry Brigade by J. B. Bickersteth
3. The Story of the Household Cavalry Vol 3 by George Arthur
4. ibid p 89
5. Evelyn Byng memoirs, p 85
6. Xth Royal Hussars Gazette Apr 35
7. History of 6th Cavalry Brigade, p 8
8. War Diary HQ 1st Corps
9. Memory Hold the Door by Buchan, p 174
10. Message from HQ Cavalry Corps 25 Oct 14
11. War Diary 3 Cavalry Division
12. ibid
13. ibid
14. Narrative by Major-Gen Sir Hugh Jeudwyne KCB, then Col GS 1st Corps filed with War Diary – PRO
15. Official History pp 337–8. Haig recorded in his diary that he watched Byng's cavalry advance with great dash, some mounted, some on foot.
16. Byng papers
17. Tribute in The Times June 35
18. Official History
19. Evelyn Byng memoirs p 109
20. The Times 23 Dec 14
21. War Diaries and Routine Orders 3 Cavalry Division and Cavalry Corps. Temporary appointments were not widely publicized which accounts for Official History implying that Allenby commanded the Cavalry Corps in the initial stages of the Second Battle of Ypres whereas, except for two days, Byng led it throughout the battle.
22. RA Geo V Q832/230
23. Letters Sir Basil Brooke to Sylvia Brooke 19 May and 6 Jun 15

24. The Passing Show – 3 Dec 17 – Byng papers
25. 'Men, Women and Things', Memories of the Late Duke of Portland KG, KCVO
26. To Sylvia Brooke

Chapter 6

1. Gallipoli Diary by Sir Ian Hamilton, Vol 1 p 302
2. ibid p 306
3. Gallipoli Diary, Hamilton, Vol 2, p 106
4. Evelyn Byng memoirs, p 106
5. Official History p 368
6. ibid pp 443–4
7. To Sylvia Brooke 15 Sep 15
8. Men, Women and Things – Portland
9. HLRO B7.13
10. Gallipoli Diary – Hamilton Vol 2 p 253
11. Brooke to Sylvia Brooke 10 Nov 15
12. Naval Memoirs of Admiral of the Fleet Sir Roger Keyes p 501
13. Brooke to Sylvia Brooke 21 Dec 15 and 24 Jan 16, Naval Memoirs –Keyes, p 511 and G. Ward Price in Daily Express 2 Jun 16
14. Vossischer Zeitung 21 Jan 16
15. To Sylvia Brooke 24 Jan 16
16. Evelyn Byng memoirs, p 88
17. Byng papers
18. Army Quarterly Sep 35

Chapter 7

1. Letter from Lt-Col Charles Evill – Byng papers
2. 28 Apr 16
3. Men, Women and Things, Portland
4. Byng papers
5. HLRO B7.14
6. RA Geo V Q832/121
7. HLRO B7.15
8. HLRO B7.18
9. History of the 120th Regiment
10. Princess Patricia's Canadian Light Infantry by Ralph Hodder-Williams (referred to subsequently as 'PPCLI – Hodder-Williams) p 131
11. Canada's Weekly 14 June 35
12. Plumer of Messines by Sir Charles Harington, p 77
13. Official History, p 238
14. Byng papers
15. Brooke to Sylvia Brooke 12 Aug 16

16. Toronto Telegram 4 Jan 21
17. Canadian Corps Training School Magazine 8 Sep 17
18. The Legionary June 1935 article by Capt W. W. Murray MC
19. Detroit News 18 Apr 22 – anon article
20. Brooke and Titchfield mention this foible as does Robt. Woollcombe in The First Tank Battle – Cambrai 1917
21. PARC – Carson file
22. RA Geo V Q832/123
23. Article by Gen Sir Brudenell-White, Australian Army – Byng papers

Chapter 8

1. The Canadian Expeditionary Force 1914–19 by Col G. W. L. Nicholson (referred to subsequently as 'CEF – Nicholson') pp 160–5
2. 'Training of Divisions for Offensive Action' – 8 May 16 PARC
3. HQ Canadian Corps Intelligence Summary 15 Sep 16 PARC
4. The Colonist – Victoria, B. C. undated – Byng papers
5. Answers – 14 Jul 17 – Byng papers

Chapter 9

1. Weekly Despatch 25 Nov 17 – Byng papers
2. RA Geo V Q1199/1
3. Canadian Defence Quarterly – Jan 26
4. In 1915, Bragg at the age of 25 won the Nobel Prize for Physics. Later he became Cavendish Professor of Experimental Physics at Cambridge. Bull invented the first sound-ranging recorder.
5. Gen A. G. L. McNaughton, PC, CH, CB, CMG, DSO was later Chief of the General Staff, President of the National Research Council, Commander of First Canadian Army in the Second World War and Minister of National Defence.
6. McNaughton Vol 1 by John Swettenham, pp 66–78
7. Vimy by Herbert Fairlie-Wood, p 78
8. To Seize the Victory by John Swettenham, p 148
9. Vimy – Wood, p 33
10. ibid p 88
11. PARC
12. Official History p 305 and PARC
13. RA Geo V Q1199/2
14. Bishop of New Westminster quoted in 'Canada' 16 Jan 17
15. Die Osterschlacht bei Arras 1917, 1 p 40
16. PPCLI – Hodder-Williams, pp 220–1
17. Interview with author, Ottawa 1965
18. Die Osterschlacht bei Arras, 1 p 81
19. Recording of CBC radio documentary 'Vimy Ridge' – PARC

20. PARC – Borden Papers MG26H1(C)WL169
21. p 450
22. Newspaper reports undated – Byng papers

Chapter 10

1. Evelyn Byng memoirs, pp 110–2
2. The Life of General Lord Rawlinson of Trent by Sir Frederick Maurice (referred to subsequently as 'Rawlinson – Maurice) p 192
3. Evelyn Byng memoirs, p 112
4. C in C message of congratulations to Third Army 12 Sep 17
5. Haig Diary 15 Oct 17
6. Liddell Hart papers
7. 'Cambrai 1917', lecture by Byng to officers of the Canadian Corps on 26 Feb 18 – Canadian Defence Quarterly Oct 27. Referred to subsequently as 'Cambrai lecture'
8. Haig Diary 15 Oct 17
9. Interview Mrs L. M. Brooke Mar 81
10. Rawlinson – Maurice, p 203
11. Haig Diary 12 Nov 17
12. Interview Lord Brookeborough Sep 81
13. The First Tank Battle – Woollcombe, p 129
14. Byng papers
15. Haig Diary 25 Nov 17
16. The First Tank Battle – Woollcombe, p 169
14. Byng papers
17. Haig Diary 26 Nov 17
18. ibid
19. 4th Corps Order No. 320 para 8a
20. The First Tank Battle – Woollcombe, p 127
21. Report by Gen McAndrew attached to Haig Diary 30 Nov
22. Haig Diary, 15 Jan 18
23. Sep 35
24. Cambrai lecture
25. Out of My Life by Field-Marshal von Hindenburg, p 290
26. Quoted in 'Through the Fog of War' by Liddell Hart, p 263
27. My War Memories by Gen Ludendorff vol 2, p 496
28. Cambrai lecture
29. Official History p IV
30. ibid p 118

Chapter 11

1. Haig Diary 9 Mar 18
2. ibid 24 Mar 18

374

3. ibid 5 Mar 18
4. HLRO B7.28 and letter of 19 Apr 18 held by Imperial War Museum
5. Haig Diary 9 Mar 18
6. ibid 25 Apr 18
7. Vanier Diary 25 Oct 32 PARC

Chapter 12

1. Haig Diary 15, 24 May, 1 Jun 18
2. HLRO B7.29
3. Haig Diary 21 Aug
4. C in C telegram OAD 911 of 22 Aug
5. Haig Diary 23 Aug
6. Haig Diary 19 Sep and History of the War Between France and Germany 1870–71 Cassel, N. D. p 43
7. Conversation Byng–Col Repington quoted in 'To Win a War' by John Terraine, 1978
8. Haig Diary 28 Sep
9. Army Quarterly Sep 35
10. Third Army Casualty Summary–Byng papers
11. Evelyn Byng memoirs, p 114
12. Weekly Despatch 1 Dec 18
13. Sunday Express 17 Mar 29
14. Haig Diary 30 Jan 19
15. Diary of Mary Sybil Tyers T.A.N.S. (1875–1960)
16. The Globe 21 Feb 19
17. Morning Post 31 Mar 19

Chapter 13

1. The Times 9 Aug 19
2. Daily Express 23 Aug 19 and 22 Nov 20
3. The Times 6 and 26 Aug 19
4. Canada Gazette 21 Dec 20
5. Byng papers
6. Morning Post 2 Jul 20
7. Rev Tubby Clayton, Founder of Toc H in Yorkshire Post
8. Menu of Dinner 29 Jan 21–Byng papers
9. Evelyn Byng memoirs, p 117
10. Byng papers
11. Government House file
12. Byng papers

Chapter 14

1. Mackenzie King Diaries—Queen's University Kingston, Ontario (referred to subsequently as 'King Diary')—13 Apr 26
2. ibid 2 Sep 21
3. Memory Hold the Door—Buchan, p 174
4. 'Arthur Meighen Vol 2—And Fortune Fled' by Roger Graham (referred to subsequently as 'Meighen—Graham') pp 171–4
5. King Diary 29 Dec 21
6. ibid 2 Jan 22
7. ibid 31 Jan 22
8. ibid 3 Feb 22
9. Letter Byng to Currie 4 Dec 21—Currie papers PARC
10. Evelyn Byng memoirs, p 17
11. Montreal Gazette 25 Feb 22
12. Inside Government House by H. Willis-O'Connor and Madge MacBeth (referred to subsequently as 'Inside Government House'), p 20
13. Letter Mrs H. Detmege (in 1922, Mrs Adrian Keyes) to Mrs H. F. Wood
14. In 1971 and 72 author had series of interviews with Miss Eva Sandford before her death. Subsequent references to them will be shown as 'Sandford'
15. Inside Government House, pp 19 and 26
16. Interview Mme Georges Vanier Jun 79
17. 3 Jan 23 Vanier papers
18. Interview Mme Vanier
19. Evelyn Byng memoirs, p 169
20. Free Press Bulletin 19 June 22
21. To Calgary Rotary Club reported Calgary Herald 7 Jul 22
22. 11 Sep 22
23. Government House file
24. Manchester Guardian 5 Mar 24
25. Letter from Mr Ellis B. Little to author 11 Jun 79
26. Government House file. See also 'Rideau Hall' by R. H. Hubbard, p 155
27. Kaslo, B. C. 6 Aug 24
28. 24 May 24
29. Inside Government House, p 21
30. RA Geo V Q1199—24 Jan 24
31. Sandford
32. King Diary 10 Nov 24
33. Sandford
34. Diary of Arctic Tour—Major P. Hodgson loaned by R. H. Hubbard, Government House and PARC Steele Papers MG30A17 Vol 7
35. Letter Hodgson to Vanier 6 Mar 26—Vanier papers

Chapter 15

1. King Diary 21 Oct 22

2. ibid 1 Dec 24
3. ibid 23 Nov 24
4. ibid 19 Jan 24
5. ibid 4 Sep 25
6. ibid 30 Oct 25
7. Byng to Secretary of State for Dominion Affairs 17 Jul 26
8. Memo of interview Byng–Hon Charles Murphy 29 Sep 26–Murphy papers PARC
9. Vanier by Robert Speaight, p 123
10. Byng to Secretary of State for Dominion Affairs 17 Jul 26
11. Memorandum by W. F. Sladen, Secretary to Governor-General 18 Jun 26 PARC
12. King Diary 3 Nov 25
13. ibid 4 Nov 25
14. ibid 8 Nov 25
15. ibid 19 Nov 25
16. ibid 30 Nov 25
17. ibid 8 Dec 25
18. Byng to Secretary of State for Dominion Affairs 30 Jun 26
19. King Diary 12 Dec 25
20. Sandford
21. King Diary 11 Jan 26
22. 22 Dec 25–Buchan Papers, Queen's University, Kingston, Ontario
23. 31 Dec 25–Currie Papers PARC
24. King Diary 24 Jan 26
25. ibid 8 Feb 26
26. ibid 17 Feb 26
27. ibid 3 Mar 26
28. ibid 6 Mar 26
29. ibid 11 Apr 26
30. William Lyon Mackenzie King–The Lonely Heights Vol 2 by H. Blair Neatby, pp 130–143
31. Byng interview with Murphy 29 Sep 26
32. Interview Mme Vanier–arranged through her father Judge Archer
33. King Diary 26 Jun 26
34. ibid
35. ibid
36. ibid
37. ibid 27 Jun 26
38. Byng papers PARC MG 27IIIA2
39. 29 Jan 26 quoted in King George V, His Life and Reign by Harold Nicolson, pp 476–7
40. Byng papers PARC MG 27IIIA2
41. Meighen by Graham, p 419. Dr Graham quotes from a letter to him from Arthur Meighen dated 21 Aug 56
42. The Royal Power of Dissolution by Eugene Forsey, p 241
43. 6 Jul 26–Currie papers PARC

44. Buchan papers–Queen's University, Kingston
45. Vanier papers PARC
46. Interview Mme Vanier
47. King Diary 21 Sep 26
48. Interview Mme Vanier

Chapter 16

1. Evening News 16 Jun 26
2. 25 Oct 26 O'Connor papers PARC
3. King Diary 18 Oct 26
4. Evening Standard 27 Oct 26
5. Montreal Gazette 28 Sep 26
6. 30 Mar and 14 Apr 27–Currie papers PARC
7. 20 Dec 27–O'Connor papers PARC
8. ibid 16 Dec 26
9. Inside Government House, p 39 et seq
10. Byng to Vanier 15 Feb 28–Vanier papers PARC
11. Byng to O'Connor 2 Mar and 21 Jul 27–O'Connor papers PARC
12. Army Quarterly Sep 35
13. Daily Telegraph 17 May 27
14. The Times 12 Jul 28
15. ibid
16. Hicks to Byng 21 Jun 28–Byng papers
17. Letter Byng to Buchan 19 Jun–Buchan papers, Queen's University, Kingston
18. 19 Jun 28–Byng papers
19. 20 Jun 28–Byng papers
20. Sandford
21. 20 Jun 28–RA Geo V KA217/4
22. Hicks to Byng 21 Jun 28–Byng papers
23. 22 Jun 28–Buchan papers, Queen's University, Kingston
24. The Times 3 Jul 28
25. Daily Herald 4 Jul 28
26. Hansard 12 Jul 28
27. 3 Jul 28
28. 7 Jul 28
29. both 3 Jul 28
30. 14 Oct 28
31. Byng to O'Connor 2 Nov 28–O'Connor papers PARC
32. Light and Shade at Scotland Yard by H. M. Howgrave-Graham, p 11 (referred to subsequently as 'Howgrave-Graham')
33. Interview–author with Lady Bigham (formerly Miss Drysdale) 10 Feb 80
34. ibid
35. Howgrave-Graham pp 12–15
36. Evelyn Byng memoirs, p 179

37. Unpublished memoirs A. F. Orchin – Byng's valet – loaned to author – (referred to subsequently as 'Orchin memoirs')
38. Howgrave-Graham p 15
39. Sunday Express 6 Jan 29
40. Howgrave-Graham p 16
41. Orchin memoirs
42. Evening News 3 Dec 28 and Sunday Express 6 Jan 29
43. DNB
44. Eva Sandford, Mme Vanier, Lady Bigham
45. Evelyn Byng memoirs p 221 and Glasgow Evening Citizen 21 Aug 29
46. Orchin memoirs
47. Interview author with Albert Orchin 31 May 80
48. O'Connor papers PARC

Chapter 17

1. Vanier Diary PARC – 2 Jul 30
2. ibid 6 Jul 30
3. Interview Mme Vanier 14 Jun 79
4. Vanier Diary PARC 26–29 Jul 30
5. 3 Aug 30
6. Vanier Diary PARC – 29 Jul 30
7. 15 Aug 30 – Currie papers PARC
8. Interview Mme Vanier 14 Jun 79
9. Vanier Diary PARC 1 to 5 Aug 30

Chapter 18 and Epilogue

1. Daily Record 21 Aug 30
2. Vanier papers PARC
3. Orchin memoirs
4. 1 Mar 30 Vanier papers PARC
5. Interview Mme Vanier 14 Jun 79
6. Letter P. Hodgson to Vanier 27 Jun 31 – Vanier papers PARC
7. Currie to Byng 8 Jul 31 – Currie papers PARC
8. The Times 25 Sep 31
9. 29 Sep 31 – Byng papers
10. Interview Mme Vanier 14 Jun 79
11. King Diary 11 May 32
12. ibid 12 May
13. Evelyn Byng memoirs, p 62
14. Byng to O'Connor 11 Aug 33 – O'Connor papers PARC
15. Sussex Daily News 19 Oct 33
16. 10th Royal Hussars Gazette 1934–36
17. Sandford

18. Buchan to Byng 1 Oct 31 – Byng papers
19. 21 Jun 35 – O'Connor papers PARC
20. Interview 14 Jun 79 with Mme Vanier who was present

Bibliography

Unpublished Sources

Byng papers – scrapbooks in possession of Julian Byng, Esq. of Wrotham Park.
At the Public Archives of Canada, the Borden, Byng, Currie, Meighen, Murphy, Steel, Vanier and Willis-O'Connor papers.
At Queen's University Archives, Kingston, Ontario, the Buchan papers and the Mackenzie King Diaries (microfiche).
At the Public Record Office of Northern Ireland, the Brookeborough papers.
At the National Library of Scotland, the Haig diaries.
At the Staff College, Camberley, the Staff College Register.
A. F. Orchin – unpublished memoirs.
W. N. Willis – unpublished memoirs and correspondence with author.
At the Royal Archives, Windsor Castle – correspondence related to Lord Byng.
At the House of Lords Records Office, the Blumenfeld papers.

Official Histories

The History of the War in South Africa 1899–1902 (4 vols.)
Official History of the Great War:
   Military Operations France and Belgium – 1914 to 1918
   Military Operations Egypt and Palestine
   Military Operations Gallipoli
The Canadian Expeditionary Force 1914–19

Public Documents

At the Public Record Office, Kew
  War Diaries, 3 Cavalry Division 1914–15
             Cavalry Corps 1915
             1st Corps 1914

4th Corps 1914
9th Corps 1915–16
17th Corps 1916
Canadian Corps 1916–17
Third Army 1917–18
At the Public Archives of Canada
War Diaries and Operations Files – Canadian Corps

Published Sources

Adye, Sir John, *Soldiers and Others I have Known*, 1925
Arthur, Sir George, *Life of Lord Kitchener* (3 vols.) 1920
   The Story of the Household Cavalry, Vol. 3, 1926
Ascoli, David, *The Queen's Peace*, 1979
Birdwood, Field-Marshal Lord, *Khaki and Gown*, 1941
Bickersteth, J. B., *History of the 6th Cavalry Brigade*, Baynard Press, N.D.
Brander, Michael, *The 10th Royal Hussars*, 1969
Browne, Douglas G., *The Rise of Scotland Yard*, 1956
Buchan, John, *Memory Hold The Door*, 1941
Byng, Viscountess, of Vimy, *Up The Stream of Time*, 1946
Byrne, L. S. R. and Churchill, E. L., *Changing Eton*, 1937
Churchill, W. S. *London to Ladysmith Via Pretoria*, 1900
   My Early Life, 1930
De Wet, C. R., *Three Years War*, 1902
Dundonald, Earl of, *My Army Life*, 1926
Eton College, *Eton School Lists*, 1877
Falls, Cyril, *Julian Hedworth George Byng*, D.N.B. 1931–40
Farrar-Hockley, Anthony, *Goughie*, 1975
Forsey, E. A., *The Royal Power of Dissolution of Parliament in the British Commonwealth*, 1943, 1968
French, Gerald, *Goodbye to Boot and Saddle*, 1951
   The Martyrdom of Admiral Byng, 1961
French, Field-Marshal, the Viscount, of Ypres, *1914*, 1919
Fuller, J. F. C., *The Last of the Gentlemen's Wars*, 1937
   Tanks in the Great War 1914–1918, 1920
Gough, Gen Sir Hubert, *Soldiering On*, 1954
Graham, Roger, *Arthur Meighen, 'And Fortune Fled'*, 1963
Grange, Baronees Ernest de la, *Open House in Flanders*, 1929
Hamilton, Gen Sir Ian, *Gallipoli Diary* (2 vols.), 1920
Harrison, Michael, *Clarence*, 1972
Harington, Gen Sir Charles, *Plumer of Messines*, 1935
Hillcourt, William, *Baden-Powell, The Two Lives of a Hero*, 1964
Hindenburg, F. M. von, *Out of My Life*, 1920
Hodder-Williams, Ralph, *Princess Patricia's Canadian Light Infantry, 1914–19*, 1923
Howgrave-Graham, H. M., *Light and Shade at Scotland Yard*, 1947

Hubbard, R. H., *Rideau Hall*, 1977
Hutchison, Bruce, *The Incredible Canadian*, 1953
Keyes, Admiral of the Fleet Sir Roger, *Naval Memoirs*, 1934
Liddell, Col R. S., *The Tenth Royal Hussars*, 1891
Liddell Hart, B. H., *Through the Fog of War*, 1938
   The Tanks, 1959
Lloyd George, David, *War Memoirs* (6 vols.) 1933–6
Ludendorff, Gen E., *My War Memories 1914–1918*, 1920
Maurice, Sir Frederick, *The Life of General Lord Rawlinson of Trent*, 1928
McKee, Alexander, *Vimy Ridge*, 1966
Moorehead, Alan, *Gallipoli*, 1956
Neatby, H. Blair, *William Lyon Mackenzie King* (2 vols.) 1963
Neuendorf, Gwen, *Studies in the Evolution of Dominion Status*, 1942
Nicolson, Harold, *King George V, His Life and Reign*, 1952
Pemberton, W. Baring, *Battles of the Boer War*, 1964
Pickersgill, J. W., *The Mackenzie King Record*, 1968–70
Pitt, Barrie, *1918, The Last Act*, 1962
Portland, Duke of, *Men, Women and Things*, 1937
R. A. C. Tank Museum, *Illustrated Record of the Development of the British Armoured Fighting Vehicle – Tanks 1915–18*, 1967
Royle, Chas., *The Egyptian Campaign, 1882–1899*, 1900
Sixsmith, E. K. G., *British Generalship in the Twentieth Century*, 1970
   Douglas Haig, 1976
Sheridan, Michael, *Rowton Houses*, 1956
Selby, John, *The Boer War*, 1969
Smithers, A. J., *Sir John Monash*, 1973
Speaight, Robert, *Vanier*, 1970
Stacey, C. P., *A Very Double Life*, 1977
Swettenham, John, *McNaughton*, Vol. 1 1968
   To Seize the Victory, 1965
Symons, Julian, *Buller's Campaign*, 1963
Terraine, John, *Douglas Haig – The Educated Soldier*, 1963
   To Win A War, 1978
Thwaites, Norman, *Velvet and Vinegar*, 1932
Times History of the War in South Africa Vols. 2–6, 1900–2
Toland, John, *No Man's Land*, 1980
Tweedsmuir, Lady, *John Buchan by His Wife and Friends*, 1947
Tylden, Major G., *Armed Forces of South Africa*, 1954
Urquhart, H. M., *Arthur Currie, The Biography of a Great Canadian*, 1950
Willis-O'Connor, H., *Inside Government House*, 1954
Wilson, H. W., *With the Flag to Pretoria* (2 vols.) 1901
Wood, Herbert Fairlie, *VIMY!*, 1967
Woollcombe, Robert, *The First Tank Battle – Cambrai 1917*, 1967
Worthington, Larry, *Amid the Guns Below*, 1965

Index

386

decorations, 155; significance of his victory to Canadian independence, 166–7; his successes at Arleux and Fresnoy, 167–8; his reluctance to leave Canadian Corps, 168; ordered to command Third Army, 168; farewell to Canadian Corps, 169–70; CAMBRAI, 171–212; refuses to join Evelyn at lunch given by King of Belgians, 171; orders 4th Corps to attack and 3rd Corps to defend south flank, 192; in battle for Bourlon, 194–6; orders counterattacks to forestall further German advance, 202; selects new winter defensive line, 203; accused wrongly of blaming his troops, 206–8; criticized by Lloyd George, 208; criticized unjustly in Official History, 210–1; his achievement at Cambrai and its significance for the future, 208–9, 211–2; GERMAN OFFENSIVE, 1918, 213–39; reinforces 4th and 6th Corps, 218; orders initial withdrawal in Flesquières Salient, 219; orders 5th Corps from Salient, 220; coordinates operations with Gough, 220–3; takes 7th and Cavalry Corps under command, 229; at army commanders' conference at Doullens, 231; orders withdrawals to cease, 231; OFFENSIVE OPERATIONS, 1918, 241–58; comment on Lloyd George, 244; in Battle of Albert, 242–6; closes on Hindenburg defences, 247–9; in Battle of Havrincourt, 249–50; in Battle of Hindenburg Line, 250–1; in crossing of the Selle, 251–2; in final advance, 254–6; refuses to attend victory parade in Brussels, 258; deals with Calais mutiny, 260–1; in Victory Parade, London, 261–2; appointed chairman of United Services Fund, 263; his policies lead to formation of Royal British Legion, 264; retires from army, 265; created Baron Byng of Vimy and Thorpe-le-Soken, 265; awarded grant of £30,000, 265; builds club for ex-soldiers, 265; GOVERNOR-GENERAL OF CANADA, 267–300; appointed Governor General, 267–8; first misunderstanding with Mackenzie King, 276; visits Toronto and Quebec, 277; and Casselman appointment, 278–9; doubts raised about unquestioning approval of requests of Prime Minister, 279; and the Vaniers, 283–6; in Yukon, 291–2; his controversial visit to Sydney, 292–3; appointed colonel of 10th Hussars, 295; difficulties with Prince of Wales (Edward VIII), 296–7; travels to Arctic, 298–300; and Eskimos, 299; CONSTITUTIONAL CRISIS OF 1926, 301–324, 360–1; supports Mackenzie King in disagreements with Britain, 302–3, 311; distinctive Canadian flag, 304; becoming a Canadian nationalist, 304; King unwise to

continue in power, 306–7; tries to maintain friendly feeling for King, 307; suggests King and Meighen cooperate, 310; views sovereign as King of Canada, 310; reminds King of their agreement on dissolution, 315; considers King's request for dissolution unconstitutional, 316; his position after King's resignation, 319–20; his departure, 324; METROPOLITAN POLICE 325–58; created viscount, 325; returns to Thorpe, 326; offered commissionship of Metropolitan Police, 332–3; declines, 333; accepts, 335; at Scotland Yard, 337–40; friendship with Vanier, 347–55; heart attack, 349–51; Riviera, 355–6; RETIREMENT, 358–65; arranges visit to Canada, 358; in Jamaica and California, 358–9; tour of Canada, 359–62; last meeting with Currie, 362; promoted Field Marshal, 362–3; 364; death and funeral, 364–6

Byng, Lady Mary, 277
Byng, Robert, 2
Byng, Robert George, 2
'Byng Boys', 127, 166, 360
Byng of Vimy, Evelyn Viscountess (née Evelyn Moreton); meets Byng, 24; family background, 25; childhood in Ottawa, 25; associated with Kitchener, 26; marriage, 47–8; and Delhi Durbar, 51; miscarriages, 52; leader of Cairo society, 59; buys Thorpe Hall, 60; intuition about return to Egypt, 61; visits Belgian Royal Family and earns Byng's disapproval, 171; attends entry of King of Belgians into Brussels and misses Byng's return to Thorpe, 258–9; visits battlefields, 266–7; and Mackenzie King, 274, 307–9, 322, 351, 361, 367–8; and Household, 283; profanity, 283; donates cup to National Hockey League, 286; visits Sydney, N.S., 292–3; home and garden, 326–7, 359; tries to persuade Byng to accept commissionership of Metropolitan Police, 334; inherits fortune, 337; unaware of Byng's heart trouble, 343; in South Africa, 345; relations with Byng, 351; anxiety over Byng, 343, 354; and Eva Sandford, 359, 367
Bystander, The, 113

C Beach, 103
Cabaret Rouge, 111
Cairo, 57, 59–61
Calais, 6, 241, 260–1; mutiny at, 260, 261
Calgary, 288, 291, 358–9
Cambrai—See Battle of, 172–212, also 220, 237, 247–8, 250–1, 258, 266
Cambrai, Battle of, 172–212
Cambridge, Duke of, 23

389

390

391

395

Armed Forces

397

398

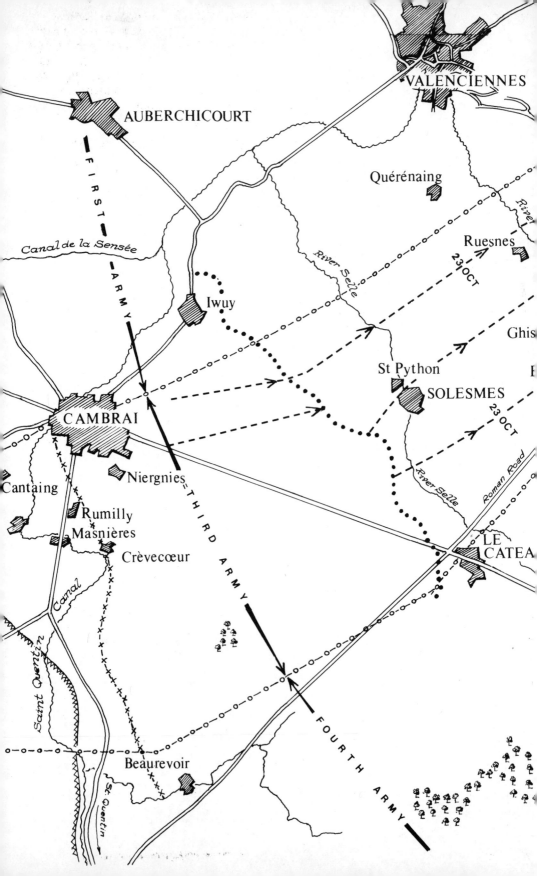